Ancient World Studies
The Book of
ISAIAH

Seek the LORD while He may be found;
call upon Him while He is near.
Isaiah 55:6

Ancient World Studies the Book of Isaiah
Copyright © Cheryl Anderson and Suzanne Hagelin, 2013
Varida Publishing & Resources LLC
PO Box 688, Woodinville, WA 98072
www.varida.com

All rights reserved.
Copying is only allowed within these parameters:
Churches that buy a master copy of this study may make copies
for their church members with written permission from the publisher as long as the
copies are not sold for profit.

All Bible quotations are from the New American Standard Version
unless specified otherwise.

Scripture taken from the NEW AMERICAN STANDARD BIBLE, © Copyright The Lockman Foundation 1960, 1962, 1963, 1968, 1971, 1972, 1973, 1975, 1977, 1988, 1995. Used by permission.

Quotations designated (NIV) are from THE HOLY BIBLE: NEW INTERNATIONAL VERSION®. NIV®. Copyright © 1973, 1978, 1984 by International Bible Society. Used by permission of Zondervan Publishing House. All rights reserved.

Scripture quotations marked (NLT) are from the HOLY BIBLE, New Living Translation, copyright © 1996. Used by permission of Tyndale House Publishers.

Scripture quotations marked "NKJV™" (or NKJ) are taken from the New King James Version®. Copyright © 1982 by Thomas Nelson, Inc. Used by permission.   All rights reserved.

Ancient World Studies the Book of Isaiah was written by Cheryl Anderson and Suzanne Hagelin. Special thanks to Sarah Park and Kathy Albright for their contributions. Historical summaries written by Suzanne Hagelin.

ISBN: 978-1-937046-00-2

PREFACE

These are the basic goals we have chosen for this study:

- to study consecutively through the book of Isaiah, chapter by chapter and verse by verse.
- to let scripture interpret scripture and to add little commentary or opinion.
- to draw out first the meaning in context, scripturally and historically.
- to provide historical background, summaries and other helps.
- to draw out Messianic prophecies and in this way glorify Christ.
- to give the student a clear grasp of what Isaiah prophesied and the impact it had on the world of his day.

We encourage you to enrich your study with commentaries and added research on the themes and parables in Isaiah. We have tried to stick to the straightforward, obvious interpretation of the passage as much as possible.

We trust the Lord will bless you as you study His Word.

> For as the rain and the snow come down from heaven,
> and do not return there without watering the earth and
> making it bear and sprout, and furnishing seed to the sower
> and bread to the eater;
> So will My word be which goes forth from My mouth;
> It will not return to Me empty, without accomplishing what I desire,
> and without succeeding in the matter for which I sent it.
> Isaiah 55:10-11

Before you begin your study of Isaiah,
we recommend that you read the overview of the
<u>History of the Ancient World</u>
which is located in the appendix at the end of your study
on page 380. It is helpful for understanding the scope of
God's revelation to the nations long ago.

Ancient World Studies the Book of Isaiah
Contents

- Study Description	4
- Maps, Timelines and Study Helps	5
- Introduction	11
- Lessons 1 – 30	15
- Conclusion	377
- Appendix including Historical Outlines and optional studies	379

Lesson	Chapters	Title	Page
1	1-2:11	God's Plea to His Children	15
2	2:11-4	Humbling the Proud	27
3	5-6	The Lord's Vineyard	39
4	7-9	The Threat of Invasion	51
5	10-12	The Root of Jesse	65
6	13-14	The Lord Judges Babylon	75
7	15-17	Judgment on Moab and Damascus	85
8	18-20	Egypt and the Land of Whirring Wings	95
9	21-22	Edom and Jerusalem	105
10	23-25	Tyre, a Curse and a Promise	115
11	26-27	Gathering His People	127
12	28-29	Ephraim's Captivity, Jerusalem's Warning	137
13	30-31	Don't Turn to Egypt!	149
14	32-33	God's Wrath on the Nations	159
15	34-35	The Recompense of God	171
16	36-37	A Mighty Deliverance	183
17	38-40	The Comfort of the Lord	195
18	41-42	The Lord's Case	207
19	43-44	Called By Name	219
20	45-47	Cyrus Comes, Babylon Falls	231
21	48-50	Inscribed on the Palms of My Hands	243
22	51-52	Awake, O Zion!	257
23	53	The Portrait of Our Redeemer	269
24	54-55	Enlarge Your Tents	283
25	56-57	Prepare the Way For My People	295
26	58-59	The Fasting God Desires	307
27	60-61	The Favorable Year of the Lord	321
28	62-63	My Delight is in Her	335
29	64-65	Found by Those Who Did Not Seek Me	349
30	66	New Heavens and a New Earth	363

Study Description

This study is organized in a five-day format with four daily sections. Maps, timelines and other study helps are found in the front of the study while historical outlines and optional studies are at the end.

- ## Draw near to God and He will draw near to you... James 4:8

    In the beginning of our lesson each day, we have a short section designed to help draw us into God's presence and prepare our heart for the study of the Word.

- ## Study to show yourself approved... 2 Timothy 2:15

    In this section we study and draw out the meanings of the passage of the day.

- ## Prove yourselves doers of the word... James 1:22

    This section of the lesson is practically helping us to apply what we learned in the Word of God.

- ## In everything, by prayer and petition... Philippians 4:6

    At the end of our time, we bring our needs to the Lord and pray about what we have learned.

Notes and Explanations

Isaiah has a number of repeated themes. Every time we cover these, the following markers will be on the right hand side of the page. You may wish to mark these verses in your Bible using this symbol. At the end of the year, you have the option of summarizing what you learn about each one.

Prophecies about the Messiah — **(M)**

The Day of the Lord — **(D)**

The Holy One of Israel — **(H)**

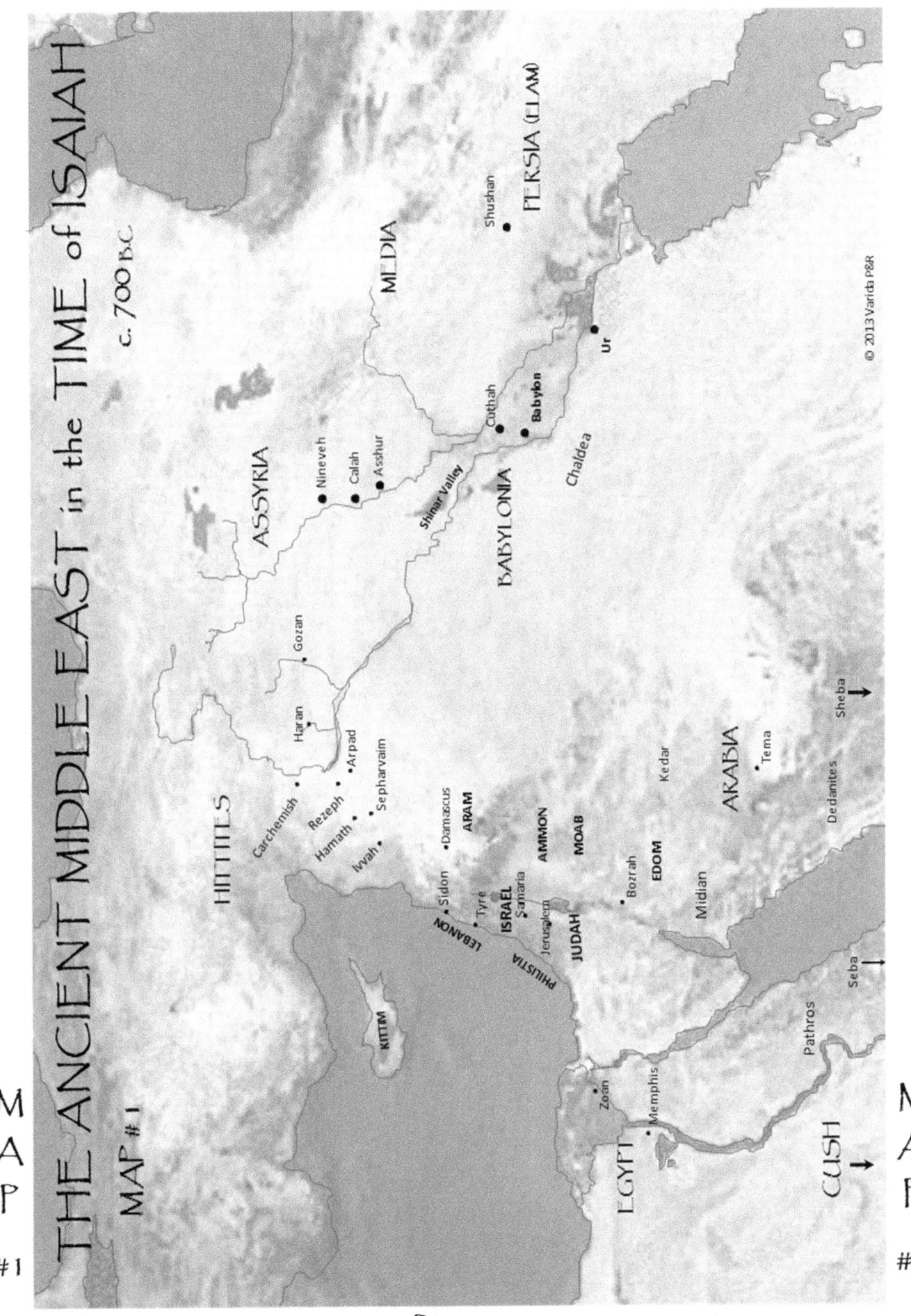

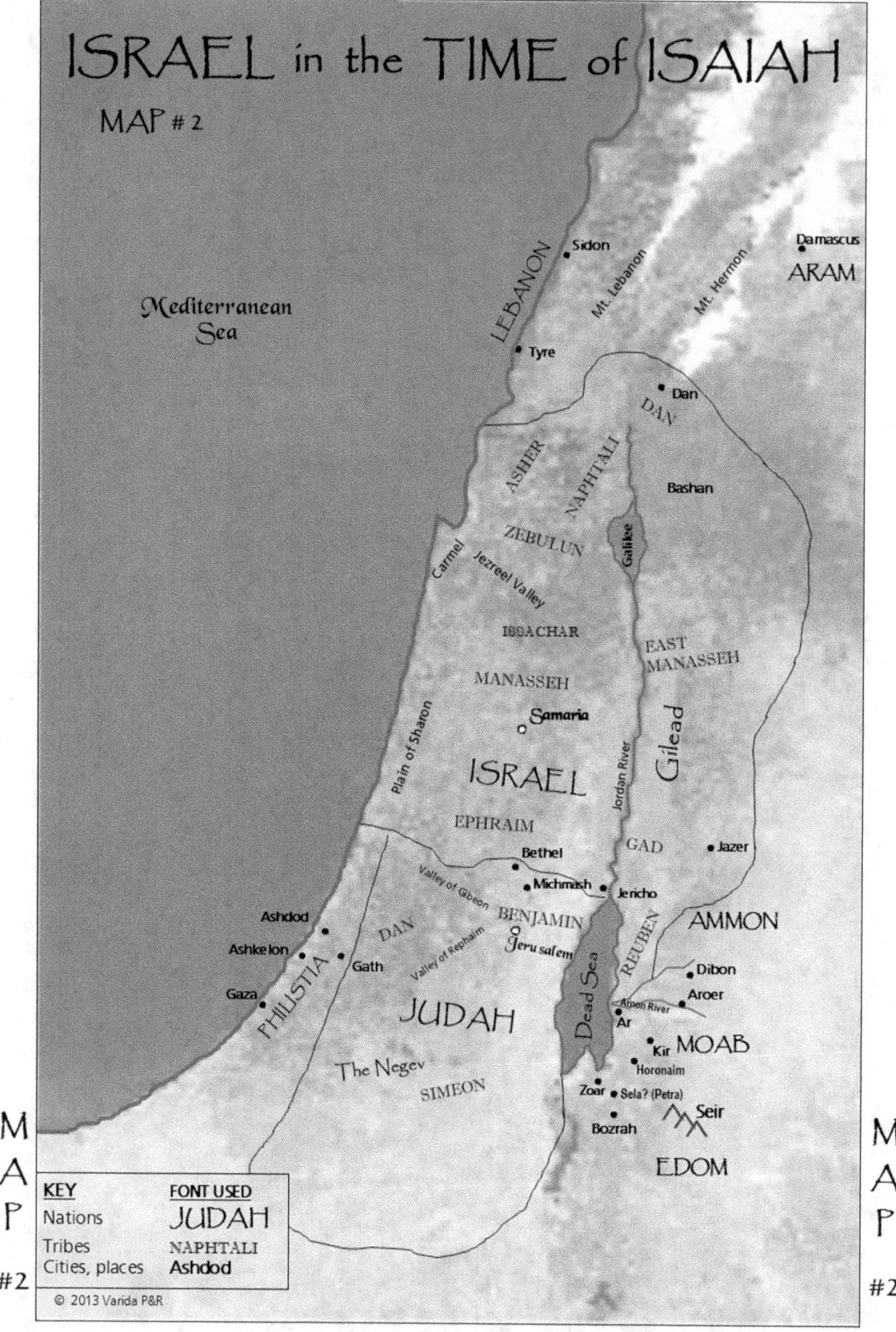

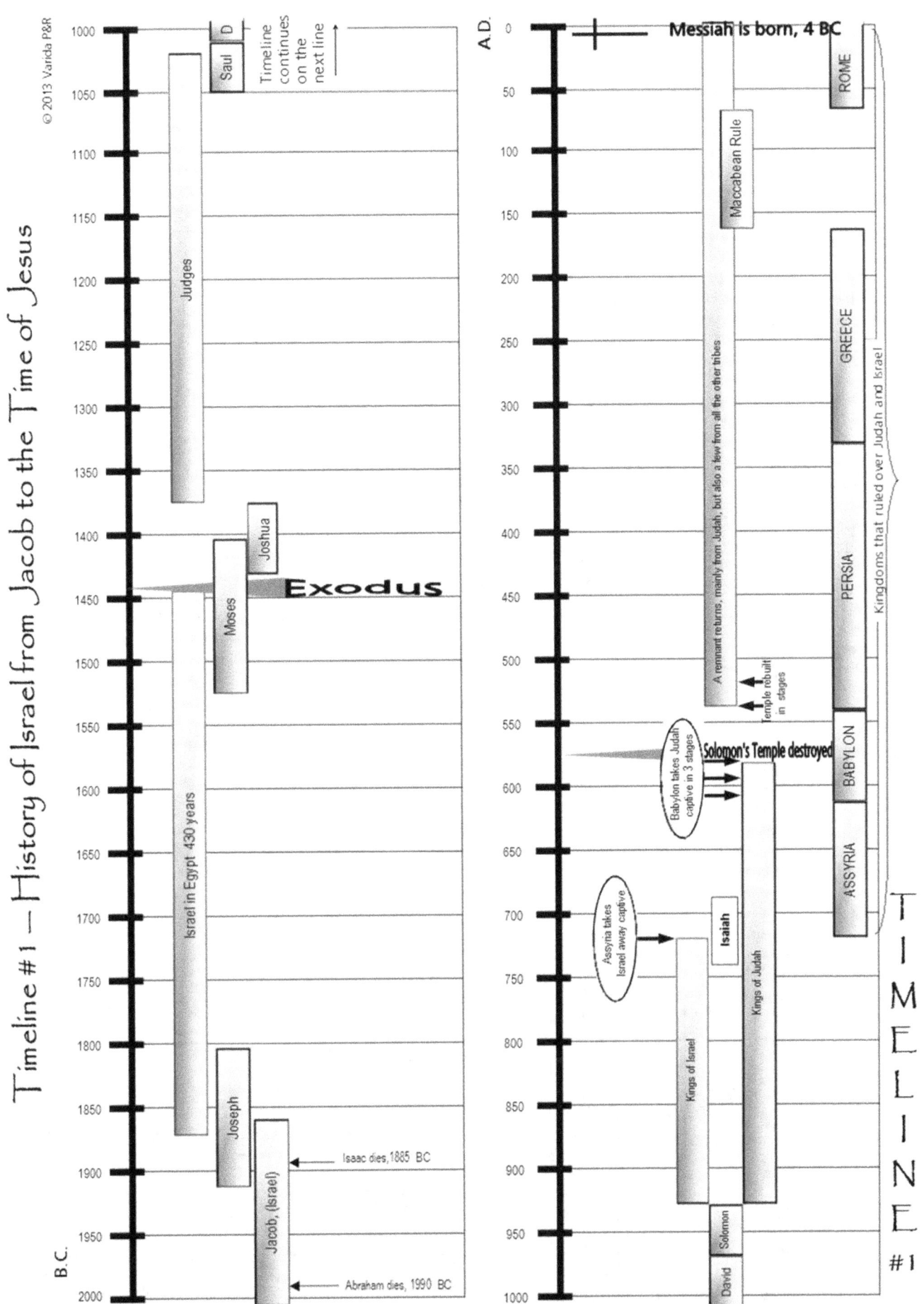

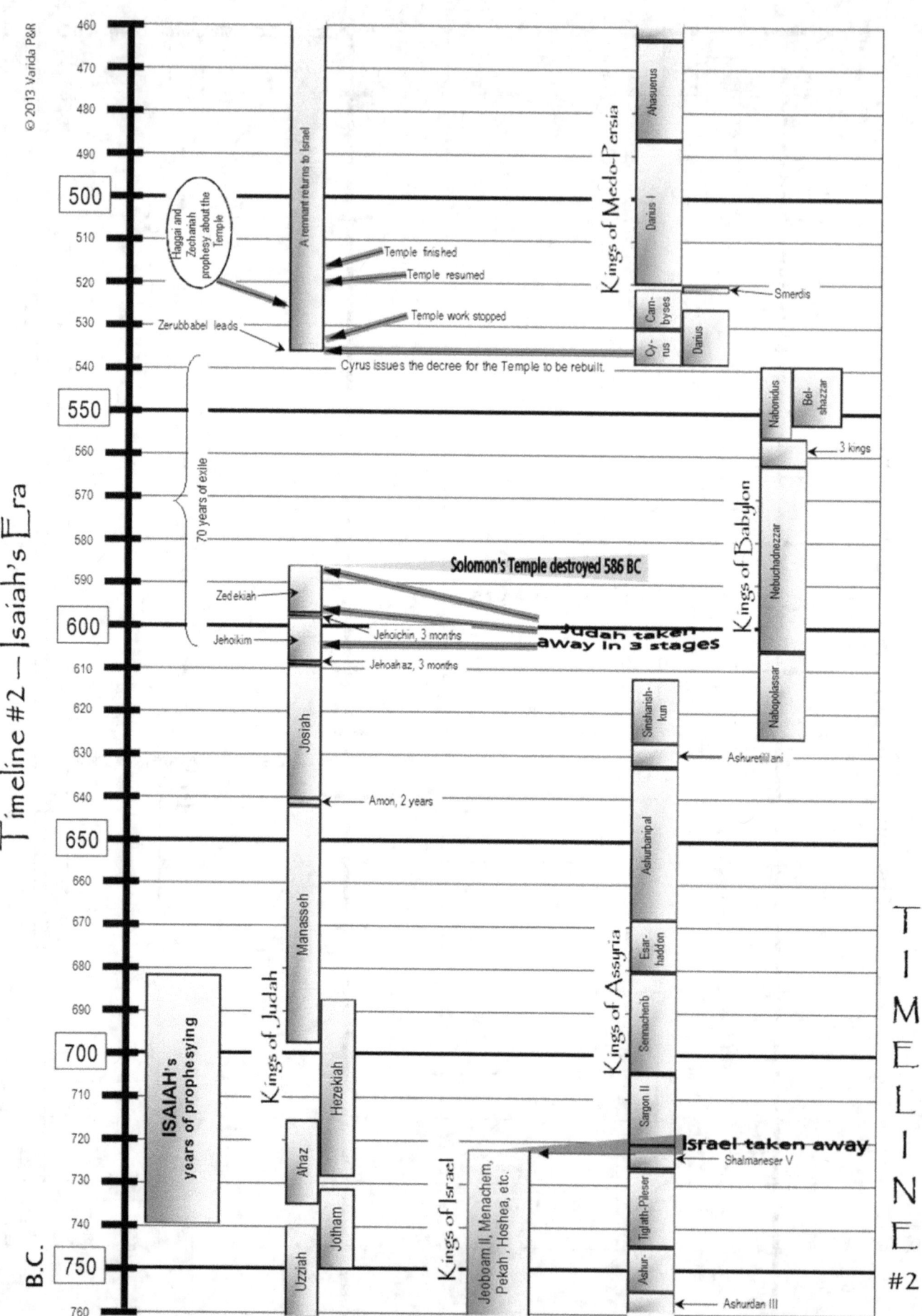

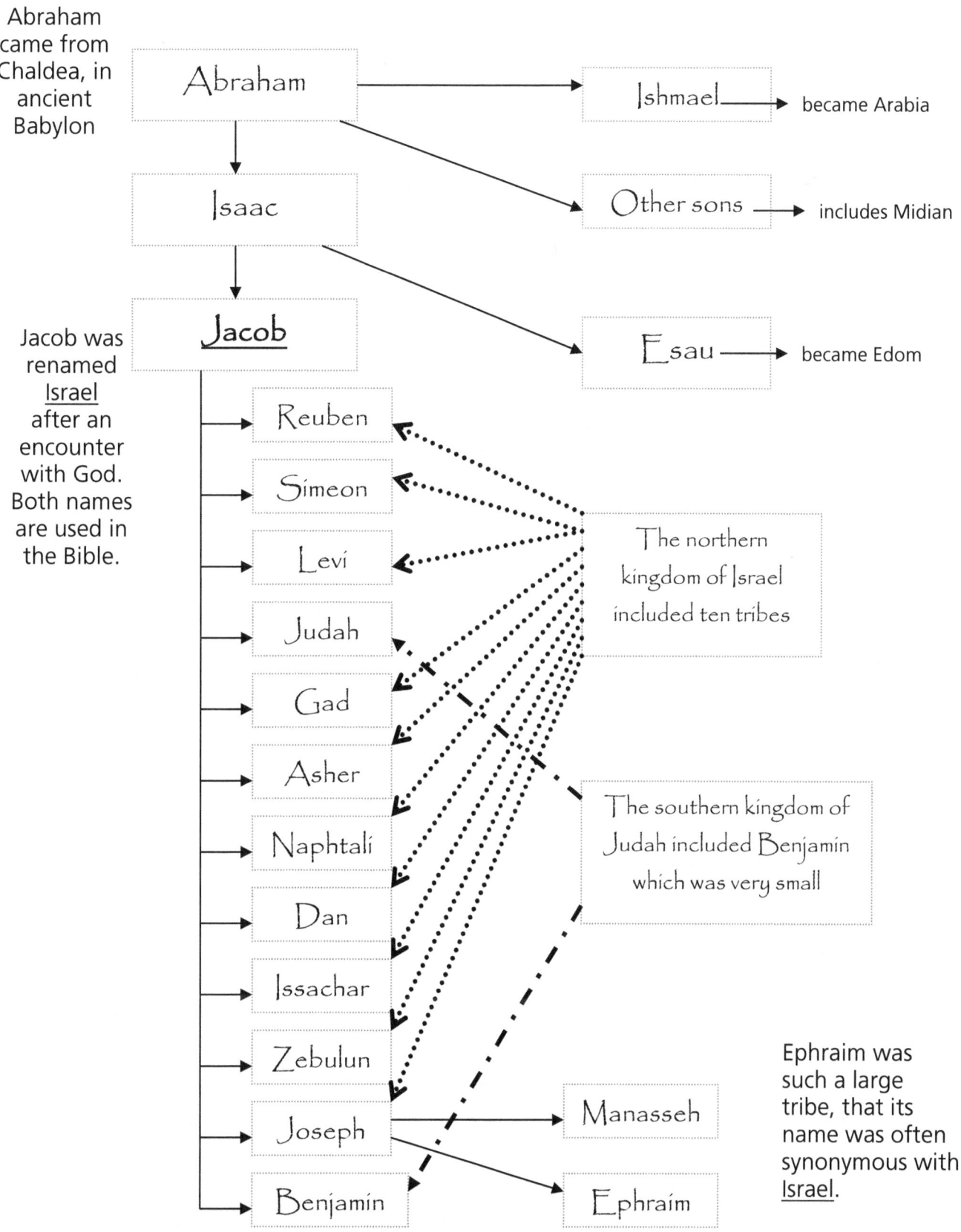

Introduction to the Study of Isaiah

"True prophets are like good doctors: they diagnose the case, prescribe a remedy, and warn the patient what will happen if the prescription is ignored."(Wiersbe)

Isaiah, the son of Amoz, is considered one of the mightiest prophets in the history of Israel. He lived in Jerusalem, the main city of the tribe of Judah and Jewish tradition says he was a member of the royal family. His name means, "The Lord is Salvation". He was married to a prophetess and had two sons. He was so completely devoted to the Lord that he was willing to humble himself and walk around in a loincloth, virtually naked, for three years, to be a sign to Judah of the nakedness and shame of putting their hope in the wrong place. Historical tradition tells us that the wicked King Manasseh killed him by having him sawn in two (referred to in Hebrews 11:37).

The book of Isaiah has 66 chapters, which have a remarkable parallel to the Bible with its 66 books. The first 39 chapters of Isaiah are about the law and judgment; so are the 39 books in the Old Testament. The next 27 chapters of Isaiah emphasize grace and hope like the message of the 27 books of the New Testament.

Isaiah is full of amazing prophecies. Some were fulfilled in the days they were prophesied, some in later years in history such as where Isaiah predicts in chapters 44 and 45 that the King of Persia, Cyrus, will bring back the remnant of his people about 180 years before it took place, even before Cyrus was born! Some prophecies are still waiting to be fulfilled. Yet so many people still refuse to believe!

*But though He had performed
so many signs before them, yet they were not believing in Him.
John 12:37*

Some of the main themes of Isaiah are:

The Holy One of Israel
The Servant
Salvation
Messianic prophecies
The Day of the Lord
Judgment
Hope and comfort

When Isaiah prophesied there was often a present application and a future interpretation. In our study we will look for both.

The Lord had provided so abundantly for Israel when He brought them into the Promised Land. He knew that their welfare depended on remembering the Lord and avoiding pride and self-sufficiency. He warned them from the beginning:

Then it shall come about when the LORD your God brings you into the land which He swore to your fathers, Abraham, Isaac and Jacob, to give you, great and splendid cities which you did not build, and houses full of all good things which you did not fill, and hewn cisterns which you did not dig, vineyards and olive trees which you did not plant, and you eat and are satisfied,
then watch yourself, that you do not forget the LORD who brought you from the land of Egypt, out of the house of slavery.
Deuteronomy 6:10-12

But Israel did forget and the Lord sent Isaiah to remind them.

Historical Backdrop

Isaiah prophesied during the reign of four kings of Judah: King Uzziah, King Jotham, King Ahaz and King Hezekiah. He died during the reign of King Manasseh, the son of Hezekiah, as was mentioned before.

<u>King Uzziah</u> was a godly and powerful king, greatly blessed by the Lord, but he ended up allowing pride to cause him to stumble.

Uzziah was sixteen years old when he became king, and he reigned fifty-two years in Jerusalem; He did right in the sight of the LORD according to all that his father Amaziah had done. He continued to seek God . . . and as long as he sought the LORD, God prospered him.
2 Chronicles 26:3-5

But when he became strong, his heart was so proud that he acted corruptly, and he was unfaithful to the LORD his God, for he entered the temple of the LORD to burn incense on the altar of incense. Then Azariah the priest entered after him and with him eighty priests of the LORD, valiant men. They opposed Uzziah the king and said to him, "It is not for you, Uzziah, to burn incense to the LORD, but for the priests, the sons of Aaron who are consecrated to burn incense. Get out of the sanctuary, for you have been unfaithful and will have no honor from the LORD God." But Uzziah, with a censer in his hand for burning incense, was enraged; and while he was enraged with the priests, the leprosy broke out on his forehead before the priests in the house of the LORD . . . and they hurried him out of there, and he himself also hastened to get out because the LORD had smitten him.
2 Chronicles 26:16-20

Isaiah was called and commissioned by the Lord in the year of Uzziah's death, an event that apparently had a profound effect on him. Perhaps the king was an idol to Isaiah, or maybe he feared him, for it wasn't until Uzziah was off the throne that Isaiah was able to see how God wanted to use his life.

In the year of King Uzziah's death I saw the Lord sitting on a throne, lofty and exalted, with the train of His robe filling the temple.
Isaiah 6:1

<u>King Jotham</u> was also a good king.

Jotham was twenty-five years old when he became king, and he reigned sixteen years in Jerusalem. And his mother's name was Jerushah the daughter of Zadok. He did right in the sight of the LORD, according to all that his father Uzziah had done; however he did not enter the temple of the LORD.... So Jotham became mighty because he ordered his ways before the LORD his God.
2 Chronicles 27:1-2,6

<u>King Ahaz</u> was a wicked king.

He departed totally from the spiritual qualities of the previous kings, and he forsook God and plunged into idolatry and made images for Baal. Besides offering sacrifices on all of the high places, he also sacrificed his children to Moloch in the valley of Hinnom. This brought the hand of judgment against him. The King of Israel (in the north) and the King of Aram (Syria) united their forces and marched against Judah. 120,000 men lost their lives in that battle. On their retreat from the battle, Israel carried off 200,000 Judean women and children as captives. As the armies returned, Oded the prophet of God to Israel, went out to meet the army and reproved them for wanting to enslave their brothers. His warning was heeded and the people were returned.

But King Ahaz still rejected God and did not turn to Him for help. He turned instead to the king of Assyria and tried to purchase help with payment from the Temple treasure. He became a servant to this heathen king who never ended up helping him. That's what can happen with our fears and idols, they can enslave us.

<u>King Hezekiah</u> was a good king who clung to the Lord and followed Him wholeheartedly.

Hezekiah became king when he was twenty-five years old; and he reigned twenty-nine years in Jerusalem.. He did right in the sight of the LORD, according to all that his father David had done. In the first year of his reign, in the first month, he opened the doors of the house of the LORD and repaired them.
2 Chronicles 29:1-3

Hezekiah restored the temple worship. He also refused to pay tribute to the king of Assyria, an alliance that had been displeasing to the Lord, so Assyria threatened to come and conquer Jerusalem.

At this time Judah was experiencing great prosperity. But the Assyrian army was encamped in the north, threatening invasion of the northern kingdom Israel. The king of Assyria was a brutal king. He was known for skinning people alive and for leading his captive's away with hooks through their noses.

Notice the difference between Ahaz' response to his dilemma and King Hezekiah's response. Both needed an ally, but Ahaz made himself partner with the world while Hezekiah sought the Lord as his refuge. The scripture says:

> Do not be bound together with unbelievers; for what partnership
> have righteousness and lawlessness, or what fellowship has light with darkness?
> Or what harmony has Christ with Belial, or what has a believer in common with an unbeliever?
> Or what agreement has the temple of God with idols? For we are the temple of the living God...
> 2 Corinthians 6:14-16

When the King of Assyria sent a letter threatening to destroy the cities of Judah and called for surrender, King Hezekiah took the letter and spread it out on the altar before the Lord and poured his heart out before the Lord crying out to Him for deliverance. Then God sent the prophet Isaiah to Hezekiah with the message that Assyria would not come into the city. He believed God and trusted in Him for His help, not in the world, not in others. And the Lord rewarded his trust with a powerful and mighty deliverance.

King Manasseh was the next king and he was the worst king in the history of Judah.

Amazingly though, scripture says that he repented and God forgave him (2 Chronicles 33:11-18). Jerusalem was still held accountable for the terrible evil they did during his reign.

> Alas, sinful nation, A people laden with iniquity, A brood of evildoers, children who are corrupters!
> They have forsaken the LORD, They have provoked to anger, The Holy One of Israel,
> They have turned away backward.
> Isaiah 1:4

These kings were the political leaders of their time. The spiritual leaders were the priests. The prophets spoke into both the priests' and the kings' lives with messages from God.

Originally

God had intended for the sacrifices described in Moses' Law, in the books of Exodus and Leviticus, to teach men that without the shedding of blood there would be no forgiveness of sins.

> And according to the Law, one may almost say, all things are cleansed
> with blood, and without the shedding of blood there is no forgiveness.
> Hebrews 9:22

The symbolic meaning of the law had been lost. Instead of being obedient to God's laws the people were satisfied with an outward show of obedience. The law was meant to be a teacher to lead them to their need for a savior.

> Therefore the Law has become our tutor to lead us to Christ,
> so that we may be justified by faith.
> Galatians 3:24

> "What are your multiplied sacrifices to Me?" says the LORD.
> I have had enough of burnt offerings of rams and the fat of fed cattle;
> And I take no pleasure in the blood of bulls, lambs or goats.
> When you come to appear before Me, who requires of you this trampling
> of My courts? Bring your worthless offerings no longer, incense is an
> abomination to Me. New moon and sabbath, the calling of assemblies –
> I cannot endure iniquity and the solemn assembly.
> I hate your new moon festivals and your appointed feasts,
> They have become a burden to Me; I am weary of bearing them.
> Isaiah 1:11-14

God wanted their hearts. But they were a stubborn, rebellious people who turned away from God, so the Lord allowed a time of suffering and warned of exile to come. Yet if they would return to the Lord, He would forgive them and bring them back into the Promised Land. These warnings that the prophet Isaiah prophesied in this book are what we will be studying this year.

> For You do not delight in sacrifice,
> otherwise I would give it; You are not pleased with burnt offering.
> The sacrifices of God are a broken spirit; A broken and a contrite heart,
> O God, You will not despise.
> Psalm 51:16-17

God's Plea to His Children
Isaiah chapter 1 – 2:11
Lesson 1

DAY 1 — Introduction

➢ **Draw near to God and He will draw near to you... James 4:8**

Read Psalm 1, and ask God to make you like a tree firmly planted by rivers of water.

MEMORY VERSE Isaiah 1:18

"Come now, and let us reason together," Says the LORD,
"Though your sins are as scarlet, they will be as white as snow;
Though they are red like crimson, they will be like wool."

➢ **Study to show yourself approved ... 2 Timothy 2:15**

These visions concerning Judah and Jerusalem came to Isaiah son of Amoz during the reigns of Uzziah, Jotham, Ahaz, and Hezekiah--all kings of Judah.
Isaiah 1:1

1. Look at the maps provided in the front of your study and locate Israel, Judah, Aram, and Assyria. You may want to lightly color them in with colored pencils. Review the **Isaiah timeline** located in the front of your study. Notice who ruled during his lifetime.

Read the "**Introduction to Isaiah**" on page 11, if you haven't already done so. It will help bring coherency. Isaiah prophesied for about 70 years during the reigns of four kings of Judah. Using the introduction you just read, fill in the main points you learn about each king including the length of his reign, its spiritual climate and major events. You may read the chapters in II Chronicles that refer to them if you have time. *(We are not including King Manasseh because Isaiah died early in his reign.)*

King Uzziah (II Chronicles 26)

King Jotham (II Chronicles 27)

King Ahaz (II Chronicles 28)

King Hezekiah (II Chronicles 29)

➤ <u>Prove yourselves doers of the word . . . James 1:22</u>

2. Make a plan for how you will fit this study into your daily schedule and write it down here.

➤ <u>In everything, by prayer and petition . . . Philippians 4:6</u>

    Renew your commitment to be in the Word this year. Ask the Lord to help you follow through. Listen and obey the prompting of the Holy Spirit to come to Him when He calls you, to lay aside the urgent for the necessary.

    Ask the Lord to keep you faithful to Him all the days of your life, that you would never turn aside to the left or the right.

Open my eyes, that I may behold wonderful things from Thy law.
Psalm 119:18

~ ~ ~ ~   **DAY 2**   ~ ~ ~ ~
Spiritual Sickness

➤ <u>Draw near to God and He will draw near to you . . . James 4:8</u>

For You do not delight in sacrifice, otherwise I would give it; You are not pleased with burnt offering. The sacrifices of God are a broken spirit; A broken and a contrite heart, O God, You will not despise.
Psalm 51:16-17

God wants us to worship Him in Spirit and truth, with sincerity of heart. Ask the Lord to make you a genuine seeker of Him.

Practice your memory verse:

"Come _____, and let us _____ together," Says the LORD,

"Though your sins are as _____, they will be as white as _____;

Though they are red like _____, they will be like _____."

Isaiah 1:18

➤ <u>Study to show yourself approved . . . 2 Timothy 2:15</u>

    The first chapter of Isaiah is a well-rounded introduction to the message of his entire book. The kingdom was prosperous during Uzziah's reign and he was a powerful and respected king in the ancient world. The people must have thought they were doing so well. Isaiah's message was bold from the very beginning. What a wonderful example he was, and still is, for the people of God!

    He begins with a scathing criticism of Judah's devotion to God. He sets the time period in the first verse and then describes both their problems and the remedy.

3. Read Isaiah 1:1-10. Answer the following questions using verses 1-4.

Who does the Lord call to witness and who is His complaint against (v.2a)?

What have they done (v.2b)?

Who does the Lord compare His people to and how (v.3)?

How are they described and what have they done according to verse 4?

4. Read Isaiah 1:5-6. This is not literally physical sores but is speaking of sin as leprosy. The sin in their life is so rampant that it has consumed them from head to toe. List the symptoms of this sick patient Isaiah describes.

5. The disease referred to here is fake ritual, as described later in the chapter in verses 10-15. Why does God despise this?

6. What does Jesus say about empty ritual and hypocrisy in Matthew 23:27-28?

7. Read Isaiah 1:7-10.
How do verses 7-8 describe what will happen to Zion (a name for Judah)?

What would have been their future if the Lord hadn't intervened (v.9)?

Who does the Lord compare them to in verse 10 and why do you think He does?

Genesis 18 and 19 tell the story of how the Lord destroyed Sodom and Gomorrah, two ancient cities of Canaan, because of their great sin. They were located under the Dead Sea.

➤ <u>Prove yourselves doers of the word ... James 1:22</u>

8. Look again at Isaiah 1:3. Even animals recognize the hand that feeds them. Do you? Is your security something you take for granted? Is it based on your ability to provide for yourself and your shrewd financial plan? What is the source of your sustenance?

9. Read the following scriptures and write a prayer of thanks to God for being your Provider. Genesis 22:14, I Corinthians 4:7, James 1:17.

10. The Lord desires "*truth in the innermost being*" (Psalm 51:6) and "*true worshipers*" (John 4:23). What are things you say and do that lack true sincerity?

11. Read these scriptures and ask the Lord to search your heart and expose any insincerity that is unwanted weight. Make a note of what speaks to you.

I Corinthians 5:7-8

Colossians 3:22-24

12. How can you keep your heart pure from deceit?

Jeremiah 17:9-10

Psalm 119:9-11

➢ <u>In everything, by prayer and petition . . . Philippians 4:6</u>

The Lord loves who you are. Be yourself before God. Tell Him now all the deep things of your heart. He already knows and wants to be close to you.

*Doing the will of God from the heart,
With good will render service, as to the Lord, and not to men...
Ephesians 6:6-7*

~ ~ ~ ~   **DAY 3**   ~ ~ ~ ~
The Remedy

➢ <u>Draw near to God and He will draw near to you. . . James 4:8</u>

*How blessed is he whose help is the God of Jacob, whose hope is in the LORD his God,
Who made heaven and earth, the sea and all that is in them; Who keeps faith forever;
Who executes justice for the oppressed; Who gives food to the hungry. The LORD sets the prisoners free. The LORD opens the eyes of the blind; The LORD raises up those who are bowed down; The LORD loves the righteous; The LORD protects the strangers; He supports the fatherless and the widow, But He thwarts the way of the wicked. The LORD will reign forever, Your God, O Zion, to all generations.
Praise the LORD!
Psalm 146:5-10*

God's heart is always for the underdog. Which of the people mentioned in this scripture can you identify with? Let these promises comfort you. Ask Him to give you His heart for the meek and lowly.

Practice your memory verse:

"_____ now, _____ let ____ reason _____," Says ____ LORD,
"_____ your _____ are ____ scarlet, _____ will ___ as _____ as _____;
Though _____ are ____ like _____, they _____ be _____ wool."

_____ 1: ____

> ## Study to show yourself approved... 2 Timothy 2:15

Yesterday we saw how Judah's rebellion against God has left them in a terrible state spiritually. Today we will see in greater detail both the charges against Judah and the hope the Lord offers them.

13. Read Isaiah 1:11-20. In verses 11-15, the Lord mentions various religious practices the people follow. What are they and how does the Lord view them?

verse 11

verse 12

verse 13

verse 14

verse 15

14. Why does God not hear their prayers (v. 15)?

15. Consider the Lord's advice to them in verses 16-20.
List the things He tells them to do in verses 16-17.

How does the Lord appeal to them in verse 18?

What promise is offered in verse 19?

What warning is given in verse 20?

16. Look up the scriptures and fill in the following chart, which covers the Lord's exhortations to the people. Listen to what God is saying to your heart. What are you to do?

reference	scripture's teaching	your thoughts
Psalm 9:9-10		
Psalm 10:17-18		
Psalm 34:14		
Psalm 37:3		
Psalm 68:5		
1 Timothy 5:3		
James 1:27		
1 John 1:9		

➤ <u>Prove yourselves doers of the word . . . James 1:22</u>

17. Who are the oppressed? How can you help them? Who is a defenseless orphan that you know?

18. What is your responsibility socially to those who are oppressed, orphans, widows and the defenseless? What are you doing to help?

19. From your own experience explain why it is much harder to fulfill the moral requirements of Isaiah 1:16-17 than just go through the motions mentioned in Isaiah 1:10-15?

➤ <u>In everything, by prayer and petition . . . Philippians 4:6</u>

Ask the Lord to give you His heart for these neglected people groups. Obviously, they are really on God's heart. May the things that are on God's heart be on our hearts also!

*If a brother or sister is without clothing and in need of daily food,
and one of you says to them, "Go in peace, be warmed and be filled,"
and yet you do not give them what is necessary for their body, what use is that?
James 2:15-16*

~ ~ ~ ~ **DAY 4** ~ ~ ~ ~
A Promise of Healing

➤ <u>Draw near to God and He will draw near to you. . . James 4:8</u>

*Be gracious to me, O God, according to Your lovingkindness;
according to the greatness of Your compassion blot out my transgressions.
Wash me thoroughly from my iniquity and cleanse me from my sin. For I know my transgressions,
and my sin is ever before me. Against You, You only, I have sinned and done what is evil in
Your sight, so that You are justified when You speak and blameless when You judge.
Psalm 51:1-4*

Ask the Lord to forgive and cleanse you, to make you pure, so that you can receive all that He has for you today.

Practice your memory verse:

"Come _____, and ____ us _____ together," _____ the _____, "Though _____ sins _____ as _____, they _____ be ___ white ___ snow; _____ they ____ red _____ crimson, _____ will ___ like _____."

Isaiah ___:18

> ## Study to show yourself approved... 2 Timothy 2:15

Today as we finish studying Isaiah chapter 1, the Lord explains what He will do to free His people of their rebellion and what it will cost them.

20. Read Isaiah 1:21-23. Make a comparison of Jerusalem's past and present conditions.

past	present

21. Read Isaiah 1:24-31. Answer the following questions.

What names are given the Lord in verse 24 and what will He do?

What word picture does He use to describe what He will do to His people (v.25)?

What will the Lord restore in the city and what will the city be called (v.26)?

What does He plan for Zion (Jerusalem) according to verse 27?

In contrast, what does He say in verse 28?

22. What else awaits the sinners mentioned in verse 28 according to the following verses?

verse 29

verse 30

verse 31

*Note – verse 29 refers to the sinful idolatry connected with these places.

23. Read the following scriptures and write down the promises God gave about His forgiveness.

Psalm 103:12

Isaiah 1:18

Jeremiah 31:34

Micah 7:19

Page 21

24. Read Isaiah 1:24-26. According to the dictionary '**dross**' means "…the scum formed by oxidation at the surface of molten metals… worthless material that should be removed…" What does this tell you about the sin in our lives and the process God uses for sanctification?

> Prove yourselves doers of the word … James 1:22

25. Look at Isaiah 1:27-31. How often do you refuse to come to the Lord? You know you ought to but you'll find a friend, family member, to talk to instead. Write a safe guard, a principle for yourself so you'll try to always turn to the Lord first.

26. Notice how many times rebellion is mentioned in this chapter. Why do you think people turn their backs on the One who loves them?

27. What dross has been coming up this week? The Lord really wants to pinpoint that area, and give you mercy and grace to overcome. You may want to share with the group and keep each other accountable in prayer.

> In everything, by prayer and petition … Philippians 4:6

Ask the Lord to make you pure like silver and gold and to remove any dross in your life. Dross dims the surface. God wants us to shine for Him. Pray about all the things He stirred in your heart through the Word.

*Therefore let us draw near with confidence to the throne of grace,
so that we may receive mercy and find grace to help in time of need.
Hebrews 4:16-5:1*

~ ~ ~ ~ **DAY 5** ~ ~ ~ ~
God's Power

> Draw near to God and He will draw near to you… James 4:8

*Now it will come about that in the last days
The mountain of the house of the LORD will be established as the chief of the mountains,
and will be raised above the hills; and all the nations will stream to it. And many peoples will come and say, "Come, let us go up to the mountain of the LORD, to the house of the God of Jacob;
That He may teach us concerning His ways and that we may walk in His paths."
Isaiah 2:2-3*

Come into the Lord's presence right now and ask Him to teach you His ways that you might walk in His truth.
Write your scripture memory verse:

> <u>Study to show yourself approved... 2 Timothy 2:15</u>

As we read the book of Isaiah we need to remember that many of the portions of scripture have present day application and also future interpretation. Be looking for both.

What a wonderful day it will be when the Lord returns to the earth, sets up His kingdom and rules peacefully for a thousand years! No more anti-war demonstrations. Zion will be the center of the world and nations will stream to it. The Lord Himself will judge between the people.

In this portion of the chapter, Isaiah begins with a description of the last days. This is probably a reference to the thousand year reign of Christ mentioned in Revelation 20:4-6. Then, having described how the nations will seek the glory of the Lord, Isaiah goes back to a plea to his own people in the house of Jacob to return to the Lord, and a description of the evil they are pursuing.

28. Read Isaiah 2:1-11. Use Isaiah 2:1-5 to answer the following questions.

Who is this passage about (verse 1)?

What time frame does it refer to (verse 2a)?

What will happen to the mountain of the house of the Lord (v.2)?

What will people say about it (v.3a)?

What will go forth from the Lord's mountain (3b)?

What impact will the Lord have on the world in those days (v.4)?

How does Isaiah plead with his people in verse 5?

29. Look at Isaiah 2:6-9.

Why has the Lord abandoned his people (v.6)?

How does verse 7 describe their prosperity?

What sins have they indulged in according to verse 8?

What effect does this sin have on them (v.9)?

What does Isaiah predict the people will do and why (v.10)?

What effects will the Lord's coming have 'in that day' (v.11)?

30. How is verse 6 like people today?

31. The key phrase in this passage is "filled with" or "full of". In the following chart, make a note of what the Bible teaches about these sins. In the last column write how you think these sins are practiced in our world today.

filled with	scripture reference	what the Bible teaches	parallel today
influences from East, soothsayers (verse 6)	Leviticus 19:26 Deuteronomy 18:9-14		
silver, gold, treasures (verse 7a)	Deuteronomy 8:11-14		
horses, chariots (verse 7b)	Deuteronomy 17:16		
idols (verse 8)	Leviticus 26:1		

32. In Isaiah 2:10-11, we see the power of God. Look up these verses and write down what they say about God's almighty power.

Deuteronomy 3:24

I Chronicles 29:11-12

Job 36:5, 42:2

Psalm 93:1

And I heard, as it were, the voice of a great multitude
and as the sound of many waters and as the sound of mighty peals of thunder,
saying, "Hallelujah! For the Lord our God, the Almighty, reigns.
Revelation 19:6

➢ Prove yourselves doers of the word... James 1:22

33. The Lord didn't want them to multiply horses for themselves because they stopped trusting in Him. What or who do you trust in? Have you accumulated things, people, skills or accomplishments that you can lean on instead of the Lord?

34. We should be encouraged by Isaiah 2:10-11 because rather than being terrified by the Lord's almighty power, we can have great hope and confidence. How do the following scriptures explain His power that is available to us?

II Corinthians 13:4

Ephesians 1:19

Some boast in chariots and some in horses,
But we will boast in the name of the LORD, our God.
Psalm 20:7

35. What a joy it is to know that we have such a mighty God to strengthen us and help us to stand! Is there any area that you need God's power in today? Explain.

➢ <u>In everything, by prayer and petition . . . Philippians 4:6</u>

   The house of Jacob had filled their land and their lives with many things, but we are called to: *"Be filled with the Spirit."* (Ephesians 5:18)

Is your life filled with other things? Commit them to the Lord.
Ask Him to fill you so that the fruit of the Holy Spirit spills out to those around you.

~~~~~~   Prayer Requests   ~~~~~~

Humbling the Proud
Isaiah chapters 2:11 - 4
Lesson 2

DAY 1 — The Proud Brought Low

➢ **Draw near to God and He will draw near to you... James 4:8**

Humble yourselves in the presence of the Lord, and He will exalt you.
James 4:10

Take some time now to humble yourself before the Lord. Acknowledge His greatness and His wonderful love for you.

MEMORY VERSE   Isaiah 2:11

The proud look of man will be abased
And the loftiness of man will be humbled,
And the LORD alone will be exalted in that day.

➢ **Study to show yourself approved... 2 Timothy 2:15**

In the second half of Isaiah chapter 2, the Lord explains what He meant in verse 11. "In that day" He will humble the proud by His appearing. Remember that this key phrase refers to a day of reckoning for the nations, when judgment is brought on the kingdoms Isaiah talks about and also in the end-times when the Lord deals with the nations of the earth.

Read Isaiah 2:11-22. Notice how many times in this passage the words 'proud', 'lofty', 'high', and 'lifted' occur (*optional: underline them*).

1. What will the Lord accomplish 'in that day' and why is this important (v.11)?

2. Who or what is the Lord against according to these verses?

verse 12

verse 13

verse 14

verse 15

verse 16

3. Why is it inappropriate for these things to be lifted up and yet it is entirely appropriate for God to be exalted?

I say to everyone among you not to think more highly of himself than he ought to think;
but to think so as to have sound judgment,
Romans 12:3

4. Answer the following questions about Isaiah 2:17-22.
   What will happen to these things that are lifted up (v.17-18)?

   Where will men go and why (v.19 and 21)?

   How will men respond to the Lord's appearing in verse 20?

   What is Isaiah's advice to them in verse 22?

5. In Isaiah 2:22 we see the brevity of man. Read these scriptures and describe man's life.
   Psalm 49:10-12

   Psalm 49:17-18

   Psalm 144:3-4

6. Why do we grasp so much for man's approval when his life is so brief? Do we even realize we are doing this? Share your thoughts about this.

> <u>Prove yourselves doers of the word . . . James 1:22</u>

7. Today there are many things raised up against the knowledge of God that are meant to blind people to the truth and glory of the Lord. How can you apply the following scripture in your life?

*We are destroying speculations and every lofty thing raised up
against the knowledge of God...
II Corinthians 10:5*

8. The Lord is against the lofty and the proud, but He is not against you. Read Romans 8:31-32 and write down how God has demonstrated He is <u>for</u> you.

9. Meditate on the phrase, **"The Lord alone . . . "** (Isaiah 2:11,17). Is the **Lord alone** enough for you? Explain.

10. What does the Lord advise us in verse 22 and how can you personally apply it?

> <u>In everything, by prayer and petition . . . Philippians 4:6</u>

Ask the Lord to help you to stop looking to man whose life is so short, but instead to look to Him. Declare to Him that He alone is enough for you.

*Cease striving and know that I am God; I will be exalted among the nations;
I will be exalted in the earth.   Psalm 46:10*

DAY 2
The Day of the Lord

➤ <u>Draw near to God and He will draw near to you... James 4:8</u>

*Two women will be grinding at the mill; the one will be taken, and one will be left.
Therefore be on the alert, for you do not know which day your Lord is coming.
But be sure of this, that if the head of the house had known at what time of the night
the thief was coming, he would have been on the alert and would not
have allowed his house to be broken into. For this reason you also must be ready;
for the Son of man is coming at an hour when you do not think He will.
Who then is the faithful and sensible slave whom his master put in charge
of his household, to give them their food at the proper time?
Blessed is that slave whom his master finds so doing when he comes.
Truly I say to you that he will put him in charge of all his possessions.
Matthew 24:41-47*

Ask the Lord to help you live your life as if He were coming today! He might!!!

Practice your memory verse:

*The _____ look of man will be _____
And the _____ of man will be humbled,
And the LORD alone will be _____ in that _____.
Isaiah 2:11*

➤ <u>Study to show yourself approved ... 2 Timothy 2:15</u>

The Day of the Lord is a major theme in the book of Isaiah. We have set aside today's lesson to focus on what the scripture teaches about it.

11. Look up these scriptures and write down what they say about "The Day of the Lord".

Isaiah 2:10-11, 17-20

Ezekiel 30:3

Joel 2:1-3

Amos 5:18-20

Obadiah 1:15

Zephaniah 1:14-18

Malachi 4:1-6

Revelation 6:12-17

12. We are also looking to a future fulfillment of the "Day of the Lord". This is called the "last days". What do the following verses teach about the last days?

I Corinthians 15:51-57

II Peter 3:10

Revelation 20:6

Revelation 20:11-15

> *The pride of man will be humbled, and the loftiness of men*
> *will be abased; and the Lord alone will be exalted in that day...*
> *Isaiah 2:17*

Praise God we won't be in the final judgment! We have a great hope to look forward to:

> *For the Lord Himself will descend from heaven with a shout,*
> *with the voice of the archangel and with the trumpet of God,*
> *and the dead in Christ will rise first. Then we who are alive and remain*
> *will be caught up together with them in the clouds to meet the*
> *Lord in the air, and so we shall always be with the Lord.*
> *Therefore comfort one another with these words.*
> *1 Thessalonians 4:16-18*

> ***Note** – When Jesus rose from the dead, He gave all those who would believe in Him eternal life. We are baptized into His death (Romans 6:3), made alive together with Him and raised with Him (Ephesians 2:5-6). That is why we are a part of the <u>first</u> resurrection. Jesus said, "*I am the resurrection and the life...*" John 11:25

➤ <u>Prove yourselves doers of the word . . . James 1:22</u>

13. Read Matthew 25:1-13 about the parable of the ten virgins. In this parable some of them were ready and some were not. How are you making yourself ready for the Lord's return?

➤ <u>In everything, by prayer and petition . . . Philippians 4:6</u>

We don't need to be afraid of the Lord's return or the future. But we do need to be ready. Ask the Lord to make you ready. Pray for those who don't know Jesus and aren't ready.

> *Let us rejoice and be glad and give the glory to Him,*
> *For the marriage of the Lamb has come and His bride has made herself ready.*
> *Revelation 19:7*

~ ~ ~ ~   **DAY 3**   ~ ~ ~ ~
Far From God

➤ <u>Draw near to God and He will draw near to you . . . James 4:8</u>

Meditate on the Wisdom of God. Listen to Him speak to your heart as you read His Word:

> *Oh, the depth of the riches both of the wisdom and knowledge of God!*
> *How unsearchable are His judgments and unfathomable His ways!*
> *Romans 11:33*

> *For wisdom is better than jewels; and all desirable things cannot compare with her.*
> *Proverbs 8:11*
> *He who gets wisdom loves his own soul; he who keeps understanding will find good.*
> *Proverbs 19:8*

> *Let your heart hold fast my words; Keep my commandments and live;*
> *Acquire wisdom! Acquire understanding! Do not forget nor turn away*

from the words of my mouth. Do not forsake her, and she will guard you;
Love her, and she will watch over you. The beginning of wisdom is: Acquire wisdom;
And with all your acquiring, get understanding. Prize her, and she will exalt you;
She will honor you if you embrace her. She will place on your head a garland of grace;
She will present you with a crown of beauty.
Proverbs 4:4-9

The acquisition of wisdom is above that of pearls.
Job 28:18

And to man He said, "Behold, the fear of the Lord, that is wisdom;
And to depart from evil is understanding.'"
Job 28:28

But if any of you lacks wisdom, let him ask of God,
who gives to all generously and without reproach, and it will be given to him.
James 1:5

Ask the Lord to give you wisdom beyond your years, wisdom to understand and do His will.

Practice your memory verse:

_____ proud _____ of _____ will _____ abased

_____ the _____ of _____ will _____ humbled,

_____ the _____ alone _____ be _____ in _____ day.

_____ 2: ___

> ## Study to show yourself approved … 2 Timothy 2:15

The people of Judah and Jerusalem were far from God and sinning against Him openly. The Lord warns them of a fierce judgment that He is bringing against them. The kind of ravages He describes are the sufferings that take place when a city is under siege. It never happened in Isaiah's lifetime and it's possible that the Lord postponed it because they repented. Over a hundred years later, Babylon inflicted this punishment on Jerusalem three times.

This passage also describes their lack of leadership, and their shameful treatment of the poor.

14. Read Isaiah 3:1-15. Answer the following questions.

What will the Lord remove from Jerusalem and Judah (verse 1)?

Who will be removed according to verses 2-3 and what kind of leadership do they represent?

Who will God replace them with (v.4)?

What will be the result of this leadership in verse 5?

How do verses 6-7 describe the desperate state the people will be in as they look for leadership?

Why do you think there's so much apathy and a lack of leadership?

Why were they judged according to verse 8?

How does verse 9 describe their attitude towards their sin? What do you think it means?

15. Look at Isaiah 3:8 again. Why are our actions and speech so important?
   James 1:22-26

   James 3:2, 6

16. Contrast Isaiah 3:9 with the following scriptures. What does the Lord require of me when I sin?
   Psalm 51:16-17

   Micah 6:8

17. Read Isaiah 3:10-11. What does it say the righteous and the wicked will receive?

18. When people sin they usually reap in another season and this leads them to think they are off the hook and won't get caught but in Numbers 32:23 it says *"...you have sinned against the LORD; and be sure your sin will find you out..."*
   What does Galatians 6:7-9 say?

19. Read Isaiah 3:12-15.

   How does the Lord describe the leaders in verse 12?

   What is the Lord's response (v.13)?

   What fault does the Lord find in them in verses 14-15?

20. The Lord wants us to take care of the poor. Look up these scriptures. Notice the Lord's tender mercy toward the poor. Write down what the Lord is saying to you.
   Leviticus 5:7

   Leviticus 14:21-22

   Deuteronomy 14:28-29

   Deuteronomy 15: 7-11

Matthew 5: 42

I Timothy 6:18

Hebrews 13:16

I John 3:17-18

➤ <u>Prove yourselves doers of the word . . . James 1:22</u>

21. What would happen to you if you lost your greatest source of support, other than the Lord? Do you need to change any of your attitudes? Ask God to teach you to rely on Him and not trust in man.

22. How can we apply this teaching about caring for the poor in our society where people stand on a street corner asking for money? What wisdom do we need to apply to be a help to them? What are some practical suggestions?

23. God is not only generous with provision but He is generous with grace, mercy, forgiveness, understanding and love, which He lavishes (monsoons) on us.
Are you generous? Are you making provision for other's inadequacies? How?

➤ <u>In everything, by prayer and petition . . . Philippians 4:6</u>

Ask the Lord to give you a generous heart.
Ask God to give you a broken heart over the things that breaks His heart

*Each one must do just as he has purposed in his heart,
Not grudgingly or under compulsion, for God loves a cheerful giver.
2 Corinthians 9:7*

~ ~ ~ ~ # DAY 4 ~ ~ ~ ~
The Women of Israel

➤ <u>Draw near to God and He will draw near to you. . . James 4:8</u>

*Charm is deceitful and beauty is vain,
But a woman who fears the LORD, she shall be praised.
Proverbs 31:30*

Consider the qualities the Lord has shaped in you that are worthy of praise. Thank Him for these things and ask the Lord to continue to make you someone who fears Him.
Practice your memory verse:

The _____ look ____ man _____ be _____
And _____ loftiness ____ man _____ be _____,
And ____ LORD _____ will _____ exalted _____ that _____.
Isaiah ___:11

> ## Study to show yourself approved... 2 Timothy 2:15

In the last portion of Isaiah chapter 3, the Lord describes the women of Jerusalem and how He will deal with them.

24. Read Isaiah 3:16-26. The women really had a lot of outward adornments.

How does their behavior show their pride (v.16)?

What will the Lord do to them (v.17)

List the things that the Lord will take away from them according to verses 18-23. ⓓ

What five things will the Lord remove and what will He replace them with in verse 24?

instead of	there will be

What other kinds of loss will they suffer (v.25)?

How will they end up (v.26)?

25. In the Middle East, in those days, a person's dress showed their position in life. Shaving the head was a sign of mourning. A rope belt, sackcloth and branding were apparently signs of slavery. Look up the following scriptures. How are we to be dressed?

Proverbs 31:25

Luke 12:35

Luke 24:49

Romans 13:14

1 Corinthians 10:31

Ephesians 4:24

Ephesians 6:11

1 Timothy 2:9-10

1 Peter 3:3-6

1 Peter 5:5b

26. Look at 1 Peter 3:3-6 again. Since God looks at the heart, does it matter how we dress? Explain your answer.

➤ Prove yourselves doers of the word... James 1:22

27. Look at 1 Corinthians 8:13. Does your clothing ever cause a brother or sister to stumble? Explain.

How does Romans 14:19 shed light on what our attitude should be?

28. We should also be careful of becoming legalistic about clothing and letting a critical spirit develop in our hearts. What do the following verses teach you about that?
Matthew 23:27-28

Colossians 2:20-23

29. Are you content with what you have? Or do you complain in your heart about your clothing? Give the Lord permission to change your wardrobe. Be willing to take another aside. Let them know if they should be more discreet in their choice of clothing.

30. Look at the description of the woman in Proverbs 31:10-31. Choose one area that you want to grow in. Share with the group and commit it to prayer.

➤ In everything, by prayer and petition... Philippians 4:6

Pray, "Lord in all I do, may I be pleasing to You." Listen to Him. Is He telling you something? Write it down.

I always do the things that are pleasing to Him... John 8:29

DAY 5
The Branch

> ➤ <u>Draw near to God and He will draw near to you... James 4:8</u>

You are my hiding place; You preserve me from trouble;
You surround me with songs of deliverance.
Psalm 32:7

God takes seriously His protection and care over your life. He is your hiding place in trouble. Take a moment to remember times when He has been your refuge and give thanks.

Write your memory verse:

➤ <u>Study to show yourself approved... 2 Timothy 2:15</u>

Isaiah chapter 4 begins in verse 1 with the desperate condition of the women in Jerusalem after He judges them. Then He proceeds to describe His glorious restoration of Jerusalem through the Branch of the Lord. This captures the grace that will cover the Lord's people during Jesus' thousand-year reign (Revelation 20:4-6).

31. **Read Isaiah Chapter 4:1-6.** It was a reproach in Israel to be unmarried or barren. "In that day", (referring to the Lord's judgment on the nations and/or the end times), there will be 7 women for every man. How will the women handle this tragic situation according to verse 1?   Ⓓ

  Why does Isaiah 3:25 say that there are so few men?

32. In Isaiah 4:2-4, the survivors are the remnant. They will be made holy.

  How does verse 2a describe the Branch of the Lord?   Ⓜ

  What will the survivors receive in verse 2b?

  How does verse 3 describe those who are left in Zion?

  What does God do in verse 4 to make them holy?

33. Read Isaiah 4:5-6.

  How will the Lord overshadow Zion in verse 5?

  What does the cloud and fire remind them of? What does it represent?

Page 36

The LORD was going before them in a pillar of cloud by day to lead them on the way, and in a pillar of fire by night to give them light, that they might travel by day and by night. He did not take away the pillar of cloud by day, nor the pillar of fire by night, from before the people.
Exodus 13:21-22

What will the Lord shelter them from according to verse 6 and what do you think it represents?

34. In the midst of this suffering the Lord offers hope. The Branch of the Lord in verse two refers to Jesus. Look up the following scriptures. Write down what it says about "The Branch" Jesus.

Isaiah 11:1-5

Jeremiah 23:5-6

Zechariah 3:7-10

John 15:1

➤ Prove yourselves doers of the word ... James 1:22

35. In Isaiah 4:5-6 it describes the Lord's protection and covering over His people. Summarize what these scriptures teach about this.

Psalm 18:2

Psalm 27:5

Psalm 46:1

Psalm 91:1-11

Psalm 121:1-8

35. A storm was brewing for the children of Israel. Where do you run when you're facing a storm? Who do you cry out to? Jesus wants to be a shelter for you. He will welcome you when you cry out to Him. In Matthew 8:25 it says: *And they came to Him, and awoke Him, saying, "Save us, Lord; we are perishing!"*

> <u>In everything, by prayer and petition... Philippians 4:6</u>

Thank the Lord for His protection and care over your life. Pray for people you know that need His covering. Use some of the scriptures in question 34 to guide you in your prayers.

You hide them in the secret place of Your presence from the conspiracies of man...
Psalm 31:20

~~~~~   Prayer Requests   ~~~~~

The Lord's Vineyard
Isaiah chapters 5 - 6
Lesson 3

DAY 1 — The Vineyard

➤ *Draw near to God and He will draw near to you...* James 4:8

> *He who gives attention to the Word shall find good,*
> *And blessed is he who trusts in the Lord.*
> *Proverbs 16:20*
>
> *The one on whom seed was sown on the good soil,*
> *This is the man who hears the word and understands it;*
> *who indeed bears fruit, some hundredfold, some sixty, and some thirty.*
> *Matthew 13:23*

Ask God to give you a hunger for His Word and for it to bear fruit in your life.

MEMORY VERSE — Isaiah 5:16

But the LORD of hosts will be exalted in judgment,
And the holy God will show Himself holy in righteousness.

➤ *Study to show yourself approved ... 2 Timothy 2:15*

In this chapter the Lord uses the word picture of a vineyard to describe His people Israel and Judah. He contrasts His investment in them and His expectations for them with the sinful fruit they actually produced. The rest of the chapter describes their behavior in detail and its consequences.

1. Read Isaiah chapter 5:1-7. Answer the following questions.

Who do you think is singing and what is he singing about (verse 1)?

How did the Lord care for His vineyard (v.2a)?

What did He expect and what did He obtain (v.2b)?

Who does the Lord appeal to in verse 3?

What does He ask them in verse 4?

List all the things that will happen to the fruitless vineyard according to verses 5-6.

How does verse 7 explain the interpretation of this analogy?

Page 39

2. Read the following scriptures and make a note of the care they received from God and the fruit they bore.

scripture	care received	fruit
Proverbs 24:30-34		
Isaiah 27:2-3		
Jeremiah 2:21		

3. Read Isaiah 5:7a again. This is a picture of how God feels about His people. Look up '**delightful**' in the dictionary and write what it means. How does this bless your heart?

4. Notice God's heart for the vineyard. God is not stingy. Does He only give what the vineyard deserves?

5. Read Ezekiel 19:10-14. This prophecy was given over a hundred years later when the Jews were in captivity in Babylon. How does it describe the Lord's judgment against Israel and Judah given in Isaiah 5:5-6?

➢ Prove yourselves doers of the word ... James 1:22

6. Read Matthew 21:33-44. What more did God give for the vineyard, that was hidden in Isaiah's day? What fruit does He expect now and how does your life bear this fruit?

7. The word 'expected' is repeated two times in Isaiah 5:2 and 4. Also in Isaiah 5:7 God looked for, (expected), justice and righteousness. In verse 2 He provided a wine vat with full intention of a fruitful harvest. In 2 Peter 1:3 it says that He has provided everything we need for life and godliness. Read John 15:1-11. What is God expecting from your life?

8. Commit yourself to being a healthy branch in the vineyard. You need these things:
   1. Abide in Jesus and be nourished with His word.
   2. Give the Lord permission to prune away any thing that is not pleasing to Him.
   3. Pray about everything and cultivate a life of joy.

> ## In everything, by prayer and petition... Philippians 4:6

How blessed is the man who does not walk in the counsel of the wicked,
nor stand in the path of sinners, nor sit in the seat of scoffers!
But his delight is in the law of the LORD, and in His law he meditates day and night.
He will be like a tree firmly planted by streams of water, which yields
its fruit in its season, and its leaf does not wither;
and in whatever he does, he prospers.
Psalm 1:1-3

Pray earnestly for sweet fruit to grow in your life that you would be like a tree firmly planted by rivers of water.

~ ~ ~ ~   # DAY 2   ~ ~ ~ ~
The First Three Woes

> ## Draw near to God and He will draw near to you... James 4:8

Read and ponder these verses:

But know that the LORD has set apart the godly man for himself;
the LORD hears when I call to Him.
Psalm 4:3

I love those who love me;
and those who diligently seek me will find me.
Proverbs 8:17

Blessed is the man who listens to me,
watching daily at my gates, waiting at my doorposts.
For he who finds me finds life, and obtains favor from the LORD.
Proverbs 8:34-35

Ask the Lord to help you to listen, watch, and wait for Him.

Practice your memory verse:

But the _____ of hosts will be _____ in judgment,
And the holy _____ will show Himself holy in _____.
Isaiah 5: ___

> ## Study to show yourself approved... 2 Timothy 2:15

    In Isaiah chapter 5 there are six woes listed that capture the sins of the people that offend the Lord. This is the worthless fruit described in the parable of the vineyard. Today we will look at the first three of them.

9. Read Isaiah 5:8-19. Answer the following questions.

    What sin is described in verse 8?

    What judgment will the Lord bring on them because of it (v.9-10)?

    What sin is described in verse 11?

> Woe is defined as:
> "grievous distress,
> misery or trouble;
> misfortune, calamity,
> affliction,"
> (from Dictionary.com).

How does verse 12 describe how they spend their time and what they overlooked?

What will happen to the people and why (v.13)?

Sheol is the Old Testament word for the place where the soul went after death.

What judgment is described in verse 14?

What will be the result of this judgment in verses 15-16?

Who will benefit from the judgment on Jerusalem (v.17)?

What sin is described in verses 18-19?

10. How is Matthew 7:13 an explanation of Isaiah 5:14?

11. Use Isaiah 5:12-19 to fill in the following chart. For each woe look up the verses in the last two columns and take notes on what the scriptures teach.

Woe	Sin	Judgment verses	Scriptures' Teaching	Scriptures' Warning
1	v. 8 greed	v. 9-10	Leviticus 25:23-28	1 Timothy 6:6-11
2	v. 11 drunkenness	v. 13	Ephesians 5:18	Proverbs 20:1, 23:29-35
3	v.18 falsehood	v. 24-25	Zechariah 8:16-17 Ephesians 4:15	Psalm 5:6, 12:1-3 Jeremiah 9:5-9

➢ <u>Prove yourselves doers of the word ... James 1:22</u>

12. People today are still suffering woe (grief) because of their sin. This is why Jesus went to the cross – to free them. The secret to being a light to people caught in these traps is to walk in the virtue which is the opposite of their sin. This is also the best way to find victory over these sins in our lives. What do the following scriptures teach us?

<u>The opposite of greed is generosity.</u>

Psalm 84:11

Proverbs 3:9-10

Proverbs 21:26

Proverbs 28:27

Malachi 3:10-12

2 Corinthians 9:6-8

Opposite of drunkenness is being filled with the Holy Spirit.
John 7:38

Romans 8:11

The opposite of falsehood is speaking the truth.
Proverbs 8:6-8, 12:17

Ephesians 4:25

Colossians 3:9

13. Let the Lord examine your hearts ask Him which of these qualities are you weak in.

Make a decision to do something proactive about it. For example: if you struggle with greed or materialism then purpose in your heart to take a God size step of faith. Do something you couldn't possibly do in your own flesh. Give something away -- your money, time, a possession..... Let the Lord lead you.

➤ In everything, by prayer and petition... Philippians 4:6

Ask the Lord to make you a generous person, one who is filled with His Holy Spirit, speaking the truth in love.

*God is able to make all grace abound to you, so that always having all sufficiency
in everything, you may have an abundance for every good deed.
2 Corinthians 9:8*

~ ~ ~ **DAY 3** ~ ~ ~ ~
Three More Woes

➤ Draw near to God and He will draw near to you... James 4:8

The fear of the Lord is an awe and respect for Him, different from other kinds of fear. If you're struggling with the wrong kind of fear right now, tell the Lord. He already knows it. "*For He cares for you.*"

*The name of the LORD is a strong tower; the righteous run to it and are safe.
Proverbs 18:10*

*Fear of man will prove to be a snare, but whoever trusts in the LORD is kept safe.
Proverbs 29:25*

Practice your memory verse:

_____ the _____ of _____ will _____ exalted _____ judgment,
_____ the _____ God _____ show _____ holy _____ righteousness.
_____ 5:___

> ## Study to show yourself approved ... 2 Timothy 2:15

Yesterday we studied the first three woes that would come on the people of Jerusalem because of their sin. Today we will study the second three woes that the Lord declares against them in the last portion of Isaiah chapter 5. Then He describes the Assyrian army that is coming.

14. Read Isaiah 5:20-30. Answer the following questions.

What sin is described in verse 20?

What sin is described in verse 21?

What sin is described in verses 22-23?

What else does the Lord have against them according to verse 24b?

How does Isaiah describe the judgment coming on the people for these sins in verses 24-25?

15. Fill in the following chart about the second three woes, (Isaiah 5:20-23). For each one look up the verses in the last two columns and take notes on what the scriptures teach.

Woe	Sin	Judgment verse	Scriptures' Teaching	Scriptures' Warning
4	v. 20 calling evil good, and good evil	v. 24-25	Proverbs 17:15	Malachi 2:17 Luke 16:15
5	v. 21 pride	v. 24-25	Deuteronomy 8:11-17	Proverbs 11:2, 16:18
6	v. 22-23 injustice	v. 24-25	Exodus 22:21-22 Leviticus 19:15	Exodus 22:23-24 Psalm 12:5

Page 44

16. Answer the following questions using **Isaiah 5:26-30**. This is a picture of the Assyrian Army. It is interesting that the Lord uses the lioness to describe them since this animal was so important to the Assyrians.

How does the Lord summon the Assyrians and how do they respond (v.26)?

How are the soldiers in this army described (v.27)?

What are their weapons and military assets like (v.28)?

What analogy is used to describe its manner when it attacks (v.29-30a)?

Describe what it will be like in the land when they attack (v.30b).

> ## Prove yourselves doers of the word... James 1:22

17. Yesterday we saw that the best way to deal with sin in our own lives and is to pursue the opposite of that sin. How do the following scriptures equip us to do this?

<u>The opposite of calling evil good is to uphold the truth of God.</u>

John 3:21

John 8:32

Ephesians 5:6-11

<u>The opposite of pride is humility.</u>

Proverbs 16:18-19

Proverbs 29:23

James 4:10

<u>The opposite of injustice is being fair and just.</u>

Proverbs 21:3

Jeremiah 7:5-7

Micah 6:8

> ## In everything, by prayer and petition... Philippians 4:6

Ask the Lord to reveal your heart and motives to you. Let Him show you if there are any of these sins in your life. Ask Him to make you someone who upholds God's truth, who is humble and fair. He longs to conform you to His image.

> ... Wait until the Lord comes who will both bring to light the things hidden in the darkness and disclose the motives of men's hearts; and then each man's praise will come to him from God.
> 1 Corinthians 4:5

DAY 4
A Sanctified Tongue

➤ <u>D</u>raw near to God and He will draw near to you... James 4:8

Let the words of my mouth and the meditation of my heart be acceptable in Your sight O Lord, my rock and my Redeemer.
Psalm 19:14

Our words flow from the thoughts of our heart. Take a moment to let the Lord purify your heart.

Practice your memory verse:

But ____ LORD ____ hosts ____ be _____ in _____,
And ____ holy ____ will ____ Himself ____ in _____.
Isaiah ___:16

➤ <u>S</u>tudy to show yourself approved... 2 Timothy 2:15

In chapter 6 Isaiah sees God's holy presence in His throne room. This vision contrasted so greatly with his own condition, that he cried out in grief at his sin. But no sooner had he admitted his sin than he was cleansed of it. That is when God commissioned him to prophesy to His people about their hardness of heart, their future exile and the holy seed that remains.

18. Read Isaiah Chapter 6. Today we will be focusing on verses 1-7. Look at your Isaiah timeline to see the historical context of this vision.

According to verse 1a, when did Isaiah have this vision?

How did Isaiah describe the Lord in verse 1b?

What creatures did he see and what were they like (v.2)?

What do they continually say to one another in verse 3?

How is the temple affected by the Lord's presence (v.4)?

> *Note - For further study on the throne room of God, read Revelation 4 and Ezekiel 1.

How is Isaiah affected by the Lord's presence (v.5)?

Who responded to Isaiah's cry and what did he do (v.6-7)?

Page 46

19. Consider what an incredible experience this was for Isaiah. This vision of the Lord impacted him for the rest of his life. What do these scriptures teach us about the privilege of being in the Lord's presence?

Psalm 16:11

Psalm 21:6

20. In God's presence, Isaiah is woefully aware of his sin, specifically the sin of his lips. What do the following verses teach us about our words?

Matthew 12:34-37

Matthew 15:11, 18

Luke 6:44-45

21. Look up the following scriptures and write down what the Lord says to you.

Proverbs 10:19-21

Proverbs 10:31-32

Proverbs 12:18

Proverbs 15: 1-2

Proverbs 15:4, 7

Proverbs 15:23, 26, 28

Proverbs 16: 13

Proverbs 17: 28

Proverbs 22:11

Proverbs 31:26

James 3:1- 11

> ## Prove yourselves doers of the word... James 1:22

22. The scriptures hold up a high standard for our speech. Specifically, how is the Lord convicting you and what can you do about it?

23. Choose one or two of the scriptures from today's lesson and commit them to memory.

> *Keep your tongue from evil and your lips from speaking lies.*
> *Turn from evil and do good; seek peace and pursue it.*
> *Psalm 34:13-14*

> *I said, "I will guard my ways, lest I sin with my tongue;*
> *I will restrain my mouth with a muzzle,*
> *Psalm 39:1*

➤ In everything, by prayer and petition... Philippians 4:6

Ask the Lord to put a watch over your mouth to guard what comes out, and ask the Holy Spirit to convict you when to hold your tongue. Pray for a transformed heart.

> *Let the words of my mouth and the meditation of my heart*
> *be acceptable in Your sight, O LORD, my rock and my Redeemer.*
> *Psalm 19:14*

> *Let your speech always be with grace, as though seasoned with salt,*
> *so that you will know how you should respond to each person.*
> *Colossians 4:6*

Jesus is our example. He lived in this world yet never failed with His tongue. We, on the other hand, often sin with our tongues. God knows our needs. He knows we're weak in this area. He wants to help us. Cry out to Him. With God nothing is impossible.

> *We do not have a high priest who is unable to sympathize with our weaknesses, but we have one who has been tempted in every way, just as we are-yet was without sin. Let us then approach the throne of grace with confidence, so that we may receive mercy and find grace to help us in our time of need.*
> *Hebrews 4:15-16*

~ ~ ~ ~   **DAY 5**   ~ ~ ~ ~
Isaiah's Calling

➤ Draw near to God and He will draw near to you... James 4:8

> *For the eyes of the LORD move to and fro throughout the earth*
> *that He may strongly support those whose heart is completely His.*
> *2 Chronicles 16:9a*

God is looking for willing and available servants. You're not disqualified because of your lack or weaknesses. He looks at the heart. He will prepare you if you are willing. Ask the Lord what He would have you do.

Write your memory verse:

➤ Study to show yourself approved... 2 Timothy 2:15

Today we will continue in chapter 6 with Isaiah's vision of God and his commissioning to the people of Judah. Once the Lord cleansed Isaiah of his sin, he felt free to volunteer to serve Him.

24. Read Isaiah 6:8-13. Answer the following questions.

What did the Lord say in verse 8 and how did Isaiah respond?

What instructions did the Lord give him in verses 9-10?

> Isaiah 6:9-10 is quoted several times in the New Testament. For example:
> Matt 13:14-1
> Acts 28:26-27

In verse 11, Isaiah asks for how long will he have this difficult job. Write down the Lord's answer. (verses 11-12)

What encouragement does the Lord give Isaiah to balance the sorrow of His previous words (v.13)?

(M)

Note -- Isaiah 6:13 is actually a messianic prophecy about Jesus. The tenth portion refers to those who remain faithful to the Lord. The holy seed or stump refers to the root of Jesse (Isaiah 11:1), also called the Branch in Isaiah 4:2

25. Read I Samuel 3:1-10 and Acts 9:10-17. What do both of these stories have in common and how are they like Isaiah's response to God's call?

26. In Isaiah 6:9-10, God describes a people who have hardened their hearts. Read John 12:37-41. Does God harden a person's heart? Is that fair?

> "As one hears the Word today, it always accomplishes one of two things; either a drawing to God and learning to love and serve Him better, or a further hardening and rejection. We are either better for having heard God's Word or worse. The process of hardening of the heart is not a mystery nor is it a miracle enacted by God, but a natural process begun and carried on and completed by the sinner himself. It is a continuous process. No one ever came to the condition of a hardened heart suddenly. It is produced by repeated neglect of truths and shunning God's calling through the Holy Spirit. A hardened heart is one of immovable feelings through active opposition to God. How many carelessly tamper with the truth of God's Word. It is a serious matter!" (Mrs. T.M. Constance)

27. Look up the following scriptures. What do they teach us about hardening of the heart?

Psalm 81:11-12

Proverbs 28:14

Mark 16:14

Acts 7:51

Hebrews 3:12-13

As in water face reflects face, so the heart of man reflects man.
Proverbs 27:19

> ### Prove yourselves doers of the word... James 1:22

28. Isaiah was called to something that he wouldn't necessarily see a lot of fruit in. We all want to be an impact player and make a big difference. But is there an area in your life that the Lord is calling you to be faithful in, obedient, and maybe not see the outcome? Are you willing to be faithful with a happy heart? Resting, waiting – or are you complaining? Let the Lord search your heart.

For who hath despised the day of small things? .... Zechariah 4:10a

29. Are you condoning sin in your heart that could bring hardening? Explain.

> ### In everything, by prayer and petition... Philippians 4:6

Make yourself available to God. "Here I am. Send me." Ask God to guard your heart against hardening or unbelief. Ask Him to keep you soft and pliable toward Him.

Watch over your heart with all diligence, for from it flow the springs of life.
Proverbs 4:23

~~~~~   Prayer Requests   ~~~~~

The Threat of Invasion
Isaiah chapters 7 – 9
Lesson 4

DAY 1 — Take Care and Be Calm

> ➤ **Draw near to God and He will draw near to you... James 4:8**

We have been given such a glorious hope, yet sometimes we get discouraged. The Lord has given us so many promises to strengthen our hearts and build up our hope. Pray the following scripture into your life.

> *... We have not ceased to pray for you and to ask that you may be filled*
> *with the knowledge of His will in all spiritual wisdom and understanding,*
> *so that you will walk in a manner worthy of the Lord, to please Him in all respects,*
> *bearing fruit in every good work and increasing in the knowledge of God;*
> *strengthened with all power, according to His glorious might,*
> *for the attaining of all steadfastness and patience, joyously giving thanks to the Father,*
> *who has qualified us to share in the inheritance of the saints in Light.*
> *Colossians 1:9-12*

MEMORY VERSE Isaiah 9:6

For a child will be born to us, a son will be given to us;

and the government will rest on His shoulders;

and His name will be called Wonderful Counselor,

Mighty God, Eternal Father, Prince of Peace.

> ➤ **Study to show yourself approved ... 2 Timothy 2:15**

Isaiah received his commission to prophesy in the year Uzziah, King of Judah died. He was a good king who followed the Lord all of his days, though he became proud in his old age and behaved presumptuously. He was humbled and disciplined for it by the Lord. His son Jotham who became king in his place, also walked in the Lord's ways and was faithful all his life (2 Chronicles 26-27).

With a heritage like that Jotham's son, King Ahaz, had every reason to trust in the Lord, but he chose the opposite. 2 Kings 16:1-4 tells us that Ahaz did evil in the sight of the Lord, sacrificing and burning incense to idols on the high places, on hills and under trees. He even sacrificed his own son by fire. He imitated the evil pursued by the kings of Israel (the northern kingdom).

In Isaiah chapter 7 we see that the kings of Aram and Israel have come up against Judah to conquer it. Ahaz is going around Jerusalem to see how he must prepare the city for a siege and the Lord sends Isaiah to meet him. Remember as you read this that Ahaz has rejected the Lord and followed the religious practices of the very kings who are coming to destroy him. Now, instead of simply handing him over to the enemy, the Lord promises to deliver him. He proves that the gods of other nations are no match for the Lord.

1. Read the "History of Aram" in the history appendix at the back of the study (page 384). Make a note of anything that helped you to understand better the climate in which this chapter takes place.
Look up Aram and its capital city on the map in the front of the study.

2. Read Isaiah chapter 7:1-9.

In verse 1, who was planning on invading Judah and what would the end result be?

How did King Ahaz and his people feel about this (v.2)?

What instructions did the Lord give Isaiah (v.3)?

What message did He want him to give the king (v.4)?

What were the enemies planning (v.5-6)?

What promise does the Lord make in verse 7?

In verse 8, the Lord mentions the king and capital of Aram. What prophecy does He give about Israel (Ephraim)?

Then He mentions the king and capital of Israel in verse 9. He follows it with a warning to Ahaz. What is this warning?

Why do you think the Lord linked these nations together with His warning to Ahaz in verses 8-9?

3. In Isaiah 7:3, the Lord had Isaiah take his young son with him to meet the king, who was named Shear-yashub. This name means, "A remnant will return." What message do you think the Lord wanted to convey to King Ahaz through this baby's name?

Note - Around this time, Ahaz had already lost in battle against Israel and Aram and over 200,000 captives had been taken (2 Chronicles 28:8). He may have been referring to them.

4. In verse 9, the Lord has a prophecy spoken directly to Ahaz, "...*If you will not believe, you surely shall not last...*" What do you think it means? (Remember how we saw that unbelief is connected to the hardening of the heart in Isaiah 6.)

> <u>Prove yourselves doers of the word... James 1:22</u>

5. Notice that when the Lord gave the promise, the army didn't instantly disappear. What problems are 'encamped' against you right now? Give the reasons you have for hoping in the Lord and write down any promises in His Word that comfort you about it.

6. Are you resting in the Lord in the midst of your situation? How can you grow in this today?

> <u>In everything, by prayer and petition . . . Philippians 4:6</u>

> *"Be still, and know that I am God . . ." Psalm 46:10*
>
> *". . . Blessed are those who have not seen and yet have believed." John 20:29*

Do you find yourself wanting to see the answers to your prayers before you will rest in the Lord and trust Him? He is worthy of our trust! Pray to the Lord, committing yourself to believing His promises before you see them and choosing to hope and rest. Give thanks and praise Him for His faithfulness!

~ ~ ~ ~ <u>DAY 2</u> ~ ~ ~ ~

Immanuel Is Promised

> <u>Draw near to God and He will draw near to you. . . James 4:8</u>

Meditate on this name, Immanuel (*God with us*), that was given for Jesus over 700 years before He was born. He has fulfilled this amazing name in so many ways! He became one of us and lived like we do. *"He learned obedience from the things which He suffered"*, though He certainly didn't need to. We were created in His image and He took on our fallen image so that He could share His perfect image with us. In what ways is He with you today?

Practice your memory verse:

For a _____ will be _____ to us, a son will be _____ to us;

and the _____ will rest on His _____;

and His _____ will be called _____ Counselor,

Mighty God, _____ Father, Prince of _____.

Isaiah 9:___

> <u>Study to show yourself approved . . . 2 Timothy 2:15</u>

Yesterday we studied the Lord's reassuring promise about the coming war with Aram and Israel as well as His personal warning to Ahaz to not be unbelieving. Today, as we finish chapter 7, we see the Lord using Isaiah's son as a prophetic witness to Judah. He connects the boy's growing up (v.16), with the timing of an invasion in the near future by the Assyrian army that will be used by God to deliver them from the current threat. In the middle of this encounter between prophet and king, the Lord gives an amazing prophecy about the coming Messiah.

7. Read Isaiah chapter 7:10-25.   Answer the following questions focusing on verses 10-14.

What did the Lord tell Ahaz to do in verses 10-11?

What was Ahaz's response (v.12)?

How did Isaiah react to Ahaz's answer (v.13)?

What messianic promise does the Lord give in verse 14?

8. "Ask the Lord..." Isaiah said, "I will not ask..." Ahaz answered. And he must have felt very righteous in quoting scripture and saying he wouldn't test the Lord. Why do you think the Lord was displeased? Look up the following scriptures to help you understand why.

	scripture	insight given
the purpose of a sign	Deuteronomy 18:20-22	
rejecting a sign	Isaiah 30:9-11 John 10:37-38	
testing the Lord	Deuteronomy 6:16 Psalm 95:8-9 *	
the correct heart response	John 7:17	

*Note – At Massah, the Israelites tested God by demanding water and doubting His presence among them (Exodus 17:7).

9. Read Matthew 1:18-25 and explain how this promise was fulfilled.

10. Read Isaiah 7:15-16. Here, in verse 16, the Lord turns back to the boy in Isaiah's arms. Verse 15 could refer to either him or the Messiah.

What food will the boy eat when he reaches the age of refusing evil and choosing good? (v.15)

What time frame does the prophecy in verse 16 give for the destruction of the two kings, of Aram and Israel?

*Note – In his prophecy Isaiah says that the two enemy kings will be forsaken before the boy is mature enough to choose between good and evil. In this culture, children were thought to become directly accountable to God at the age of 13 and this was celebrated with a bar-mitzvah (for a boy) or bat-mitzvah (for a girl). This prophecy about the kings was fulfilled before 13 years were completed. Isaiah's firstborn son wasn't old enough to discern between good and evil when the two kings were wiped out.

11. The Lord warns them about what He is going to do and describes the effect two armies will have on the land of Judah when they gather there. Using Isaiah 7:17-25, answer the following questions.

Who is the Lord going to bring against them? (verse 17)

Who are the two armies? (verse 18)

What analogies did the Lord use and what do they mean? (v.18-19)

What word picture did the Lord use to describe the effect the armies will have on the land of Judah and what does it mean? (v.20)

What will they live off of after the armies are gone? (verses 21-22)

What condition will the land end up in? (v.23-25)

12. This story takes an unexpected turn. The Lord has offered deliverance to Ahaz in the guise of the king of Assyria and instead of trusting in this promise, he takes matters into his own hands. Read 2 Kings 16:7-9 and explain what he did.

13. The Lord had already promised to deliver him and He didn't back down, but notice Ahaz's response to God's faithfulness. Read what Ahaz did next according to 2 Kings 16:10-18. How do you think the Lord must have felt about that? What effects do you think it had on the people Ahaz ruled?

> <u>Prove yourselves doers of the word . . . James 1:22</u>

14. Have you ever responded to the Lord the way Ahaz did in Isaiah 7:12? Explain.

15. Ask the Lord if there is any area right now in which the Lord is calling you to a step of faith and you are resisting Him. Make a decision to overcome it.

If we are faithless, He remains faithful, for He cannot deny Himself. . . 2 Timothy 2:13

16. Look again at the warning that is given to Ahaz in Isaiah 7:9. The truth we glean from this is that faith is essential to laying hold of God's promises. What promise do you need to claim today?

"Without faith it is impossible to please Him..." Hebrews 11:6

> <u>In everything, by prayer and petition . . . Philippians 4:6</u>

Ask the Lord to give you a willing heart so that you will know what His will is. He is able to guide you. "*My sheep know my voice*," Jesus said in John 10:27. Pray for direction and <u>expect</u> an answer. Make up your mind to submit to the answer.
Give Him praise and thanksgiving for His faithfulness.

My sheep hear My voice, and I know them, and they follow Me...
John 10:27

~ ~ ~ ~ # DAY 3 ~ ~ ~ ~
Warning

> <u>Draw near to God and He will draw near to you. . . James 4:8</u>

The LORD spoke to me with his strong hand
upon me, warning me not to follow the way of this people.
He said: "Do not call conspiracy everything that these people call conspiracy;
do not fear what they fear, and do not dread it. The LORD Almighty
is the one you are to regard as holy, He is the one you are to fear,
He is the one you are to dread, and He will be a sanctuary . . . ."
Isaiah 8:11-14

Apparently Isaiah was being affected by the threat to Jerusalem and the fears of the people around him. The Lord felt it necessary to remind him not to fear what everyone else feared and to keep his eyes on the Lord. Then the Lord would be a safe place for him. Entrust your fears to the Lord. Ask Him to anchor you in His peace and to help you keep your eyes on Him.

Practice your memory verse:

_____ a _____ will ___ born ___ us, __ son ____ be _____ to ____;
and _____ government _____ rest ___ His _____;
and _____ name _____ be _____ Wonderful _____,
Mighty _____, Eternal _____, Prince ___ Peace.
_____ 9: __

➤ Study to show yourself approved ... 2 Timothy 2:15

Isaiah chapter 8 is another prophecy about the Assyrian army and the destruction it will cause. It begins with the birth of Isaiah's second son and the prophetic name the Lord gives him. Then it explains why Israel will fall and Judah will not. The Lord gives Isaiah a strong, personal warning and contrasts those who fear God with those who don't.

17. **Read Isaiah chapter 8.**

What was Isaiah supposed to write on a tablet (v.1)?

What kind of witnesses did the Lord choose (v.2)?

Isaiah's wife, a prophetess, gave birth to a second son. What name did the Lord give him (v.3)?
*Note – this is the Hebrew form of the phrase he wrote on the tablet in verse 1.

What reason did God give for this name (v.4)?

18. According to verses 5-6, the Lord was going to bring judgment on Samaria (which is the capital of Israel) because they preferred Rezin, the king of Aram, to the waters of Shiloah. These waters flow next to the city of Jerusalem and represent the truth they should have been living by which flowed from the worship of God in Jerusalem.

In verses 5-6, what do you think Rezin represented to Israel?

Explain briefly what verses 7-8 say will happen to Judah – notice how the Lord uses the analogy of water to describe it.

19. The Lord reveals to the people of Jerusalem that Assyria is coming not only to destroy their enemy but also to afflict them (see 2 Chronicles 28:20).

What does Isaiah 8:9-10 tell us about the enemies' plans against Judah?

Why will this happen according to verse 10b?
*Note -- This phrase is identical in Hebrew to the name "Immanuel" given in Isaiah 7:14.

20. The Lord spoke strongly to Isaiah in verses 11-16.

What does the Lord tell him to avoid (v.11-12)?

What advice does the Lord give him (v.13-14a)?

What warning does He give to the people of Jerusalem (v.14b-15) if they do not honor the Lord as He advises in verse 13?

What exhortation does the Lord give in verse 16?

What is Isaiah's response to the Lord in verse 17?

What does Isaiah say about his children in verse 18?

21. Why do you think the Lord's words to Isaiah were so strong?

Note – There was a plot to conquer Judah and put someone else on the throne (Isaiah 7:6).

22. What did the people tell Isaiah to turn to for advice and how did he react (v.19)?

How does Isaiah say they should consult their God and why (v.20)?

What will happen to the people who ignore Isaiah's advice (v.21-22)?

> ## Prove yourselves doers of the word... James 1:22

23. Isaiah's children were signs to the nation. Have you surrendered your children to the Lord for His purposes? Consider, this includes any children in the Lord that you are called to disciple and pray for. What are some practical ways that you can do this?

24. Can you relate to Isaiah's troubled heart that needed a strong exhortation from the Lord? Are there any conspiracies or plans of men that you are frightened of? What is the Lord's advice to you (verse 13-14a)?

25. Verses 16 and 20 refer to the word of God. How can you make the law and the testimony a foundation for your life?

26. Name some sources people turn to today, apart from God, for wisdom and direction. Have you turned to any of these and what was the result? Make up your mind to turn only to God.

➢ <u>In everything, by prayer and petition . . . Philippians 4:6</u>

Pray over the things you mentioned in the last question. If you have dabbled in any of these and haven't yet dealt with it in prayer then find someone to pray with about it. Any territory that has been given over to Satan needs to be reclaimed and consecrated in prayer. Pray for someone the Lord brings to mind that needs to be delivered from some of these things.

We have renounced secret and shameful ways . . .
2 Corinthians 4:2a

~ ~ ~ ~ **DAY 4** ~ ~ ~ ~
The Kingdom

➢ <u>Draw near to God and He will draw near to you . . . James 4:8</u>

Jesus answered and said, "My kingdom is not of this world.
If My kingdom were of this world, then My servants would be fighting
so that I would not be handed over to the Jews;
but as it is, My kingdom is not of this realm."
John 18:36

Does your heart get overly burdened by struggles that are of this world? Let Him search your heart today and show you if you are getting sidetracked from His kingdom. Ask Him to fill you with joy as He reveals His heart and His plans to you today.

Practice your memory verse:

For ___ child _____ be _____ to ____, a _____ will _____ given ____ us;
_____ the _____ will _____ on _____ shoulders;
_____ His _____ will _____ called _____ Counselor,
_____ God, _____ Father, _____ of _____.
Isaiah ___:6

➢ <u>Study to show yourself approved . . . 2 Timothy 2:15</u>

Isaiah chapter 9 begins with a great promise for two provinces in the Northern kingdom of Israel. It talks about the light that will dawn in this land, the victory they will have and the glorious kingdom the Son of David will rule. It includes some of the most loved prophecies about the Messiah among Christians today.

27. Read Isaiah chapter 9:1-7. In our map of Israel (*located in the front of your study*), look up where the lands of Zebulun and Naphtali are. Also look up Galilee (i.e. the sea) and the land on the other side, east of the Jordan. With a colored pencil, draw a circle around this area.

Answer the following questions.

How was Galilee treated formerly and how will that change (verse 1)?

What will happen to those who live there (v.2)?

Isaiah calls this area "Galilee of the Gentiles" prophetically because over the years, other nations had gradually begun invading and occupying this land (II Kings 10:32-33). This continued in Isaiah's lifetime more aggressively, (II Kings 15:29, 1 Chronicles 5:26), until all the people of Israel were taken away into captivity and other people groups had been brought to live in their place.

How will the Lord bless them (v.3)?

What deliverance will He give them (v.4)?

At some point after the captivity in Babylon, and before the time of Christ, the children of Israel came back to live in this area and yet the people of Judah looked down on them.

How does verse 5 describe what will happen to their oppressors? Considering the context, who do you think they are?

This is why the Pharisees criticized Jesus saying: "...Search, and see that no prophet arises out of Galilee." John 7:52b

28. How is Isaiah 9:2 fulfilled in Matthew 4:12-17?

29. How does Isaiah 9:6-7 describe the Messiah and His government?

30. Notice the names given to Jesus. Write in your own words what each of them means.

Wonderful Counselor	Psalm 33:11	
Mighty God	Jeremiah 32:17-19	
Eternal Father	John 14:6-11	
Prince of Peace	John 14:27	

31. Make a note of what you learn about the Messiah's reign from the following scriptures.

His government	Daniel 2:44 Daniel 7:13-14	
David's throne	Psalm 89:35-37 Luke 1:31-33	

Justice and righteousness	Isaiah 11:3-5 Revelation 19:11	
Zeal of the Lord	Isaiah 42:13 Isaiah 59:15-17 John 2:13-17	

32. What do the following verses tell us about this Kingdom that Jesus rules over?

Matthew 5:3, 10

John 3:3-7

John 18:36-37

> ## Prove yourselves doers of the word... James 1:22

> *And He called a child to Himself and set him before them, and said, "Truly I say to you, unless you are converted and become like children, you shall not enter the kingdom of heaven. "Whoever then humbles himself as this child, he is the greatest in the kingdom of heaven. And whoever receives one such child in My name receives Me..."*   Matthew 18:2-4

33. *God welcomes anyone into His kingdom. Have you personally received His invitation?*
"... God our Savior wants all men to be saved and to come to a knowledge of the truth."
(1 Timothy 2:3-4)

34. Is God your wonderful counselor? When in need of advice, do you turn to Him or to others?

35. Are you experiencing God's peace? The Prince of Peace wants to give you peace that surpasses understanding in your circumstances. Read John 16:33 and Philippians 4:7.

36. Ask the Lord how He wants you to serve Him in building His kingdom today. Write down some practical things you think He wants you to do.

> ## In everything, by prayer and petition... Philippians 4:6

God is your Eternal Father. Our earthly fathers are imperfect and fail us from time to time, but God, our Heavenly Father, never fails us. Spend some time now giving Him all the burdens of your heart. He longs to be with you. Pray for His kingdom to come as Jesus taught us. Offer yourself to do His will.

Our Father in heaven, hallowed be your name
your kingdom come, your will be done on earth as it is in heaven...
Matthew 6:9-10

DAY 5
The Anger of the Lord

> ## Draw near to God and He will draw near to you... James 4:8

The anger of the Lord is very real, but so is His lavish grace. He offered His grace freely to the sons of Israel from the beginning even though the good news of salvation through Jesus the Messiah had not yet been revealed. Consider this beautiful passage in Hosea, which was prophesied to them around this same time period:

> *Return, O Israel, to the Lord your God,*
> *For you have stumbled because of your iniquity...*
> *I will heal their apostasy. I will love them freely,*
> *For My anger has turned away from them...*
> *Hosea 14:1,4*

Take a moment to remember the way His grace has covered you. Ask the Lord to remind you of how He has lavished His grace upon you. Let your heart be comforted and any doubts be washed away.

Write out your memory verse:

> ## Study to show yourself approved... 2 Timothy 2:15

The second half of Isaiah chapter 9 is a message to the northern kingdom of Israel. The Lord points out their pride in the face of the danger that is coming against them. Their enemies attack them on the right and on the left but they don't turn back to the Lord. So the Lord tells them plainly that He will have no pity on them and the judgment that is coming will not be turned back. The tragedy is that the same hand which brings destruction is the hand which offers mercy if they will only return to the Lord!

37. Read Isaiah chapter 9:8-21. Jacob is another name for Israel. Manasseh and Ephraim are two tribes within Israel that inherited large portions in the land. Check your map of Israel in the front of your study and notice the area that belonged to them. Samaria is the capital city.

The message in verse 8 is for Jacob. How are the people responding to it (v.9)?

What do they intend to do after the destruction comes (v.10)?

Who does the Lord raise up against them in verses 11-12?

How do the people respond to these attacks (v.13)?

Who will the Lord cut off, according to verses 14-15?

What kind of leadership do they provide (v.16)?

What attitude will the Lord have in verse 17 and why?

38. Remember how we studied the Lord's heart for the widows and the orphans in lesson 1? Look up these scriptures and consider how distressing it must be for Him to withhold His mercy!
Genesis 6:6-7

Deuteronomy 5:29

Isaiah 48:18

Luke 19:41-42

39. Continue answering the questions about the passage.
What will the wickedness of the people do in Isaiah 9:18-19?

How do the people of Ephraim and Manasseh treat each other, according to verses 20-21?

40. What do the following verses say about the anger of the Lord?
Psalm 30:5

Psalm 78:21-22

Psalm 78:31-38

Psalm 86:15

2 Peter 3:9

Revelation 14:9-11

41. From what you learned in the previous question, why do you think it says in Isaiah 9:12,17, 21, that the Lord's anger is still not turned away? Look at the following verses for help.
1 Kings 21:27-29

Jonah 3:10

Revelation 9:20-21

42. Read Hebrews 3:7-19. Explain under what circumstances we may encounter the Lord's anger.

43. Read Psalm 103:8-13. What encouragement does it give you?

> ## Prove yourselves doers of the word... James 1:22

44. Now that you've got a better idea of what the people were like, it's easier to understand the Lord's exhortation to Isaiah to not be afraid (Isaiah 8:12). What would have happened to Isaiah's witness if he had succumbed to fear? Is there any area in your life where you are letting your weakness hinder your effectiveness?

45. Is there any area of your life in which you may be provoking the Lord to anger? He longs to be gracious to you. Write down what it is and how you will deal with it. Ask for prayer.

> ## In everything, by prayer and petition... Philippians 4:6

Right now, give thanks for the grace of God that protects you from His anger. Ask Him to reveal areas of doubt, weakness and unbelief in your life and to give you promises in the Word that apply. Make a conscious decision to trust the Lord and believe in His promises and don't be discouraged if you feel like you are wavering. <u>Choose</u> to rely on the Lord and He will be faithful.
Pray and pour out your heart to God for all the things you need today.

Now to Him who is able to do far more abundantly beyond all that we ask or think, according to the power that works within us, to Him be the glory in the church and in Christ Jesus to all generations forever and ever. Amen.
Ephesians 3:20-21

~~~~~   Prayer Requests   ~~~~~

The Root of Jesse
Isaiah chapters 10 – 12
Lesson 5

DAY 1
Justice

> ## Draw near to God and He will draw near to you... James 4:8

Today we are going to be looking at how important justice is to the Lord. The people of Israel had completely lost touch with the truth and their ignorance was bringing a terrible destruction upon them. Ask the Lord to give you a spirit of wisdom and revelation in the knowledge of Him. Ask Him to enlighten the eyes of your heart.

> *My people are destroyed for lack of knowledge...*
> *Hosea 4:6*

Take a moment to quiet your heart before Him, committing your cares to Him. It is time to listen. He is going to share His heart with you today and these things are precious to Him.

MEMORY VERSE   Isaiah 11:9

They will not hurt or destroy in all My holy mountain,

for the earth will be full of the knowledge of the LORD

as the waters cover the sea.

> ## Study to show yourself approved... 2 Timothy 2:15

In chapter 10, Isaiah continues his proclamation against Israel that was begun in the previous chapter, (Is 9:8-21), which we studied last week. Now the Lord is getting more specific. He particularly hates the injustices described in Isaiah 10:1-2 and explains the judgment coming against those who practice them in verses 3-4. These prophecies were probably given in the few years between the birth of Isaiah's second son and the coming of the Assyrian army.

1. Read Isaiah 10:1-4. List the things that the Lord is against in verses 1-2.

2. What does the Lord say will happen to those who do these things (verses 3-4)?

3. It is clear that the Lord is bringing judgment on these nations for their lack of justice. In Psalm 37:28 it says "... *For the LORD loves justice...*"

What do the following verses say about justice?

Deuteronomy 10:17-18

Deuteronomy 16:18-20

Page 65

Deuteronomy 27:19

Proverbs 21:3

Proverbs 28:5

> *The LORD loves righteousness and **justice**.*
> *Psalm 33:5*

4. According to Matthew 23:23, how did Jesus feel about justice?

5. We are accountable before the Lord to uphold justice as He does, but we are not to judge others. Only God is a righteous judge. What do the following scriptures teach us about that?

Matthew 7:1-5

1 Corinthians 5:12, 6:1-2

James 4:11-12

> ➤ <u>Prove yourselves doers of the word... James 1:22</u>

6. Have you been unjust in any area where you have authority? Consider not only your job and your children, but also areas such as paying bills and taxes. Perhaps you haven't done anything that the world would disapprove of but your conscience bothers you. What do you think the Lord would have you do?

7. In Proverbs 18:17 it says, "*The first to plead his case seems just, until another comes and examines him.*" It is easy to pass judgment against someone in your heart, without hearing both sides of the story. How can you grow in applying justice in your every day life?

8. Are there any areas you have neglected or avoided that the Lord wants you to be more diligent in because He desires to uphold justice through you?

> ➤ <u>In everything, by prayer and petition... Philippians 4:6</u>

Pray about the things you learned today and areas in your heart the Lord is shedding light on. Ask the Lord to work within you and strengthen what pleases Him. Ask Him to transform you where needed. Commit yourself to learning the ways of justice without neglecting mercy and kindness.

> *To do righteousness and justice is desired by the LORD rather than sacrifice.*
> *Proverbs 21:3*

~ ~ ~ ~ # DAY 2 ~ ~ ~ ~
Judgment on Assyria

➤ Draw near to God and He will draw near to you... James 4:8

As you draw near to the Lord today, consider the high honor He gives us when choosing to use us. Assyria abused the privilege of being a tool for the Lord and was judged for it. We want to learn from their poor example so that we can avoid the same mistake. Read the words of this verse and pray that the Lord would make you faithful.

"Well done, good and faithful slave. You were faithful with a few things, I will put you in charge of many things; enter into the joy of your master."
Matthew 25:21

Practice your memory verse:

_____ will not hurt or _____ in all My holy _____,

for the _____ will be full of the _____ of the LORD

as the _____ cover the _____.
Isaiah 11:9

➤ Study to show yourself approved... 2 Timothy 2:15

In this part of the chapter the Lord explains why He is going to judge Assyria after He has finished dealing with Israel, and what will happen to the army they are so proud of. The king of Assyria was allowed to succeed over Samaria, the capital of Israel (called a godless nation in verse 6), because they were worshiping idols. This led him to a serious mistake. He assumed that he could destroy Jerusalem just as easily and considered the Lord to be as weak as the idols of other nations. We will see more of this story later on in the book of Isaiah.

Read Isaiah 10:5-34.

9. Read the History of Assyria found at the back of your study in the appendix, page 385. Make a note of anything you find helpful or interesting, or that you have questions about.

10. In Isaiah 10:5-14, the Lord explains why He is going to punish Assyria. Fill in the following chart to clarify what the passage is talking about.

The mission God gave Assyria (v.5-6)	
Assyria's intent (v.7)	
Assyria's boasting (v.8-9)	
Assyria's view of the God of Jerusalem (v10-11)	
When the Lord will punish the king of Assyria and why (v.12)	
The king of Assyria's sin and boasting (v.13-14)	

11. Now we'll look at the Lord's answer to Assyria's boasting and judgment in Isaiah 10:15-19. How does God explain their foolishness (v.15)?

What will He do to the king's warriors and worldly glory (v.16)?

Who will reveal Himself and what will He do (v.17?)

What judgment will He bring on the Assyrian king (v.18-19)? *Note- the trees refer to men.*

12. In verses 17 and 20, we see the contrast between the effect the Holy One has on the enemy and on His people, the remnant of Israel. What do these verses teach us about Him?

Exodus 24:17

Deuteronomy 4:24

Deuteronomy 9:3

13. Fill in the following chart using Isaiah 10:20-27.

God's purpose for Israel (v.20)	
God's promise for Israel (v.21-22)	
God's advice to the people of Zion, *i.e. Jerusalem* (v.23-24)	
God's promise about Assyria (v.25)	
God's comparison with past events (v.26)	
God's analogy of their deliverance (v.27)	

Note – Verse 26 refers to the victory the Lord gave Israel through Gideon in Judges 7:25, and to the destruction of Egypt by God, led by Moses in Exodus 14:25-27.

14. List the towns Assyria will overcome on its way to Jerusalem (v.28-32).

15. In verses 33-34, God returns to the analogies of trees and an axe. What does He prophesy?

Note – Lebanon was a land was full of majestic cedar trees and it is symbolic of the men of Assyria (Ezekiel 31:3 "...Assyria was a cedar in Lebanon...").

16. Wasn't the Lord using Assyria to do His will in judging nations, especially Israel and Judah? Is the Lord being unfair to turn and judge them? (Check Matthew 7:2)

17. "In that day" is used twice in chapter 10, in verses 20 and 27. What do these verses say about the Day of the Lord?

> **The Day of the Lord**, is a day of judgment and dealing with the nations. It often had two applications, one for the people of Israel and Judah in their day, and one for the 'end times'. In these cases, some aspects of the prophecy have been fulfilled and others haven't.

***BONUS**: For more about God's judgment on Assyria, read the books of Jonah and Nahum, which represent two different periods of their history about 150 years apart.*

➤ <u>Prove yourselves doers of the word... James 1:22</u>

18. Look at Isaiah 10:20 again. Isn't it astonishing to think of people relying on the one who struck them? Have you ever done that? Who do you rely on?

19. What are some mistakes that Assyria made when being used by God that you can avoid?

How will you avoid them?

What can you learn from Galatians 6:1-4?

➤ <u>In everything, by prayer and petition... Philippians 4:6</u>

Ask the Lord to search your heart and equip you to build up others gently. Pray that He would give you the right heart and attitude when you need to give correction.

*In the same way you judge others, you will be judged,
and with the measure you use, it will be measured to you.
Matthew 7:2*

~ ~ ~ ~ # DAY 3 ~ ~ ~ ~
The Qualities of the Messiah

➤ <u>Draw near to God and He will draw near to you... James 4:8</u>

Today you will be studying a vivid portrait of the Messiah, our Lord Jesus. Ask the Lord to open the eyes of your heart so that you may see Him clearly, and to open your spiritual ears so that you may hear what the Spirit wants to say to you. Ponder these verses and ask yourself, what qualities make the Lord so beautiful?

Your eyes will see the King in His beauty... Isaiah 33:17a

*One thing I have asked from the Lord, that I shall seek;
That I may dwell in the house of the Lord all the days of my life,
To behold the beauty of the Lord, and to meditate in His temple.
Psalm 27:4*

Practice your memory verse:

They _____ not _____ or _____ in _____ My _____ mountain,
_____ the _____ will ___ full ___ the _____ of _____ LORD
___ the _____ cover _____ sea.
_____ 11:___

> ## Study to show yourself approved ... 2 Timothy 2:15

After discussing the injustice of Israel and the arrogance of Assyria, the Lord must have felt the people needed hope. The Immanuel that He mentioned in chapters 7 and 8, and the influence His government will have on the earth are described more carefully.

Read Isaiah chapter 11:1-9.

20. Jesse (v.1) was the name of King David's father. The Messiah was prophesied to be David's son and that's why it was clear that this passage is a reference to the Messiah. How does Isaiah 11:2 describe the Spirit that would be on Him?

Ⓜ

> **The root of Jesse** is another name for the promised Son of David, the Messiah. The word root in Hebrew is "netzer" and is the same root of the word "Nazareth", the town where Jesus grew up. It is thought that Matthew 2:23 was referring to this prophecy in Isaiah 11:1.

21. According to Isaiah 11:3-4:

What would be His delight (v.3a) and what does Proverbs 8:13 say about it?

Describe the justice that He would uphold (v.3-4a).

How would He punish the guilty (v.4b)?

22. What evidence of the qualities of the Messiah, described in Isaiah 11:1-5, do you see in Jesus' life? Read the definition given for each characteristic. Then look up the following scripture references and make a note of how He displays each one.

quality	evidence in Jesus' life
wisdom – knowledge applied in just actions	Matthew 22:15-22
understanding – perceive the meaning, grasp	Luke 2:46-47
counsel – advice given to direct the conduct of another	Mark 10:17-23
strength – mental, physical or moral power, force, vigor	Luke 4:28-30
knowledge – acquaintance with facts, truths or principles	Matthew 24:24-25

fear of the Lord – to have reverence for God leading to obedience	Matthew 4:1-10
righteousness – free from guilt or sin according to moral law	John 8:46, 19:4
fairness – free from bias, dishonesty or injustice	John 5:30
faithfulness – steadfast in affection or allegiance, adhering to promises or duty	John 6:37-40

23. How does Isaiah 11:6-9a describe the earth during the Messiah's reign? Include what the animals will eat.

24. Write down the reason given for this wonderful change in verse 9b:

25. What do these verses say about where the knowledge of God comes from?

Proverbs 1:7

Proverbs 2:6

> *...Let him who boasts boast of this, that he understands and knows Me...*
> *Jeremiah 9:24a*

➤ <u>Prove yourselves doers of the word...James 1:22</u>

26. Of all the qualities of Jesus that are mentioned here, which ones do you admire the most and which ones would you like to emulate the most? Why?

27. A question to ponder: How much would you say that the knowledge of God fills your home and your life? Do you desire more?

28. What areas in your life that are weak and need to be filled with the knowledge of God? Write a prayer asking the Lord to do this for you.

Page 71

> In everything, by prayer and petition... Philippians 4:6

Ask the Lord to build the qualities of Jesus into your life. Pray for these qualities to grow in your family, your church and others. Ask the Lord to give you a single-hearted desire to seek His kingdom first. Pray that the knowledge of God would fill your life.

Thy kingdom come, Thy will be done...
Matthew 6:10

For the Lord gives wisdom; from His mouth come knowledge and understanding...
For wisdom will enter your heart, and knowledge will be pleasant to your soul...
Discretion will guard you, understanding will watch over you...
Proverbs 2:6,10,11

~ ~ ~ ~ ## DAY 4 ~ ~ ~ ~
Gathering the Scattered

> Draw near to God and He will draw near to you... James 4:8

He who is not with Me is against Me;
And he who does not gather with Me scatters.
Matthew 12:30

Let the Lord examine your heart this morning in the light of this scripture. His heart is to gather the lost and He has promised someday to come for us and gather all of those who are His in the clouds. How do the desires of your heart line up with His? Are your thoughts and goals pointing in the same direction? How do you spend your time and money? Let the Lord shape your goals for your own life, for your family and those who are in your realm of influence. Just take a moment to invite Him to work.

Practice your memory verse:

_____ will _____ hurt ___ destroy ___ all _____ holy _____,

for ____ earth _____ be _____ of ____ knowledge ___ the _____

as ___ waters _____ the _____.

Isaiah ____:9

> Study to show yourself approved... 2 Timothy 2:15

Yesterday we looked at the description of the Messiah in His role as the ruler of the earth and we saw the effect He had on all creatures. Today we will look at the second half of the chapter in which the Lord explains what will happen with His people and the territory they will possess. In verse 11 it talks about recovering His people for the second time – and this was before they had even been scattered the first time!

Read Isaiah 11:10-16.

29. Before we study this passage, look up all the places mentioned in verse 11 on your map located at the front of the study. Try to picture what the Lord means when He talks about these places in this passage.

30. Answer the following questions using Isaiah 11:10-16.

What will the root of Jesse mean to the nations (v.10)?

Ⓓ

Ⓜ

What places will the Lord gather His people from (v.11-12)?

What current (in their day) problems will no longer exist (v.13)?

What land will they possess (v.14) and what does it represent today?

> The prophecies about a remnant returning to the land of Israel have been fulfilled twice in history, in the time of Ezra when the Jews returned to the land after Babylon was conquered (Ezra 2:1-58), and during the 20th century after Israel became a nation again in 1948. The greatest fulfillment of it will happen when Jesus returns a second time and sets up His kingdom. (Revelation 20:6)

31. In Isaiah 11:15, it mentions destroying the tongue of the Sea of Egypt. This is probably a reference to a branch of the Red Sea. Then it mentions 'The River' and in the Bible this refers to the Euphrates. The Lord is comparing the freedom the people will have to return to Israel from Assyria to the time in their past when they left Egypt. How does it describe what will happen to 'The River'?

What will God make for His people who remain in Assyria (Isaiah 11:16)?

➤ Prove yourselves doers of the word... James 1:22

32. In Isaiah 11:10-16, we see how God planned to restore His people who had been sent far away because of their sin. He has done even more for us to restore us from the sin that separated us from Him. Do you know of anyone who is in exile because of sin? Do you share the Lord's heart of longing for them to be restored? How can you be a source of restoration to them?

➤ In everything, by prayer and petition... Philippians 4:6

Ask the Lord to make you a gatherer. Ask Him to help you pray this morning for whatever is burdening you and whomever He has put on your heart today.

Already he who reaps is receiving wages and is gathering fruit for life eternal; so that he who sows and he who reaps may rejoice together.
John 4:36

~ ~ ~ ~ <u>DAY 5</u> ~ ~ ~ ~
Rejoicing in the Lord

➤ Draw near to God and He will draw near to you... James 4:8

Take a moment to consider the trials you are dealing with right now. In this brief life, we have troubles and tribulations that are unworthy to be compared with the glory that will be revealed to us. Lord, grant us eternal perspective! Strengthen our hope and our conviction of the glory that is to come. Stir our hearts today to look into the future and rejoice in You.

"In an outburst of anger I hid My face from you for a moment,
But with everlasting lovingkindness I will have compassion on you,"
Says the LORD your Redeemer.
Isaiah 54:8

Write your memory verse:

➢ <u>Study to show yourself approved . . . 2 Timothy 2:15</u>

In Isaiah chapter 12 the Lord tells His people how they will sing and rejoice in Him for His salvation and for His mighty deeds. He encourages them that no matter what judgment they may face, the end will be wonderful.

33. Read Isaiah chapter 12:1-6. In that day, why will they be thankful (v.1)?

34. What has God become to them and what will they do in response (v.2-3)?

God is...

I will...

35. List the things that they will exhort one another to do in verses 4-6.

36. How is the Holy One described in verse 6?

➢ <u>Prove yourselves doers of the word . . . James 1:22</u>

37. Isaiah 12:4-6 calls them to be a bold and powerful witness before the world, making known all God has done in many ways. What does Matthew 5:14-16 say about this?

38. Look at the list you made in question 35. Which ones have you been practicing recently? Which ones do you want to grow in?

39. How has God been "great in your midst" (v.6)? Who will you tell today?

➢ <u>In everything, by prayer and petition . . . Philippians 4:6</u>

Pray through this chapter, giving thanks and finding joy in what the Lord has done for you. Commit all your needs and cares to Him.

For great in your midst is the Holy One of Israel.
Isaiah 12:6

~~~~~ Prayer Requests ~~~~~

The Lord Judges Babylon
Isaiah chapters 13 – 14

Lesson 6

DAY 1   Offending and pleasing the Lord

➤ <u>Draw near to God and He will draw near to you… James 4:8</u>

The Lord is long suffering and patient. He waits for people to turn from their evil ways and He gives them clear warnings. We should never take His grace and His patience for granted. Ask the Lord to increase your desire to please Him.

*Therefore we also have as our ambition,
whether at home or absent, to be pleasing to Him.
2 Corinthians 5:9*

MEMORY VERSE   Isaiah 14:24

The LORD Almighty has sworn, "Surely, as I have planned, so it will be, and as I have purposed, so it will stand."

➤ <u>Study to show yourself approved … 2 Timothy 2:15</u>

In Isaiah chapter 13, we find the "Oracle of Babylon". This prophecy covers the time when the Lord brought the Medes and Persians against Babylon in 538 BC, to judge them for their deeds as a nation, long after Isaiah's death (Isaiah 13:17, Daniel 5:30-31). It calls this the "Day of the Lord". However, this prophecy is also foreshadowing a time period that hasn't happened yet when the Lord will deal with all the nations on earth (v. 11).

1. Look at timeline #2 about Isaiah's era in the front of your study. Write down the time periods for each of the following kingdoms:

Assyria

Babylon

Medes and Persians

This prophesy about the destruction of Babylon is being given at the height of Assyria's power, before Babylon rose to power, before they conquered Assyria, and before the children of Israel were exiled there for 70 years.

2. Read the "**History of Babylon**" in the appendix page 386 at the back of your study and make a note of any questions you have or facts you want to remember.

    In the days that Isaiah was prophesying, Babylon was a distant province of Assyria and his prophecies wouldn't be fulfilled for a couple hundred years. The people must have wondered why it was being given. But the Lord knew that the day would come when these prophecies would comfort a broken and humbled people who were seeking Him and He wanted them to have the witness of fulfilled prophecies against Assyria and other nations as evidence of His faithfulness.

Page 75

3. Read Isaiah chapter 13:1-16.

   How does the Lord summon the conquering army (v.2)?

   How does He describe them in verses 3-5?

4. What do verses 6-13 say about the Day of the Lord?

why they should wail verse 6	
the peoples' reaction verses 7-8	
the Day of the Lord in verse 9	
evidence in the sky verse 10	
who will be judged and why verse 11	
the people left verse 12	
the Lord's emotions, and their effect, verse 13	

5. What will happen to the people of Babylon (verses 14-16)?

> Psalm 137:8-9 shows that the Babylonians were receiving the same treatment they had given the Jews.

➢ <u>Prove yourselves doers of the word... James 1:22</u>

6. Babylon had resisted the Lord and judgment was inevitable. It is easy for us to become anxious when we read these things but we shouldn't fear the wrath of God. 1 Thessalonians 5:9 makes it clear that we are destined for salvation, not wrath. On the other hand, our behavior does matter. Ephesians 5:10 says we should "... try to learn what is pleasing to the Lord." What do the following verses teach us about pleasing Him?

   John 4:23-24

   Romans 8:8-9

   Romans 15:1-3

   Colossians 3:23

   1 Thessalonians 4:1-3

   Hebrews 11:6, 13:15-16

> In everything, by prayer and petition... Philippians 4:6

Pray for the Lord to develop these habits and qualities into your life. Ask Him which one you need the most. "... *the prayer of the upright is His delight.*" (Proverbs 15:8b)

> *... Whatever we ask we receive from Him,*
> *because we keep His commandments and do the things that are pleasing in His sight.*
> *1 John 3:22*

~ ~ ~ ~ <u>DAY 2</u> ~ ~ ~ ~

Babylon in the Day of the Lord

> Draw near to God and He will draw near to you... James 4:8

Read the following Psalm out loud and give thanks for the promises in it. Ask the Lord to anchor the ones you need the most in your heart today.

> *God is our refuge and strength, a very present help in trouble.*
> *Therefore we will not fear, though the earth should change*
> *And though the mountains slip into the heart of the sea;*
> *Though its waters roar and foam,*
> *Though the mountains quake at its swelling pride. Selah.*
> *There is a river whose streams make glad the city of God,*
> *The holy dwelling places of the Most High.*
> *God is in the midst of her, she will not be moved;*
> *God will help her when morning dawns.*
> *The nations made an uproar, the kingdoms tottered;*
> *He raised His voice, the earth melted. The LORD of hosts is with us;*
> *The God of Jacob is our stronghold. Selah.*
> *Come, behold the works of the LORD, Who has wrought desolations in the earth.*
> *He makes wars to cease to the end of the earth; He breaks the bow*
> *and cuts the spear in two; He burns the chariots with fire.*
> *"Cease striving and know that I am God; I will be exalted among the nations,*
> *I will be exalted in the earth." The LORD of hosts is with us;*
> *The God of Jacob is our stronghold. Selah.*
> *Psalm 46*

Practice your memory verse:

The _____ Almighty has _____, "Surely, as I have _____,

so it will be, and as I have _____, so it will _____."

Isaiah 14:23

> Study to show yourself approved... 2 Timothy 2:15

Today we will continue studying Isaiah chapter 13 to see what the army of the Medes will be like and the state the city of Babylon will be left in on the Day of the Lord.

7. Read Isaiah 13:17-22.

Who does it say the Lord will bring against Babylon (v.17a)?

What will their attitude be regarding wealth (v.17b)

What will their attitude be regarding young men and children (v.18)

How is Babylon described and what will be its fate (v.19)?

Who will live there or go there (v.20)?

What kinds of animals will live there (v.21-22a)?

How much time is allotted to Babylon (22b)?

8. In Isaiah 13:19 it says that Babylon will be like Sodom and Gomorrah. What happened to them according to Luke 17:28-29?

9. In the passage we read yesterday, it mentions the Day of the Lord. Today we will look at it again. In Isaiah 13:10 it talks about the sun, moon and stars being dark. This is a reoccurring end times prophesy mentioned in numerous places. Look up the following samples and make a note of what they say:

Joel 2:2, 3:15

Matthew 24:29

Revelation 6:12-14

10. As we study this oracle against Babylon, we need to also apply it to the end times. Babylon is a symbol of the false religion that will deceive the whole world (Revelation 14:8). This is only fitting since it was the birthplace of the first rebellion after the flood (Genesis 11:1-9).
How does Revelation 17:3-6 describe Babylon?

11. What will happen to this city according to Revelation 18:2-8?

➢ <u>Prove yourselves doers of the word... James 1:22</u>

12. We do not want to be swept away by the judgment that is coming on the earth. What advice does the Lord give His people in Revelation 18:4?

13. Is there any area where you are being influenced by the world or where you need to hold up your guard? What are some practical ways you can separate yourself from the world?

14. We are called to live in the world but not be tainted by it. In John 17: 11,15, Jesus said we are in the world, but we are not of the world (i.e. we don't belong to it any more.) In James 4:4 it says "...*Therefore whoever wishes to be a friend of the world, makes himself an enemy of God...*" How can you befriend people in the world for the sake of the gospel without befriending the world?

➤ <u>In everything, by prayer and petition... Philippians 4:6</u>

Confess to the Lord any sins, habits or situations where you have compromised with the world. Ask Him to cleanse you and free you. Ask Him to help you to do whatever it takes to live in a manner worthy of your calling.

Ask the Lord to make you alert and ready for whatever lies ahead. Pray for those who aren't ready.

~ ~ ~ ~ ## DAY 3 ~ ~ ~ ~
Freedom from the Oppressor

➤ <u>Draw near to God and He will draw near to you... James 4:8</u>

A day is coming when we no longer suffer under any oppression, weakness or trial. Commit your cares to the Lord and give thanks. Let Him encourage you with this hope. Make up your mind to wait for the fulfillment of His promises.

Practice your memory verse:

_____ LORD _____ has _____, "Surely, _____ I _____ planned, _____ it _____ be, _____ as ____ have _____, so _____ will _____."

Isaiah ____:24

➤ <u>Study to show yourself approved... 2 Timothy 2:15</u>

Isaiah chapter 14 has several sections. Today we will look at verses 1-11. This passage covers how the Lord will bring His people back to the land, which He did after the fall of Babylon. Then it goes into a 'taunt against the king of Babylon' referring to both the human king and also to Satan (the power behind the king of Babylon) and how he fell from heaven (v.12).

15. **Read Isaiah 14:1-11.** What will the Lord do for His people according to verses 1-3?

verse 1

verse 2

verse 3

16. How will they taunt the King of Babylon (v.4-5)?

> This taunt against the King of Babylon is not just cruel mocking. It helps them to realize that they are free and he has no power over them any longer.

How did he used to treat the nations (v.6)?

How does the earth respond to his destruction (v.7)?

Why were they full of joy?

17. What do the cypress and cedar trees say in verse 8?

Remembering that these represent men, what do you think their words mean?

18. In verse 9 it mentions *Sheol*. This is the Old Testament name for the place of departed spirits. How do verses 9-11 describe the reaction of the departed spirits to the king's fall?

19. In the middle of this taunt, there is a beautiful promise. In Isaiah 14:7 it says *"The whole earth is at rest and is quiet; they break forth into shouts of joy."* As much as we long for God's blessing, He longs for it more. He takes joy in caring for us. Jeremiah 32:41 talks about this same period of restoration. What does it say gives the Lord joy?

20. Zephaniah 3:17 says we are the Lord's source of joy. This really adds insight to Jesus' statement in Matthew 25:23 "Enter into the joy of your Master." What do the following verses say about the Lord's joy and our sharing in it?

Psalm 16:11

Psalm 87:7

Luke 15:7

John 15:11

Galatians 5:22

> ## Prove yourselves doers of the word...James 1:22

21. God's people taunted the king of Babylon in Isaiah 14:4-5, when the Lord dealt with him. What do you think is an appropriate response when a cruel enemy is defeated?

22. Are you lacking joy? Look at question 20. What can you do about it?

23. In 1 Thessalonians 2:20 it says *"You are our glory and joy."* because Paul had entered into His master's joy. His heart had become aligned with the heart of God, he was others-focused, rejoicing in their salvation. Where is your heart invested? Do you find joy in God's will?

➤ <u>In everything, by prayer and petition... Philippians 4:6</u>

Consider how you bring joy to the heart of God. Consider also how you have hurt Him, but instead of letting that discourage you, turn your heart to Him. For everything you have done wrong, just believe "He has taken care of that." Jesus has taken care of all of our sin and in its place is His joy. Don't let your heart be troubled. Believe in Jesus! Today He wants to share His joy with you. You are His joy! Ask Him to give you joy.

The LORD your God in your midst, the Mighty One, will save; He will rejoice over you with gladness, He will quiet you with His love, He will rejoice over you with singing."
Zephaniah 3:17

~ ~ ~ ~ **DAY 4** ~ ~ ~ ~

Star of the Morning

➤ <u>Draw near to God and He will draw near to you... James 4:8</u>

...not My will, but Yours be done.
Luke 22:42

This is how Jesus prepared His heart for the task that lay ahead of Him. Take some time to surrender your will to the Lord. Offer yourself to Him. This is the worship that pleases Him.

Practice your memory verse:

The _____ Almighty _____ sworn, "_____ , as __ have _____ , so ___ will ___, and ___ I _____ purposed, ___ it _____ stand."
_____ 14:___

➤ <u>Study to show yourself approved... 2 Timothy 2:15</u>

24. Read Isaiah 14:12-23. In this passage we discover the real power behind the king of Babylon. Verse 12 makes it very clear that it is Satan. He is called the Star of the Morning (in the Latin: Lucifer) and it says he fell from heaven. According to verses 12-14, what were the purposes in Satan's heart?

I will _____
I will _____
I will _____
I will _____
I will _____

> Star of the Morning: *The Hebrew word is "hellel" or 'shining one' and it is not the same name that is given to Jesus in Revelation 22:16. Stars of God in verse 13, is thought to be a reference to the angels (Job 38:7, Daniel 8:10).*

25. What happened to Satan because of these evil purposes (v.12)?

26. What do these verses show us about Satan's heart?
Genesis 3:4-5

Matthew 4:1-10

27. Make a note of what you learn about Satan and spiritual forces from the following scriptures.

Luke 10:17-20

Ephesians 2:1-2

Ephesians 6:12

Colossians 2:15

James 4:7

1 Peter 5:8-9

28. Read 1 John 3:7-10. How can we tell the difference between the children of God and the children of Satan?

29. The king of Babylon had taken on Satan's purposes and now he must share in his fall. Fill in the following chart using Isaiah 14:15-23.

Where he would end up instead of becoming like the Most High (v.15)	
What people would say about him (v.16-17)	
What will happen to his body (v.18-19)	
Why he won't have a kingly burial (v.20)	
What his children will inherit (v.21)	
What the Lord says He will do to Babylon (v.22-23)	

➢ Prove yourselves doers of the word... James 1:22

30. Read Isaiah 14:13-14 again. Do any of your heart attitudes reflect the thoughts in this passage? Is there any area where you need to humble yourself and relinquish what you want to the Lord? Do you ever say "I will..." when you know the Lord is leading differently?

31. Look at question 27 again. Understanding the Lord's power over the enemy and our part in the spiritual battle is strengthening. How is the Lord encouraging you to apply this truth?

➢ In everything, by prayer and petition... Philippians 4:6

Pray over all the things that spoke to you today. Ask the Lord for His Spirit to rule over you. Surrender your will to the Lord. Don't be troubled by the enemy's attacks or any trials you are going through. Jesus has won the victory for us.

You are from God, little children, and have overcome them;
because greater is He who is in you than he who is in the world.
1 John 4:4

~ ~ ~ ~ # DAY 5 ~ ~ ~ ~
Philistia is Judged

> ## Draw near to God and He will draw near to you... James 4:8

*Behold, I am the LORD, the God of all flesh;
is anything too difficult for Me?
Jeremiah 32:27-28*

We often lose our perspective when we are discouraged and our troubles seem overwhelming. We need reminding that the Lord can handle anything. It's as if He were saying to us, "Have you forgotten I created everything? Are your problems too great for me?" Today as we read about two nations He chooses to deal with, that were serious problems for Judah, remember that He is still the same today. Cast your cares on Him today and quiet your heart before Him. Stir your heart to trust in Him and rest.

Write down your memory verse:

> ## Study to show yourself approved... 2 Timothy 2:15

In the second half of Isaiah chapter 14, the Lord returns to the current powers that are oppressing Judah. He gives a prophecy about how the Lord will break Assyria in His own land (i.e. Judah), which is fulfilled later in Isaiah 36 and 37, during Isaiah's lifetime; and another prophecy about Philistia warning them not to rejoice over the king's death because their own judgment is coming also.

32. **Read Isaiah 14:24-32.** Answer the following questions.

What assurance does the Lord give in verse 24?

What does He plan to do in verse 25?

33. The Lord is planning to make an example of Assyria. Who else will be judged in the same way? What does verse 26 say?

What questions does Isaiah pose in verse 27?

34. The Lord emphasizes in verse 27 that no one can resist His hand. Make a note of what the following verses say about this.

Job 42:2

Proverbs 21:30

Isaiah 43:13

35. Look at Isaiah 14:28-32 and answer the following questions.

When did this prophecy come (v.28)?

What does the Lord warn Philistia not to do and why (v. 29)?

Who will the Lord take care of and how? Who will be destroyed (v. 30)?

What emotions will Philistia experience when the 'smoke from the north' comes (v.31)?
(*This is a reference to Judah, which lies north and east of them.*)

When messengers are sent to Judah to ask what happened, what will be said to them (v. 32)?

36. What do the following verses tell us about the history of war with Philistia (the Philistines) in Isaiah's time? Look at where these kings are on timeline #2 in the beginning of the study.

King	scripture	what it says
Uzziah	2 Chronicles 26:6	
Ahaz	2 Chronicles 28:18-19	
Hezekiah	2 Kings 18:8	

    The Philistines were rejoicing when Ahaz died because his father Uzziah, (the serpent in this prophecy), had fought against them and gained a lot of territory from them. In Ahaz's time they regained this territory and conquered portions of Judah. Now with Ahaz's death, they must have thought their victory was secure but the Lord is warning them that one of Uzziah's descendants, (the viper), would rise up and win against them again. This was fulfilled by Hezekiah in 2 Kings 18:8.

➢ <u>Prove yourselves doers of the word . . . James 1:22</u>

37. In both of these prophecies the Lord points out that He was making an example of them to other nations. Assyria was a warning of judgment that would come to the world and Zion was an example of His protection. What kind of example does your life portray to the world?

38. The same refuge that was offered to Judah (Isaiah 14:32) is given freely to us. How does Romans 8:38-39 describe our safety and how we are loved?

➢ <u>In everything, by prayer and petition . . . Philippians 4:6</u>

Take some time to commit your problems, no matter how large, to the Lord's care. Ask the Lord to make your life an example of His grace and mercy. Pray also for some of the great needs and troubles you are concerned about in the world, for wars, leaders, natural disasters, etc.

~ ~ ~ ~ ~ ~ Prayer Requests ~ ~ ~ ~ ~ ~

Judgment on Moab and Damascus
Isaiah chapters 15 – 17
Lesson 7

DAY 1   The Lord Grieves

➤ **Draw near to God and He will draw near to you... James 4:8**

The Lord has done so much to make it possible for people to be spared. Consider these verses and ask the Lord to give you a better appreciation of His love for people, even in the midst of judgment. Let Him soften your heart and give you compassion for the lost.

> "For I have no pleasure in the death of anyone who dies," declares the Lord GOD.
> "Therefore, repent and live."
> Ezekiel 18:32

> ... How often I wanted to gather your children together,
> just as a hen gathers her brood under her wings, and you would not have it!
> Luke 13:34

MEMORY VERSE   Isaiah 17:7

In that day man will have regard for his Maker,

and his eyes will look to the Holy One of Israel.

➤ **Study to show yourself approved... 2 Timothy 2:15**

In Isaiah chapters 15 and 16, Isaiah proclaims the word of the Lord to Moab. This prophecy was fulfilled in Isaiah's lifetime, three years after it was given, when Assyria conquered Moab. A small remnant of Moabites was to survive. This was surely a powerful illustration for Judah of what God required and how He would follow through on His prophecies about them, as well.

1. <u>Locate</u> Moab on your map that is at the beginning of the study. You may want to color it in with a light colored pencil or mark it in some way. <u>Read</u> the history of Moab, located in the appendix, page 390, at the back of your study. Make a note of anything you consider important, or any questions you have.

2. **Read Isaiah chapter 15** and answer the following questions:

What two cities are mentioned in verse 1? What does it say will happen to them and in what time frame?

What places are mentioned in verses 2-5 and 8?

3. Who will the people turn to in their distress (v.2)?

4. What signs of mourning do the people display?
verse 2

verse 3

verse 4

verse 5

5. What does the Lord say will happen:
To the Nimrim River (v.6a)?

To the vegetation of the land (v.6b)?

To their possessions (v.7)?

To the waters of Dimon (v.9a)?

6. How far does the distress spread (v.8)?

How will the survivors be treated (v.9b)?

> The waters of Dimon mentioned in verse 9 are thought to be a play on the Hebrew word for blood and the name of the city: Dibon.

7. In verse 5, the speaker says "My heart cries out for Moab…" *(NAS)* In context it seems to be the Lord expressing this emotion since He is the one speaking, *(Notice also in Isaiah 16:10b-11a)*. Perhaps as the Lord expresses His grief, Isaiah also shared it with Him. Why do you think the Lord felt this way?

➢ <u>Prove yourselves doers of the word … James 1:22</u>

8. Who or what do you turn to when disaster strikes?

9. How do you feel when you have to discipline or punish someone? Are you the kind of person that relishes seeing someone 'get what they deserve'? Do you share the Lord's grief?

10. Does the Lord share His emotions with you? Or are you always the one doing the talking? Ask Him to give you a deeper friendship with Him, to make you a kindred spirit – someone He can share His heart with.

➢ <u>In everything, by prayer and petition … Philippians 4:6</u>

Consider how much sorrow the Lord has as He looks across the earth and sees the evil and violence that fills it. Lift up your heart to Him and worship Him. Give Him thanks for His kindness and longsuffering. It costs Him greatly. Your prayers bring Him joy. That is humbling! Don't withhold the small amount of comfort that you can offer Him. He values it.

… the prayer of the upright is His delight.
Proverbs 15:8

~ ~ ~ ~ # DAY 2 ~ ~ ~ ~
The Lord's Heart for Them

> ➤ <u>Draw near to God and He will draw near to you... James 4:8</u>

In Isaiah 53 it says that Jesus was a man of sorrows and acquainted with grief. We often connect this with what He suffered on the cross, but it also includes His heart for the lost and those who must be judged. Notice how He felt when the leaders of Jerusalem didn't recognize His coming and embrace Him for who He really was, their Messiah:

> *When He approached Jerusalem, He saw the city and wept over it, saying,*
> *"If you had known in this day, even you, the things which make for peace!*
> *But now they have been hidden from your eyes. For the days will come upon you*
> *when your enemies will throw up a barricade against you, and surround you*
> *and hem you in on every side, and they will level you to the ground*
> *and your children within you, and they will not leave in you one stone upon another,*
> *because you did not recognize the time of your visitation."*
> Luke 19:41-44

Practice your memory verse:

In that day _____ will have _____ for his _____ ,

and his _____ will look to the _____ One of _____ .

Isaiah 17:7

> ➤ <u>Study to show yourself approved... 2 Timothy 2:15</u>

Isaiah chapter 16 continues the oracle of Moab begun in the previous chapter that we studied yesterday. It states plainly that Moab's greatest problem was its pride. As a solution, the Lord recommends that the Moabites go back to paying tribute to Judah as a way of humbling themselves before Him. This would bring them under the protection of the throne of David. The judge in the tent of David (v.5) is a reference to the Messiah.

11. Read Isaiah chapter 16:1-11. Answer the following questions.

Who should they send the lamb to and by what way (v.1)?

Who will turn to Zion for help and what are they compared to (v.2)? *Note – the Arnon River was the border between their lands.*

What will they ask the people of Zion for (v.3-4a)?

12. What promises do verses 4b-5 give and what do you think they mean?

When the Lord makes mention of both the tribute and King David, He is reminding them of a time in their past they may well wish to forget. In 2 Samuel 8:2, we are told that David put two thirds of their people to death after he conquered them. Those who lived paid him tribute. This continued through the reign of Ahab, king of Israel, when they paid tribute with many lambs, 2 Kings 3:4. The Lord seems to be advising them to submit again to Judah, which would be humbling and then they will find that the throne of the descendent of David will be established in lovingkindness. This was how they could find hope in the Lord God of Israel.

13. What is Moab being judged for (verse 6)?

14. What judgment is predicted in verses 7-8?

15. How does the Lord feel about this judgment and why?
verse 9

verse 10

verse 11

16. In the midst of this prophecy of judgment, we saw in verse 5 a hint of hope for Moab, one of the Gentile nations. How do these verses explain more about God's heart for the nations?
Isaiah 45:22

Isaiah 55:6-7

Lamentations 3:31-33

John 3:15-17

➢ <u>Prove yourselves doers of the word... James 1:22</u>

17. Moab is being advised to ask Judah for help (Isaiah 16:1-4). This shows that they, and the gods they take pride in, aren't strong enough to defeat their enemies. It would be humbling and probably difficult for them. Are you in a position right now where you need to ask for help? Explain.

18. In Isaiah 16:11, what is the vivid image given for how the Lord feels about Moab? Can you relate to this word picture? Have you ever experienced anything like that?

19. Can you feel the Lord's compassion and grief for Moab in verse 11? His heart is resonating like the strings of a harp. Sometimes music can help to express the burdens of the heart. Sometimes it is the only way to express "*groanings too deep for words*" (Romans 8:26). How can you cultivate this kind of compassion for others?

> In everything, by prayer and petition... Philippians 4:6

Ask the Lord to give you a heart of compassion for people around you and people in the world. Pray for them. He wants to share His heart, both the joy and the sorrow, with those who are willing. Ask the Lord to stir the hearts of many people to prayer and to pour out a Spirit of grace and supplication on the earth.

For I have no one else of kindred spirit who will genuinely be concerned for your welfare.
Philippians 2:20

~ ~ ~ ~ ## DAY 3 ~ ~ ~ ~
Pride, the Sin of Moab

> Draw near to God and He will draw near to you... James 4:8

Pride is not merely being overly aware of your own self. And humility isn't putting your self down. Pride is thinking more highly of yourself than you deserve, it is believing a lie. Humility is believing the truth about yourself as you really are, as the Lord sees you. Ask the Lord to prepare your heart and open up your understanding so that you will have sound judgment and view yourself accurately. Pray for His word to take root deep within you and transform you today.

... I say to everyone among you not to think more highly of himself
than he ought to think; but to think so as to have sound judgment...
Romans 12:3

Practice your memory verse:

In _____ day _____ will _____ regard _____ his _____ ,
and _____ eyes _____ look ____ the _____ One ____ Israel.
_____ 17:___

> Study to show yourself approved... 2 Timothy 2:15

Read Isaiah chapter 16:1-14. Today we will finish looking at verses 12-14 and then focus on Moab's main problem – their pride.

20. In verse 12 it mentioned their high place. This is a reference to a temple to their false god. How does it describe the way they would respond to the threat that is coming? Will it be effective?

21. This prophecy was probably given in the time of Hezekiah (2 Kings 18:9), when Assyria was threatening all the nations around them. How much time do they have left according to verses 13-14?

22. Moab's pride is described as an excessive pride and verse 6 mentions his arrogance, and his fury. What does Jeremiah 48:29-30 say about them?

23. Read 2 Kings 3:26-27. What did the king of Moab do that inspired the fury of the people of Moab? How does this help you to understand the grief they brought to the Lord?

24. What do the following verses say about pride?
Deuteronomy 8:11-14

1 Samuel 2:3

Psalm 101:5

Proverbs 8:13

Proverbs 16:18

Proverbs 29:23

I John 2:15-16

➢ <u>Prove yourselves doers of the word . . . James 1:22</u>

25. Do you struggle with anger or pride? Explain.

26. In 1 Corinthians 6:12 it says that though everything is permissible for me, not everything is beneficial. There are many areas in our daily lives where we have freedom to make choices. Consider this, what are some small ways in your daily life that you can choose the more humble way? Let the Spirit of God search your heart and guide you. He may have a suggestion for you that wouldn't be a humbling thing for anyone else, but it will be very effective for you.

27. Another aspect to consider is giving honor to others. Is there someone you have neglected to honor that the Lord is bringing to mind? Is there someone you have always considered less than yourself? Ask the Lord to search your heart and help you repent of that. Ask Him to show you how you can give honor to that person.

28. What do you learn about boasting from these scrciptures?
1 Corinthians 3:21, 4:18-20, 5:6-8

James 4:13-16

➤ In everything, by prayer and petition... Philippians 4:6

Ask the Lord to give you a humble, teachable heart. *He resists the proud but gives grace to the humble (1 Peter 5:5).* Pray for those who are proud and resisting Him.

O LORD, my heart is not proud, nor my eyes haughty; nor do I involve myself in great matters, or in things too difficult for me. Surely I have composed and quieted my soul; like a weaned child rests against his mother, My soul is like a weaned child within me. O Israel, hope in the LORD from this time forth and forever.
Psalm 131

~ ~ ~ ~ ## DAY 4 ~ ~ ~ ~
Sharing in the Judgment

➤ Draw near to God and He will draw near to you... James 4:8

Do not be bound together with unbelievers; for what partnership have righteousness and lawlessness, or what fellowship has light with darkness? Or what harmony has Christ with Belial, or what has a believer in common with an unbeliever?
2 Corinthians 6:14-15

Today we are going to see how those who are bound together in unholy alliances share in the judgment they bring. Take a moment to ask the Lord to quiet your heart and teach you what He wants you to learn today. Ask Him to make you salt and light and to keep you from bonding together with those who are in darkness.

Practice your memory verse:

_____ that _____ man _____ have _____ for _____ Maker,
_____ his _____ will _____ to _____ Holy _____ of _____ .
Isaiah ____ :7

➤ Study to show yourself approved... 2 Timothy 2:15

Isaiah chapter 17 begins with a prophecy of judgment against Damascus, the capital of Aram (modern day Syria), and continues with a judgment against the northern kingdom of Israel. We might ask, why would the Lord begin with an oracle against Damascus and end up discussing Israel? This was probably because of Israel's recent alliance with Aram against Judah, which displeased the Lord.

The key to this link is found in verse 3 where the Lord says "*And the remnant of Aram; They will be like the glory of the sons of Israel...*" He then begins to describe how the glory of Israel will fade.

29. Read the history of Israel located in the appendix, page 389, at the back of your study. Make a note of facts you want to remember or questions you have.

30. Read Isaiah chapter 17:1-6. Answer the following questions.

What will happen to Damascus (v. 1)?

The cities of Aroer were located across the Jordan on the border of Moab and belonged to Israel. What would happen to them (v.2)?

What will Ephraim and Damascus each lose in that day (v.3)?

What will happen to Jacob in verse 4? (This also applies to Damascus.)

31. The Lord uses word pictures to describe what will happen to them. He refers to gleanings. This is what was left after the harvest. What does He say and what do you think He means?

verse 5

verse 6

32. What do the following verses tell us will happen to these two nations?
Isaiah 8:4

Amos 1:3-5

> ## Prove yourselves doers of the word... James 1:22

33. The most significant illustration of a bad alliance in the Bible is seen in mixed marriages, ("...*they mingled with the nations and learned their practices*", Psalm 106:35). Read the following scriptures and write down what you learn about this.

Exodus 34:15-16

Deuteronomy 7:2-6

Psalm 106:35-39

Proverbs 22:24-25

1 Corinthians 7:39

1 Corinthians 15:33

James 4:4

34. Have you bound yourself to any partnerships or agreements that will compromise your walk with God? If you are in doubt about a particular relationship or partnership, ask yourself this: What are your goals? How do they compare with their goals?

Can two walk together, unless they are agreed?
Amos 3:3 (NKJ)

35. In 1 Corinthians 5:9-10, it says, *"I wrote you in my letter not to associate with immoral people; I did not at all mean with the immoral people of this world, or with the covetous and swindlers, or with idolaters, for then you would have to go out of the world."*
Explain what you think the balance should be between these two principles.

> ## In everything, by prayer and petition... Philippians 4:6

Ask the Lord to examine your relationships and to point out to you any areas where you have compromised His standards. Ask Him to give you a repentant heart and a willingness to do whatever it takes to set things right. Seek wise counsel and prayer support if you need it.
Pray for people you know who are heading towards trouble.

Then Solomon formed a marriage alliance with Pharaoh king of Egypt, and took Pharaoh's daughter...
1 Kings 3:1

Now King Solomon loved many foreign women along with the daughter of Pharaoh...
For when Solomon was old, his wives turned his heart away after other gods...
1 Kings 11:1-4

"Woe to the rebellious children," declares the LORD,
"Who execute a plan, but not Mine, And make an alliance,
but not of My Spirit, In order to add sin to sin..."
Isaiah 30:1

~ ~ ~ ~   ## DAY 5   ~ ~ ~ ~
Reaping What Has Been Sown

> ## Draw near to God and He will draw near to you... James 4:8

Do not be deceived, God is not mocked; for whatever a man sows, this he will also reap.
For the one who sows to his own flesh will from the flesh reap corruption,
but the one who sows to the Spirit will from the Spirit reap eternal life.
Galatians 6:7-8

The time you spend studying the Word of God is a valuable way of sowing to the Spirit. Ask the Lord today to work within you and bring a rich harvest from this investment. Take a few moments to quiet your heart and commit your cares to Him so that you can focus on the Word.

Write down your memory verse:

> ## Study to show yourself approved... 2 Timothy 2:15

Today we will finish looking at the judgment that is coming on Damascus that will be shared by Israel, "in that day". This phrase "in that day", repeated three times in this chapter, is referring to the day when the Lord deals with these two nations. It also foreshadows a time when He will deal with <u>all</u> the nations.

36. Read Isaiah chapter 17:7-14 and answer the following questions.
What change of heart will take place when the Lord brings this judgment (v.7)?

How will their attitude change towards their idols (v.8)?

Page 93

What condition will their land be in (v.9)?

What is their sin (v.10a)?

What kind of plants did they plant and what harvest will they reap (v.10b-11)?

37. The last few verses broaden in their perspective and look at 'the nations'.
How do verses 12-13a describe the nations and the 'many peoples'?

What will the Lord do to them and how does Isaiah describe it (v.13b-14a)?

Who will receive this punishment (v.14b)? *note - the word 'us' refers to Judah in this verse.

> <u>Prove yourselves doers of the word ... James 1:22</u>

38. What kind of seed are you sowing and what sort of a harvest do you expect to reap?

*He who goes to and fro weeping, carrying his bag of seed,
Shall indeed come again with a shout of joy, bringing his sheaves with him.
Psalm 126:6*

> <u>In everything, by prayer and petition ... Philippians 4:6</u>

*Let us not lose heart in doing good, for in due time we will reap if we do not grow weary.
Galatians 6:9*

Make up your mind to continue sowing to the Spirit and pursuing the things of God. Ask Him to strengthen you and give you diligence to persevere so that you will receive all that He has promised. Commit your needs to Him with confidence.

~ ~ ~ ~ ~ ~   Prayer Requests   ~ ~ ~ ~ ~ ~

Egypt and the Land of Whirring Wings
Isaiah chapters 18 – 20

Lesson 8

DAY 1
Correction

> ## Draw near to God and He will draw near to you... James 4:8

Sometimes we misinterpret the Lord's quiet. He may seem distant, cold, or unfeeling. We read His patience as indifference and His discipline as anger and we rob ourselves of the greatest comfort He offers – trusting and waiting for Him. But He carries our sorrows so deeply. He is so certain of what He must do to deliver us, that He won't be discouraged from dealing with the things that bind us. Consider your life today and begin to trust Him more. Commit yourself to Him. He is your God. There is no other.

Cease striving and know that I am God.
Psalm 46:10

MEMORY VERSE Isaiah 19:24-25

In that day Israel will be the third party with Egypt and Assyria,

a blessing in the midst of the earth, whom the LORD of hosts has blessed, saying,

"Blessed is Egypt My people, and Assyria the work of My hands,

and Israel My inheritance."

> ## Study to show yourself approved... 2 Timothy 2:15

Chapter 18 is a prophecy about a nation in Africa that isn't clearly identified. It says that it "... *lies beyond the rivers of Cush...*". This would be south and/or east of the rivers of Cush (Ethiopia). The most likely assumption is that it is referring to Cush itself. Isaiah follows this prophecy in chapter 19 with an oracle against Egypt and then in chapter 20, mentions Egypt and Cush as the two nations Judah had trusted in that would be judged. We know it is a land renown in the world of that day, a land of power and influence, and the Lord plans to deal with it.
It probably takes place in the immediate future during the Assyrian conquest.

1. **Read Isaiah chapter 18.** The people and their land are described in verses 1-2 and 7. What does it tell you about them?

the people	the land

**** *The reference to whirring wings (or 'buzzing wings' in NKJ) is cryptic. It could have been an informal name based on something as ordinary as the sound of a local insect.*

Page 95

2. In verse 2b, what does the Lord tell the messengers to do?

What does He tell the messengers of the nations to look for to know when this land's judgment has come (verse 3)?

3. Look at verse 4. The Lord is using analogies that they can identify with. They must be a farming society that has a hot climate like the one He uses in His word pictures. How does the Lord describe what His gaze will be like when He turns towards them?

4. In verses 5-6, the Lord uses another analogy, that of a blossoming vine, to explain the war that is coming and what will happen to their people.

What does verse 5 say and what do you think it means?

What age group(s) specifically do you think the pruning applies to?

What will happen to the people according to verse 6?

During what seasons will the war last (v.6)?

5. What will be the end result of this judgment according to verse 7 and what do you think it represents?

6. Isaiah 18:7 speaks of a gift of homage being brought to the Lord. Why is it important to offer this homage before it is required of them?

> Psalm 2:11-12

> Philippians 2:10-11

➤ <u>Prove yourselves doers of the word . . . James 1:22</u>

7. What advice would you give to the people of the land of "whirring wings" if you could speak to them before the Lord's judgment came?

8. Look at question 6 again. Have you given Jesus the homage that is His due? How can you honor His lordship now?

➤ <u>In everything, by prayer and petition . . . Philippians 4:6</u>

All discipline for the moment seems not to be joyful, but sorrowful; yet to those who have been trained by it, afterwards it yields the peaceful fruit of righteousness.
Hebrews 12:11

Pray for those who are experiencing the Lord's correction that their faith would not fail and for the Lord to strengthen them and supply all their needs. Choose to trust the Lord's hand upon them.

~ ~ ~ ~ # DAY 2 ~ ~ ~ ~
Division

> ## Draw near to God and He will draw near to you... James 4:8

The Lord has called us to unity. When we are close to the Lord we have fellowship with others who are close to the Lord. Our differences become small when we focus on Jesus. Ask the Lord to search your heart today and reveal any attitudes or grievances or anything in you that would bring division in His body. Pray for a humble, teachable heart.

... all of you, clothe yourselves with humility toward one another, for God is opposed to the proud, but gives grace to the humble.
1 Peter 5:5

... Put on love, which is the perfect bond of unity.
Colossians 3:14

Practice your memory verse:

In that day _____ will be the third _____ with Egypt and _____, a _____ in the midst of the _____, whom the LORD of hosts has _____, saying, "Blessed is Egypt My _____, and Assyria the _____ of My hands, and Israel My _____."
Isaiah 19:24-25

> ## Study to show yourself approved... 2 Timothy 2:15

In chapter 19, Isaiah prophesies against the ancient land of Egypt. The Lord hasn't given up on them. He revealed Himself to them and judged their idols long before in the time of Moses. Now He says He is coming to them again. No wonder the idols are trembling!

9. Read the History of Egypt located in the appendix at the back of your study on page 388.

10. Read Isaiah 19:1-10. According to verse 1 explain:

How the Lord arrives -

The idols' response -

The Egyptians response -

In verse 2, the word 'against' is used five times. It speaks of a breakdown of society on several levels, social, political and familial. Who is against whom? List all five.

11. This division and warfare in Egypt is extremely destructive. According to verse 3:
What happens to their spirit and their plans?

Who do they turn to instead of the Lord?

12. Who does the Lord hand them over to (v.4)?

13. What do the following verses teach us about division?
Matthew 12:25

Romans 16:17-18

1 Corinthians 1:10

1 Corinthians 12:24-25

14. In this oracle against Egypt, the Lord destroys first of all their unity. Second, He targets the heart of their economy and wealth.
What will happen to their waters, rivers, canals and streams (v.5-6)?

What will happen to the Nile, it's vegetation and fields (v.7)?

What is the response of the fishermen (v.8)?

How do the weavers respond (v. 9)?

What and who else is affected (v.10)?

> ➤ <u>Prove yourselves doers of the word . . . James 1:22</u>

15. What did Jesus pray for us in John 17:21-23?

16. How does 1 John 1:6-7 help us understand why it isn't always this way?

17. What are some practical ways you can be a source of unity in the body? See Ephesians 4:1-6.

> ➤ <u>In everything, by prayer and petition . . . Philippians 4:6</u>

Ask the Lord to heal broken relationships and division in the body. Let Him show you specific situations He wants you to pray for. Pray with faith and confidence because your prayers will make a difference. Commit yourself to serving the Lord and being a blessing to His people.

Only conduct yourselves in a manner worthy of the gospel of Christ... that you are standing firm in one spirit, with one mind striving together for the faith of the gospel...
Philippians 1:27

~ ~ ~ ~ **DAY 3** ~ ~ ~ ~
Foolish Advisers

> Draw near to God and He will draw near to you... James 4:8

Who do you turn to for counsel? What would the Lord say about your advisers? Jesus warned us solemnly that there would be people we can't trust who try to lead us astray with their teaching. He said we would know them by their fruits, that is, their deeds. Ask the Lord to give you insight today and to deliver you from any teachings or people in your life that are destructive. You are accountable before God for the advice you take.

Who is this that darkens counsel by words without knowledge?
Job 38:2

Practice your memory verse:

In _____ day _____ will ____ the _____ party _____ Egypt _____ Assyria, ___ blessing ____ the _____ of ____ earth, _____ the _____ of _____ has _____, saying," _____ is _____ My _____, and _____ the _____ of _____ hands, _____ Israel _____ inheritance."
_____ 19: _____

> Study to show yourself approved... 2 Timothy 2:15

18. Read Isaiah 19:11-16. Yesterday we saw how disunity and economic disaster have come upon Egypt. Today, the Lord exposes one of Egypt's greatest weaknesses, its leaders, and He brings charges against them.

Note – *The Hebrew word 'prince' means one who has power; a ruler or leader.* (Strong's)

How does God describe Pharaoh's advisers, the princes of Zoan and Memphis, in verses 11a+13a?

How do they describe themselves (v.11b)?

What challenge does God give to Pharaoh's advisers in verse 12?

What charges does He bring against them in verses 13b and 14?

What word picture does the Lord use to explain how Egypt looks to Him (v.14b)?

What does verse 15 say will happen?

Read Isaiah 9:14-15. Explain who this verse is talking about.

What will the end result be of their terrible leadership according to Isaiah 19:16?

19. What do the following verses say about the world's wisdom?

Isaiah 44:24-25

1 Corinthians 1:19-20

20. What were the wise men of Egypt lacking according to Proverbs 9:10?

> ➤ Prove yourselves doers of the word... James 1:22

21. What do the following verses teach you about seeking wise counsel?

Psalm 1:1a

Psalm 32:8

Psalm 33:10-11

Proverbs 11:14

Proverbs 12:15

22. Are you listening to counsel that is ungodly? Have you chosen advisors whose lives are ungodly? What kind of fruit will their counsel bear?

23. What is your realm of influence or example? In what areas do you exercise leadership?

24. What leadership qualities do you admire most?

25. How do you need to grow as a leader and an example?

26. What practical steps will you take to grow as a godly advisor and leader?

> ➤ In everything, by prayer and petition... Philippians 4:6

Ask the Lord to make you diligent to seek His counsel and to give you godly, faithful advisers. Ask Him to make you someone who gives wise counsel. Pray for an ever-increasing love of the Word of God.

Your statutes are my delight; they are my counselors.
Psalm 119:24

Pray for the Lord to develop leadership qualities in you. Ask Him to make you an example worthy of imitating.

... In speech, conduct, love, faith and purity,
show yourself an example of those who believe.
1 Timothy 4:12

~ ~ ~ ~ **DAY 4** ~ ~ ~ ~
My People

➤ <u>D</u>raw near to God and He will draw near to you... James 4:8

The Lord desires to gather people for His own from all the nations. What does it mean to be the people of the Lord? Read the following verse aloud. Underline the parts that bless you the most.

*And they shall be My people, and I will be their God;
and I will give them one heart and one way, that they may fear Me always,
for their own good, and for the good of their children after them. And I will make
an everlasting covenant with them that I will not turn away from them, to do them good;
and I will put the fear of Me in their hearts so that they will not turn away from Me.
And I will rejoice over them to do them good, and I will faithfully plant them in this land
with all My heart and with all My soul.*
Jeremiah 32:38-41

Practice your memory verse:

_____ that _____ Israel _____ be _____ third _____ with _____
and _____, a _____ in _____ midst _____ the _____,
whom _____ LORD _____ hosts _____ blessed, _____,
"Blessed _____ Egypt _____ people, _____ Assyria _____ work _____
My _____, and _____ My _____."
Isaiah ___:24-25

➤ <u>S</u>tudy to show yourself approved... 2 Timothy 2:15

In the last part of Isaiah chapter 19, the Lord talks about how the Egyptians will eventually worship Him and He will deliver them. He also mentions the three greatest nations that Judah is concerned with: Egypt, their ally, Israel, their enemy and Assyria, the kingdom that is conquering the known world. He proclaims that a day is coming when all of these nations will worship the Lord together.

27. Read Isaiah 19:16-25. Remember that "in that day" is a reference to the end times as well as a day of judgment on the nations. Use the following questions to record the things that will happen to Egypt "In that day".

Reviewing verse 16, what state will the Egyptians be in and why? Ⓓ

What will their attitude be towards Judah (v.17)?

What will happen to their cities (v.18)?

What will there be in Egypt and what do you think it means (v.19)?

Why will they build these things (v.20a)?

Describe who the Lord will send to them in answer to their cry (v.20b)?

28. The Lord makes His purpose very clear in verses 21-22. What does He say?

verse 21

verse 22

29. Remember that Assyria is the greatest threat at the time when Isaiah was prophesying. Israel was an enemy. Egypt was Judah's ally, also a great nation. Each one of them had their own religious system of idol worship. What does Isaiah say in these verses?

verse 23

verse 24

verse 25

30. Assyria was located in modern Iran. Can you picture Iran, Egypt and Israel worshiping the Lord together? What do you think the people's reaction might have been to these prophecies?

31. In Isaiah 19:25, the Lord uses names that traditionally belong only to Israel. Egypt and Assyria are now going to share in them. What do they reveal about their new relationship with God?

name	traditional use	now used for	your thoughts
My people	Exodus 6:7	Egypt	
work of My hands	Isaiah 64:8	Assyria	
My inheritance	I Kings 8:51-53	Israel	

*Note – The fulfillment of this prophecy applies to all of Israel, not just the northern kingdom.

➢ <u>Prove yourselves doers of the word... James 1:22</u>

32. In Isaiah 19:20, the Lord delivers them. How has He been a Savior and a Champion in your life? How has He delivered you from your oppressors?

33. These three nations listed in Isaiah 19:25, were all powerful, pagan nations (even Israel because they had abandoned the Lord and gone after pagan idols). Perhaps this promise of the Lord seemed almost too amazing to believe. What nations do you know of that have religious and cultural ways which are an overwhelming obstacle to the gospel?
What hope can you glean from this verse?

34. What does John 10:16 say about this?

➢ <u>In everything, by prayer and petition... Philippians 4:6</u>

    Pray for those nations that you listed in question 33. Ask the Lord to drive back the darkness that hinders them from understanding the gospel. Lord, pour out your Holy Spirit and send forth workers into the harvest.

*All the ends of the earth will remember and turn to the LORD,
And all the families of the nations will worship before You.
Psalm 22:27*

~ ~ ~ ~ # DAY 5 ~ ~ ~ ~
Sharing the Shame

➤ <u>Draw near to God and He will draw near to you... James 4:8</u>

Sometimes the Lord calls us to share in someone else's sorrow or shame. He allows us to go through difficult trials. Jesus prepared His heart for suffering by surrendering to the will of God. Ask the Lord to give you the same heart. No one can rob you of what you give willingly.

*... If when you do what is right and suffer for it you patiently endure it,
this finds favor with God.
1 Peter 2:20*

Write down your memory verse:

➤ <u>Study to show yourself approved... 2 Timothy 2:15</u>

In Isaiah chapter 20, after the fall of Samaria, the commander of the Assyrian army arrives to attack Ashdod, a Philistine city on the West coast bordering Judah. The Philistines were apparently expecting to be relieved by the armies of Egypt and Cush. Judah watched anxiously as this war unfolded. Egypt was also their ally and Ashdod was about 32 miles away from Jerusalem. Imagine the entire Assyrian army sweeping down the coastline, that close to your home! But Isaiah warns them vividly that the outcome will not be good.

The Lord asks Isaiah to perform a sign to verify that the prophecy is from God (Deut. 18:21-22).

35. Read Isaiah chapter 20. Look up Philistia and Ashdod on the map of Israel in the front of your study. You may want to mark this with a colored pencil. Look at timeline # 2 in the front of your study. It will help you figure out the time frame.

What city is conquered, which Assyrian king is mentioned and what is the time frame (v.1)?

What does the Lord tell Isaiah to do (v.2)?

Who is the sign against (v.3)?

What does it mean will happen (v.4)?

What will be the result of this event (v.5)?

Who is this referring to and what do they say (v.6)?

36. How does Isaiah's sign of nakedness show the foolishness of hoping in something other than the Lord?

37. The war apparently lasted three years and during that time, Isaiah bore the shame of the captives of Egypt and Cush, both proud and powerful nations. What does this tell you about the Lord that He would have His servant walk this way?

38. Does this give you a glimpse of Isaiah's character? How would you describe him based on what you know so far?

So they went on their way... rejoicing that they had been considered worthy to suffer shame for His name. Acts 5:41

39. What can you glean from these verses?

Matthew 16:24

Luke 6:22-23

2 Corinthians 12:7-9

> ## Prove yourselves doers of the word... James 1:22

40. Isaiah was called to a radical obedience. Have you ever been called to something similar?

41. What does it mean to share in someone's shame?

42. Read Hebrews 12:2. How did Jesus overcome shame?

43. How can you come alongside someone who is suffering with shame? They have a great need for hope and forgiveness. These stories may be helpful.

Luke 18:10-14

John 8:3-11

> ## In everything, by prayer and petition... Philippians 4:6

Pray for people you know who are bearing shame or disgrace. Ask the Lord to give you a heart of compassion for them and a willingness to come alongside them to help them bear the burden.

And so Jesus also suffered outside the city gate to make the people holy through His own blood. Let us, then, go to Him outside the camp, bearing the disgrace He bore. (NIV)
Hebrews 13:12-13

~~~~~ Prayer Requests ~~~~~

Edom and Jerusalem
Isaiah chapters 21 – 22
Lesson 9

DAY 1 — Keeping Watch

> Draw near to God and He will draw near to you... James 4:8

Are you getting sleepy or complacent in your faith? The Lord warns us in the same way He warned His people who would be in exile in Babylon. Stay alert so that you will avoid the snares of the world. Wait before the Lord for a moment and let Him show you where you need to be stirred.

*Keep watching and praying that you may not enter into temptation;
the spirit is willing, but the flesh is weak.
Matthew 26:41*

MEMORY VERSE   Isaiah 21:8 (NIV)

*And the lookout shouted, "Day after day, my lord,
I stand on the watchtower; every night I stay at my post."*

> Study to show yourself approved... 2 Timothy 2:15

In Isaiah chapter 21, there are three oracles of judgment. The first is about the fall of Babylon (Isaiah 21:9) to the Medean and Persian armies in 538 BC, fulfilled about 140 years after Isaiah's death.

Isaiah compares the coming of the Medes and Persians (Elam) to the windstorms of the Negev. The Negev is a part of southern Judah that is very dry – in fact, Negev means 'dry land'. At times, sandstorms blow in from the Sahara desert carrying huge quantities of warm sand that darken the sky and obscure the vision for miles around. Clothes washed and hung to dry in these storms dry in half an hour or less and smell of sand. The windstorms leave a fine layer of sand on everything, even in closed rooms. At times, if the wind is fierce enough, it becomes like sandpaper scouring away at everything.

1. Read Isaiah 21:1-10. Answer the following questions.

How is the coming judgment described (v.1)?

What is Isaiah's opinion of the vision God has shown him (v.2a)?

What observation does he make about the people the vision is about (v.2b)?

Who is the Lord bringing and what will God accomplish through them (v.2c)?

Write down the effect the vision has on Isaiah in verses 3-4.

2. In Isaiah 21:3-4, Isaiah experienced physical symptoms similar to what the King of Babylon would suffer when the prophecy was fulfilled. How is this described in these scriptures?
Jeremiah 50:43, 51:31

Daniel 5:5-6

3. At the time when this prophecy was being fulfilled, Belshazzar, the king of Babylon, hosted a feast for a thousand of his nobles (Daniel 5:1) while outside the city walls the army of the Medes and the Persians laid siege. What does Isaiah 21:5 say Babylon's captains are doing when the attack comes and what does the prophet cry out to them?

4. How do these verses describe the army coming against Babylon?
Isaiah 13:17-18

Jeremiah 50:42

5. The Lord wanted them to be watching for the fulfillment of His prophecies. Answer the following questions from Isaiah 21:6-10.

Who does the Lord appoint and what is he supposed to do (v.6)?

What is he supposed to watch for and how should he respond when he sees it (v.7)?

How is the lookout responding to this commission (v.8)?

In verse 9 the lookout sees what he has been watching for. What response does he hear (v.9)?

What word does Isaiah add to this prophecy (v.10)?

> ➤ <u>Prove yourselves doers of the word . . . James 1:22</u>

6. Consider how this prophecy affected Isaiah (in Isaiah 21:3-4). Why do you think the Lord shared this burden with him? Are you willing to share the burdens of the Lord?

7. The Lord is portraying a drastic contrast between His servants who are watchful and alert and the people of Babylon who are feasting as their doom draws near. Why do you think it is so important to the Lord that His people be watching for the fulfillment of His prophecies?

8. In what ways is the Lord calling you to be watchful?

9. How can you apply Isaiah 21:8 to your life?

> ➤ <u>In everything, by prayer and petition . . . Philippians 4:6</u>

What prophecies and purposes of the Lord come to mind right now that haven't yet been accomplished? Pray over these promises and ask the Lord to make you faithful and help you keep watch.

Indeed, none of those who wait for Thee will be ashamed...
Psalm 25:3

Not one of the good promises which the LORD had made
to the house of Israel failed; all came to pass.
Joshua 21:45

DAY 2
Edom's Question

> Draw near to God and He will draw near to you... James 4:8

A heart at peace gives life to the body, but envy rots the bones. (NIV)
Proverbs 14:30

Are there any areas of your heart that need peace? Ask the Prince of Peace. Do you struggle with envy? Let the love of Christ fill your heart and wash it away. Ask the Lord to use His word today to free you and transform you.

Practice your memory verse:

And the _____ shouted, "Day after _____, my lord, I _____ on the _____; every _____ I stay at my _____."
Isaiah 21:8

> Study to show yourself approved... 2 Timothy 2:15

The second oracle in Isaiah chapter 21 is about Edom and is very brief, covering only two verses. The context of this passage is during the time of the captivity of Judah in Babylon.

10. Read the History of Edom in the appendix, page 387, located at the end of your study. Make a note of anything that interests you or any questions you have. Locate Edom on your map in the beginning of the study.

11. Read Isaiah 21:11-12. This is a rather strange oracle about Edom that becomes a little clearer when you compare it with other scriptures. A voice calls from Seir, the mountainous area of Edom, asking the watchman a question, (probably the same watchman that is mentioned in verse 8, i.e. the one watching for the Lord's words to be fulfilled).

What is he asking and what do you think he means (v.11)?

What is the answer and what do you think it means (v.12)?

12. The context of this passage is during the time of the captivity of Judah in Babylon. Judah is supposed to look forward to the destruction of Babylon and a time of restoration for the remnant of their people. They have been encouraged to watch for these promises. Edom's interest has a different intent. They seem to be asking how long Judah's suffering will continue. Read the following verses and make a note of Edom's attitude towards God's people.

Ezekiel 35:5

Ezekiel 35:10-13

Ezekiel 36:5

Amos 1:11

Obadiah 1:10-12

13. Now that you have looked up these verses, it is probably easier to understand the context of what the voice from Edom said. They were enjoying and benefiting from Judah's suffering. What do you think they were really asking? What was their purpose?

➤ <u>Prove yourselves doers of the word . . . James 1:22</u>

14. Read Hebrews 12:15-17. There are several interesting points about Esau in this scripture. It implies that he was defiled by bitterness. And he was truly sorry for losing the blessing, but he had no repentance for what he had done.
Have you ever confused sorrow and tears for repentance? Explain.

Have you let others convince you of their motives with tears instead of deeds?

15. Have you enjoyed someone else's trouble or thought that they were getting what they deserved? Before you say "no", consider how common this sentiment is in our popular culture today. Movies often appeal to a sense of 'getting what they deserve'. We are encouraged to laugh at our enemies and jeer at their suffering.

What does Proverbs 24:17-18 say?

16. Edom had a culture based on a deep animosity and envy towards Judah. This hardened their hearts towards them and stifled their compassion. What kind of things have hindered your compassion in the past – perhaps still are?

➤ <u>In everything, by prayer and petition . . . Philippians 4:6</u>

Pray for a compassionate heart towards those who are reaping what they have sown. Ask the Lord to give you a humble heart. Ask Him to free you of anything that is stifling your compassion.

Rejoice with those who rejoice, and weep with those who weep.
Be of the same mind toward one another; do not be haughty in mind,
but associate with the lowly. Do not be wise in your own estimation.
Romans 12:15-16

~ ~ ~ # DAY 3 ~ ~ ~ ~
Arabia's Opportunity

➤ <u>Draw near to God and He will draw near to you... James 4:8</u>

*Dear children, let us not love with words or tongue
but with actions and in truth. (NIV)
I John 3:18*

We never know what opportunities the Lord will send our way to be a blessing to others. We do know that "apart from Him we can do nothing". Ask the Lord to work in your heart today and equip you for the needs of the day. Pray for a renewed love for the Lord and a new filling of His Holy Spirit.
Take a moment to consider your need for Him and then let the word wash you and equip as you study.

Practice the memory verse.

*And _____ lookout _____, "Day _____ day, _____ lord,
___ stand _____ the _____; every _____ / _____ at _____ post."
_____ 21:___*

➤ <u>Study to show yourself approved... 2 Timothy 2:15</u>

The third oracle in Isaiah chapter 21 is about Arabia, but it isn't a prophecy of judgment on them. It is a gently worded request from the Lord asking for mercy towards the fugitives who will be coming their way. It may be referring to the time when Nebuchadnezzar attacks Kedar, an Arabian tribe, as mentioned in Jeremiah 49.

17. Read Isaiah 21:13-17. Several tribes of Arabia are mentioned here, Tema and Kedar, two tribes from the sons of Ishmael; and Dedan, a tribe from a son of Abraham by Keturah, his second wife. The Dedanites were merchants who usually traveled in caravans for the purpose of trade and this passage mentions their need to stay overnight in Arabia, a dry and desert land.

Look up Tema, Kedar and Dedan, on your map of the Ancient Middle East.

Who was traveling and where would they spend the night (v.13)?

What were the Temanites encouraged to do (v.14)?

Why were they asked to do this (v.15)? (It is clear they are being asked to give aid for free.)

Where would the refugees come from (v.16)?

18. What was going to happen within a year in verses 16-17?

19. There is one other prophecy about war against Kedar, which is probably referring to the same time period. What does Jeremiah 49:28-33 say will happen when Nebuchadnezzar, the King of Babylon, attacks them?

➤ <u>Prove yourselves doers of the word... James 1:22</u>

20. In verse 14, Arabia was told to bring water and bread to the fugitives who were fleeing from Kedar. They were expected to do this willingly and cheerfully. How do you respond when you see a need and you have something you could share? Are you reluctant to use your limited resources? Let the Lord search your heart about this.

21. Or do you generously give with a desire to be a blessing? What do these verses teach us?
Proverbs 3:27-28

Matthew 7:12

James 2:12-16

1 John 3:17

➤ <u>In everything, by prayer and petition... Philippians 4:6</u>

Pray for the needs of those around you and ask the Lord to make you a cheerful giver. Lord, grant us today, opportunities to share with others and help us to recognize them.

Yes, brother, let me benefit from you in the Lord; refresh my heart in Christ.
Philemon 1:20

~ ~ ~ ~ ## DAY 4 ~ ~ ~ ~
Jerusalem's Folly

➤ <u>Draw near to God and He will draw near to you... James 4:8</u>

Deliver those who are being taken away to death,
And those who are staggering to slaughter -- Oh, hold them back!
Proverbs 24:11

The time we spend in the word and waiting on the Lord is so valuable. He equips us to be like lighthouses to those around us. Ask Him to strengthen and encourage you today. Ask Him to make you bold and forgetful of self so that you will be able to warn those who are heading into danger. Turn to the scriptures now with the expectation of receiving all you need.

Practice your memory verse:

_____ the _____ shouted, "_____ after _____, my _____, I _____ on _____ watchtower; _____ night ___ stay ___ my _____."

Isaiah ____:8

> ## Study to show yourself approved... 2 Timothy 2:15

Isaiah chapter 22 is about Jerusalem. It takes place during the reign of Hezekiah in Isaiah's lifetime. The Assyrian army is coming their way and they are getting ready to resist them, but the Lord sees that they are neglecting the most important preparations of all and exhorts them. The second half of the chapter is a personal prophecy against one man in the king's household.

22. **Read Isaiah 22:1-14.** The Valley of Vision is a reference to Jerusalem (see verses 9-10).

What are the people doing in verse 1 and why do think they did this?

How did the mood of the city change and why (v.2)?   *Note – the second part of this verse may refer to famine because of a siege.

What did their rulers do and what happened to them (v.3)?

How did Isaiah feel about this prophecy (v.4)?

What has the Lord planned for this day (v.5)?

23. In Isaiah 22:6, Elam and Kir are mentioned. Elam was a part of Persia and Kir was a city of Medea, both of which were under Assyria's domination at that time. They were probably included in the Assyrian army.

How did they prepare for battle (v.6)?

What would the people of Jerusalem see when they looked out from the city walls (v.7)?
*Note – perhaps this is why they are all on the housetops in verse 1.

What did God do according to verse 8a?

24. How are the people of Jerusalem preparing for the threat coming against them?

verse 8b

verse 9

verse 10

verse 11a

25. What did they neglect according to Isaiah 22:11b?

26. King Hezekiah built an underground conduit, 1750 ft. long, that joined the water from the Siloam Pool within the city, to the Gihon Spring that was outside the walls of the city. This impressive project has been excavated and can be visited today. He was preparing for the invasion of Assyria. What do the following verses say about the preparations Hezekiah made?

2 Kings 20:20

2 Chronicles 32:2-5

27. What had the Lord called the people to in Isaiah 22:12?

How were they actually acting in the face of the impending war (v.13)?

28. What perspective does Lamentations 4:12 give on why they might have reacted this way?

29. What sobering warning did the Lord give them in Isaiah 22:14?

30. When Judah was preparing for the army of Assyria, they were being very wise according to worldly standards. It must have been a real jolt to hear a prophecy like this one. If it had come from anyone else, they may have rejected it, but Isaiah was a famous man of God. The people of Jerusalem had seen other prophecies of his come true, such as the fall of the northern kingdom of Israel during the reign of Ahaz. When he came to them with this prophecy, weeping and grieving over what was to come, what effect do you think it had on them?

> In some ways this is a very encouraging prophecy because the people of Jerusalem really took it to heart and repented. The frightening predictions in verses 2-5 never took place! We will be studying the continuation of this story in detail in Isaiah chapters 36-37.

➢ <u>Prove yourselves doers of the word . . . James 1:22</u>

31. What do the following verses say?
Jeremiah 5:1

Jeremiah 26:3

Acts 3:19

32. Isaiah dearly loved his people and interceded for them with tears. How has the Lord called you to be an intercessor? Ask Him to show you.

➢ <u>In everything, by prayer and petition . . . Philippians 4:6</u>

Turn to the Lord and pray for those who are reaping the consequences of their sin. Ask the Lord to bring them to repentance. Ask Him also to soften your heart in any area where you have sinned and need to repent. Take a moment to give the Lord praise, honor and glory for His great compassion and lavish forgiveness. Pray for opportunities to draw people from their sin into His grace.

"For I have no pleasure in the death of anyone who dies,"
declares the Lord GOD. "Therefore, repent and live."
Ezekiel 18:32

~ ~ ~ ~ # DAY 5 ~ ~ ~ ~
Replacing the Ungodly Leader

➢ <u>Draw near to God and He will draw near to you... James 4:8</u>

*I searched for a man among them who would build up the wall
and stand in the gap before Me for the land, so that I would not destroy it...
Ezekiel 22:30*

When a person's life is fully committed to serving the Lord, he is ready at any time to step into whatever new role God has for him. You need to be ready to step into the roles He has for you. Make up your mind to accept the daily life and training the Lord is giving you. Ask Him to grant you a willing spirit so that when He has need of you, you will rise to the challenge, whether great or small.

Write down your memory verse:

➢ <u>Study to show yourself approved... 2 Timothy 2:15</u>

In the second half of Isaiah chapter 22, we see a stark contrast between two very different men. The first is Shebna, the man in charge of Hezekiah's royal court, whose life has brought shame on his master's house,. It is quite possible that the Lord considers him personally responsible for the flagrant arrogance the people of Jerusalem were displaying in Isaiah 22:13.
   The second is Eliakim, a diligent, godly man whose his life was fully committed to the Lord – a worthy leader. "My servant" the Lord calls him. He was ready when God had need of him.

33. **Read Isaiah 22:15-25**. Answer the following questions.

What is Shebna's position (v.15)?

What has he done that offends God in verse 16?

What will the Lord do to him according to verses 17-18?

What did the Lord call him in verse 18d?

What else will the Lord do to him (v.19)?

34. The Lord has already chosen a replacement for Shebna's job (v.20). His name is Eliakim, the son of Hilkiah. What will the Lord do for him according to the following verses?

verse 21

verse 22

verse 23

verse 24

**Notice how Eliakim brings "glory to his father's house" (v.23b)
but Shebna brought shame on his master's house (v.18d).*

Page 113

35. In verses 20 and 25 it says "*in that day*" which is a reference to the Day of the Lord. What do you think the peg that gives way "*in that day*" might represent in verse 25?

36. It is clear from scripture that Hezekiah and his household took Isaiah's prophecy to heart and acted on it. What positions do these men hold in Hezekiah's court after the switch, according to Isaiah 36:3?

37. In Isaiah 22:21, the Lord gives us insight into the character qualities that appeal to Him in Eliakim. He says he will become a father to the inhabitants of Jerusalem. What do you think that means in this context? In other words, what will he do that fills a fatherly role in their lives?

38. Revelation 3:7 describes Jesus. What does it say about Him? Eliakim is a picture of the Messiah.

➢ Prove yourselves doers of the word ... James 1:22

39. Hezekiah's father had been a lousy example. It's possible all the inhabitants of Jerusalem were lacking the example of a godly father. The Lord provided what was needed through one man. Are you in need of godly examples in your life? Explain.

40. Are you the kind of person the Lord could raise up to be a godly example for a community? What qualities do you have that the Lord can use? What qualities do you want to grow in?

41. What does 2 Timothy 2:21 say?

➢ In everything, by prayer and petition ... Philippians 4:6

For I gave you an example that you also should do as I did to you
John 13:15

Pray for your leaders. Ask the Lord to bless their relationship with Him and to fill them with His Spirit. Pray for them to walk according to their conscience. Ask the Lord to keep them from temptation and deliver them from evil. Pray that they would be good examples.

Offer yourself to the Lord to be an example and a blessing wherever He needs you.

~~~~~~   Prayer Requests   ~~~~~~

Tyre, a Curse and a Promise
Isaiah chapters 23 – 25

Lesson 10

DAY 1 — The Stronghold of Tyre

> ### Draw near to God and He will draw near to you... James 4:8

Do you feel safe? Think about why. There are many things we put our trust in but only One that is worthy of our trust. Ask the Lord to show you today, as you study His Word, any area where you are trusting in someone or something other than Him. He wants to establish you on solid ground – on Jesus.

For no man can lay a foundation other than the one which is laid, which is Jesus Christ.
1 Corinthians 3:11

MEMORY VERSE   Isaiah 25:8

He will swallow up death forever.
The Sovereign LORD will wipe away the tears from all faces;
He will remove the disgrace of His people from all the earth.
The LORD has spoken. (NIV)

> ### Study to show yourself approved... 2 Timothy 2:15

Isaiah chapter 23 is a prophecy about the Lord's judgment on Tyre and Sidon, the two greatest cities of Phoenicia (Lebanon). It will be fulfilled more than a hundred years after Isaiah's death, when Babylon invades. At the time when this prophecy was made, Chaldea (Babylon) was an inferior province of Assyria, which was the most powerful kingdom in the world. In an indirect way, this prophecy showed that Tyre would NOT be conquered by Assyria.

1. Read the History of Tyre and Sidon in the appendix, page 391, located at the end of your study. Make a note of anything that interests you or any questions you have. Locate these cities on your map in the beginning of the study.

2. Read Isaiah chapter 23:1-9. Remember that these cities are seaports.
What news do the ships of Tarshish (Spain) hear and how does it affect them (v.1)?   *Note- this news comes from Cyprus, which is one of Tyre's colonies.*

Who is addressed in verse 2 and how are they to respond?

What was their business (v.3)?

> The phrase *'the grain of the Nile'* refers to the abundant harvests Egypt obtained from the yearly flooding of its banks which deposited a rich silt in its fields.

Page 115

What does the sea say in verse 4 and why do you think this would bring shame on Sidon?

How will Egypt react to the report (v.5)?

What are the people told to do in verse 6?

How do verses 7-8 describe the city and the people of Tyre before they fell?

3. In verse 8, the question is asked "Who has planned this against Tyre?" What is the answer given in verse 9? Why?

> Prove yourselves doers of the word... James 1:22

4. Did you notice who was upset when Tyre was destroyed? All those who benefited from its commerce. Did you pick up on the words like 'revenue' and 'market' (or something similar depending on your translation)? Compare it to a stock market crash. Would you be wailing with the 'ships of Tarshish' or ashamed with Sidon? Think about this honestly for a moment. How would something like that affect you? Could you honestly say with Job "*The LORD gave and the LORD has taken away. Blessed be the name of the LORD.*" *(Job 1:21)*?

5. What does Proverbs 18:11 say?

6. What is the point in the story Jesus told in Luke 12:16-21?

7. Contentment is a wonderful gift (1 Timothy 6:6). How can you become a person who is not driven by wealth or materialism?

8. Is the Spirit of God convicting you in any way about these things? Share and ask for prayer.

> In everything, by prayer and petition... Philippians 4:6

Ask the Lord to reveal if there are any fortresses in your heart that you rely on instead of Him. He alone is the stronghold that will not fail us in times of trouble. If we trust in Him, we will not be devastated when disasters strike the world around us. Pray that He would make you a light and a witness of Him as well so that you will draw others to His refuge when they are struggling.

He only is my rock and my salvation, My stronghold; I shall not be shaken.
Psalm 62:6

The LORD is my rock and my fortress and my deliverer,
My God, my rock, in whom I take refuge; my shield and the horn of my salvation, my stronghold.
I call upon the LORD, who is worthy to be praised, and I am saved from my enemies.
Psalm 18:2-3

~ ~ ~ ~ # DAY 2 ~ ~ ~ ~
The Lord's Purpose For Tyre

➢ <u>Draw near to God and He will draw near to you... James 4:8</u>

The Lord has a purpose for everything. He can use your mistakes as well as your successes. He can bring good out of your sorrows, trials and weaknesses as well as your joys and strengths. Take a moment to offer yourself to Him today.

...You greatly rejoice, though now for a little while you may have had to suffer grief in all kinds of trials. These have come so that your faith-- of greater worth than gold, which perishes even though refined by fire-- may be proved genuine and may result in praise, glory and honor when Jesus Christ is revealed. (NIV)
1 Peter 1:6-7

Practice your memory verse:

He will _____ up death _____.

The _____ LORD will wipe away the _____ from all faces;

He will remove the _____ of His people from all the _____.

The LORD has _____.

Isaiah 25:8

➢ <u>Study to show yourself approved ... 2 Timothy 2:15</u>

Yesterday we studied the beginning of the judgment on Tyre. We saw how it affected a variety of nations who were dependent on Tyre's commerce. Today we continue reading about what God intends to do to this city.

9. **Read Isaiah 23:10-18.** Answer the following questions.

What are the people of Tarshish told to do (v.10)?

Note – In verse 10 it says "There is no more restraint." or "strength" in the NKJ. The word in Hebrew is literally 'girdle**'. The idea is that when the girdle is removed they are weakened, defenseless. The people of Tarshish have lost their security, their defense.*

10. What does verse 11 say the Lord has done?

11. What does the Lord say to Tyre in verse 12?

> The Lord had intended for Israel to conquer Canaan over a thousand years before. He had given the city of Tyre and its region to the tribe of Asher (Joshua 19:29), but they had never conquered it.

12. In verse 13, the Lord describes the land that will conquer Tyre. What does it say Assyria did to it?

*Note – Assyria had destroyed Babylon and considered it of little value, but here the Lord predicts its rise to power.

13. Verse 14 echoes the cry in verse 1. What does it say?

14. In verses 15-18, Isaiah prophesies of Tyre's restoration.

How long will Tyre remain forgotten (verse 15)?

What analogy does the Lord use to describe Tyre's restoration (v.16)?

What will the Lord do for Tyre in verse 17a?

What will they do in response (v.17b)?

What will happen to her wages (v.18)?

*Note -- The period of Tyre's exile parallels Judah's captivity in Babylon. It's interesting that the Lord allows this nation to return at about the same time that Judah returns. He explains His reasons in verse 18. When the people of Judah returned to the land and wanted to rebuild the Temple, they got their supplies from Tyre and Sidon, just as Solomon had done centuries before. Years later, Tyre had a flourishing Christian community and may have been a great support to the persecuted church in Judea in the time of the apostles.

➢ <u>Prove yourselves doers of the word ... James 1:22</u>

15. The Lord has a purpose in everything He does. What do the following verses say?
Proverbs 16:4

Micah 4:12

Romans 8:28

16. The Lord also has a purpose for everything in your life. What areas do you want Him to bring good out of? Are there areas in your life that you find it difficult to see God's hand in?

17. When you consider world events today, are you troubled by what you see happening? How does today's lesson help you put it into perspective? What questions do you have?

➢ <u>In everything, by prayer and petition ... Philippians 4:6</u>

Pray for God's perspective for the world. Ask Him to help you see His hand in world events. In the mighty battle going on around the world for the souls of men, He calls us to prayer so that His kingdom would be built.

For our struggle is not against flesh and blood, but against the rulers, against the powers, against the world forces of this darkness, against the spiritual forces of wickedness in the heavenly places. Therefore, take up the full armor of God, so that you will be able to resist in the evil day, and having done everything, to stand firm........ With all prayer and petition pray at all times in the Spirit, and with this in view, be on the alert with all perseverance and petition for all the saints.
Ephesians 6:12-13,18

DAY 3
The Weight of Sin on the Earth

➤ <u>Draw near to God and He will draw near to you... James 4:8</u>

Jesus said that His yoke is easy and His burden is light. If you are feeling weighed down by many burdens or sins, this is not the Lord's will for you. Even if the world is full of evil, sin and shame, we have been called to an abundant life. Ask the Lord to lift you up and encourage you with His word.

For this is the love of God, that we keep His commandments;
and His commandments are not burdensome.
1 John 5:3

Write down your memory verse:

He _____ swallow _____ death _____ .
The _____ LORD _____ wipe _____ the _____ from _____ faces;
_____ will _____ the _____ of _____ people _____ all _____ earth.
_____ LORD _____ spoken.
_____ 25: ___

➤ <u>Study to show yourself approved... 2 Timothy 2:15</u>

Isaiah chapter 24 is about the destruction of the earth. It refers to the Lord's judgment in the end-times.

18. Read Isaiah 24:1-12 and answer the following questions.

What will the Lord do to the earth (v.1)?

This disaster will level people so that all social distinctions are forgotten. Who is mentioned in verse 2?

What will be the extent of the damage (v.3)?

How does verse 4 describe what will happen to the earth?

19. In verse 5, Isaiah explains clearly why this judgment is coming. Who is to blame and what charges does the Lord bring against them?

20. What does it say will happen because of these charges (v.6)?

21. How do the following verses show why the land is under a curse?
Numbers 35:33

Psalm 106:37-40

22. Notice how many times the earth is mentioned in Isaiah 24:1-6 and what is said about it. The earth is under a curse because of the sin of its inhabitants. The Lord is holding all the people of the world accountable for what they know of Him and the earth (the planet) suffers for their evil.

What did they know and disobey of the Lord's standards?

   Genesis 9:1-6

   Romans 1:18-32

How is the earth affected by their sin?

   Romans 8:19-22

God created the earth to be inhabited (Isaiah 45:18). It is not a sin to clear land or to kill animals to provide food and shelter. God gave everything for us to enjoy and take care of so that our children would also be blessed. The purpose of caring for the earth is for the sake of our children.

What does Genesis 1:28, 2:15 say about this?

23. How does Isaiah 24:7-12 describe the effect this judgment will have on them and their joy?

   verse 7

   verse 8

   verse 9

   verse 10

   verse 11

   verse 12

> In verses 7-11, Isaiah is using wine as an analogy of what the people have invested their hearts in. Notice how they grieve over the destruction of their wine, *"There is an outcry in the streets concerning the wine"*. Revelation uses this analogy when referring to the false religion of the world and its immoral practices. It makes it clear that people committed acts of immorality and merchants became rich because of their wine (Revelation 18:3).

➢ <u>Prove yourselves doers of the word... James 1:22</u>

24. A curse is devouring the earth and some people are laboring very hard to protect it without understanding the heart of the problem. How can you apply the wisdom of the scriptures you studied today to these concerns?

25. Are you conscientious about your stewardship on earth? Can you see any areas where you can make a difference?

➢ <u>In everything, by prayer and petition . . . Philippians 4:6</u>

Pray for those who have a heart to take care of the earth. Ask the Lord to use this desire to draw them to the Creator who first entrusted the earth to us. Pray for opportunities to share the hope that is within you.

For the creation was subjected to frustration, not by its own choice, but by the will of the one who subjected it, in hope that the creation itself will be liberated from its bondage to decay and brought into the glorious freedom of the children of God. We know that the whole creation has been groaning as in the pains of childbirth right up to the present time.
Romans 8:20-22 (NIV)

~ ~ ~ ~ <u>DAY 4</u> ~ ~ ~ ~

Hope in the Day of Destruction

➢ <u>Draw near to God and He will draw near to you . . . James 4:8</u>

The Lord doesn't want us to be afraid of disaster. He shows us in His word repeatedly to trust in Him and be at peace. We are encouraged to rejoice in our trials. Ask the Lord to strengthen your hope and faith today as you study this passage about judgment.

*God is our refuge and strength, a very present help in trouble.
Therefore we will not fear, though the earth should change
And though the mountains slip into the heart of the sea.*
Psalm 46:1-2

Write down your memory verse:

_____ will _____ up _____ forever.
____ Sovereign _____ will _____ away ____ tears _____ all ____ ;
He ____ remove ____ disgrace ___ his _____ from ___ the _____ .
The _____ has _____ .
Isaiah ____ :8

➢ <u>Study to show yourself approved . . . 2 Timothy 2:15</u>

Today we continue studying the prophecy about the destruction of the earth. This prophecy applies to the Day of the Lord (see verse 21 'in that day'). You may want to review the questions you answered yesterday about the first half of chapter 24.

26. Read Isaiah 24:13-23. Answer the following questions using verses 13-16.

How does verse 13 summarize what will be left among the peoples? *(Probably referring to the numbers of people who survive the devastation.)*

What will these people do (v.14)?

What does Isaiah exhort the listener/reader to do (v.15)?

What is heard from the ends of the earth (v.16a)?

What is distressing Isaiah in verse 16b?

27. There is a striking contrast between the righteous and the wicked in these verses. What is the difference between the way the two groups respond to the Lord's judgment on the earth (v.14-16)? Why do you think Isaiah says '*Woe to me*'?

28. Continue answering the following questions using verses 17-23.

How does Isaiah warn the treacherous in verses 17-18?

How do verses 19-20a describe what happens to the earth and what do you think it represents?

Why will the earth fall (v.20b)?

Two groups will be punished '*in that day*'. Who are they (v.21)?

What will be done to them (v.22)?

What will happen when the Lord of hosts reigns on Mount Zion (v.23)?

29. In verses 19-20 the earth is described as shaking violently. What do you learn about the earth quaking in the day of the Lord's judgment from these scriptures?

Nahum 1:5-6

Zechariah 14:5

Revelation 6:12-14, 16:18

30. God has provided a solution for the curse brought on the inhabitants of the world by sin. What do these verses say about being cleansed of our sin?

Hebrews 9:22

Hebrews 10:19-22

I Peter 1:18-19

> <u>Prove yourselves doers of the word . . . James 1:22</u>

31. There were two kinds of people identified in this chapter of Isaiah, those who sang to the Lord in the midst of the devastation, and those who dealt treacherously. How do you respond to disaster?

32. Write down what you want your response to be when you are in trials.

> <u>In everything, by prayer and petition . . . Philippians 4:6</u>

Ask the Lord to make you a worshiper who always glorifies Him no matter what your circumstances are. Pray for those around you who are going through trials. Ask the Lord to make you a light to others who are looking for hope in a dying world.

Prove yourselves to be blameless and innocent, children of God above reproach
In the midst of a crooked and perverse generation, among whom you appear as lights in the world . . .
Philippians 2:15

DAY 5
Death is Swallowed Up

➤ <u>Draw near to God and He will draw near to you... James 4:8</u>

Do you ever feel uncertain or afraid of death? Fear isn't God's will for you. The Lord hated death so much that He went to the cross to free us from it. How much more will He free you from all the things you fear! Let Him search your heart today and help you see the fears you are wrestling with.

Because God's children are human beings-- made of flesh and blood-- Jesus also became flesh and blood by being born in human form. For only as a human being could he die, and only by dying could he break the power of the Devil, who had the power of death. Only in this way could he deliver those who have lived all their lives as slaves to the fear of dying.
Hebrews 2:14-15 (NLT)

Write down your memory verse:

➤ <u>Study to show yourself approved... 2 Timothy 2:15</u>

Isaiah chapter 25 is a song of praise to God. It includes a magnificent promise about the Lord swallowing up death for all time – the promise of eternal life. At the end, a brief prophecy about Moab is added.

33. **Read Isaiah chapter 25.** Answer the following questions.

Why does Isaiah exalt the Lord in verse 1?

What has God done that Isaiah appreciates (v.2)?

What was the result of what God did in verse 2 (see verse 3)?

How does the Lord protect the helpless and the needy (v.4) and what does He protect them from?

What is the storm this verse refers to (v.4c)?

What does Isaiah say God does in verse 5?

34. Verses 6-9 cover one of the most amazing promises God had ever given. It wasn't meant for just the people of Jerusalem but "*for all peoples*". What do these verses say?

verse 6

verse 7

verse 8

verse 9

Page 123

35. How do the following verses shed light on the glorious promises God has given us in Isaiah 25:6-8?

prepare a lavish banquet	Revelation 19:9	
remove the covering veil	2 Corinthians 3:13-16	
victory over death	Romans 6:9-10	
wipe tears away	Revelation 7:17	
remove the reproach	Colossians 1:22	

36. When we studied Isaiah chapters 15 and 16 (in lesson 7), we covered the judgment on Moab. Here at the end of Isaiah 25, we find them mentioned again, perhaps tying it to the beginning of the chapter where God is praised for destroying a fortified city (v.2).

Use Isaiah 25:10-12 to answer the following questions.

What will happen to Moab in verse 10?

What will Moab's response to this humbling be (verse 11a)?

What will the Lord accomplish (verse 11b)?

What will the Lord do in verse 12?

> *The Lord uses very powerful imagery to show what will be the end of Moab because of their pride. Having been offered so spectacular a promise as victory over death, they choose to spread out their arms and try to stay afloat in their own strength.*

> ➤ Prove yourselves doers of the word... James 1:22

Jesus said that those who believe in Him would never see death. He was referring to their souls. When He spoke of the body, He said they fell asleep. The disciples also used this phrase to describe the death of believers. Paul affirmed confidently that to be apart from the body was to be present with Christ. He was speaking of his soul or spirit. Even though our bodies will sleep, our spirits will be with Christ the moment we die and when our bodies are resurrected they will be transformed into new bodies like Jesus'.

37. We are often more affected by the world's views than we realize but the word of God is powerful for the renewing of the mind. We have printed out the following scriptures about death. Read them out loud in an attitude of prayer. Underline the parts you consider the most important. You can make notes in the margins if you wish.

Even though I walk through the valley of the shadow of death, I fear no evil, for You are with me; Your rod and Your staff, they comfort me.
Psalm 23:4

Precious in the sight of the Lord is the death of His godly ones.
Psalm 116:15

Truly, truly, I say to you, he who hears My word, and believes Him who sent Me, has eternal life, and does not come into judgment, but has passed out of death into life.
John 5:24

Truly, truly, I say to you, if anyone keeps My word he will never see death.
John 8:51

For the law of the Spirit of life in Christ Jesus has set you free from the law of sin and of death.
Romans 8:2

*But when this perishable will have put on the imperishable,
and this mortal will have put on immortality, then will come about the saying that is written,
"Death is swallowed up in victory. O death, where is your victory?
O death, where is your sting?" The sting of death is sin...*
1 Corinthians 15:54-56

*But we do not want you to be uninformed, brethren, about those who are asleep, so that you will not grieve as do the rest who have no hope. For if we believe that Jesus died and rose again, even so God will bring with Him those who have fallen asleep in Jesus. For this we say to you by the word of the Lord, that we who are alive and remain until the coming of the Lord, will not precede those who have fallen asleep. For the Lord Himself will descend from heaven with a shout, with the voice of the archangel and with the trumpet of God, and the dead in Christ will rise first. Then we who are alive and remain will be caught up together with them in the clouds to meet the Lord in the air, and so we shall always be with the Lord.
Therefore comfort one another with these words.*
1 Thessalonians 4:13-18

... I was dead, and behold, I am alive forevermore, and I have the keys of death and of Hades.
Revelation 1:18 (Jesus is speaking)

*Behold, the tabernacle of God is among men, and He will dwell among them,
And they shall be His people, and God Himself will be among them,
And He will wipe away every tear from their eyes; and there will no longer be any death;
There will no longer be any mourning, or crying, or pain; the first things have passed away.*
Revelation 21:3-4

38. Do you have any fears or misconceptions about death that the Lord is targeting today?

39. In the verses you just read, what gives you the greatest joy? Write a prayer thanking God for it.

➢ <u>In everything, by prayer and petition ... Philippians 4:6</u>

*If the Spirit of Him who raised Jesus from the dead is living in you,
He who raised Christ from the dead will also give life to your
mortal bodies through His Spirit, who lives in you.*
Romans 8:11

Ask the Lord to give you more understanding of how great a salvation He has given us, and how powerful His Spirit is within us. Commit yourself to Him and ask Him to rule over you. Give thanks to Him for all He has done. He has done incredible things and He is so good to us!!

~~~~~ Prayer Requests ~~~~~

Gathering His People
Isaiah chapters 26 – 27
Lesson 11

DAY 1 — A Mind At Peace

➤ <u>Draw near to God and He will draw near to you... James 4:8</u>

*Trust in the LORD with all your heart and do not lean on your own understanding.
In all your ways acknowledge Him, and He will make your paths straight.
Proverbs 3:5-6*

Trusting the Lord is directly linked to you experiencing God's peace. Tell the Lord you're weak in this area and ask Him to help you trust Him more.

MEMORY VERSE   Isaiah 26:3 (NKJ)

*You will keep him in perfect peace,
whose mind is stayed on You, because he trusts in You.*

➤ <u>Study to show yourself approved ... 2 Timothy 2:15</u>

Chapter 26 continues the song of praise that Isaiah began in the previous chapter. He praises God for the city He provides for the righteous, the afflicted and the helpless. This is what the people of Judah will inherit "*In that day...*"

1. **Read Isaiah 26: 1-6.** Answer the following questions about verses 1-6.

   What will the people of Judah sing about in that day according to verse 1?

   Who may enter (v.2)?

   What attitude are they characterized by (v.3) and why?

   What exhortation do they give in this song (v.4)?

   What has God done that brings them joy (v.5-6)?

   Note –This may refer to Moab in Isaiah 25:10-12.

2. What are some of the ways Isaiah 26:1-6 would be fulfilled according to these scriptures?
   Nehemiah 6:15-16

   Psalm 12:5

   Isaiah 25:2-4

   Zechariah 2:5

   Revelation 21:10-12

3. Isaiah 26:3, uses the phrase "*perfect peace*". In Hebrew it says "shalom shalom". Shalom means peace. It also means perfect, whole, complete, or sound. Here are some other definitions.

    peace -   a mind free of anxiety or distress, a state of tranquility

    keep -   guard, hold, maintain, be faithful to

    mind -   the conscious part of a person, intellect, reason

    stayed -   standing firm, remaining; persevering

Rewrite Isaiah 26:3 in your own words using these definitions for a guide.

4. Our minds can be a real battleground and we need to learn how to live daily in the perfect peace God gives us. How can we train our minds in the discipline of the Lord?

Psalm 94:19

Romans 8:6

Romans 12:2

2 Corinthians 10:5

Colossians 3:2

Hebrews 4:12

➢ *Prove yourselves doers of the word ... James 1:22*

5. In Isaiah 26:4, it admonishes us to trust in the Lord forever, for He is our everlasting rock. Practically speaking, what does trusting God look like in the life of the believer?

6. In what other things might we trust besides the Lord?

7. Do you recognize when your thoughts are getting out of hand? Have you developed poor mental habits that are so deeply ingrained that you feel powerless to change them? Consider the scriptures in question 4 and make a practical plan to renew your mind. Write it here.

8. Read David's advice to his son Solomon and Paul's counsel to the Philippian believers in the following scriptures. What can you glean from them?

1 Chronicles 28:9

Philippians 4:6-7

➢ *In everything, by prayer and petition ... Philippians 4:6*

    Ask the Lord to help you grow in knowing and trusting Him as your Everlasting Rock. Take time today to place God at the center of your thoughts and imaginations. Pray now that you will keep your mind stayed on Him; pray and trust Him for all your needs and with all your concerns.

Do not let your heart be troubled; believe in God, believe also in Me.
Peace I leave with you; My peace I give to you; not as the world gives do I give to you.
Do not let your heart be troubled, nor let it be fearful.
John 14:1,27

DAY 2
Longing For God

➢ <u>Draw near to God and He will draw near to you... James 4:8</u>

*As the deer pants for the water brooks, So my soul pants for You, O God.
My soul thirsts for God, for the living God; When shall I come and appear before God?
Psalm 42:1-2*

God longs for you. Do you long for Him? Ask Him to give you a thirst for more of Him.

Practice your memory verse:

You will _____ him in perfect _____, whose mind is _____ on You, because he _____ in You.
Isaiah 26: ___

➢ <u>Study to show yourself approved... 2 Timothy 2:15</u>

In Isaiah 26:7-13, our passage for today, the Lord describes the heart of the righteous, how they long for Him and some of what He does for them. He contrasts their attitude with that of the wicked.

9. Read Isaiah 26:7-13. Answer the following questions.

How do the righteous people of Judah describe the path they have chosen (v.7a)?

What do they pray for in verse 7b?

How do they describe their longing for God (v.8-9a)?

How do the inhabitants of the world learn God's ways (v.9b)?

How do the wicked respond to the Lord's favor (v.10)?

How does verse 11 contrast what the Lord's enemies see and don't see?

What does verse 12 say the Lord does for us?

Who has ruled over them according to verse 13a?

What can only God help them with (v.13b)?

10. Verse 7 says, "*The way of the just is uprightness...*", (NKJ). Define uprightness in your own words. What are some synonyms for uprightness?

11. Why is it, do you suppose, that the grace of God does not always bring the wicked to repentance? (Isaiah 26:9b-10a)

Psalm 78 demonstrates this pattern very vividly, that when God punished them they returned to Him and when He shows them favor they rebel. Read these portions to get the idea.

Psalm 78	what God did	how they responded
verses 14-17		
verses 33-35		
verses 38-40		
verses 52-59		

12. Look up the following scriptures. How do they describe a heart that thirsts for God?

Psalm 17:15

Psalm 27:8

Psalm 63:1,6

Psalm 73:25

Psalm 84:2

Luke 6:12

13. How do the following verses explain that the Lord "*performed for us all our works*" (Isaiah 26:12)?
2 Corinthians 9:8

Ephesians 2:10

➤ *Prove yourselves doers of the word ... James 1:22*

14. Look at Isaiah 26:8-9a again. How does your devotion to God compare to this description? Do you thirst for the Living God? Do you seek Him for Himself, or only for what He can do for you?

15. Look again at Isaiah 26:12-13. How can you lay hold of the grace you need to love Him more?

➤ *In everything, by prayer and petition ... Philippians 4:6*

Meditate on and pray the following passage into your life. Ask the Lord to give you a greater thirst for Him.

Your name, even Your memory, is the desire of our souls.
At night my soul longs for You, indeed, my spirit within me seeks You diligently...
Isaiah 26:8b-9a

DAY 3
Resurrection of the Dead

➤ <u>Draw near to God and He will draw near to you... James 4:8</u>

*Blessed be the God and Father of our Lord Jesus Christ,
who according to His great mercy has caused us to be born again to a living hope
through the resurrection of Jesus Christ from the dead.
1 Peter 1:3*

Of all the people on earth, we have the greatest reason to rejoice. We have been born again to a living hope!! We know what our future is and Who we will spend eternity with. Our precious Savior, our wonderful Lord, the love of our lives will be in our midst giving us light and joy. He is the longing of our souls!!

Practice down your memory verse:

_____ will _____ him ____ perfect _____,

whose _____ is _____ on _____, because ____ trusts ____ You.

_____ 26: ___

➤ <u>Study to show yourself approved... 2 Timothy 2:15</u>

    The last half of Isaiah chapter 26 covers some of the most powerful prophecies in the whole book. It discusses Israel's distress over the earth's deliverance, the Lord's answer and the resurrection of the body.

16. Read Isaiah 26:14-21.

What lament is expressed in verse 14?

What has the Lord done for the nation in verse 15?

How did the people respond to the Lord's chastening (v.16)?

How does Isaiah describe God's people in verses 17-18a?

What conclusion did they reach in verse 18b?

17. Read Hebrews 12:11. What is God's purpose in chastening His people (Isaiah 26:16)?

18. Isaiah confesses the failure of Judah to bring forth children spiritually. Why do you think they thought they should be able to accomplish deliverance for the earth? What do you think they were lacking?

19. What promise does the Lord give them in verse 19 in answer to their distress?

20. How do the following scriptures expand on the teaching of the resurrection of the dead?
    Isaiah 25:8a

    Daniel 12:2

    Matthew 27:52-53

    John 5:28-29

    John 11:25

    Romans 6:5

    1 Corinthians 15:42-44

21. Isaiah 26:20-21 continues the description of what will happen. This is an end-times reference. What does the Lord tell His people to do in verse 20 and for how long?

    What is He going to do and why (v.21)?

22. In Jesus' time, there was a sect of the Jews called the Sadducees. They only acknowledged the first five books of the Bible as being the word of God. They rejected this passage in Isaiah about the resurrection of the dead. Read Matthew 22:23-33 and explain how Jesus proved them wrong.

➤ Prove yourselves doers of the word ... James 1:22

23. Look at Isaiah 26:16-18 again. Can you identify with this lack of fruitfulness? Have you ever been discouraged in a task that you knew was worthy and good in the Lord's sight? Verse 19 is the Lord's powerful response to this lament. How does it comfort you?

24. How can you become more fruitful? What encouragement do the following scriptures give you?
    Romans 8:11

    2 Corinthians 5:17

    Galatians 2:20

25. In view of this wonderful promise of the resurrection of the body, do you need to adjust any of your priorities? Have you placed undue importance on this fleshly body and neglected eternal things?

> In everything, by prayer and petition... Philippians 4:6

*Jesus said to her,
"I am the resurrection and the life. He who believes in me will live,
even though he dies; and whoever lives and believes in me will never die.
Do you believe this?"
John 11:25-26*

Jesus is asking you also, do you believe this? This resurrection power is available to you today. Lift up your heart to the Lord and seek His help with confidence. Give Him thanks for all He has done in you and for you. Worship Him with all your heart!

~ ~ ~ ~ **DAY 4** ~ ~ ~ ~
Battling the Lord

> Draw near to God and He will draw near to you... James 4:8

Make peace with God. He loves you. Stop resisting Him. He is offering you grace and forgiveness.

*I have no wrath. Should someone give Me briars and thorns in battle,
Then I would step on them, I would burn them completely.
Or let him rely on My protection, Let him make peace with Me,
Let him make peace with Me.
Isaiah 27:4-5*

Practice your memory verse:

You _____ keep _____ in _____ peace,
_____ mind _____ stayed _____ You, _____ he _____ in _____.
Isaiah ____:3

> Study to show yourself approved... 2 Timothy 2:15

Isaiah chapter 27 continues the **"in that day"** theme, beginning with the promised destruction of Leviathan. It continues with a description of what will happen with His vineyard. The outcome will be very different than it was when He first described it in Isaiah 5:2-6. At that time, it did not yield the expected fruit, in spite of His tending.

26. Read Isaiah 27:1-6. Answer the following questions.

How does verse 1 describe Leviathan and what does it say will happen to him?

How does the Lord care for His vineyard in verses 2-3?

Describe the Lord's response when someone comes against Him in battle (v.4)?

Why do you think the Lord points out that He has "no wrath" in verse 4?

What does He offer them instead of battle (v.5)?

Page 133

27. What does the Lord promise concerning Jacob or Israel in verse 6?
Note – this is a reference to the gospel spreading and bearing fruit throughout the world.

28. Write a description of Leviathan from Job chapter 41.

> **Leviathan** is the Hebrew name given to a great sea monster described in Job. Apparently it is a fitting description for Satan. Revelation gives this name to him and Isaiah seems to as well.

29. In Isaiah 27:1, Leviathan is also called the "*dragon*". The dragon is referred to one other time in Isaiah and 14 times in Revelation. What do the following verses say about the dragon's future?

Revelation 12:9

Revelation 20:10

30. Read Luke 10:18-20. What authority has Jesus given us? What should we rejoice in?

➤ Prove yourselves doers of the word ... James 1:22

31. Look at Isaiah 27:4 again. Do you find yourself battling the Lord sometimes? Do you offer Him thorns and briars when you come to Him? He isn't angry with you. How can you apply verse 5 and make peace with Him?

32. In Isaiah 27:6, it says that Jacob will take root and bear fruit. Jesus made it clear that we who believe are the branches of this plant and we need to abide in Him to bear fruit (John 15:5). What do these verses say about where should our roots be?

Colossians 2:7

Ephesians 3:17

➤ In everything, by prayer and petition ... Philippians 4:6

Do you have any huge, seemingly unconquerable monsters (problems, issues, concerns) in your life? Pray over them giving them to God to fix or conquer. Believe that He will accomplish what concerns you. Rest in the hope of your salvation and in your victory in Christ!

*Who is the one who overcomes the world,
but he who believes that Jesus is the Son of God?
1 John 5:5*

~ ~ ~ ~ **DAY 5** ~ ~ ~ ~
The Lord's Threshing

➤ <u>Draw near to God and He will draw near to you... James 4:8</u>

*Beloved, do not be surprised at the fiery ordeal among you,
which comes upon you for your testing, as though some strange thing were happening
to you; but to the degree that you share the sufferings of Christ, keep on rejoicing,
so that also at the revelation of His glory you may rejoice with exultation.*
1 Peter 4:12-13

The Lord has a purpose in all of His testing. Look for the joy beyond the trial, the promised outcome. He longs to share His glory with us. He will separate the precious from the worthless in your life and it is worth it!! Trust Him and don't resist Him.

Write down your memory verse:

➤ <u>Study to show yourself approved... 2 Timothy 2:15</u>

In the second half of Isaiah 27, Isaiah explains how Jacob, (i.e. the northern kingdom of Israel), will be chastened, forgiven and restored. They were taken away into exile because of their sin and now Isaiah explains the process necessary for the fruitfulness described in verse 6 to take place.

33. Read Isaiah 27:7-13.

What question does Isaiah ask in verse 7?

Note -- Isaiah 27:7 is basically asking if Jacob has been struck in the same way their enemies were. The answer is meant to be a clear "No." God did not strike them with plagues like He did Egypt when He led them out of slavery. He didn't wipe them out completely.

How did He deal with His people according to verse 8?

What will be the result of this chastening (v.9a)?

What does the Lord expect Jacob to do in verse 9b?

After the Lord's discipline, what will the cities be like according to verse 10-11a?

What are they lacking and what is God's response (11b)?

What will the Lord do in verse 12? *Note – the area described is the land promised to Israel, but only occupied during Solomon's reign.*

What else will happen "in that day" (v.13)?

34. How is verse 8 explained by 2 Kings 17:6-18?

35. How was Isaiah's prophecy in 27:9 fulfilled according to 2 Kings 23:14-20?

Note – The Lord couldn't bring His people back until the altars and idols were destroyed.

36. In Isaiah 27:12, it says the Lord will start His threshing. What does the word "thresh" mean? What is the purpose of God's threshing?

37. What does John the Baptist say Jesus will do in Matthew 3:11-12?

38. Isaiah 27:13 speaks of the Lord's scattered people gathering to worship Him in His holy mountain. How do the following scriptures add to this beautiful promise?

Isaiah 11:11-12

Ezekiel 20:39-41

Zephaniah 3:9-12

> ➢ <u>Prove yourselves doers of the word ... James 1:22</u>

39. In Isaiah 27:9, we saw that the Lord still needed to demolish the idols' altars even though the people were no longer there. Ask the Lord to search your heart and see if there is any 'baggage' in your life from old sins. This could be attitudes, fears, habits, possessions that have links to the past, etc. What is He telling you?

> ➢ <u>In everything, by prayer and petition ... Philippians 4:6</u>

O my threshed people, and my afflicted of the threshing floor!
What I have heard from the LORD of hosts, the God of Israel, I make known to you.
Isaiah 21:10

Ask the Lord to give you a trusting, humble heart whenever you encounter times of threshing. He longs only to separate the wheat from the chaff and purify you. Pray for those you know who are being threshed. Pray for many to be saved so they will be the Lord's wheat "in that day".

~ ~ ~ ~ ~ ~   Prayer Requests   ~ ~ ~ ~ ~ ~

Ephraim's Captivity, Jerusalem's Warning
Isaiah chapters 28 – 29

Lesson 12

DAY 1 — The Lord, our Strength

➢ <u>Draw near to God and He will draw near to you... James 4:8</u>

What is the source of your strength? What do you turn to when you feel weak? Is it caffeine? Sleep? Food? Encouraging words from a friend? Isaiah 40:31 says:

> But those who wait on the Lord shall renew their strength;
> they shall mount up with wings like eagles. They shall run and not be weary,
> they shall walk and not faint.

Take time today to wait on the Lord. Ask Him to teach you to wait. Allow Him to renew your strength.

MEMORY VERSE   Isaiah 28:16

Therefore thus says the Lord God,

"Behold, I am laying in Zion a stone, a tested stone, a costly cornerstone, for the foundation, firmly placed. He who believes in it will not be disturbed."

➢ <u>Study to show yourself approved... 2 Timothy 2:15</u>

Isaiah chapter 28 begins with a scathing indictment against the drunkards of Ephraim. He condemns their judges, priests and prophets. He speaks of the storm coming against them and gives a message of hope for the remnant who survive. Remember that "Ephraim" and "Israel" are names that refer to the ten tribes who established the Northern Kingdom whose capital was Samaria.

1. Read Isaiah 28:1-8. Answer the following questions.

Who is this woe pronounced against and how are they described (v.1)?

Describe the agent the Lord has brought against them (v.2).

What will happen to them according to verses 3 and 4?

What will the Lord become to the remnant of His people "in that day" (v.5)?

Who will He strengthen and what will He give them (v.6)?

2. There is a stark contrast between what the Lord wants (in verse 6) and what actually exists at this time in verse 7. Who else is sharing in the sin of the leaders of Ephraim and how does it affect their work (v.7)?

How does the Lord describe the environment they work in (v.8)?

3. Summarize the sins of Ephraim in this passage.

4. What do the following Scriptures say about their sin?
   Proverbs 16:18

   Proverbs 20:1

   Proverbs 23:31-33

   Ephesians 5:18

5. Isaiah 28:5 uses the image of a crown to portray what the Lord will mean to His people in that day. What do the following verses teach about crowns?
   Isaiah 62:3

   1 Thessalonians 2:19

   2 Timothy 4:8

   James 1:12

   1 Peter 5:4

   Revelation 3:11

> Prove yourselves doers of the word . . . James 1:22

6. The beauty of Ephraim is like a fading flower, it says in Isaiah 28:1 and 4. What a contrast to the glorious diadem the Lord will be to them 'in that day'! The beauty of earthly, temporal flowers fading is compared with the promise of eternal glory. How have you experienced this in your life?

7. The Lord used the force of "*mighty overflowing waters*" to bring down the proud crown of Ephraim. In contrast, the 24 elders in heaven willingly cast their crowns at the Lord's feet (Revelation 4:10). Where are you today? Willingly humbling yourself before the Lord, or is force needed?

> In everything, by prayer and petition . . . Philippians 4:6

*In that day the LORD of hosts will become a beautiful crown
And a glorious diadem to the remnant of His people.
Isaiah 28:5*

Pray that the Lord would reveal Himself to you as your crown and your glory. Ask Him to revive your love for Him and show you how you can treasure Him more. Give thanks for all the blessings He has given you and then, one by one, tell Him He is more precious to you than any of them. Ask Him to make you single-hearted in your devotion to Him.

~ ~ ~ ~ **DAY 2** ~ ~ ~ ~
The Precious Cornerstone

➤ <u>Draw near to God and He will draw near to you… James 4:8</u>

*The stone which the builders rejected has become the chief corner stone.
This is the LORD'S doing; it is marvelous in our eyes.
Psalm 118:22-23*

Jesus is the foundation and cornerstone of our faith. Everything in our lives should be built on Him. It must be of faith. Pray that He would stir your faith. Ask the Lord to anchor you in Him today and to make your life one with lasting value.

Practice your memory verse:

Therefore thus says the _____ God:
"Behold, I am laying in _____ a stone, a tested _____,
a costly _____, for the foundation, firmly _____.
He who _____ in it will not be _____."
Isaiah 28:16

➤ <u>Study to show yourself approved… 2 Timothy 2:15</u>

Yesterday in Isaiah 28 we read about how the rulers, priests and prophets of Ephraim had rendered themselves worthless. Now, because of their error, there is no one left to hear the words of the Lord. Therefore, God will exercise judgment through a foreign people (verse 11). The rulers of Jerusalem watch and mock Israel's plight because they have made a pact with Assyria (2 Kings 16:7-18), but God has a message for them as well.

8. Read Isaiah 28:9-22. Because the rulers of Jerusalem have rendered themselves incapable of hearing the Lord's wisdom, He has greatly simplified His teaching for them.

What age group are these instructions appropriate for (v.9)?

Referring to verses 10-11, describe God's method of educating His people.

Verse 12 explains why He resorts to these measures. What did He offer them and what was their response?

Verse 13a repeats again the training they will be given. What will be the result (v.13b)??

Who are the scoffers the Lord is warning in verse 14?

How do they describe the pact they have made with Assyria in verse 15a?

What was their security (v.15b)?

9. Flood waters are used to describe the army in verses 15, 17 and 18. Read Isaiah 8:7-8. How was the Assyrian army like a flood?

10. Continue answering the questions on Isaiah 28:16-22.
    On what should they have been relying (v.16)?   *Note – this is a Messianic prophecy.

    Against what would they be measured (v.17a)?

    What will happen to the refuge they have chosen (v.17b)?

    What will happen to their pact with the Assyrians (v.18)?

    What will the army do to them when it passes through and how often will it come (v.18b-19)?

    What word picture does the Lord paint in verse 20?

11. What do you think God meant by this picture (v.20)?

12. In verse 21, two mighty victories of the Lord are mentioned as examples of what He will do. Make a note of God's divine intervention.
    God fights against the Amorites in Gibeon - Joshua 10:6-11

    God broke through against the Philistines at Mt. Perizim - 2 Samuel 5:19-20

    In the second half of Isaiah 28:21, how does He describe the work He will do and what do you think He means?

13. Verse 22 is a strong warning from the Lord, both for the people of Judah and for us. Re-write this verse in your own words.

14. What do you learn about the cornerstone mentioned in Isaiah 28:16 from these scriptures?
    Psalm 118:22

    Isaiah 8:14

    Matthew 21:42-45

    Acts 4:10-12

    Romans 9:31-33

    1 Corinthians 3:11

    Ephesians 2:20-22

    1 Peter 2:4-8

➢ <u>Prove yourselves doers of the word... James 1:22</u>

Isaiah's contemporaries made a pact with Assyria and put their trust in that instead of the Lord. It's interesting that the people in Jesus' day were similar. The Pharisees and religious rulers of His day put their trust in their connections with Rome instead of in the Messiah, the cornerstone.

> *Therefore the chief priests and the Pharisees convened a council, and were saying, "What are we doing? For this man is performing many signs. If we let Him go on like this, all men will believe in Him, and the Romans will come and take away both our place and our nation."*
> *John 11:47-48*

The Pharisees knew Isaiah well. They should have taken heed to Jesus' warning about rejecting the chief cornerstone (Luke 20:17-19).

15. Consider what you learned in question 14. What is the purpose of a cornerstone? What does it mean to have Christ as your cornerstone?

16. The work God did is described as unusual and extraordinary. How is God doing the extraordinary in your life? Or are you settling for mediocrity?

> *We urge you, brethren, to excel still more... 1 Thessalonians 4:10*

➢ <u>In everything, by prayer and petition... Philippians 4:6</u>

> *I love You, O LORD, my strength. The LORD is my rock and my fortress and my deliverer, My God, my rock, in whom I take refuge; my shield and the horn of my salvation, my stronghold.*
> *Psalm 18:1b-2*

Pray these verses, thanking God that He is your solid rock, your sure foundation, a precious cornerstone. Thank Him that you can build your life on Him.

~ ~ ~ ~ **DAY 3** ~ ~ ~ ~
A Time of Threshing

➢ <u>Draw near to God and He will draw near to you... James 4:8</u>

> *If any of you lacks wisdom, let him ask of God, who gives to all generously and without reproach, and it will be given to him.*
> *James 1:5*

Are you in need of a bountiful supply of wisdom today? Ask God and then remember to listen and look for His answers throughout the day. Realize that His hand is upon you and that everything has a purpose.

Practice your memory verse:

Therefore _____ says _____ Lord _____, "Behold, ___ am _____ in _____ a _____, a _____ stone, ___ costly _____, for _____ foundation, _____ placed. _____ who _____ in ___ will ___ be _____."

Isaiah ___:16

Page 141

> ## Study to show yourself approved... 2 Timothy 2:15

Today we will cover the last part of Isaiah chapter 28 that explains what the Lord wants to accomplish with the judgment He is bringing on Israel and Judah. The concept of threshing which He touched on in Isaiah 27:12, is explained in more depth.

17. Read Isaiah 28:23-29. Answer the following questions to draw out the meaning of the parable.
What exhortation is given in verse 23?

Note – This refers to more than listening. It reflects a heart attitude that leads to action. "Everyone who hears these words of Mine and acts on them, may be compared to a wise man who built his house on the rock..." Matthew 7:24

What question is asked in verse 24 and what is the obvious answer?

What follows after the plowing (v.25)?

Why does the farmer do this (v.26)?

Verse 27 compares the appropriate and the inappropriate methods of harvesting two herbs. What does it say?

How is grain harvested for bread (v.28)?

What concern limits the threshing (v.28b)?

What reassurance does Isaiah give in verse 29?

18. This story is a parable. The plowing of the soil is temporary. It's followed by the peaceful sowing of seed and the growing season. The threshing is also a temporary process. It only continues as long as is necessary. What do you think the Lord is trying to tell them?

> ## Prove yourselves doers of the word... James 1:22

19. Look up the following passages and record what "threshing" means in each one.
Matthew 3:12

Matthew 13:37-43

Luke 22:31-32

20. Notice how the Lord describes different harvesting techniques for the different crops mentioned in Isaiah 28:27-28. He wants us to apply this to the way He works in our lives. Are you experiencing threshing right now? How? What is the Lord harvesting?

21. Are you able to accept the Lord's threshing in your life? Remember that "*His counsel is wonderful and His wisdom great*" (Isaiah 28:29). We can choose to resist or cooperate with the Lord when He threshes us. Tell Him you are willing to accept His work in your heart.

➤ <u>In everything, by prayer and petition . . . Philippians 4:6</u>

Think about the magnitude of God's love for you and His wonderful works. In prayer, cast all your cares on Him for He cares for you. He is your wonderful, always available, wise counselor.

> Many, O LORD my God, are the wonders which You have done,
> and Your thoughts toward us; there is none to compare with You.
> If I would declare and speak of them, they would be too numerous to count.
> Psalm 40:5

~ ~ ~ ~ **DAY 4** ~ ~ ~ ~
God's Chastening

➤ <u>Draw near to God and He will draw near to you . . . James 4:8</u>

Hebrews 12:11 says,
> "Now no chastening seems to be joyful for the present, but painful:
> nevertheless, afterward it yields the peaceable fruit of righteousness
> to those who have been trained by it." (NKJ)

Think about your response to chastening. Do you desire the peaceable fruit of righteousness in your life? Are you willing to be trained by God's chastening? Pray and submit yourself to Him.

Practice your memory verse:

_____ thus _____ the _____ God: " _____, I ____ laying ____ Zion __ stone, __ tested _____, a _____ cornerstone, _____ the _____, firmly _____. He _____ believes ___ it _____ not ____ disturbed."

_____ 28: _____

➤ <u>Study to show yourself approved . . . 2 Timothy 2:15</u>

In Isaiah chapter 29, Isaiah warns Judah and Jerusalem of God's impending discipline. Ariel (verse 1) means "Lion of God". It is a reference to the king of Judah as well as the city his throne is in, Jerusalem. It is interesting to note that Sennacherib, the Assyrian king coming against them, used to hunt lions for sport and his palace walls were covered with base reliefs of this practice. You can see them at the British Museum in London.

22. Read Isaiah 29:1-8. Let's look at the history behind the name, Ariel, or "Lion of God".

How does Genesis 49:9-10a describe the king who would come from the tribe of Judah?

How does Numbers 24:9a identify the nation of Israel?

How does Revelation 5:5 clarify who the Lion of Judah is?

23. Describe the discipline the Lord is bringing on them (Isaiah 29:1-4).
What does God remember the city Ariel for (v.1a)?

What does the Lord tell them to do in verse 1b and what do you think He means?

What will He bring to them (v.2)?

What will He do according to verse 3?

What results will this have (v.4)?

24. Though the judgment He is bringing on Jerusalem is hard, the Lord promises them that He will also judge the nation He uses.
What will happen to their enemies and how fast (v.5)?

What judgment will the Lord bring directly on them Himself (v.6)?

How does verse 7 reassure the people of Jerusalem?

How does the Lord describe those who wage war against Mt. Zion in verse 8?

25. Explain the analogy the Lord uses in Isaiah 29:8. What do you think it means?

> *Note – When Jacob, the patriarch, also known as Israel, was an old man, he called his sons together and prophesied over them. He predicted that his son Judah would rule over the other brothers calling him a lion (Genesis 49:9-10). When the people of Israel were brought up out of Egypt, they were recognized as the Lion of God, because the Lord was with them. When David was king over all Israel, he was called the Lion of Judah and his capital city, Jerusalem, was the Lion of God. Jesus, the son of David, of the tribe of Judah, the king of Israel, inherited this name and Jerusalem, His city, did as well. This woeful cry "O Ariel!" in verse 1 is particularly poignant. It is so much like Jesus' lament:*
> *O Jerusalem, Jerusalem, the city that kills the prophets and stones those sent to her! How often I wanted to gather your children together, just as a hen gathers her brood under her wings, and you would not have it!   Luke 13:34*

26. What does Isaiah 10:5,12 say about these attackers?

➤ <u>Prove yourselves doers of the word... James 1:22</u>

27. The Lord warns them of how He will humble them in Isaiah 29:4. Then they will be in a condition to turn to the Lord in their heart, ready to *"whisper from the dust"* the prayer He has been waiting to hear. God listens to the prayer of the heart. How can this truth strengthen your prayers?

28. In Isaiah 29:8, the Lord describes the fleeting satisfaction the enemies of the Lord will have. What do the following verses say about **earthly** satisfaction?

Proverbs 14:14

Proverbs 27:20

Ecclesiastes 1:8

Ecclesiastes 5:10

29. What do the following verses say about **godly** satisfaction?

Psalm 17:15

Psalm 65:4

Psalm 107:9

Proverbs 19:23

Jeremiah 31:14

Matthew 5:6

30. Can you see the connection between what you set your heart on and being satisfied? What kind of satisfaction do you pursue?

➢ <u>In everything, by prayer and petition... Philippians 4:6</u>

Prayer is powerful, even when it is whispered from the dust. Pray for those who are being humbled by God and give thanks for the good fruit that comes from God's chastening. Ask the Lord to draw His enemies to Himself as He frustrates their empty plans.

I now rejoice, not that you were made sorrowful, but that you were made sorrowful to the point of repentance; for you were made sorrowful according to the will of God...
2 Corinthians 7:9

~ ~ ~ ~ <u>DAY 5</u> ~ ~ ~ ~
Hearts That Are Far Away

➢ <u>Draw near to God and He will draw near to you... James 4:8</u>

God's desire is not for us to know <u>about</u> Him, but for us to <u>know</u> Him. To know Him personally, we must seek Him sincerely. Hebrews 11:6 says,

*...For he who comes to God must believe that His is,
and that He is a rewarder of those who diligently seek Him.*

If your desire is to know God, pray and purpose in your heart to diligently seek Him. Look for Him today even in the unlikely places, the uncomfortable circumstances and in the usual conversations.

Write down your memory verse:

➢ <u>Study to show yourself approved... 2 Timothy 2:15</u>

In Isaiah chapter 29, the Lord points out Judah's superficial worship. This was the main complaint God made when Isaiah first began to prophesy (chapter 1). He connects it to their total lack of spiritual discernment and understanding. Then He describes what He will do to restore them.

31. Read Isaiah 29:9-24. Answer the following questions using verses 9-13.
What is their condition and what effect does it have on them (v.9)?

What has the Lord done to them (v.10)?

How does this affect their ability to understand prophecy (v.11)?

What does 1 Corinthians 2:14 say about this?

32. Continuing with the passage: Who will they turn to and how does it help (Isaiah 29:12)?

Why does the Lord say He will do this (v.13)?

How does John 4:24 say the Lord wants to be worshiped?

33. Jesus quoted Isaiah 29:13 in the gospels. Read Mark 7:1-16 and explain how He applied it and to whom.

What does Matthew 15:12-14 add to the story?

34. How does Isaiah 29:14 say that God will handle them?

Verse 14 talks about their wisdom. What do these verses say about this?
1 Corinthians 1:25

1 Corinthians 3:19

35. The counselors at this time in Judah's history were promoting alliance with Egypt as the only way to survive Assyrian attack. Knowing Isaiah would disapprove, they attempted to hide their counsel from him, but God knew.

Who does the Lord describe in Isaiah 29:15 and what do they say to themselves?

How does the Lord expose their foolishness in verse 16?

36. God intends the prophecy in Isaiah 29:17 to be proof of His foreknowledge. What event does He predict and how does Isaiah 37:24 confirm it?

37. What will happen "on that day" according to the following verses in Isaiah 29?

verse 18

verse 19

verses 20-21

38. What did the Lord promise concerning the house of Jacob in Isaiah 29:22-24?

➢ <u>Prove yourselves doers of the word... James 1:22</u>

39. The Jews hadn't stopped worshipping God outwardly. What was lacking? How can you avoid falling into a similar rut – going through the motions of church?

40. The hardness of their hearts had deadened them to the truth. How does this happen according to these verses?

John 12:35-40

2 Corinthians 4:3-4

2 Timothy 4:3-4

41. Do you ever hide your plans from the Lord, the way God's people did in verse 15? Why or why not? He knows all and loves you!

42. The people Isaiah was writing to had somehow lost their fear of the Lord. In Matthew 22:37-40 Jesus said, "...*You shall love the Lord your God with all your heart, with all your soul and with all your mind.*" How do <u>you</u> love God with all your heart, mind and soul?

43. How does Isaiah 29:24 comfort you concerning those who err and criticize you?

44. Isaiah 28:24 reveals again the kind intentions of God in the midst of His chastening. "*Those who err in mind will know the truth, and those who criticize will accept instruction.*" Ask the Lord if you are "erring in mind" or criticizing. Write down any areas where you need more truth and instruction.

➢ <u>In everything, by prayer and petition... Philippians 4:6</u>

Ask the Lord to awaken you spiritually and to give you a tender, hungry heart that listens to Him. Ask Him to keep you close to Him, and to keep your faith genuine – your heart sincere.

For You do not delight in sacrifice, otherwise I would give it;
You are not pleased with burnt offering. The sacrifices of God are a broken spirit;
A broken and a contrite heart, O God, You will not despise.
Psalm 51:16-17

~ ~ ~ ~ ~ ~ ~   Prayer Requests   ~ ~ ~ ~ ~ ~ ~

Don't Turn To Egypt!
Isaiah chapters 30 – 31

Lesson 13

DAY 1 — Confidence in Men vs. Confidence in God, part 1

➤ <u>Draw near to God and He will draw near to you... James 4:8</u>

Sometimes something in the past looks more desirable than the present. Sometimes we wish we could go back in time or go back to a place that we remember being easier, more fulfilling or fun. But our memories are not always terribly trustworthy and we tend to remember only what we want to remember. God is trustworthy; He is worthy to be trusted. The question is, do you trust Him with your present and your future? Do you trust Him with the decision of whether to go back or to move forward? Do you believe that He does indeed work all things together for good for those who love Him and who are called according to His purpose? Make this a matter of prayer today. Begin now to trust God to know your best and to move you in that direction.

The steps of a good man are ordered by the LORD, and He delights in his way. (NKJ)
Psalm 37:23

MEMORY VERSE   Isaiah 30:18b

For the Lord is a God of justice;
Blessed are all those who wait for Him.

➤ <u>Study to show yourself approved ... 2 Timothy 2:15</u>

In Isaiah chapter 30, the Lord returns to His complaint about those who are hiding their plans from Him (see Isaiah 29:15). They are making an alliance with Egypt instead of listening to Him. He exposes their foolishness. The prophecy in Isaiah 8:7-8 regarding the capture of Judah by Assyria can no longer be dismissed or ignored.

1. Read Isaiah 30:1-8. Use the following questions to draw out what is being said.

Who is the Lord declaring "woe" against in verse 1 and why?

What are they doing in verse 2?

What will they reap because of it (v.3)?

Who did they send to the cities of Egypt (v.4)?

How will they let them down (v.5)?

What was the traveling like through the Negev (i.e. south of Judah) in verse 6a?

What sort of bribe/tribute do they take along (v. 6b)?

What does the Lord call Egypt and why (v.7)?

What does the Lord tell Isaiah to do in verse 8 and why?

2. Fill in the following chart comparing wise counsel, which is what the Lord offered them, with man's plans, which they were acting on.

Wise Counsel	Man's Plans
Psalm 33:11	Psalm 33:10
Proverbs 2:6-8	Proverbs 16:9
Proverbs 19:20-21	Daniel 4:35

3. With these verses in mind, how would you summarize Judah's behavior? What predictions can you make about Judah's future?

4. What do the following scriptures teach you about alliances that are displeasing to the Lord?
2 Chronicles 20:35-37

Proverbs 13:20

2 Corinthians 6:14-18

➤ Prove yourselves doers of the word... James 1:22

5. "Woe to the rebellious children," says the Lord, "Who take counsel, but not of Me, and who devise plans, but not of My Spirit..."(Isaiah 30:1). As a parent, family member or friend, how do you respond to a rebellious child? Use Scripture to support your answer and share with your group to provide encouragement.

6. Whose counsel have you listened to? What has the outcome been or what will it be?

➤ In everything, by prayer and petition... Philippians 4:6

If your desire is to, be like a tree firmly planted by streams of water, which yields its fruit in its season, whose leaf does not wither and who prospers in whatever he does, you must learn to hear God's voice.
Pray through this psalm and ask God to help you listen to Him and turn away from ungodly counsel.

Blessed is the man who walks not in the counsel of the ungodly,
nor stands in the path of sinners, nor sits in the seat of the scornful;
but his delight is in the law of the Lord, and in His law he meditates day and night.
He will be like a tree firmly planted by streams of water, which yields its fruit in its season
And its leaf does not wither; and in whatever he does, he prospers.
Psalm 1:1-3

~ ~ ~ ~ **DAY 2** ~ ~ ~ ~

Confidence in Men vs. Confidence in God, part 2

➤ <u>D</u>raw near to God and He will draw near to you... James 4:8

*For thus the Lord GOD, the Holy One of Israel, has said,
"In repentance and rest you will be saved, in quietness and trust is your strength."
Isaiah 30:15*

Troubled thoughts and doubt can rob us of our peace and make it harder to trust God. Quietness and rest are often linked. Lift the eyes of your heart to the Lord and ask Him to quiet you. Let Him give you the rest you need today. He is willing and He will give it to you if you ask.

Practice your memory verse:

For the _____ is a God of _____;
_____ are all those _____ wait for Him.
Isaiah 30:18b

➤ <u>S</u>tudy to show yourself approved... 2 Timothy 2:15

Yesterday we read about how Judah was turning to Egypt for help against Assyria. Today we will look at how the Lord describes them and what will happen because they reject His counsel. Isaiah 30:8 tells us that the Lord had Isaiah write it down for <u>us</u> so that it would be "*a witness forever*".

7. **Read Isaiah 30:9-17.** Look at this description of the God's people.

How does God describe the people of Judah in verse 9?

What do they say to His prophets (v.10-11)?   (H)

What have they done according to verse 12?

8. Why would anyone put their trust in oppression and guile and rely on them as Isaiah 30:12 says? What are the assumptions that lead to such foolishness according to the following verses?

Psalm 73:3-5

Isaiah 47:10a

*They have said, "The LORD does not see, nor does the God of Jacob pay heed."
Pay heed, you senseless among the people; and when will you understand, stupid ones?
Psalm 94:7-8*

9. What analogy does the Lord use to describe what will happen because of their sin (Isaiah 30:13)?

What does He compare their collapse to and what does it communicate to you (v.14)?

What advice had the Lord given them (v.15a)?   (H)

What did they decide to do instead (v.15b-16a)?

How will the enemy respond to their flight (16b)?

How well will their armies fight (v.17)?

> When the Lord gave the children of Israel His commandments in Moses' Law, He promised to bless them abundantly for obedience. He also warned them of the repercussions of disobeying (Deuteronomy 28:15).
> One of the curses that would fall on them was defeat at the hand of their enemies.
> "The LORD shall cause you to be defeated before your enemies; you will go out one way against them, but you will flee seven ways before them, and you will be an example of terror to all the kingdoms of the earth."
> Deuteronomy 28:25.
> "How could one chase a thousand, and two put ten thousand to flight, unless their Rock had sold them, and the LORD had given them up?"
> Deuteronomy 32:30

10. In Isaiah 30:10-11, we see that the people of Judah would rather trust in men than in God, and would rather hear deceptive words than the truth. What do these scriptures teach about this?

Jeremiah 5:31

Zechariah 7:11

Romans 16:17-18

2 Timothy 4:3-4.

11. Isaiah 30:15 says that the people were unwilling to accept the Lord's rest. We also underestimate how important His rest is. What do these verses teach us about entering the Lord's rest?

Psalm 116:7

Matthew 11:28-30

Hebrews 4:10-11

What hinders the disobedient from entering God's rest according to Hebrews 3:18-19?

➤ <u>Prove yourselves doers of the word . . . James 1:22</u>

12. Are you resting in the Lord? What hinders you from entering His rest today?

➤ <u>In everything, by prayer and petition . . . Philippians 4:6</u>

> *Give thanks to the LORD, for He is good. . . Oh let those who fear the LORD say,*
> *"His lovingkindness is everlasting." From my distress I called upon the LORD;*
> *The LORD answered me and set me in a large place. The LORD is for me; I will not fear;*
> *What can man do to me? The LORD is for me among those who help me;*
> *Therefore I will look with satisfaction on those who hate me.*
> *It is better to take refuge in the LORD than to trust in man.*
> *Psalm 118:1,4-8*

Pray now. Give your burdens to the Lord and trust Him alone to answer and to help. Keep God at the forefront of your mind today. Be careful not to forget that He alone is in control of your life.

~ ~ ~ ~ **DAY 3** ~ ~ ~ ~
The Lord's Longing

> ## Draw near to God and He will draw near to you... James 4:8

The Lord longs to be gracious to you. He is a good shepherd. He will never leave you or forsake you. Listen to Him and follow.

Pray over your troubles, your waywardness, your doubt and your pain and entrust it all to Him.

> *... You will weep no longer.*
> *He will surely be gracious to you at the sound of your cry;*
> *when He hears it, He will answer you.*
> *Isaiah 30:19*

Practice your memory verse:

For _____ Lord _____ a _____ of _____ ;
Blessed _____ all _____ who _____ for _____ .
Isaiah ____:18b

> ## Study to show yourself approved... 2 Timothy 2:15

The second part of Isaiah chapter 30 reveals the longing God has for His people. It isn't too late for them to avoid the judgment they are bringing on themselves. He reassures them of His restoration.

13. Read Isaiah 30:18-26.

How is the Lord described? What does He want to do for Israel (v.18)?

How does He encourage those who weep in Zion (v.19)?

What has He given them and who does He promise to reveal (v20)?

What guidance will they receive (v.21)?

Ⓜ

14. So, despite their disobedience and despite their rejection, the Lord is still willing to restore them. What does that tell you about His character?

15. *"Your eyes will behold your Teacher."* How do these verses show that Jesus fulfilled Isaiah 30:20?

John 3:2

John 13:13

16. Continue answering questions about Isaiah 30 focusing on verses 22-26.

What will they do to their idols (v.22)?   *Notice the wealth they represent.*

What blessings from the Lord will follow this purification process (v.23-24)?

In verse 25, what else will happen on the day "the towers fall"?

*Note – This may refer to the destruction of the strongholds of their enemies. It is worth mentioning that they had built incense altars to idols on every lofty mountain and every high hill. Surely this water was cleansing the land.

What will the sun and moon be like when the Lord heals His people (v.26a)?

How will He heal them (v.26b)?

How does Revelation 22:5 add understanding to this?

17. What insight do you gain from these verses about the water mentioned in Isaiah 30:25?

Zechariah 14:8

John 7:38

> ➤ <u>Prove yourselves doers of the word . . . James 1:22</u>

18. Isaiah 30:18-26 is full of beautiful promises. Make a note of the ones you need today.

19. How have you personally experienced the Lord's longing to be gracious to you and His patient waiting to have compassion on you (v.18)?

20. The Lord has provided guidance for us. Are your ears alert to His gentle voice? If you get off track, listen and you will hear Him behind you calling "*This is the way, walk in it,*" (v.21).

> ➤ <u>In everything, by prayer and petition . . . Philippians 4:6</u>

Pray for the Lord to stir a longing for Him in your heart. Pray for people you know who need the Lord to teach them to walk. Ask the Lord to open doors for you to reach others on His behalf so that the longing of His heart can be satisfied – that they could be saved, healed, reconciled to the Lord.

Now all these things are from God, who reconciled us to Himself through Christ and gave us the ministry of reconciliation.
2 Corinthians 5:18

DAY 4
The Name of the Lord

> ### Draw near to God and He will draw near to you... James 4:8

The name of the LORD is a strong tower; the righteous runs into it and is safe.
Proverbs 18:10

Remember how the apostle John rested his head on Jesus' chest? When you get scared, who do you call for or who do you run to? Real safety is keeping yourself as close to the Lord as possible. It is there that you can be assured that He is in control of all. Pray as you begin today and draw near to God.

Practice your memory verse:

_____ the _____ is ___ God ____ justice;
_____ are _____ those _____ wait _____ Him.
_____ 30: ___

> ### Study to show yourself approved... 2 Timothy 2:15

This chapter of Isaiah speaks of the period of time between the capture of Israel by Assyria and the attack on Judah. We know from earlier in this chapter, that Judah fears Assyria, has sought help from Egypt and does not have confidence in God's ability to deliver them.

21. Read Isaiah 30:27-33. Answer the following questions.

Where does the Lord's name come from (v.27a)?

How is He described in the rest of verse 27?

What is His breathe like and what does it do to the peoples (v.28)?

What will it be like for God's people as they go to the mountain of the Lord (v.29)?

What will be heard and seen according to verse 30?

Who is this display intended for and how will they respond (v.31)?

What will accompany the Lord's rod of punishment according to verse 32?

What has been prepared for the king of Assyria (v.33)?   *Note – Topheth is a place of burning. It's a type of the lake of fire in Revelation 20:15.

Page 155

22. In verse 27, Isaiah refers to God as the name of the Lord. In the New Testament we see Jesus linked with the name of the Lord. What do the following Scriptures say about His name?

Exodus 20:7

Psalm 124:8

Mark 11:9

Acts 4:12

Philippians 2:9-10

23. Isaiah 30:28 describes the breath of the Lord like an overflowing torrent that reaches to the neck. Read the following verses and describe the breath of God.

Job 4:8-9

Isaiah 11:4b

Isaiah 30:33

2 Thessalonians 2:8

24. It's interesting that in Isaiah 30:32, the Lord says He will include music in His battle against Assyria. According to 2 Chronicles 20:22, what place does music play in the warfare of the Lord?

> ## Prove yourselves doers of the word... James 1:22

25. How can you run to the name of the Lord for safety?

26. Notice how in Isaiah 30:29, the Lord says they will have songs in the night. What does this mean to you? How does the Lord comfort you with songs? Read Psalm 42:8.

> ## In everything, by prayer and petition... Philippians 4:6

*When I remember You on my bed, I meditate on You in the night watches,
For You have been my help, and in the shadow of Your wings I sing for joy.
Psalm 63:6-7*

Pray that in every circumstance, you would go to the mountain of the Lord, to the rock of Israel. Ask for gladness of heart and songs in the night.

~ ~ ~ ~ # DAY 5 ~ ~ ~ ~
In Whom Do You Trust?

> ## Draw near to God and He will draw near to you... James 4:8

"Things are not always as they appear." Do you ever get bogged down with seeing life through worldly eyes and forget to keep your eternal perspective? Do you ever look at situations, forgetting that it has a God given purpose? Pray as you begin your study that God would show you His purpose for all that you go through today and that He would help you to grow in trusting Him.

To everything there is a season, a time for every purpose under heaven: (NKJ)
Ecclesiastes 3:1

Write down your memory verse:

➢ <u>Study to show yourself approved . . . 2 Timothy 2:15</u>

Isaiah chapter 31 begins with another "woe" pronounced against those who put their trust in Egypt. Remember that Assyria went to war against the Philistines and then Egypt and Cush, for three years (Isaiah chapter 20). Isaiah walked around naked for three years as a witness to their defeat and shame. During that time he prophesied against Jerusalem's alliance with Egypt and called them to repentance. In this chapter we see the most amazing prophecies yet given about Assyria's defeat.

27. Read Isaiah 31:1-9. Answer the following questions.

What are the people doing that brings woe and who are they avoiding (v.1)?

What is the Lord like and what will He do (v.2)?

How do the Egyptians compare to the Lord (v.3)? What kind of help will they provide?

What will the Lord be like when He wages war on Mt. Zion (v.4)? *Notice how the Lord is making a connection again with the Lion of Judah, as He did in Isaiah 29:1.*

How will He protect Jerusalem (v.5)?

What plea does Isaiah give the people in verse 6?

What prediction does he make about the idols they were trusting in (v.7)?

What amazing prophecy is given about the Assyrian army and the young men left behind in Assyria (v.8)?

What will destroy Assyria's rock (or confidence) in verse 9?

28. Read what the following verses say about trusting God vs. trusting in the appearance of might.

Deuteronomy 20:1

Psalm 33:16-22

Proverbs 21:31

29. What does Psalm 115:3-8 teach us about the foolishness of worshipping idols?

30. In Isaiah 31:9, once again the Lord is using the imagery of fire to explain what He will be like to the Assyrians. What do these verses say?

Deuteronomy 4:24

Isaiah 10:16-17

Isaiah 30:27,30,33

> Prove yourselves doers of the word... James 1:22

31. In Ezekiel 14:4 God makes it clear that people set up idols in their hearts. 1 John 5:21 says, "*Little children, guard yourselves from idols.*" How can you guard yourself from idols such as money, power, position, possessions, etc?

You shall not make for yourself an idol, or any likeness of what is in heaven above or on the earth beneath or in the water under the earth. You shall not worship them or serve them; for I, the LORD your God, am a jealous God, visiting the iniquity of the fathers on the children, on the third and the fourth generations of those who hate Me...
Exodus 20:4-5

32. Did you notice how the Lord promised to deliver Jerusalem even though they were walking in disobedience? How does that encourage you in your life?

33. Israel relied on horses, trusted in chariots, and believed in other nations, but God was wanting them to rely, trust and believe in Him.
Write out Proverbs 3:5-6 here. Write down some things you need to trust God with. Acknowledge Him in these areas and don't rely on your own understanding.

> In everything, by prayer and petition... Philippians 4:6

How great is Your goodness, which You have stored up for those who fear You, Which You have wrought for those who take refuge in You, before the sons of men! You hide them in the secret place of Your presence from the conspiracies of man; You keep them secretly in a shelter from the strife of tongues.
Psalm 31:19-20

Thank God for His goodness that He has laid up for you!
Thank Him that He will keep you in His secret shelter!

~ ~ ~ ~ ~ ~   Prayer Requests   ~ ~ ~ ~ ~ ~

God's Wrath on the Nations
Isaiah chapters 32 – 33

Lesson 14

DAY 1 — The King Who Rules Righteously

➤ <u>Draw near to God and He will draw near to you... James 4:8</u>

As children are growing, it is often necessary to go through their closets and clear out the old things to make room for the new. Once they are grown, it is easy to go for years just adding the new, forgetting to take out the old. Spiritually, is it time to clean out some closets in your life? Are you hanging onto old habits, thoughts, teaching or traditions that interfere with receiving new information from the Lord? Pray as you begin today. Pass on the old "stuff" to the Lord and prepare yourself to receive all that He has for you today.

Therefore we were buried with Him through baptism into death, that just as Christ was raised from the dead by the glory of the Father, even so we also should walk in newness of life. (NKJ)
Romans 6:4

MEMORY VERSE   Isaiah 32:17 (NKJ)

The work of righteousness will be peace, and the effect of righteousness, quietness and assurance forever.

➤ <u>Study to show yourself approved... 2 Timothy 2:15</u>

In chapter 32, Isaiah begins with a description of the godly leaders the Lord will provide when His King comes to rule. It is a reference to the Messiah's reign, though it also refers to any king who upholds God's standard. The influence these leaders have on the nation is powerful.

1. Read Isaiah 32:1-8. These verses describe a future new leadership for the nation. These are quite a contrast to the leaders you read about in Isaiah 28:7-8.

Who will reign and what will characterize their reign (v.1)?

Ⓜ

What will they be like (v.2)?

What effect will it have on those they govern (v.3-4)?

What will "no longer" be said (v.5)?

How is the fool described in verse 6?

How is the rogue (*scoundrel or schemer*) described in verse 7?

How is the noble (*or generous*) person described in verse 8?

Page 159

2. Isaiah 32:1-2 paints a beautiful picture of the kind of king God desires. What do you learn about it from these scriptures?

how he rules - Isaiah 11:4-5

what he and his leaders are like - Isaiah 25:4

Jesus is the perfect fulfillment of this prophecy

    Matthew 8:24-26

    John 4:10-14

3. When the King reigns righteously, He will have princes ruling with Him (verse 1). What do you learn about that from these verses?

1 Corinthians 6:2a

2 Timothy 2:12a

Revelation 3:20-21

4. In Isaiah 32:3-4, a change for the better takes place. What was their condition before and after?

before	*after*
Isaiah 28:10-12	Isaiah 29:18-19, 24
Isaiah 29:9-13	Isaiah 32:3-4 (our passage today)

Read how this change took place:

"The Spirit of the Lord is upon Me, because He anointed Me to preach the gospel to the poor. He has sent me to proclaim release to the captives, and recovery of sight to the blind, to set free those who are oppressed..." Luke 4:18

"... I am Jesus... I am sending you, to open their eyes so that they may turn from darkness to light and from the dominion of Satan to God, that they may receive forgiveness of sins and an inheritance among those who have been sanctified by faith in Me." Acts 26:15b, 17b-18

> Isaiah 32:4 speaks of the transformation that will take place in the minds of the hasty when Jesus reigns and His truth is the standard for the earth. This will lead to truth on the lips as well. It will no longer be necessary for the Lord to speak to them with stammering lips as He did in Isaiah 28:11.

5. In Isaiah 32:3, their spiritual sight is recovered. How can someone's spiritual sight be dimmed? Look up the following scriptures.

John 8:12

John 12:46

2 Corinthians 4:4-6

➤ <u>Prove yourselves doers of the word . . . James 1:22</u>

6. How can you apply the following scriptures to help one whose spiritual eyes or ears are dulled? How do they encourage you?

Romans 15:1-2

Galatians 6:1

Hebrews 12:12-13

7. Isaiah 32:2 shows us that we are meant to share in Jesus' ministry. Are you a refuge from the wind or a shelter from the storm? Do you refresh people who are parched? How do you need to grow in this area?

8. "*No longer will the fool be called noble,*" Isaiah 32:5 says. There are many fools and rogues who are applauded in our world today. What should your attitude be towards them?

9. Isaiah 32:8 says that "*...noble men devise noble plans.*" God shows us that He approves of making noble plans and it is a fruit of His instruction. Are there any visions or plans in your heart that He wants to encourage you in? Explain.

➤ <u>In everything, by prayer and petition . . . Philippians 4:6</u>

Ask the Lord to make you a refuge, a shelter and like streams of water in a parched land. Pray for yourself and others that you would have eyes to see, and ears to hear and that you would discern truth. Pray for a deepening love of the word of God. Ask the Lord to fill your heart with truth so that your mouth would overflow with words that glorify Jesus.

The mouth of the righteous flows with wisdom
Proverbs 10:31a

~ ~ ~ ~ # DAY 2 ~ ~ ~ ~
Complacency

➤ <u>Draw near to God and He will draw near to you. . . James 4:8</u>

Keep watching and praying that you may not come into temptation;
The spirit is willing, but the flesh is weak.
Mark 14:38

We need to guard our hearts against complacency and mediocrity. Ask the Lord to keep you alert and watchful, ready for Him.

Practice your memory verse:

The work of _____ will be peace, and the _____ of righteousness, _____ and assurance _____.

Isaiah 32:17

> ## Study to show yourself approved... 2 Timothy 2:15

In the second half of chapter 32, the Lord targets specifically the wealthy women among His people. He contrasts the state of destruction the land will be in after His judgment, with the blessing that is available when He pours out His Spirit on the people. He calls on them to rise up from their complacency and intercede for the nation with sackcloth and mourning!

10. Read Isaiah 32:9-20. Answer the following questions.

Who is the Lord speaking to in this passage (v.9)?

When will the trouble come upon them (v.10a)?

What does the Lord say about the harvest (v.10b)? What do you think He means?

What does the Lord exhort them to do (v.11-12)?

What will happen to the land of His people (v.13-14)?

11. Psalm 107:33-34 shows the connection between the condition of a land and the people who live in it. What does it say and how does this shed light on Isaiah 32:13-14?

12. What does it mean to be complacent? Why would this be a cause for warning?

13. Continue answering questions about Isaiah 32:15-20

What will God give and what effect will it have (v.15)?

How will the people be changed by the pouring out of the Spirit (v.16-17)?

How will God's people dwell because of this change (v.18)?

What does verse 19 say?

What promise is offered them in verse 20?

> *Isaiah 32:19 refers back to the judgment mentioned in verses 12-14. In the NLT version it says:*
> *"Even though the forest will be destroyed and the city torn down..."*
> *as if to say, even then it won't be too late for the Lord's promises (v.15-18) to be fulfilled.*

14. Isaiah 32:15-17 describes a wonderful change brought about by the Holy Spirit. This was always God's heart for His people. How was this promise fulfilled?

Acts 2:1-4

Acts 10:45

15. In Isaiah 32:17 it teaches us that because of the pouring out of the Holy Spirit, there will be quietness and confidence forever. What do you learn about confidence from these scriptures?

Psalm 78:7

Proverbs 14:26

Acts 4:13

Philippians 3:3

16. In Isaiah 32:18 it says that people will live in peaceful habitations, secure dwellings and undisturbed resting places. How is this like heaven? Read Revelation 7:15-17.

➤ Prove yourselves doers of the word... James 1:22

17. Isaiah 32:9-14 describes the depressing result of women who are complacent, while Isaiah 32:15-20 describes the fruitful conditions that exist when the Spirit is poured out. According to Galatians 5:16, what is the result of walking in the Spirit? How is walking in the Spirit accomplished?

18. Do you have a complacent attitude about something where the Lord is perhaps warning you to rise up? What is it? What action should you take? Read 1 Corinthians 10:12.

19. Galatians 5:22-23 lists the fruits of God's Spirit. Write them down and put a star next to those you particularly need help with today.

➤ In everything, by prayer and petition... Philippians 4:6

When we respond to the Lord's call to pray, He moves powerfully on our behalf. Pray against complacency. Ask Him to pour out His Spirit and bring in justice and righteousness in your home and your land. This will bring the peace, quietness and confidence He longs to give us.

Therefore be careful how you walk, not as unwise men but as wise,
making the most of your time, because the days are evil.
Ephesians 5:15-16

DAY 3
Sowing and Reaping

> ## Draw near to God and He will draw near to you... James 4:8

You reap what you sow. Usually you sow in one season and reap in the next. Have you considered what you are sowing in your relationships this season? Think about your spouse, children, family and friends. Are you sowing the kinds of seeds that you will be anxious to reap? Pray and ask God to show you what you are sowing and to forgive you for past mistakes. Ask Him to reveal Himself to you through His Word today and to give you the grace to sow good seeds.

Every way of a man is right in his own eyes, but the LORD weighs the hearts. (NKJ)
Proverbs 21:2

Practice your memory verse:

The _____ of _____ will ____ peace, _____ the _____ of

_____, quietness _____ assurance _____.

Isaiah ____ :17

> ## Study to show yourself approved... 2 Timothy 2:15

Isaiah chapter 33 begins with another "woe" pronounced on the "destroyer". It is likely that this was referring to the Assyrian army but it was meant to be instructive for all those who deal treacherously. In this prophecy, Isaiah prays for his people. If they put their trust in the Lord, He will honor their trust and they will begin to reap His blessings.

20. Read Isaiah 33:1-6.

In this "woe" against the destroyer, what have they sown? (v.1a)?

What do they now reap? (v.1b)?

After the pronouncement of this woe, Isaiah records a prayer (v.2). What is his petition to the Lord?

What effect does the sound of the Lord's coming have (v.3)?

How is the gathering of the Lord's spoil described and what do you think it means (v.4)?
Note – locusts devour everything in their path.

What qualities and works of God are the people remembering in verse 5?

What will the godly people inherit according to verse 6?

21. In this passage, Isaiah pronounces the sixth and last woe of this section (chapters 28-33). Altogether, he has recorded sixteen. Woe is defined as: *"grievous distress, misery or trouble; misfortune, calamity, affliction,"* (from Dictionary.com). Let's look at all the "woes." Who were the recipients? Briefly explain what God is warning them of?

Isaiah 3:8-9	Isaiah 10:1
Isaiah 3:11	Isaiah 10:5
Isaiah 5:8	Isaiah 28:1
Isaiah 5:11	Isaiah 29:1
Isaiah 5:18	Isaiah 29:15
Isaiah 5:20	Isaiah 30:1
Isaiah 5:21	Isaiah 31:1
Isaiah 5:22	Isaiah 33:1

22. All of those mentioned in the chart of woes are warned that grief will come on them because of their deeds. The Lord has no joy in seeing the wicked receive the inevitable outcome of their evil. What do you learn about God's heart from these verses?

Lamentations 3:31-33

Ezekiel 18:23, 32

23. Previously, these people were unwilling to wait for God (Isaiah 30:15-16). Now Isaiah writes *"We have waited for You..."* (Isaiah 33:2). What heart attitude does this represent and how do you think the Lord will respond to it?

24. Isaiah 33:6 says that God will be the stability of your times. His stability transcends the turmoil of the times. Why is that? Read Matthew 7:24-25.

> ## Prove yourselves doers of the word... James 1:22

25. Read Galatians 6:7. Write it here. Explain how this is a reasonable result of actions.

26. What do the following verses add to this?

Proverbs 24:12

Galatians 6:8-9

27. Isaiah waited for God in 33:2. Why are we supposed to wait for the Lord? What blessings and benefits do you see in waiting in these verses?

Psalm 27:14

Psalm 37:34

Proverbs 20:22

> In everything, by prayer and petition... Philippians 4:6

Lord, teach me to wait on You. I long to be quiet, resting at Your feet.

My soul, wait in silence for God only, for my hope is from Him
Psalm 62:5

~ ~ ~ ~ **DAY 4** ~ ~ ~ ~
Walking Righteously

> Draw near to God and He will draw near to you... James 4:8

The Lord is described as a consuming fire. He is beautiful in His holiness but without the covering of Jesus as our righteousness, He would be terrifying.
Isn't it wonderful how we can approach Him unafraid? Let Him draw you today. He wants to continue to transform you into the image of His Son so that He can keep you close to His heart and have fellowship with you.
Doesn't your heart long for Him? He is the desire of our souls.

Therefore, since we are receiving a kingdom that cannot be shaken, let us be thankful, and so worship God acceptably with reverence and awe, for our "God is a consuming fire."
Hebrews 12:28-29

Practice your memory verse:

_____ work ____ righteousness _____ be _____,
and _____ effect ___ righteousness, _____ and _____ forever.
_____ 32: ____

> Study to show yourself approved... 2 Timothy 2:15

In yesterday's study, Isaiah prophesied Assyria's punishment from God and Judah's return to Him. Today, Isaiah speaks of the devastation that will take place and the resulting fear of the Lord.

28. Read Isaiah 33:7-16.

Who is upset and what are they doing in verse 7?

Why has travel ceased? What attitude does the destroyer have (v.8)?

Lebanon is the region of Tyre and Sidon. Sharon, Bashan and Carmel are parts of northern Israel that Assyria captured earlier. What condition are they in because of the destroyer (v.9)?

29. Now the Lord has had enough. What does He say He will do now (v.10)?

What has the destroyer produced and what will the Lord do to him (v.11)?

What will happen to these people who are like thorns (v.12)?

Who is the Lord revealing Himself to and what does He want them to acknowledge (v.13)?

30. What is Isaiah's description of the sinners in Zion (v.14a)?

What questions are distressing them (v.14b)?

31. What is the answer to their questions, in verse 15?

32. What is the future for the one who fulfills these qualities (v.16)?

33. Read Psalm 15:1-5. Note any additional character qualities of those who may dwell with the Lord.

➢ <u>Prove yourselves doers of the word . . . James 1:22</u>

When the people saw the Lord arise and bring judgment on the destroyer, they became afraid. Their reaction was similar to Isaiah's in chapter 6 when he cried out "Woe is me for I am a man of unclean lips!" These people are terrified because they are sinners and they knew they were unfit to live in the presence of God. It is at that moment that there is hope for their salvation. As long as they are comfortable with their sinful lives, there is no hope for them. But the moment God's holiness is revealed and they see their need, God can extend the miracle of salvation!

Blessed are the poor in spirit, for theirs is the kingdom of heaven.
Blessed are those who hunger and thirst for righteousness, for they shall be satisfied.
Matthew 5:3,6

This is the glory of the gospel! This is the pattern God chose to use in Isaiah, continually contrasting the judgment on sin with the prophecies of the Messiah. We will see this when we study the end of chapter 33 tomorrow.

34. What is necessary in order for <u>us</u> to walk righteously? We need to take off the "grave clothes" and put on the "grace clothes."

Romans 6:11-13

1 John 1:9

35. In Isaiah 33:15 it answers the question "*Who among us can live with the consuming fire?*" It says "*He who walks righteously and speaks with sincerity...*" In question **33** we added to the description of those who can live with God. Are you feeling convicted about any of these areas? Explain.

➤ In everything, by prayer and petition... Philippians 4:6

Galatians 2:20 says:

I have been crucified with Christ; it is no longer I who live, but Christ lives in me; and the life which I now live in the flesh I live by faith in the Son of God, who loved me and gave Himself for me.

Ask the Lord to reveal to you any deeds in your life that come from the old nature. Purpose in your heart to turn away from them and walk in the victory Jesus has given you. Pray now asking God for strength and conviction to walk righteously and to speak uprightly.

~ ~ ~ ~
# DAY 5
The Lord Reigns
~ ~ ~ ~

➤ Draw near to God and He will draw near to you... James 4:8

It is so easy to become overwhelmed by the cares of each day! There are a multitude of things that demand your attention at any given moment. Despite this, God already knows what you will accomplish today and what is truly necessary. He knows which items on your list need immediate attention and which ones do not. His perspective is eternal and He truly knows what matters most. Try giving Him your schedule, your list and your priorities today. Ask Him to order your day - making additions and deletions where necessary - and to give you an eternal perspective in this life.

*I will instruct you and teach you in the way which you should go;
I will counsel you with My eye upon you.
Psalm 32:8*

Write down your memory verse:

➤ Study to show yourself approved... 2 Timothy 2:15

In the end of Isaiah 33, the Lord explains how His people who were terrified of Him will end up hoping in His salvation and being forgiven for their iniquity. In one amazing verse, they go from "The Lord is our judge" to "He will save us". This is a wonderful revelation of Yeshua, the Hebrew name for Jesus which means 'salvation' – given at a time when the Lord's purpose was still a mystery.

36. Read Isaiah 33:17-24. In this portion of Scripture:

Who and what will the Lord's people see (v17)?

What will they say when they consider the terror they experienced previously (v.18)?

Who will they no longer see (v.19)?

How is Jerusalem described in verse 20?

What will the Lord be like for them (v.21)?

What names does verse 22 give the Lord?

Verse 23 refers back to verse 21 as if to explain why there will be no ships on the river of the Lord. This is a picture of man's works. None of man's efforts will hold together in the Lord's presence (Ephesians 2:8-9), but the lame who rely on the Lord will inherit great spoil.
How does verse 23 portray this word picture?

What promises are given in verse 24?

37. Verse 22 lists four capacities in which the Lord will reign. What do these scriptures add?

Judge	decides fairly whether the law has been followed, punishes law breaking	John 5:22
Lawgiver	writes the laws we are judged by	James 4:12a
Savior	rescues from harm danger, loss or death	Matthew 1:21
King	ruler, authority to make decisions about us	Revelation 17:14

As a Lawgiver, God gave us a standard by which to live. As a Judge, He evaluated our deeds and determined they were worthy of death. As a Savior, He redeemed us from the outcome of our deeds. As a King, He rules over us forever. The Bible says "*For, I, the Lord, do not change...*" (Malachi 3:5). He will always be our Lawgiver, Judge, Savior and King.
Take a moment to thank Him for who He is to you.

Page 169

> ## Prove yourselves doers of the word... James 1:22

38. Have your eyes beheld the King in His beauty (v.17)? In Psalm 27:4, David's desire was to behold the beauty of the Lord in His temple. Does your life bear witness to this desire? If not, what changes can you make today to move in that direction?

> ## In everything, by prayer and petition... Philippians 4:6

*His divine power has granted to us everything pertaining to life and godliness,
through the true knowledge of Him who called us by His own glory and excellence.
For by these He has granted to us His precious and magnificent promises,
so that by them you may become partakers of the divine nature.
2 Peter 1:3-4*

What a wealth of riches we have in our Lord!! Spend time in prayer now thanking Jesus that He is the righteous Judge, the Lawgiver, the King of Kings and the One who saves us. Thank Him for your hope of eternity and for all He has prepared for you.

~ ~ ~ ~ ~ ~   Prayer Requests   ~ ~ ~ ~ ~ ~

The Recompense of God
Isaiah chapters 34 – 35

Lesson 15

DAY 1 — A Sacrifice in Edom

➤ <u>Draw near to God and He will draw near to you... James 4:8</u>

Job 42:1-2 says, "*Job answered the LORD and said, 'I know that You can do all things, and that no purpose of Yours can be thwarted.'*" In Genesis, the Lord said to Abraham, "*Is anything too hard for the Lord?*" As you begin your study today, meditate on the sovereignty of God and His awesome ability to handle whatever circumstances you are facing. Pray now and give the Lord your fears, weaknesses, trials and burdens. Ask Him to give you a glimpse of His sovereignty and a sense of His purpose in all that you're dealing with today.

But as for me, I trust in You, O LORD, I say, "You are my God."
Psalm 31:14

MEMORY VERSE   Isaiah 35:10

And the ransomed of the LORD will return,

and come with joyful shouting to Zion, with everlasting joy upon their heads.

They will find gladness and joy, and sorrow and sighing will flee away.

➤ <u>Study to show yourself approved... 2 Timothy 2:15</u>

In Isaiah chapter 34, the Lord calls all the nations to listen as He warns them of the day of vengeance that is coming when He deals with the evil they have done. He explains how He will destroy their armies and what the land will be like after His destruction. This is a reference to a specific battle that will take place in the region of Edom in the end times. Afterwards it will not be fit for human habitation.

1. Read Isaiah 34:1-8.

What are the various names that Isaiah gives to those who need to listen to this prophecy (v.1)?

Who is the Lord against and what words are used to describe His emotions (v.2a)?

What will He do to them in verse 2b?

What will happen to their slain (v.3)?

What armies are described in verse 4 and what will happen to them?   *Note – the Hebrew word for 'hosts' is literally 'armies'.*

Page 171

2. In Isaiah 34:4, God speaks of the hosts that occupy the physical heavens. This is a reference to the stars as well as angelic beings. In the Bible, "the heavens" speaks of everything extending up and away from the earth, including the atmosphere and the rest of the universe as we know it. How do these verses add to this passage?

Psalm 102:25-26

Matthew 24:29

Revelation 6:12-17

3. Who will His sword descend upon in Isaiah 34:5?

In Isaiah 34, verses 6 and 7, the Lord describes a sacrifice. He mentions animals that were regularly offered up in the Temple. But in context, it appears to be referring to a slaughter of armies of the nations, gathered in the region of Ancient Edom. Bozrah was the capital of Edom.
What kinds of animals are listed in verses 6-7?

What reason does the Lord give for this sacrifice in verse 8?

4. In verse 2 we read that "...*the Lord's indignation is against all the nations*..." The battle described in this chapter is one example of this. How will the Lord's indignation affect the nations?

Jeremiah 10:10

Habakkuk 3:12

Zephaniah 3:8

5. What are the various ways it will affect His people?

Isaiah 26:20-21

Micah 7:9

➢ <u>Prove yourselves doers of the word...James 1:22</u>

6. Thank God that we don't have to be afraid of His indignation!! He has given us a sure hope in the name of Jesus. How do these scriptures confirm that?

Romans 10:13

1 Thessalonians 5:9

➢ <u>In everything, by prayer and petition...Philippians 4:6</u>

Give thanks to the Lord for His patience and forbearance – He is still waiting for people to repent. Ask Him to make you a light to those who are under His indignation and draw them to Jesus. Pray for the Lord's compassion for the lost.

*The Lord is not slow about His promise, as some count slowness,
but is patient toward you, not wishing for any to perish but for all to come to repentance.
2 Peter 3:9*

~ ~ ~ ~ # DAY 2 ~ ~ ~ ~
Vengeance is Mine, says the Lord

> ### Draw near to God and He will draw near to you... James 4:8

So, as those who have been chosen of God, holy and beloved, put on a heart of compassion, kindness, humility, gentleness and patience; bearing with one another, and forgiving each other, whoever has a complaint against anyone; just as the Lord forgave you, so also should you. Beyond all these things put on love, which is the perfect bond of unity.
Colossians 3:12-14

Do you ever feel like getting revenge? The Lord counsels us to love our enemies. Offer your heart to Him again. Let Him fill you with forgiveness and grace.

Practice your memory verse:

And the _____ of the LORD _____ _____,
and _____ _____ joyful shouting to Zion, _____ everlasting joy upon their _____.
They will find _____ and joy, and _____ and sighing will flee away.
Isaiah 35:10

> ### Study to show yourself approved... 2 Timothy 2:15

Today we will continue looking at Isaiah chapter 34. The second half is a description of God's judgment on the earth and the resulting destruction and devastation in the land of Edom.

7. Read Isaiah 34:8-17.

Reviewing verse 8, how is this day described?

Ⓓ

What condition will the land be left in and what do you think it means (v.9)?
Try to picture what geological phenomenon could produce this effect.

How does verse 10 describe the state of the land?

What animals will live there in verse 11a?

What plumb line or standard will the Lord stretch over this land (v.11b)?

What rulers will they have (v.12)?

What condition will their towers and cities be in (v.13)?

What other animals will live there according to verses 14-15?

Where are we told to seek confirmation of this prophecy (v.16a)?

What does the book affirm (v.16b)?

How did the Lord give the animals this land (v.17)?

8. Isaiah 34:8 is talking about a battle that will take place in the land of Edom in the end-times. What insight do these verses add?
Deuteronomy 32:35a, 41-43

Isaiah 63:4

Luke 18:7

2 Thessalonians 1:6-10

*"**Vengeance**: God's work in giving just payment for wrongdoing."* (Nelson)

9. What do the following verses say about vengeance or taking revenge?
Leviticus 19:18

Romans 12:19-20

* Note: *Edom, the nation of Esau, is now the home of various desert creatures. The land is bleak and barren, however, total fulfillment of Isaiah's prophesy will come when God pronounces His judgment upon all His enemies in the earth.*

➢ <u>Prove yourselves doers of the word . . . James 1:22</u>

10. Have you been tempted to take vengeance into your own hands? How does today's teaching strengthen you?

11. Romans 12:20 encourages us to be kind to our enemies. What did Jesus teach about that and how can you make these verses a part of your life?
Matthew 5:44-45

Luke 6:35

➢ <u>In everything, by prayer and petition . . . Philippians 4:6</u>

Ask God to give you a gracious forgiving heart so you can be loving even to those who hurt you. Pray for your enemies.

*Love your enemies, and do good, and lend, expecting nothing in return;
and your reward will be great, and you will be sons of the Most High;
for He Himself is kind to ungrateful and evil men.
Luke 6:35*

DAY 3
The Glory of God

> ➤ <u>Draw near to God and He will draw near to you... James 4:8</u>

Surely we have all been stranded somewhere - perhaps a broken down vehicle, a canceled flight, a missed bus. Whatever the case, the response is generally to seek someone who can come and rescue us. Perhaps you feel stranded today in a difficult situation, either spiritually, emotionally or physically. Our lesson today includes the phrases:

"Be strong, do not fear!...He will come and save you."
Isaiah 35:4

This verse is great for restoring our perspective! Rejoice today in the Lord's promise to come and to save you! Give Him your difficulties in prayer right now, ask Him to come and save you and be watchful for His presence today.

Practice your memory verse:

And _____ ransomed _____ the _____ will _____, and _____ with _____ shouting _____ Zion, _____ everlasting _____ upon _____ heads. _____ will _____ gladness _____ joy, _____ sorrow _____ sighing _____ flee _____.

Isaiah ___:10

> ➤ <u>Study to show yourself approved... 2 Timothy 2:15</u>

Isaiah chapter 35 contrasts the blessing God's people will receive with His judgment on the nations described in the previous chapter. This passage is messianic and was recognized as being so by the people of Jesus' day.

12. Read Isaiah 35:1-7.

Describe what the land will look like in verses 1-2a.

What will be given to it in verse 2b?

Why does this occur? (verse 2c)

13. When we read Isaiah 33:9, it mentioned Lebanon, Sharon and Carmel. How does it compare to Isaiah 35:2 and what conclusions can you draw? It may help to remember that Jesus went to these places in His time on earth.

14. What do the following verses tell us about the glory of the Lord (mentioned in Isaiah 35:2)?

Exodus 24:16-18

1 Kings 8:10-11

John 1:14

John 2:11

John 17:5

15. Continue looking at Isaiah 35:3-7.
What advice does the Lord give (v.3)?

How should we encourage the anxious (v.4)?

What miracles will be seen in verses 5-6a?

Ⓜ

What metaphor is used in verse 6b and what does it mean?

Contrast the land before and after according to verse 7.

before	after

16. How do these verses confirm that Jesus fulfilled the prophecy given in Isaiah 35:5-6?
Matthew 9:27-30

Matthew 15:30-31

Mark 7:32-37

Luke 7:20-23

John 7:37-39

➤ <u>Prove yourselves doers of the word . . . James 1:22</u>

17. Consider the verses about the glory of the Lord in question 14. Have you ever experienced the glory of the Lord? Explain. Write a brief prayer asking for the Lord to reveal His glory to you.

18. Isaiah 35:3 exhorted the strong to "*Encourage the exhausted, and strengthen the feeble,*" we are exhorted to do the same. Read the following verses. What do they add?
Romans 15:1-2

1 Corinthians 8:9

1 Corinthians 9:22

Hebrews 12:12-13

Page 176

19. Who do you know that needs encouragement and strength? How can you minister to them?

20. In Isaiah 35:4 we are told to say to those who have an anxious heart, "*Take courage, fear not. Behold your God will come... He will save you.*" How are you doing this? Are you open and sensitive to see those around you who might be feeling anxious?

➤ In everything, by prayer and petition... Philippians 4:6

Ask God to strengthen you to do His work, to enable you to make personal changes so that you can minister effectively to others, and to be sensitive and available to minister to those whom God has placed in your path.

Therefore, my beloved brethren, be steadfast, immovable, always abounding in the work of the Lord, knowing that your toil is not in vain in the Lord.
1 Corinthians 15:58

~ ~ ~ ~ **DAY 4** ~ ~ ~ ~
The Highway of Holiness

➤ Draw near to God and He will draw near to you... James 4:8

Meditate on these scriptures about the Holiness of God:

Who among the gods is like you, O LORD?
Who is like you-- majestic in holiness, awesome in glory, working wonders?
Exodus 15:11 (NIV)

Your statutes stand firm;
holiness adorns your house for endless days, O LORD.
Psalm 93:5 (NIV)

Put on the new self, created to be like God
in true righteousness and holiness.
Ephesians 4:24 (NIV)

May He strengthen your hearts so that you will be blameless and holy
in the presence of our God and Father when our Lord Jesus comes with all his holy ones.
1 Thessalonians 3:13 (NIV)

For they disciplined us for a short time as seemed best to them,
but He disciplines us for our good, that we may share His holiness.
Hebrews 12:10 (NAS)

Consider how holiness is imparted to us.
Ask God to make you holy, useful, prepared for every good work.

Therefore, if anyone cleanses himself from these things,
he will be a vessel for honor, sanctified, useful to the Master,
prepared for every good work
II Timothy 2:21

Practice your memory verse:

_____ the _____ of _____ LORD _____ return, _____ come _____ joyful _____ to _____, with _____ joy _____ their _____. They _____ find _____ and ____, and _____ and _____ will _____ away.

_____ 35: ____

➤ <u>Study to show yourself approved... 2 Timothy 2:15</u>

The last three verses of Isaiah chapter 35 talk about the highway of holiness. This is a symbol of the pathway offered to all those who seek the Lord and are walking in His ways, set apart for Him.

21. Read Isaiah 35:8-10. Complete the chart below about the "Way".

Description of the Way	What/Who is not on it	Those who travel on it

22. Isaiah 35:8 says, "*the unclean will not travel on it.*" What does 1 Corinthians 6:9-10 say makes a person unclean?

23. Isaiah 35:8 also says, "*fools will not wander on it.*" Look up the following verses and build a description of a fool.

Psalm 14:1

Proverbs 10:23

Proverbs 12:15

Proverbs 13:19b

Proverbs 14:1

Proverbs 14:8-9,16

Proverbs 15:5

Proverbs 17:21

Proverbs 18:2

Proverbs 20:3

Proverbs 28:26

Ecclesiastes 7:9, 10:3

Isaiah 32:6

Romans 1:21-22

24. Isaiah 35:9 says that lions and vicious beasts will not be found there. This represents those who would ensnare the righteous. What do you learn about them from these verses?

Psalm 10:8-11

Matt 7:15-16

1 Peter 5:8

25. What do the following verses in the New Testament teach about the Way? (i.e. the highway of holiness)

John 14:6

Acts 9:2

Acts 24:14

> The Hebrew word for highway is 'derech' which means "way". This is the word used in the New Testament for the Christian faith.

➢ <u>Prove yourselves doers of the word . . . James 1:22</u>

26. Think about the Highway of Holiness described in Isaiah 35:8-10 and also the verses about God's holiness that you read at the beginning of our lesson today. What does it mean to be holy? How can you be holy?

> *... like the Holy One who called you, be holy yourselves also in all your behavior;*
> *because it is written, "You shall be holy, for I am holy."*
> *1 Peter 1:15-16*

27. None of us wants to be a fool. Were there any aspects of the fool that you found in question **23** that you need to be on your guard against? Explain.

➢ <u>In everything, by prayer and petition . . . Philippians 4:6</u>

Praise God for His indescribable gift of holiness!! He called us to be holy and also makes it possible. Consecrate yourself to Him in every area of your life. Ask Him to search you and reveal to you the areas that need work. Pray that He would make you wise in His wisdom. Pray for those you know who are walking in foolishness. Pray this verse and claim it as a promise:

> *And I will give them one heart and <u>one way</u>, that they may fear Me always,*
> *for their own good and for the good of their children after them.*
> *Jeremiah 32:39*

~ ~ ~ ~ **DAY 5** ~ ~ ~ ~
Everlasting Joy

➢ <u>Draw near to God and He will draw near to you . . . James 4:8</u>

Christian joy is not simply happiness or cheerfulness, it is inner contentment, peace and deep gladness that is not dependent upon circumstances and does not diminish during difficulties. Isaiah 35:10 says, *"And the ransomed of the Lord shall return...They will find joy and gladness."* One day, joy will be ours. For now, our joy comes by laying aside in prayer those things that burden us. In God's presence you can experience the fullness of joy. Pray now and enter His presence.

> *You will make known to me the path of life; in Your presence is fullness of joy;*
> *In Your right hand there are pleasures forever.*
> *Psalm 16:11*

Write down your memory verse:

➢ **Study to show yourself approved... 2 Timothy 2:15**

Today we will focus on the last verse of Isaiah 35, our memory verse for the week, which talks about the joy God has reserved for His people that He has redeemed.

28. **Read Isaiah 35:1-10** again to remember the context of verse 10.

Who will return and where do they return to (v.10a)?

How are they acting and what do they find (v.10b)?

What will flee from them (v.10c)?

Who are the ransomed or redeemed of the Lord?

29. The word <u>ransom</u> means a payment given in order to redeem a prisoner, slave or captive person from bondage. Verse 10 described the people God has ransomed. What do the following verses say about this ransom?

Mark 10:45

1 Timothy 2:5-6

1 Peter 1:18-19

30. What are the ransomed of the Lord redeemed from?
Psalm 107:2

Hosea 13:14

Galatians 3:13

Ephesians 1:7

Titus 2:14

31. Sometimes it's difficult for us to grasp that our ransom has been paid. We often feel like something more needs to be done for us to be free. Review your answers in question **29**. What did Jesus mean when He said in John 19:30, "...It is finished"?

➢ <u>Prove yourselves doers of the word . . . James 1:22</u>

32. In Isaiah 35:10, the ransomed of the Lord *"find gladness and joy."* Are you experiencing the Lord's joy? What are some of the things that rob you of your joy? Give them to God.

33. Isaiah 35:10 goes on to say, *"sorrow and sighing will flee away."* What sorrow do you look forward to having "flee away"?

➢ <u>In everything, by prayer and petition . . . Philippians 4:6</u>

Lift up your heart to the Lord and give thanks for His glorious promises. Bring your sorrows and sighing to Him. He wants to carry them for you. Are there any areas where you still need His victory or deliverance? Commit them to Him in prayer. Joy is a fruit of the Spirit. Ask for joy.

*Behold, the tabernacle of God is among men, and He will dwell among them,
and they shall be His people, and God Himself will be among them, and He will wipe away
every tear from their eyes; and there will no longer be any death; there will no longer be
any mourning, or crying, or pain; the first things have passed away.
Revelation 21:3-4*

~ ~ ~ ~ ~ ~   Prayer Requests   ~ ~ ~ ~ ~ ~

A Mighty Deliverance
Isaiah chapters 36 – 37

Lesson 16

DAY 1 — National Revival

> ➤ <u>Draw near to God and He will draw near to you... James 4:8</u>

Are you longing for the presence of God? Do you feel stale in your worship and devotion? God has provided so many ways for us to come to Him. He longs for fellowship with us more than we can imagine. Humble your heart before Him and repent of your lukewarmness. Ask and you will receive, seek and you will find. He longs to fill you again with His Holy Spirit. What is holding you back?

*Therefore repent and return, so that your sins may be wiped away,
in order that times of refreshing may come from the presence of the Lord.
Acts 3:19*

MEMORY VERSE   Isaiah 37:16

O LORD of hosts, God of Israel, the One who dwells between the cherubim,

You are God, You alone, of all the kingdoms of the earth.

You have made heaven and earth. (NKJ)

> ➤ <u>Study to show yourself approved... 2 Timothy 2:15</u>

Chapter 36 opens the most amazing story in Isaiah, the siege of Jerusalem by the Assyrian army. In order to understand the spiritual climate in which it takes place, we are going to study the background in 2 Chronicles 29-31.

When Hezekiah became king, he inherited a kingdom that had been filled with blatant idolatry. He chose to follow the Lord and bring revival. In the first year of his reign he called the priests and Levites to consecrate themselves and he restored the worship of the Lord. He sent couriers into the northern kingdom of Israel and throughout Judah calling all the Lord's people to a great feast in Jerusalem, the Passover. Nothing like this had occurred since the time of Solomon. They were so filled with joy at this celebration that they feasted for two weeks instead of one. He then tore down the altars of the idols in Judah. We are told that there had never been a king who trusted the Lord like him, before or after him.

1. Turn to **2 Chronicles chapters 29-31**. If you wish, you may want to read all three chapters. Read the following portions and write a brief description of what you learn from them.

2 Chronicles 29:1-11

2 Chronicles 29:31-36

2 Chronicles 30:1-12

2 Chronicles 30:12-20

2 Chronicles 30:21-27

2 Chronicles 31:1

2 Chronicles 31:20-21

2. In your own words, describe what a national revival looks like based on this story.

3. 2 Chronicles 30:18-20 is a beautiful picture of both intercession and God's heart for those who seek Him. What do you learn about these two things from this story?

> ## Prove yourselves doers of the word ... James 1:22

4. How can you apply this principle of intercession (2 Chronicles 30:18-20) in your prayer life?

5. Thankfully, there was someone in Hezekiah's life that impressed upon him the value of trusting in the Lord. Perhaps Isaiah had an influence on him as he was growing up. Think about the impact you have on your children and other young people around you – grandchildren, neighborhood children, your children's friends, etc. What values and character qualities would you like to impart to children? What Scriptures would you like to live before them?

> ## In everything, by prayer and petition ... Philippians 4:6

Pray for God to till the soil of people's hearts, break up their fallow ground and pour out His Spirit so that revival may come to our land. Ask Him to make you an intercessor and a light on a hill.

Sow with a view to righteousness, reap in accordance with kindness; break up your fallow ground,
For it is time to seek the LORD until He comes to rain righteousness on you.
Hosea 10:12

~ ~ ~ ~   **DAY 2**   ~ ~ ~ ~
Confidence in the Lord

➤ Draw near to God and He will draw near to you... James 4:8

Take a moment today to ponder this question: *"What is this confidence that you have?"* (Isaiah 36:4) This is what the people of the world ask about you when you put your faith and trust in God. Willingly yield to God and relinquish control where needed. You are most useful to God when you are yielded to Him.

For You are my hope; O Lord GOD, You are my confidence from my youth.
Psalm 71:5

Practice your memory verse:

O LORD of _____, God of _____,
the One who _____ between the _____,
You are _____, You alone, of all the _____ of the earth.
You _____ made heaven and earth.
Isaiah 37:16

➤ Study to show yourself approved... 2 Timothy 2:15

Hezekiah had been king only 3 years when the Assyrian king, Shalmaneser, came and conquered the northern kingdom of Israel as Isaiah had prophesied (2 Kings 18:9-10) and laid siege to Samaria. His father Ahaz paid Assyria money to come and attack them, and Judah became an Assyrian vassal. But Hezekiah, we are told, rebelled against the evil king of Assyria and stopped paying tribute.

In the 14th year of Hezekiah's reign, King Sennacherib of Assyria came against him with a great army and captured all the fortified cities of Judah. Even though a great revival had taken place and Hezekiah had a heart for the Lord, he responded in a human way, speaking the name of the Lord (2 Chronicles 32:7), but relying on his own tactics. Hezekiah took gold and silver from the Lord's Temple and sent it to him saying "I'm sorry!" in the hopes that he would go away, but it wasn't enough. The army came and lay siege to the city and Rabshakeh, the king's representative, came to taunt the people of Jerusalem.

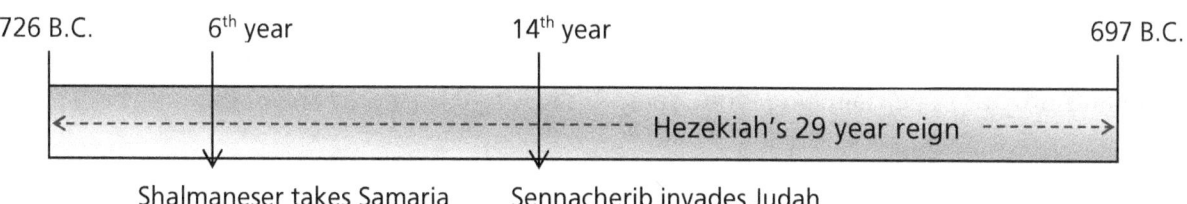

Read Isaiah 36:1-12.

6. Read 2 Kings 18:13-16. What was Hezekiah's initial response to Assyria's threat? What does this reveal about where his confidence was placed at that point?

Note -- The king of Assyria wasn't satisfied with the tribute Hezekiah sent because Jerusalem had locked its gates and prepared for a siege instead of opening up and letting their armies enter and loot the city.

7. Read 2 Chronicles 32:1-8. How did Hezekiah prepare for the attack by Assyria?

8. Read Isaiah 22:8-11. Isaiah had called the people to repent of trusting in their own strength. In chapter 22 he also prophesied of the people's arrogance in the face of death. When we studied this in Lesson 9, we saw that the people took Isaiah's warning to heart.

9. Answer the following questions about Isaiah 36:1-12.

   What historical information is given in verse 1?

   Who did the king send and where did he stand (v.2)?

   Who came out to them (v.3)?

   What question does the king have for Hezekiah (v.4)? What specifically is he attacking verbally?

   What opinion does the king have of Hezekiah's confidence (v.5)?

   Who does he assume is Hezekiah's ally and what is his opinion of them (v.6)?

   Who else does he assume they are trusting in and how does he try to undermine it (v.7)?

10. In any human warfare, emotional and mental factors are extremely important. Rabshakeh is trying to demoralize the Judeans by attacking the areas he thinks they are trusting in. How effective do you think this attack may have been on an individual level? Share your thoughts.

11. Continue answering questions about the passage in Isaiah 36:8-12.

    What offer does Rabshakeh tantalize them with in verse 8?

    How does he mock them in verse 9?

    Whose authority does he claim and what does he say is authorized to do (v.10)?

    What diplomatic step do Eliakim and Hezekiah's other representatives take in verse 11?

    What shocking response does Rabshakeh give in the ears of all the people of Judah (v.12)?

➤ Prove yourselves doers of the word... James 1:22

12. Judah's enemy attacked their confidence. *"What is this confidence that you have?"* This is exactly what Satan does to us. Why do you think this would be an effective tool in warfare, both then and in your life now?

13. Who did Hezekiah tell the people to rely on in 2 Chronicles 32:7-8? What truths in this passage would you cling to in this situation?

14. What counsel do you glean about confidence from the following scriptures?
Proverbs 3:25-26

Acts 4:13, 29

Hebrews 10:35-36

1 John 3:21-22

15. What is the Lord saying to you today and how can you apply it to your life?

➤ In everything, by prayer and petition... Philippians 4:6

Commit to the Lord in prayer the things He taught you today. Ask Him to help you make Him your confidence.

The fruit of righteousness will be peace; the effect of righteousness will be quietness and confidence forever. (NIV)
Isaiah 32:17

~ ~ ~ ~ **DAY 3** ~ ~ ~ ~
The Enemy's Challenge

➤ Draw near to God and He will draw near to you... James 4:8

When Jesus was fasting for forty days and nights in the wilderness, He became hungry and Satan was tempting Him. *"If you are the Son of God..."*, he said, tempting His confidence in the Lord and His identity in God.
Are you going through difficult times? Are you being tempted to throw away your confidence? Let the word nourish and strengthen you today. Focus your hope on the Lord and ignore the enemy's taunts.

Be strong and let your heart take courage, all you who hope in the LORD.
Psalm 31:24

Practice your memory verse:

O_____ of _____, God ___ Israel,
____ One _____ dwells _____ the _____,
You ____ God, ____ alone, ____ all _____ kingdoms ____ the _____.
You _____ made _____ and _____.
Isaiah ____:16

Page 187

> ## Study to show yourself approved... 2 Timothy 2:15

Yesterday we read the beginning of the king of Assyria's challenge to Hezekiah and the people of Jerusalem. Today we will finish studying this challenge. The enemy makes his stand quite clear. He is questioning who they will put their trust in.

16. Read Isaiah 36:13-22 and answer the following questions.

Whose words was Rabshakeh delivering and in what language (v.13)?

Who does he tell the people not to trust in and why (v.14)?

Who else does he tell them to doubt in verse 15a?

How does he quote Hezekiah in verse 15b?

What appealing alternative does he offer the people in verses 16-17?

17. Rabshakeh attacks the people's confidence in their leader several times. What words does he use against Hezekiah in these verses:

verse 14: Do not let Hezekiah... _____

verse 15: Nor let Hezekiah... _____

verse 16: Do not _____ to Hezekiah.

verse 18: Beware that Hezekiah... _____

18. Continue answering questions about Isaiah 36:18-22:

What words of Hezekiah's does Rabshakeh call misleading (v.18a)?

What question does he ask in verse 18b as proof that they can't trust Hezekiah?

What gods does he compare the Lord to in verse 19?

What challenge to their faith does he present in verse 20?

How did the people honor Hezekiah in verse 21?

Who reported these words to Hezekiah and what was their attitude (v.22)?

> Rabshakeh points out Samaria's fall. This was a very clever stab at their confidence. Samaria was the capital of the northern kingdom of Israel and they were also God's people. He implied that God had not been strong enough to deliver them, but this was not the case. They had put their trust in idols and the Lord abandoned them to their enemies (2 Kings 17:7-18).

19. Isaiah 36:21 says, "*But they were silent and answered him not a word...*" Despite their questions, fears and concerns, they were able to obey the king's command. They must have felt tempted by Assyria's offer. How do these scriptures show the wisdom of Hezekiah's command?

Exodus 14:14

Psalm 39:1

Proverbs 17:28

How was Jesus an example of this in Mark 14:60-61?

➤ <u>Prove yourselves doers of the word . . . James 1:22</u>

20. Remember Jesus fought temptation with the Word of God (Matthew 4:1-11). What scriptures do you find helpful when you need to keep silent?

21. Rabshakeh attacked the people of Jerusalem in two areas, their trust in their leader Hezekiah, and their trust in the Lord. Can you relate to this? How has the enemy attacked your confidence in your leaders or God?

22. Ask God's forgiveness for listening to the enemy and commit to trusting in the Lord despite outward circumstance.

23. What wisdom do you learn from the following verses?

Ephesians 6:13

James 4:7

1 Peter 5:8-9

24. What do you need to remember and apply from today's lesson?

➤ <u>In everything, by prayer and petition . . . Philippians 4:6</u>

Pray that you would be strong in the Lord and that you would put on the armor of God to be able to stand against the enemy. (Ephesians 6:10-20)

Put on the full armor of God, so that you will be able to stand firm against the schemes of the devil. For our struggle is not against flesh and blood, but against the rulers, against the powers, against the world forces of this darkness, against the spiritual forces of wickedness in the heavenly places.
Ephesians 6:11-12

~ ~ ~ ~ ## DAY 4 ~ ~ ~ ~
Relying on God

➤ <u>Draw near to God and He will draw near to you . . . James 4:8</u>

Meditate on, ponder, look at intently the **keeping power** of God.

I give eternal life to them, and they will never perish; and no one will snatch them out of My hand. "My Father, who has given them to Me, is greater than all; and no one is able to snatch them out of the Father's hand.
John 10:28-29

Practice your memory verse:

"___ LORD ___ hosts, _____ of _____, the _____ who _____ between _____ cherubim, _____ are _____, You _____, of _____ the _____ of _____ earth. _____ have _____ heaven _____ earth.

_____ 37: ____

> ### Study to show yourself approved... 2 Timothy 2:15

In Isaiah chapter 37, we read Hezekiah's response to the king of Assyria's challenge. Even though they are greatly distressed, they turn to the Lord and seek His help. They refuse to be tempted by the Assyrian offer of mercy and deportation.

Remember how Hezekiah had been preparing for this siege, fortifying the walls and building a conduit to the springs? Isaiah had warned him against relying on his own preparations instead of God. He called the people to true repentance and humbling. In Isaiah 32:9, he called the women at ease to repent and intercede.

Now we will see what happens when people take the Lord's warnings to heart.

25. Read Isaiah 37:1-20 and answer the following questions.

How did Hezekiah respond to the king of Assyria's challenge (v.1)?

What action did he take in verse 2?

What message did he give in verse 3 and what do you think he meant?

What hope did Hezekiah have and what did he request of Isaiah in verse 4?

26. Read the following prophecies. Explain how our passage today shows that Hezekiah took them to heart.

Isaiah 22:12

Isaiah 22:20

How was Isaiah 22:3 not fulfilled?

27. It often isn't until we are in a huge battle that we realize how small our faith is. How small Hezekiah's hope must have seemed when he sent the message to Isaiah! And yet, notice how powerful the response:

What encouragement does Isaiah give in Isaiah 37:6?

How does the Lord plan to intervene according to Isaiah 37:7?

What was the immediate fulfillment of this prophecy in Isaiah 37:8-9a?

Rabshakeh has to leave but he doesn't want Hezekiah or the people of Jerusalem to think, even for a moment, that the Lord was rescuing them. He left most of his army camped around the walls of the city. Let's look at what else he did.

28. Continue answering questions about Isaiah 37:9-20.

What did he do before he left in verse 9b?

What challenge does he give in verse 10 and who is he mocking specifically?

What does he say Assyria did to the other lands they attacked (v.11a)?

What disturbing question does he pose in verse 11b?

What cities and peoples does he list as conquered in verses 12-13?

What did Hezekiah do with the letter Rabshakeh sent (v.14)?

Who did he turn to (v.15)?

What qualities of God did he acknowledge and remember in verse 16?

What did he ask the Lord to do in verse 17?

What truth does he point out in the Assyrian message in verses 18-19a?

What reason does he give for the success of the Assyrian armies in verse 19b?

What will the outcome be when the Lord answers, according to verse 20?

29. Somehow this phrase *"Do not let your God in whom you trust deceive you..."* sounds absurd to us now as we sit and work on our study, but in the terror of the moment, it was certainly a temptation to doubt the Lord. The Lord says Rabshakeh has blasphemed Him in verse 6.

What is the definition of blasphemy? If you look at the way it is used in the Old Testament it is clear that to speak against God defiantly is blasphemy (Luke 22:63-65).

What does Numbers 15:30 say about this?

*Note – the blasphemy referred to here is not the same as the blasphemy of the Holy Spirit spoken of in the New Testament (Matthew 12:31-32).

Page 191

> ## Prove yourselves doers of the word... James 1:22

30. The first threat made to Hezekiah by Rabshakeh challenged and mocked Hezekiah's faith (Isaiah 36:4-20). The second threat made to Hezekiah was really an attack on his God. Have you ever been in a situation where someone attacked your God? What was your response? What scriptures support your response?

31. Hezekiah wasn't just desperate for the Lord's intervention. He wanted the Lord to be glorified in the eyes of the nations. Is that your heart's desire? Do you want God to be glorified or do you just want relief from your trial?

32. How is Hezekiah's response to this threatening situation and confidence in the Lord an example to you today?

> ## In everything, by prayer and petition... Philippians 4:6

Pray these verses into your life today.

> *Teach me Your way, O LORD; I will walk in Your truth; unite my heart to fear Your name.*
> *I will give thanks to You, O Lord my God, with all my heart, and will glorify Your name forever.*
> *For Your lovingkindness toward me is great,*
> *And You have delivered my soul from the depths of Sheol.*
> *Psalm 86:11-13*

~ ~ ~ ~ # DAY 5 ~ ~ ~ ~
Miraculous Intervention

> ## Draw near to God and He will draw near to you... James 4:8

Are you under attack? Are you suffering? Is your heart heavy? No matter what is happening, the Lord is a mighty champion on your behalf. He longs to tuck you under His wings and defend you. Come into His presence and pray. Cast all your cares upon Him and keep your eyes fixed on Him.

Isaiah 37:21 says,
> "...Thus says the Lord God of Israel, 'Because you have prayed to Me...'"

Align yourself with God in heart and mind. Ask Him to deal with anything that interferes with this alliance.

Write your memory verse:

> ## Study to show yourself approved... 2 Timothy 2:15

Today we will finish reading the story of the Assyrian army's siege of Jerusalem in Isaiah 37. The Lord has allowed the affront to go as far as He will tolerate and now He will show them that He is God. These were exciting times to be living in because people were believing God and taking Him at His word!

33. Read Isaiah 37:21-38.

How did the Lord respond to Hezekiah in verse 21 and why?

How has Assyria shown their scorn for Judah in verse 22?

What questions does the Lord ask the Assyrians and then answer in verse 23?

The Lord is taking Assyria's arrogance very personally. It is similar to Jesus' statement "'I tell you the truth, whatever you did not do for one of the least of these, you did not do for Me.'

How did they reproach the Lord in verses 24-25?

34. Continue answering questions about Isaiah 37:26-38.
Who is responsible for the deeds Assyria has done and what was His plan (v.26)?

What condition were the peoples they conquered in because of the Lord (v.27)?

What does the Lord know (v.28)?

What is the Assyrians' attitude about what they have accomplished (v.29a)?

What will God do to Assyria (v.29b)?

*Note – The Assyrians used to put hooks in the noses of their captives.
What sign does the Lord give Hezekiah in verse 30?

What promise does the Lord give in verses 31-32a?

Why will it take place (v.32b)?

The Lord has drawn the line. What does He say will not happen (v.33)?

What does He say WILL happen in verse 34?

Who will defend the city and why (v.35)?

> In the reign of King Ahaz, Isaiah prophesied that Assyria's army would come to Jerusalem like a flooding river. "It will overflow and pass through, it will reach even to the neck..." Isaiah 8:8. The neck refers to the walls of Jerusalem, a city that sits high on the mountains.

35. The next verse, Isaiah 37:36, is one of the most amazing verses in the book of Isaiah. It confirmed to the people the power of God and the truth of His prophecies given through Isaiah.

What does verse 36 say God did?

What did Isaiah 31:8 prophesy that God would do?

36. What did King Sennacherib do after the loss of his army, according to Isaiah 37:37-38, and what happened to him?

> ➤ Prove yourselves doers of the word... James 1:22

37. Hezekiah and the people of Jerusalem humbled themselves before the Lord. That's why the Lord intervened on their behalf. What do the following verses say about a humble heart?

Psalm 10:17

Psalm 51:17

James 4:10

1 Peter 5:5-6

Are you needing God to intervene on your behalf? Simply humble yourself and ask.

38. The Lord accomplished an incredibly miraculous deliverance for them, one that must have led to great rejoicing and amazement. But the reality of the condition of their nation after the invasion was still a great need. The Lord had already thought ahead and provided for them.
He understood that they needed time to heal and so He provided for their sustenance for three years!! Look again at Isaiah 37:30. Have you been through a major battle recently? Did you give yourself time to recover? What is the Lord saying to you?

> ➤ In everything, by prayer and petition... Philippians 4:6

Consider the problems weighing on you. Nothing is too great for the Lord to handle. Make up your mind to trust in the Lord as Hezekiah did and wait for His help. Take them to prayer right now. Let Hezekiah's prayer be an example for you. This is how it starts:

*O LORD of hosts, the God of Israel, who is enthroned above the cherubim,
You are the God, You alone, of all the kingdoms of the earth. You have made heaven and earth.
Incline Your ear, O LORD, and hear; open Your eyes, O LORD, and see; and listen to all the
words of Sennacherib, who sent them to reproach the living God...
Isaiah 37:16-17*

~ ~ ~ ~ ~ ~   Prayer Requests   ~ ~ ~ ~ ~ ~

The Comfort of the Lord
Isaiah chapters 38-40
Lesson 17

DAY 1 — The Gift of Life

➤ *Draw near to God and He will draw near to you... James 4:8*

> Your eyes have seen my unformed substance;
> And in Your book were all written the days that were ordained for me,
> When as yet there was not one of them.
> Psalm 139:16

Each day of our lives is written in the Lord's book. He holds us in the palm of His hand. He knows what you need today. Commit your day to Him and give Him the burdens of your heart.

MEMORY VERSE   Isaiah 40:8

The grass withers, the flower fades,
But the word of our God stands forever.

➤ *Study to show yourself approved... 2 Timothy 2:15*

Isaiah chapter 38 tells the story of a brush with death that Hezekiah had. It actually takes place before the great deliverance the Lord accomplished for His people in the previous chapter (see Isaiah 38:6). As you study it, consider what purpose the Lord may have had with this timing.

1. Read Isaiah 38:1-22. Answer the following questions.

What happened to Hezekiah and what message did Isaiah have for him (v.1)?

How did Hezekiah respond (v.2)?

What did he say and do (v.3)?

How did the Lord respond to Hezekiah's prayer (v.4-5)?

What else did the Lord promise to do for Hezekiah (v.6)?

What sign did the Lord promise Hezekiah to prove His word (v.7-8)?

In Isaiah 38:9-22, we find what Hezekiah wrote about his experience after he was healed. He explains how he felt, how he pleaded with the Lord and how he asked for a sign.

2. Answer these questions about what Hezekiah wrote:

> *"The sun's shadow went back ten steps on the stairway on which it had gone down..."* The Lord literally set time back a number of hours for a sign. Don't you wonder what people thought? This was a sign that would've been seen around the world.

What will he be deprived of according to verses 10-11?

How does he describe his coming death in verses 12-13?

How does he grieve in verses 14-15?

How did he plead with the Lord in verses 16-17a?

What does He say the Lord has done for him in verse 17b?

What concerns him about death (v.18)?

What does he long to do (v.19a)?

What does Hezekiah plan to tell his sons (v.19b)?

3. After pouring his heart out to the Lord, Hezekiah reaches what conclusion (v. 20)?

What remedy did Isaiah prescribe in verse 21?

What question had Hezekiah asked him at that time (v.22)?

4. Read 2 Kings 20:1-11. It makes the order of events more clear. What light does it shed on this story?

5. Read 2 Chronicles 32:24-26. How did Hezekiah respond to God's great gift to him?

> ## Prove yourselves doers of the word... James 1:22

6. Do you think this miracle had any effect on his ability to trust in God for deliverance from the Assyrians? Would it have had any effect on you?

7. Why did he turn his face to the wall? What is the significance of that action (Isaiah 38:2)?

8. In Isaiah 38:20, Hezekiah says, "*The Lord will surely save me...*" What does this tell you about God? What does this tell you about prayer that is according to God's will?

9. When do you think it is appropriate to expect healing and when should you just accept your condition? Look at these verses:

Psalm 103:3

2 Corinthians 12:7-10

James 5:16.

> ## In everything, by prayer and petition... Philippians 4:6

> *Jesus said to her, "I am the resurrection and the life;*
> *he who believes in Me will live even if he dies, and everyone*
> *who lives and believes in Me will never die. Do you believe this?"*
> *John 11:25-26*

Jesus has authority over life and death. Praise Him for every day you've been given and ask Him to help you live each day for Him.

~ ~ ~ ~   ## DAY 2   ~ ~ ~ ~
Hezekiah is Tested

> ## Draw near to God and He will draw near to you... James 4:8

> *Search me, O God, and know my heart; try me and know my anxious thoughts;*
> *And see if there be any hurtful way in me, and lead me in the everlasting way.*
> *Psalm 139:23-24*

In this verse, David asks the Lord to search him and to try (test) him. He wants the Lord to know his heart and his anxious thoughts. As you begin your study today, pray these verses. Open yourself to the Lord and confess you shortcomings and ask Him to lead you in His perfect way.

Practice your memory verse:

The grass _____, the flower _____,
But the word of our God _____ forever.
Isaiah 40:8

> ## Study to show yourself approved... 2 Timothy 2:15

Isaiah chapter 39 talks about some ambassadors from a kingdom far away that heard about Hezekiah's miraculous healing and sent a gift to him, perhaps to get the full story. Babylon, in those days, was a vassal of Assyria's, a rebellious and troublesome kingdom. They were soon to break off Assyria's yoke and grow to govern the known world. Did they investigate the miracle because they saw the sun moving back in its course? It could be.

10. Read Isaiah 39:1-8. Answer these questions.

Who sent a letter to Hezekiah and why (v.1)?

What was Hezekiah's response (v.2)?

Why do you think he did that?

What questions did Isaiah ask him and how did he respond (v.3-4)?

What message from the Lord did Isaiah give him about the wealth Hezekiah had shown (v.5-6)?

What would happen to some of his descendents (v.7)?

How was this fulfilled according to Daniel 1:1-4?

11. What was Hezekiah's response to this prophecy in Isaiah 39:8?

He seems pleased with this word spoken by Isaiah. What do you think about this? Do you agree?

12. Read 2 Chronicles 32:31. What information does it add to this story?

13. What was God's purpose in testing Hezekiah? Do you think he passed the test? Why or why not?

How do these scriptures show that he behaved unwisely?

Joshua 9:14b

Psalm 81:12

What else did Hezekiah neglect to do when the Babylonians came?

Luke 17:12-18

Romans 1:21a

14. Why do you think the Lord may have not wanted Hezekiah to show them everything?

What do you think was Hezekiah's weakness?

How did Jesus demonstrate greater wisdom in John 2:24?

15. Jerusalem and King Hezekiah were safe from Assyria, but sometime after Hezekiah's death, Jerusalem would be taken captive by Babylon. Check your timeline. When will this occur?

16. What do you learn from the following scriptures about the purpose of the God's testing?

Exodus 16:4

Exodus 20:20

Deuteronomy 8:16b-17

Judges 2:21-22

1 Corinthians 3:12-14

17. When Hezekiah heard about how some of his sons would be taken captive, he wasn't concerned for them. He cared only that "...*there will be peace and truth in my days*..." Contrast Hezekiah's heart for his children (not yet born) with these fathers in the Bible:

Abraham – Genesis 18:19

Moses' teaching about fathers – Deuteronomy 6:6-9, 20-24

Job – Job 1:5

Asaph – Psalm 78:1-7

David – Proverbs 4:3-5

➤ Prove yourselves doers of the word... James 1:22

18. Has God ever tested you in this way, waited to see if you would seek His counsel or give Him glory for the work He has done? Explain.

19. How can we best prepare ourselves for God's testing?

Psalm 119:11

Proverbs 3:5-6

James 1:2-4

20. Is there a principle for us in this story? Should we welcome everyone into our lives and share everything about ourselves openly?

➤ In everything, by prayer and petition... Philippians 4:6

The Lord tests us to purify us and to make us more like Him. Ask the Lord to help you be aware and pass the test He sets before you.

*I, the LORD, search the heart, I test the mind,
Even to give to each man according to his ways, according to the results of his deeds.
Jeremiah 17:10*

DAY 3
Preparing the Way of the Lord

➤ **Draw near to God and He will draw near to you... James 4:8**

Quiet your heart before the Lord. As you study His word today He will mold you and instruct you. Ask the Lord to reveal His glory to you and be glorified through your life.

And we, who with unveiled faces all reflect the Lord's glory, are being transformed into His likeness with ever-increasing glory, which comes from the Lord, who is the Spirit.
2 Corinthians 3:18 (NIV)

Practice your memory verse:

The _____ withers, _____ flower _____,

But _____ word _____ our _____ stands _____.

Isaiah _____:8

➤ **Study to show yourself approved... 2 Timothy 2:15**

In Isaiah chapter 40 we enter a totally new section of prophecy as mentioned in the Introduction on page 11. Up until now, there have been many messages of judgment and oracles about specific nations. Now, the Lord seems to reveal His heart much more, spending a great deal more time describing His glorious promises and the hope He offers them. Today we will read about the comfort the Lord is sending and the messenger of good news who is coming.

21. Read Isaiah 40:1-9.

What does the Lord want us to do in verse 1?

What does He add to this word in verse 2?

What does a voice call out in verse 3-4?

What will follow this preparation and who will see it (v.5)?

Ⓜ

22. In Luke 3:2-6, John the Baptist fulfilled this promise in Isaiah 40:3 when he came baptizing and calling the people to repentance. What was John the Baptist's witness according to these scriptures?

John 1:6-8

John 1:29-34

23. *"Then the glory of the Lord will be revealed,"* Isaiah 40:5 says. How was this fulfilled according to John 1:14?

24. A second voice speaks in Isaiah 40:6, saying "Call out." What does the other voice ask in response?

What is the answer given in Isaiah 40:6b-8?

What is the Lord saying about people? What point is He trying to make?

25. What is Zion exhorted to do in Isaiah 40:9?

> In Isaiah 40:9, the Hebrew says "*Behold your God*! The similarity with Pilate's quote in John 19:5 is worth noting. He said, "*Behold the man!*"

*Note – "Bearer of good news", the Hebrew word 'mevaseret', could also be translated preacher of the gospel.

26. Isaiah 40:8 says God's word stands forever. What do these scriptures teach you about God's word?

Joshua 21:45

Matthew 24:35

John 17:17

2 Corinthians 1:20

➤ <u>Prove yourselves doers of the word... James 1:22</u>

27. Isaiah 40 uses the word "call" or "calling" several times. What is the main point in each one?

verse 2

verse 3

verse 6

verse 9

Summarize what you learn from these points about sharing the gospel.

28. John the Baptist was faithful to his calling. He prepared the way of the Lord by calling the people to repentance and pointing out their sins. He baptized them with water to symbolize their desire to be purified and set apart for the Lord. He prophesied that someone much greater was coming after him and when Jesus arrived, he testified that He was the Son of God. Jesus was the glory of the Lord revealed to all flesh as Isaiah prophesied.
   This is the comfort of the Lord! Have you laid a hold of this comfort? -- Give thanks the forgiveness of your sins, the cleansing of His blood, and the glory of the Lord revealed to us.

29. John the Baptist's purpose was to prepare the way for Jesus, so that the glory of the Lord could be revealed. We have a similar purpose. How are you fulfilling that?

30. When others look at your life, is there a straight, smooth path to the Lord? What obstacles are there? Write a prayer here asking God for His help in removing obstacles.

➢ **In everything, by prayer and petition... Philippians 4:6**

God's words will outlast all of us. Ask Him to feed you from His word and help you spread the good news in the time you have.

> *In the beginning was the Word, and the Word was with God, and the Word was God. He was in the beginning with God. All things came into being by Him, and apart from Him nothing came into being that has come into being. In Him was life, and the life was the light of men. And the light shines in the darkness, and the darkness did not comprehend it.*
> *John 1:1-5*
>
> *Heaven and earth will pass away, but My words will not pass away.*
> *Luke 21:33*

~ ~ ~ ~ **DAY 4** ~ ~ ~ ~
The One Who is Coming

➢ **Draw near to God and He will draw near to you... James 4:8**

> *The LORD by wisdom founded the earth, by understanding He established the heavens. By His knowledge the deeps were broken up and the skies drip with dew.*
> *Proverbs 3:19-20*

There is no one who can compare to the Lord. Don't limit your concept of God to the finite grasp of your own mind. Humble yourself and ask the Lord to reveal more of Himself to you. Ask Him to enlarge your understanding of who He is and to increase your love for Him. Pray for a teachable, willing spirit.

Practice your memory verse:

_____ grass _____, the _____ fades,

_____ the _____ of _____ God _____ forever.

_____ 40: ___

➢ **Study to show yourself approved... 2 Timothy 2:15**

We continue studying Isaiah 40 today. Yesterday we saw that the Lord was sending a messenger to comfort His people and to prepare the way for His Messiah. Today we will read more about this Messiah. Then we will read the challenge the Lord gives His displaced people, Israel.

31. Read Isaiah 40:9-20. Use the questions to draw out the meaning of the passage.

As a recap of verse 9:

Where was Zion to go and what did they bear (v.9a)?

How were they to speak and what were they to say (v.9b)?

What were they to say (v.9c)?

How will the Lord come in verse 10?

How will He treat His flock (v.11)?

32. How does Jesus say He cares for His flock in John 10:11-14?

*Seeing the people, Jesus felt compassion for them,
because they were distressed and downcast like sheep without a shepherd.
Matthew 9:36*

33. Continue answering questions about the passage in Isaiah 40.

What questions does the Lord ask as a challenge in verse 12?

What does the Lord ask in verses 13-14 to prove that He has no equal?

What is the obvious answer to these questions?

God is omniscient, all-knowing. There is nothing we can add to His knowledge, no new information that He doesn't already know. Look up the following scriptures and summarize what you learn about His omniscience.

Psalm 44:21

Psalm 139:16

Romans 11:33

34. Continue answering questions about the passage in Isaiah 40.

What significance do the nations have in God's eyes (v.15-16)?

How does the Lord regard them (v.17)?

Verse 17 shows that the nations are no threat to God, it doesn't mean He doesn't care about them. What does Isaiah 45:22 say about His heart for them?

35. Continue answering questions about the passage in Isaiah 40.

What questions does the Lord ask in verse 18?

How does the Lord describe the alternative that some choose over Him in verses 19-20?

> <u>Prove yourselves doers of the word . . . James 1:22</u>

36. We may read through these questions with confidence and wonder in amazement how anyone could choose an idol over the Lord, but this is only because we overestimate our own spirituality. Consider these questions and comment when they apply:

Have you ever feared others and doubted the Lord because of it?

Have you ever put your trust in finances, people, your own strengths or other such securities instead of the Lord?

Have you ever doubted the Lord's counsel to you?

Isaiah 40:14 says, "*With whom did He consult and who gave Him understanding?*" There is no one who can compare with Him. No one can add to His knowledge or understanding. Ask the Lord to strengthen your trust in Him and increase your devotion to Him.

37. In Isaiah 40:11, the Messiah "*...will tend His flock, in His arm He will gather the lambs and carry them...*". Read John 21:15-17. How can you show your love for Jesus by sharing in His ministry to His flock?

38. Sometimes when we pray we want to convince the Lord to do things our way. But He says plainly, that there is no one capable of counseling Him and giving Him advice. When you pray, do you come to Him as an advisor? Or as a lamb who needs His care?

> <u>In everything, by prayer and petition . . . Philippians 4:6</u>

There is no wisdom and no understanding and no counsel against the LORD.
Proverbs 21:30

Pray for the flock, those who are hurting, those who are lost, those who are under attack. Make up your mind to pursue and live by the wisdom He gives you. Submit to Him, trust Him and rest in the peace that passes all understanding.

~ ~ ~ ~ <u>DAY 5</u> ~ ~ ~ ~
God is Above All Others

> <u>Draw near to God and He will draw near to you. . . James 4:8</u>

Isaiah 40:25 says,

'To whom will you liken Me, or to whom shall I be equal?' says the Holy One. (NKJ)

The Lord has gone to great lengths to reveal His power to us. But even more than that, He has labored to reveal His tender, personal care for us. You are kept in the palm of His hand and no one can snatch you away. Nothing is too difficult for Him to take care of.
Tell Him that there is no one like Him and put your trust in Him alone today.

Write down your memory verse:

➢ *Study to show yourself approved... 2 Timothy 2:15*

As we finish studying Isaiah chapter 40 today, the Lord continues to defend Himself. The people of Israel were doubting whether God really was better than the idols of other nations, even in exile! Rabshakeh had lumped them all into the same category (Isaiah 36:20). Were the Lord's people doing that also in their hearts?

39. Read Isaiah 40:21-31. Let's study what this passage is about.

The Lord seems astonished at their ignorance. What does He ask in verse 21?

How does He describe Himself and the inhabitants of earth in verse 22?

What does He do to powerful men (v.23)?

Describe the analogy He uses to describe their fleeting lives in verse 24?

What is the key question of this passage that He asks in verse 25?

What does He want them to know about the stars in verse 26?

40. Isaiah 40:27 gives us the reason for this speech. What has Israel been saying?

What is the Lord's strong answer in verse 28?

41. Isaiah 40:27 tells us that Israel has been saying *"My way is hidden from the LORD."* How do these scriptures add to your understanding of the Lord's perspective?

Psalm 94:7-8,11

Ezekiel 8:8-12

42. Back to Isaiah 40:29-31:

What does the Lord give in verse 29?

Describe how He contrasts this with ordinary human strength in verse 30.

What is promised to those who wait on the Lord in verse 31?

> ## Prove yourselves doers of the word... James 1:22

43. Have you behaved as if your way was hidden from the Lord? What do you learn from these scriptures?

Psalm 139:2-4

Daniel 2:22

Matthew 12:36

Mark 4:22

Hebrews 4:13

44. Isaiah 40:29 says "*He gives strength to the weary, and to him who lacks might, He increases power*". Are you doubting the power of God? How does this truth encourage you?

> ## In everything, by prayer and petition... Philippians 4:6

Lift up your eyes on high and see who has created these stars,
The One who leads forth their host by number, He calls them all by name;
Because of the greatness of His might and the strength of His power,
Not one of them is missing.
Isaiah 40:26

Pray over the areas where you are weak and let Him strengthen you. Ask Him to help you never doubt the depths of His perfect understanding, but trust in His love for you. Your ability depends on His power and not your own.

~ ~ ~ ~ ~ ~ ~   Prayer Requests   ~ ~ ~ ~ ~ ~

The Lord's Case
Isaiah chapters 41 – 42

Lesson 18

DAY 1 — The Intercession of the Lord

> **Draw near to God and He will draw near to you... James 4:8**

   We would have no hope if the Lord wasn't on our side, <u>but He is</u>. Ponder this for a moment. The One who knows everything about you is your hope and your defense!

> *What then shall we say to these things? If God is for us, who is against us?*
> *Who will bring a charge against God's elect? God is the one who justifies; who is the one who condemns? Christ Jesus is He who died, yes, rather who was raised,*
> *who is at the right hand of God, who also intercedes for us.*
> *Romans 8:31,33-34*

MEMORY VERSE   Isaiah 41:10

Fear not, for I am with you;

be not dismayed, for I am your God. I will strengthen you,

Yes, I will help you, I will uphold you with My righteous right hand. (NKJ)

> **Study to show yourself approved... 2 Timothy 2:15**

   Isaiah chapter 41 begins with the Lord calling the nations together. He is prosecuting idol worshipers and defending His people. Picture a large courtroom with the Lord as both the judge and lawyer. Historically, this prophecy was given when the northern kingdom of Israel was in exile in Assyria.

1. Read Isaiah 41:1-10. Answer the following questions.

Who does the Lord call and for what purpose do they gather (v.1)?

What question does He ask them in verses 2a?

What does this "one from the east" accomplish in verses 2b-3?

Isaiah is speaking prophetically of Cyrus, the king of Persia who will conquer Babylon in 538 B.C. long after the Assyrian empire has ceased to exist. What clues about him do you find in these verses?
Isaiah 41:25

Isaiah 45:1,13

Isaiah 46:11

Page 207

2. Continuing in Isaiah 41, what does He ask them in verse 4 and how does He answer Himself?
   *Note – This is an appropriate method of legal debate to present a question in order to answer it.

   How does the Lord describe the people of the distant lands in verses 5-6?

   What response do these nations make when they are afraid (v.7)? Read Isaiah 40:19-20 to clarify what it is talking about.

3. Notice the distinction the Lord makes between His people and the other nations, who worship idols. What names and terms of endearment does the Lord call them in verse 8?

   What do 2 Chronicles 20:7 and James 2:23 say about Abraham? What did Abraham do to earn this title?

4. Continue answering questions about the amazing promises in Isaiah 41:9-10.

   What does the Lord promise He will do for His scattered people (v.9a)?

   How does He describe them in verse 9b?

   List all the beautiful things He says to them in verse 10.

5. Isaiah 41:10 admonishes the northern kingdom of Israel, in exile, '*Do not anxiously look about you, for I am your God*'. Considering where they are at this time, why would this help them?

➤ Prove yourselves doers of the word...James 1:22

6. As believers, we have been "grafted in" to the stock of Israel (Romans 11:17). Let's personalize Isaiah 41:10.

   Why should we not fear?

   Why should we not anxiously look about us?

   What three promises can we cling to?

7. How do you need to apply these promises in your life today?

> In everything, by prayer and petition... Philippians 4:6

Give to God those things that are causing you anxiety and fear. Ask Him to carry them for you.

*Now to Him who is able to keep you from stumbling,
and to make you stand in the presence of His glory blameless with great joy,
to the only God our Savior, through Jesus Christ our Lord, be glory, majesty,
dominion and authority, before all time and now and forever. Amen.
Jude 24-25*

~ ~ ~ ~   # DAY 2   ~ ~ ~ ~
Satisfying the Thirsty

> Draw near to God and He will draw near to you... James 4:8

*As the deer pants for the water brooks, so my soul pants for You, O God.
My soul thirsts for God, for the living God; when shall I come and appear before God?
Psalm 42:1-2*

God created us with a thirst and hunger for Him. Our longing for love, acceptance, safety and identity are meant to lead us to the Lord. He is the only one who can satisfy our thirst.

Pray that the Lord would draw you to Himself and fill you to overflowing as you study His word. Ask Him to guide your thirst and to free you from turning to other sources that don't satisfy.

Practice your memory verse:

_____ not, for I am _____ you;
be not _____, for I am _____ God. I will _____ you,
Yes, I will _____ you, I will uphold _____ with My _____ right hand.
Isaiah 41:10

> Study to show yourself approved... 2 Timothy 2:15

Yesterday in Isaiah 41, we studied how the Lord confronted the nations and defended His people Israel. Today it becomes clear that the Lord is answering charges their enemies have brought against them. He defends them and promises to deal with their enemies.
Even after they've been led away into captivity, the Lord is still their Redeemer!

8. Read Isaiah 41:11-20. Answer these questions.

Fill in this chart about what will happen to their enemies according to verses 11-12.

those who	will be

How does the Lord describe Himself (v.13a)?

How does He reassure His people (v.13b)?

What promise does He give His people in verse 14?

9. Here He uses a name for them that isn't quite as endearing as the ones used in verse 8. This may refer to how they feel and how they are treated in exile.
What does Psalm 22:6-8 say?

10. In Isaiah 41:14, The Lord calls Himself their Redeemer. The Bible dictionary defines this term as:

> ... *one charged with the duty of restoring the rights of another and avenging his wrongs. This title is peculiarly applied to Christ. He redeems us from all evil by the payment of a ransom.* (Easton Bible Dictionary)

This principle comes from Moses' Law, where the nearest relative or kinsman had the right of redemption. What does Leviticus 25:25-27, 47-49 say about it?

How were these principles applied in Ruth 4:1-6?

11. Continue answering questions about Isaiah 41:15-20.

What does the Lord make Israel into (v.15a)?

What will He do with His people according to verse 15b? *Note – the mountains represent proud rulers.*

What will happen to the fruit of their threshing (v.16a)?

What will be their source of joy (v.16b)?

Who does the Lord single out in verse 17a and what is their condition?

What will He do about their need (v.17b-18)?

What will He plant and where (v.19)? What are they a picture of?

12. Look up the following verses to determine what they represent.

Psalm 92:12-14

Hosea 14:4-6

13. What is the Lord's purpose in this according to Isaiah 41:20?

Page 210

> <u>Prove yourselves doers of the word . . . James 1:22</u>

14. Isaiah 41:11-12 says enemies had been contending with Israel. Is the enemy accusing you? How do the following verses encourage you?

Zechariah 3:1-2

Romans 8:1

Revelation 12:10

15. "*I, the LORD, will answer them Myself... I will open rivers on the bare heights and springs in the midst of the valleys...*" Isaiah 41:17b-18 says. How does Amos 8:11-13 explain the thirst that God intends to satisfy?

How do the following verses describe God's provision?
Matthew 5:6

John 7:37-39

16. What are you thirsty for?

17. Do you slow down long enough to "*see and recognize, and consider and gain insight*" that the hand of the Lord is at work in your life (Isaiah 41:20)? Ask the Lord to help you recognize His work in your life.

> <u>In everything, by prayer and petition . . . Philippians 4:6</u>

> *No man can by any means redeem his brother or give to God a ransom for him—*
> *For the redemption of his soul is costly, and he should cease trying forever—*
> *But God will redeem my soul from the power of Sheol, for He will receive me.*
> *Psalm 49:7-8, 15*

We can't save any one but we can pray to the One who can. Cry out to the Redeemer of your soul for those who are lost. Pray that He would gather them into His loving arms and ransom them from their sins.

~ ~ ~ ~ **DAY 3** ~ ~ ~ ~
The Case For Idols

> <u>Draw near to God and He will draw near to you. . . James 4:8</u>

> *I am the LORD, that is My name; I will not give My glory to another,*
> *nor My praise to graven images. Behold, the former things have come to pass,*
> *now I declare new things; before they spring forth I proclaim them to you.*
> *Isaiah 42:8-9*

God does not want to share His glory with anyone or anything else – it belongs to Him alone.

Take a moment to give Him His due. Give Him glory and honor. Take a moment to meditate on all you have to be thankful for. Ask Him to speak to you through His word today – to open your eyes and your heart to who He is.

Practice your memory verse:

Fear _____, for ___ am _____ you; ____ not _____, for __ am ____ God. __ will _____ you, _____, I _____ help _____, I _____ uphold _____ with ____ righteous _____ hand.

_____ 41: ___

➢ <u>Study to show yourself approved ... 2 Timothy 2:15</u>

Yesterday in Isaiah 41, we saw how the Lord plans to refresh the afflicted and thirsty of His people. Today He exposes the nations who have accused His people and their idols. The nations have mocked the Lord because when the northern kingdom of Israel was taken into captivity for their sins, it was assumed that the Lord could not defend them and the idols of the conquering nations were stronger.

The Lord proved He wasn't weak in Isaiah 36-37 when He destroyed the Assyrian army, but now He is also proving that He is in control of everything that happens – unlike any idol of the nations.

18. **Read Isaiah 41:21-29.** Now the Lord makes His challenge to the nations more specific. The false gods of the nations are on trial. The people of these nations have put their trust in idols and the Lord is demanding they prove their idols are equal to Him.

What does the Lord say to them in verse 21?

List the proofs of their power that the Lord demands of them in verses 22-23.

This case is over quickly. What is the Lord's verdict according to verse 24?

What does the Lord call those who choose idols (v.24c)?

What prophecy does the Lord make after exposing the silence of the idols (v.25)?

> Isaiah 41:25 says "*I have aroused one from the north...*" The Persian army was going to conquer in the north first and afterwards turn south towards Babylon. It also says "*From the rising of the sun...*" referring to Cyrus, because he came from Persia in the east. This prophecy is looking ahead to the time after the fall of the Assyrian empire when Babylon was to be destroyed.

What does He ask for (again) in verse 26a?

What answer is given in verse 26b?

What did God say to Zion formerly in verse 27?

What is the result of His question in verse 28? Who steps forward to answer?

What conclusion does the Lord reach in verse 29?

19. What is a false god or an idol?

20. What else does God have to say about idols or other gods?

Exodus 20:3-5

Psalm 115:3-8

Psalm 135:15-18

Jeremiah 10:1-5

Galatians 4:8-9

1 John 5:21

21. In Isaiah 41:29, the Lord says "...*their works are worthless*..." Those who reject the Lord pursue worthless things. How do these verses describe what they seek?

Psalm 4:2

Jeremiah 10:14-15

➤ <u>Prove yourselves doers of the word...James 1:22</u>

22. Read Exodus 32:1. What caused the children of Israel to desire an idol after witnessing the miraculous works of God?

23. Sometimes people don't want to wait for God, so they substitute a quick fix, like a thing or person in the place of God. What insight do you learn from Psalm 27:4?

24. In Isaiah 41:22, the Lord asks the idols to explain what will happen, or even just what has already taken place. Even that is beyond them because they are nothing. The world's wisdom shows the same lack. It can't explain what has gone before, nor predict what will come after. Have you trusted in worldly wisdom? What does the Lord think of it and what do you think He would say to you?

What does 1 Corinthians 1:20 say?

25. Read Job 23:3-7. We have a place where we can present our lack of understanding and questions before God and be heard. How does this passage in Job comfort you?

➤ **In everything, by prayer and petition... Philippians 4:6**

Ask the Lord to guard your heart from idols. Ask Him to fill you with love for Him and that He would keep you from loving what it worthless. Ask Him to help you turn to Him first with all your problems.

Watch over your heart with all diligence, for from it flow the springs of life.
Proverbs 4:23

~ ~ ~ ~   **DAY 4**   ~ ~ ~ ~
The Servant of the Lord

➤ **Draw near to God and He will draw near to you... James 4:8**

A bruised reed He will not break and a dimly burning wick He will not extinguish...
Isaiah 42:3

Draw near to the Lord today. He is meek and lowly of heart. He will welcome you and care for you. He has compassion on you in your need and troubles. Don't be afraid or hold back.

Practice your memory verse:

_____ not, ____ / ____ with _____ ;
be _____ dismayed, ____ / ____ your _____ . / ____ strengthen _____ ,
Yes, __ will _____ you, __ will _____ you _____ My _____ right _____ .
Isaiah ____ :10

➤ **Study to show yourself approved... 2 Timothy 2:15**

Isaiah 42 begins with a glorious description of the Messiah's ministry on earth when He comes. He fulfilled this ministry during His life and continues to do so by His Spirit that He poured out at Pentecost. Our passage breaks into a song of praise in verses 10-13.

26. Read Isaiah 42:1-13. Answer the following questions. (M)

How does the Lord talk about His Servant in verse 1a?

What will the Lord do for Him in verse 1?

What will He <u>not</u> do in verses 2-3a?

What do you think the following phrases in verse 3 mean?

- a bruised reed He will not break

- a dimly burning wick He will not extinguish

What will He accomplish in verses 3b-4?

How does verse 4 explain that He will be diligent until His work is done?

27. Notice that the Servant's ministry of bringing forth justice is mentioned <u>3 times</u> in this first section. What insight does Luke 18:7-8a give you about this?

28. How does the Lord describe Himself in Isaiah 42:5?

How does He call His Servant and affirm His support for Him (v.6a)?

What purpose does He appoint His Servant for (v.6b-7)?

29. How did Jesus fulfill Isaiah 42:1-7 according to these scriptures?

Matthew 3:17

Matthew 12:11-21

Luke 22:20

John 8:12

Acts 26:18

1 Peter 2:23

30. What does the Lord affirm in Isaiah 42:8?

He states His name specifically as Jehovah or Yahweh.
Why do you think He is so particular about His name and about not giving His glory to another?

What do these verses teach about the name of the Lord?
Leviticus 19:12

Leviticus 24:11-16

Proverbs 18:10

31. What does He say He will do in Isaiah 42:9?

32. Now a song of praise is recorded in Isaiah 42:10-13.
Who is called to sing to the Lord in verses 10-12?

What are they praising Him for (verse 13)?

Note – The people who had cried out for justice are finally seeing the Lord's answer and they are filled with joy. This song is an appropriate response.

> ### Prove yourselves doers of the word... James 1:22

33. Consider the characteristics of the Servant that are mentioned in this passage. Which ones do you believe God wants to grow in you?

34. "... A bruised reed He will not break and a dimly burning wick He will not extinguish..." Isaiah 42:3 says. How has the Lord demonstrated that in your life? Share an example.

> ### In everything, by prayer and petition... Philippians 4:6

Pray through the following verses and ask the Lord to use you and make you a part of His ministry.

*I am the LORD, I have called you in righteousness,
I will also hold you by the hand and watch over you,
and I will appoint you as a covenant to the people, as a light to the nations,
to open blind eyes, to bring out prisoners from the dungeon
and those who dwell in darkness from the prison.
Isaiah 42:6-7*

~ ~ ~ ~ **DAY 5** ~ ~ ~ ~

His Plan For the Blind and Deaf

> ### Draw near to God and He will draw near to you... James 4:8

*My children, with whom I am again in labor until Christ is formed in you--
Galatians 4:19*

The Lord desires that you reach full maturity in Christ. Submit to the work of His Spirit today. Choose to believe His word and ignore your doubts. Ask Him to give you eyes to see and ears to hear.

Write down your memory verse:

> ## Study to show yourself approved...2 Timothy 2:15

Yesterday in Isaiah 42, we read about the Lord's Servant and His ministry on earth. Today the Lord explains what He has done with Israel and why. The Lord uses an unusual metaphor of a woman in labor to describe what He goes through to bring deliverance for His blind and deaf people.

35. Read Isaiah 42:14-25.

How does the Lord explain what He did before in verse 14a?

How does He describe his condition now in verse 14b?

What do you think He wants to convey by this metaphor?

List all the things God will do in verses 15 and 16 as He prepares the way for the blind.

What will happen to those who put their trust in idols (v.17)?

Who does the Lord call to in verse 18?

What odd questions does the Lord ask in verse 19?

36. In verse 19 it says "Who is so blind as he that is at peace with me?" (NASB). The NKJ actually captures the Lord's point better: "Who is blind as he who is perfect?" Israel was so confident in that they were at peace with God that they thought they were perfect. Why would Israel think they were perfect?

37. How would thinking you are perfect affect your relationship with God?

In your thoughts...

In your actions...

38. What complaint does the Lord make about Israel in verse 20?

In verse 21, what did God say He wanted to do? Why?

What condition have God's people ended up in because they disobeyed the Law (v.22)?

What is the Lord's plaintive cry to them in verse 23?

Who allowed Israel's troubles? Why? (v.24)

What happened to Jacob in verse 25 and how did he respond?

> ## Prove yourselves doers of the word... James 1:22

39. How do these scriptures help you understand Jacob's blindness?

Ezekiel 12:2

Romans 11:7-11

2 Corinthians 3:13-16
Is there an area you are blind in? What can you do about it?

40. How do these scriptures explain spiritual deafness?

Jeremiah 17:23, 44:5

Zechariah 7:11-12

Acts 7:51, 57

2 Timothy 4:3

Do you have a listening heart or are you in danger of growing deaf?

What steps can you take to develop or fine-tune a listening heart?

41. In Isaiah 42:25, it says that Israel "*paid no attention*" even though God was punishing him. Are you ignoring God's nudges, stiff arming the Holy Spirit? It may be small things like not holding your tongue, being gentle and kind, submitting to your husband. Focus your attention, look intently at the Lord and ask Him to show you your heart.

> ## In everything, by prayer and petition... Philippians 4:6

Revelation 2:29 says "*He who has an ear, let him hear what the Spirit says to the churches.*" Do you have ears to hear what the Spirit says? Ask the Lord. Pray for an outpouring of the Holy Spirit. Pray against spiritual blindness and deafness.

~ ~ ~ ~ ~ ~ ~   Prayer Requests   ~ ~ ~ ~ ~ ~

Called By Name
Isaiah chapters 43 – 44
Lesson 19

DAY 1 — Precious in His Sight

➢ **Draw near to God and He will draw near to you... James 4:8**

Since you are precious in My sight, since you are honored and I love you...
Isaiah 43:4

God loves you so much! Have you really received that message into the deepest part of you? He has chosen to value you highly because He loves you and it has nothing to do with your performance. He treasures you! As you study His word today ask Him to make that message go deeper... that you would get a new glimpse into His love for you.

Ask Him to cleanse your heart so you are ready to receive what He has for you, and to fill you again with His Holy Spirit so that you can understand His word.

MEMORY VERSE   Isaiah 43:10

"You are My witnesses," declares the Lord,
"And My servant whom I have chosen, in order that
you may know and believe Me, and understand that I am He.
Before Me there was no God formed, and there will be none after Me.

➢ **Study to show yourself approved... 2 Timothy 2:15**

In Isaiah chapter 43 the Lord continues with the theme He began in the previous chapter, the redemption of His people in spite of their sin and blindness. He assures them that even though they are living in exile and going through difficult trials, He hasn't forgotten them and He will bring them home again.

1. Read Isaiah 43:1-7. Answer the following questions about the text.

What does the Lord say about Himself in verse 1a?

What wonderful promises does He give Israel in verses 1b-2?

What reason does He give for these promises in verse 3a?

Who has He given as their ransom in verse 3b?

Why has He done this (v.4a)?

How does He say again that He spared His people (v.4b)?

(H)

2. In Isaiah 43:1 it says "*I have called you by name, you are mine...*" Why is a name so important? In some cultures parents will give their child a horrible name ("trash heap", "ugly", "not worth anything"), thinking that the evil spirits won't consider the child worth bothering with.
In American culture, we don't really understand biblical thought about names. Read the following verses and write down what you learn about the importance God places on names.

Genesis 12:2

Genesis 17:5, 15, 19

Genesis 32:24-30

Exodus 33:12, 17

3. In Isaiah 43:2, God says to Israel "*I will be with you...when you walk through the fire, you will not be scorched, nor will the flame burn you.*" This promise is meant to encourage them in trials of various kinds. Read Daniel 3:17-18,25. Explain the faith these three friends had in God and what the Lord did for them.

4. How did God give Egypt as a ransom in the past in Exodus 12:29-33, so that Israel could live?

Note – We have referred to the past for an example of giving Egypt as a ransom in their place, but this is probably a reference to the future, for example in the 6th century BC, when God arranged to have Cyrus free the Israelites to go back to Israel from Babylon. Shortly after that God let the Persians conquer Egypt, Cush, and Seba.

5. Continue answering questions about Isaiah 43.

Why does the Lord tell them not to fear (v.5a)?

From where will He gather their children (v.5b-6)?

What command does He give about them (v.6)?

Who does this include according to verse 7?

> In verse 3, the Lord was using an analogy to help Israel understand the meaning of "ransom". He gave other nations into the hands of the conquering enemy and they were spared. This doesn't mean that the other nations were unloved by Him. He made other ways for them, (see Isaiah 19:20-25). The teaching of a ransom was important because the coming Messiah would give Himself as a ransom for them. This needed to be made powerfully clear so that they could recognize Him. Isaiah mentions this again in chapter 53.

6. You been called by His name and created for His glory (v.7). What do you learn about that from the following scriptures?

called by His name	created for His glory
Acts 15:17	2 Corinthians 5:17
Revelation 3:12	1 Peter 2:9

> <u>Prove yourselves doers of the word . . . James 1:22</u>

7. In Isaiah 43:1b-2 the Lord says to Israel: "*Do not fear, for I have redeemed you; I have called you by name; you are Mine! When you pass through the waters, I will be with you; and through the rivers, they will not overflow you. When you walk through the fire, you will not be scorched, nor will the flame burn you.*" These words are also meant for you. How does the Lord want to encourage you through this passage today? What does it mean for you?

8. Isaiah 43:4 says "*...since you are precious in My sight, since you are honored and I love you...*" God declares that you are precious, honored and loved. Do you doubt that? This is how He sees you and how He wants you to see others. Are you esteeming others with the same sense of value?

> <u>In everything, by prayer and petition . . . Philippians 4:6</u>

We have so many reasons to give praise to the Lord. Instead of worrying about things, turn them into an opportunity to praise God for what He will do. Then, when God does things for you take time to thank Him. Don't forget! He has created you for His glory.
Praise Him now for His glorious promises to you.

*This will be written for the generation to come,
That a people yet to be created may praise the LORD.*
Psalm 102:18

~ ~ ~ ~   # DAY 2   ~ ~ ~ ~
Witnesses

> <u>Draw near to God and He will draw near to you . . . James 4:8</u>

The Spirit Himself testifies with our spirit that we are children of God...
Romans 8:16

Have you listened to the Lord's witness? He testifies to you that you belong to Him. What greater joy is there than that? Take a moment to think about the gift of His Holy Spirit within you and give thanks. Ask Him to teach you as you study His word today.

Practice your memory verse:

"You are My _____," declares the Lord,

"And My _____ whom I have _____, in order that

you may _____ and believe Me, and _____ that I am He.

Before Me there was no God _____, and there will be _____ after Me.

Isaiah 43:10

> <u>Study to show yourself approved . . . 2 Timothy 2:15</u>

Yesterday, Isaiah chapter 43 began with God's loving promises to Israel. Today as we continue the chapter, He reverts to the image of a courtroom. Remember that God is the final judge and all legal trials are merely a shadow of His justice. Listen to the challenge He presents and what He considers important. We will all render an account to Him someday.

9. Read Isaiah 43:8-13. Answer the following questions about the text.

Who does the Lord tell them to bring out (v.8)?

Who has gathered according to verse 9a?

How does God challenge them in verse 9b?

Who does the Lord call as His witnesses (v.10a)?

Why did He call them (v.10b)?

What does God testify about Himself (v.10c)?

In verse 11, the Lord proclaims His name. What aspect of His character does He also emphasize?

What has He done that they are witnesses to (v.12)?

What else does the Lord say of Himself in verse 13?

10. In Isaiah 43:10+12, the Lord declares "*You are My witnesses*". The people of Israel were God's witnesses! It's important to understand God's perspective here. His purpose all along was to reveal Himself to the world through His people. He gave them His testimony. He proved His testimony was true by the works He did. He expected them to proclaim His testimony.

What was God's testimony?

Exodus 31:18

Exodus 34:28

Where was it kept? Read Exodus 40:20-21.

How were they to observe it? Read Psalm 78:5-7.

11. In Isaiah 42:21, it says that God was "...*pleased for His righteousness' sake to make the law great and glorious...*" But all along He intended something much greater. Instead of commandments written in stone and kept in a golden ark, hidden within a holy place. This was only a shadow of a new covenant.

What is the Lord's testimony now? 1 John 4:14-15, 5:11

Where does He keep it? 1 John 5:10

How are we to observe it?

Matthew 24:14

Luke 21:13-15

Acts 4:33

What does Revelation 12:11 say about this testimony?

12. The old covenant was written on tablets of stone. The new one is written in hearts. Read Ezekiel 36:26. What does the Lord have to do to make way for the new covenant?

> ## Prove yourselves doers of the word... James 1:22

13. The children of Israel were appointed to be God's witnesses on earth. By keeping His commandments, which He wrote for them with His finger, they would testify to His reality. How much greater is the message of salvation!! Answer the following questions keeping in mind that <u>you</u> are the Lord's witness.

In John 8:17 Jesus said, "... *in your law it has been written that the testimony of two men is true.*" This was the standard used in Moses' Law to determine if a witness could be trusted.

What two witnesses has God provided to testify about His salvation, according to John 15:26-27?

In what other ways does God sometimes choose to testify to His message? Read Acts 14:3.

14. How are you a witness? How does your life show that you belong to the Lord Jesus?

> ## In everything, by prayer and petition... Philippians 4:6

You are a letter of Christ, cared for by us, written not with ink but with the Spirit of the living God, not on tablets of stone but on tablets of human hearts.
2 Corinthians 3:3

Ask the Lord to make you a faithful witness. Pray for opportunities to testify to His reality. Ask Him to fill you with His Holy Spirit and give you discernment of those opportunities.

~ ~ ~ ~   # DAY 3   ~ ~ ~ ~
Created For Praise

> ## Draw near to God and He will draw near to you... James 4:8

... Is anyone cheerful? He is to sing praises...
James 5:13

Sometimes simple things lift our hearts. We can be cheerful because we slept well, or ate a good meal. God has given us these small blessings to lift our hearts and we should turn them into praise. Moments of cheerfulness are a great gift. Let us rejoice in Him!

Practice your memory verse:

"You _____ My _____," declares _____ Lord,

"_____ My _____ whom _____ have _____, in _____ that

_____ may _____ and _____ Me, _____ understand _____ I _____ He.

_____ Me _____ was _____ God _____, and _____ will _____ none _____ Me."

_____ 43: _____

> Study to show yourself approved... 2 Timothy 2:15

In the end of Isaiah chapter 43, God continues presenting His case to Israel with a variety of themes. A promise of destruction of the Babylonians, their ships, armies, chariots, horses and mighty men. An encouragement to look ahead to what He will do and an exhortation to not just live in the past. He refers again to His promises about a roadway and rivers in the desert. He offers them justification and righteousness for His name's sake. He points out how greatly they need this in view of their empty sacrifices.

15. Read Isaiah 43:14-28. Answer the following questions about the text. The timeline should help you place these prophecies in their historical context.

What will He do for their sake in verse 14?

What names does the Lord give Himself in verses 14-15?

16. What does the Lord say He does in verses 16-17a?

What does He say will happen to them in verse 17b?

What does the Lord advise them and why (v.18-19a)?

What does He say He will do in verse 19b?

*Note – remember: roadway in the wilderness—highway of holiness (Isaiah 35:8), rivers in the desert (Isaiah 41:18)

Who will glorify the Lord and why (v.20-21)?

17. Psalm 102:18 confirms the truth of Isaiah 43:21 saying *"...This will be written for the generation to come, that a people yet to be created may praise the LORD..."* How does 1 Peter 2:9 add to your understanding of this privilege?

18. Continue answering questions about the text, Isaiah 43:22-28.

After describing His plan for them, what does the Lord say actually took place (v.22)?

What evidence does He give of this indictment (v.23-24a)?

What have they given the Lord instead (v.24b)?

What amazing promise does God give in response to their wearying behavior (v.25)?

> Two lambs were to be offered each day as burnt offerings in the Temple, one at dawn and one at dusk. This was required for the Lord to meet with the people (Exodus 29:38-39). It is a picture of Christ and His daily intercession for us (Hebrews 7:25, 9:11-12).

What does Ezekiel 36:21-23 add to this promise?

19. How does the Lord offer to absolve them of charges against them (Isaiah 43:26)?

What does the Lord say in Isaiah 43:27?

"*Your first forefather*" could be a reference to Adam. What does Romans 5:12 say?

What does Jeremiah 5:31 say about the "*spokesmen*" mentioned in Isaiah 43:27?

What does the Lord say He will do in Isaiah 43:28?

20. The "*princes of the sanctuary*" (verse 28) refers to the religious rulers or priests. The Lord is holding them accountable for the apostasy He is seeing in Jacob, their poor offerings (v.23-24). When He says He will pollute them, He is saying He will expose on the outside what He sees on the inside. How do the following scriptures shed light on the condition of these "*princes*"?

Malachi 1:11-13, 2:1-2

Matthew 23:27-28

21. In Isaiah 43:15, the Lord calls Himself the Creator of Israel. This Hebrew word "*bara*" is the same word used in Genesis when He created the heavens and the earth, creating something out of nothing.

What was His original creation?

Isaiah 42:5

Isaiah 45:7,12,18

What does Isaiah 65:17-18 say is His new creation?

➢ Prove yourselves doers of the word... James 1:22

22. In Isaiah 43:23b it says the Lord has not "*burdened you with offerings nor wearied you with incense*". What do you think He means? The following scriptures will add clarity.

Matthew 11:28-30

1 John 5:3

Even though the Lord does not burden His people, notice how they have burdened Him with their sin in Isaiah 43:23-24. Read Isaiah 1:14-15. Do you burden the Lord with your empty ritual or sin? Or are you a blessing to the Lord?

23. I John 5:3 tells us that God's commandments are not burdensome. Psalm 119 explains many ways in which His commandments are a great gift. We should rejoice in the Lord requirements and never think of them as a burden. Take a moment to thank God that His commandments are not burdensome.

> In everything, by prayer and petition ... Philippians 4:6

I will also praise You with a harp, even Your truth, O my God;
To You I will sing praises with the lyre, O Holy One of Israel.
Psalm 71:22

Pray for a thankful, worshipful heart. Ask the Lord to fill your heart with praise.

~ ~ ~ ~ # DAY 4 ~ ~ ~ ~
The Foolishness of Idols

> Draw near to God and He will draw near to you... James 4:8

Let your heart therefore be wholly devoted to the LORD our God...
1 Kings 8:61

When the Lord is on the throne of our hearts, we aren't stumbled by idols. Consider what it means to be wholly devoted to the Lord our God. It involves your love, your decisions, your desires, hopes and dreams. Offer yourself to the Lord today. He is waiting.

Practice your memory verse:

"_____ are _____ witnesses," _____ the _____,
"And _____ servant _____ I _____ chosen, ____ order _____
you _____ know _____ believe _____, and _____ that ___ am _____.
Before ____ there _____ no _____ formed, ____ there _____ be _____ after _____."
Isaiah ____:10

> Study to show yourself approved ... 2 Timothy 2:15

In Isaiah chapter 44 the Lord testifies to what He will do with His people Israel. Continuing with the theme of the courtroom, He establishes His own credibility as a witness. He then testifies powerfully to the absurdity of worshiping idols.

24. Read Isaiah 44:1-20. Answer the following questions about the text.

Who does the Lord call to listen (v.1-2)? What various names and descriptions does He use to describe them?

What message does He have for them in verse 2?

> **Jeshurun** is a name that God first gave to Israel in Deuteronomy 32:15. It means "upright one". It came from a song that God gave Moses to teach the children of Israel.

25. What promise does the Lord give in Isaiah 44:3-4 and what does it symbolize?

26. In Isaiah 44:3, we saw that the water poured out was the Holy Spirit. How was this fulfilled according to these scriptures?

Joel 2:28

Matthew 3:11

Luke 11:13

John 14:16,26

Acts 1:8

27. Continue answering the questions about Isaiah 44:5-20.
What are some of the ways these descendants will identify with the Lord (v.5)?

How does the Lord describe Himself in verse 6?

What standard does He establish for anyone who would confront Him and try to make themselves His equal (v.7)?

How does He again affirm His people in verse 8a?

What question does He confront them with in verse 8b?

28. What follows, in Isaiah 44:12-20, is one of the most lucid descriptions of the foolishness of idol worship in the Bible. What opening pronouncement does God make in verse 9a?

What is His assessment of their witnesses (v.9b)?

What motive of the idol makers does the Lord expose in verse 10?

Note – For a powerful example of this read Acts 19:23-30, especially verse 25.
What is God's evaluation of them in verse 11?

How does the man prepare to make his idol (v.12)?

How does he work the wood in verse 13? *Notice the creativity involved.*

Where do his supplies come from (v.14)?

What uses does the man have for the tree and how are they described (v.15-17)?

What is the spiritual condition of the idol worshiper (v.18)?

What obvious reasoning is completely lacking in this man (v.19)?

What is his state and what reason does God give for it (v.20)?

Page 227

> ## Prove yourselves doers of the word... James 1:22

29. In Isaiah 44:10, it referred to the idol makers' motives. Read Luke 16:13 and ask the Lord if this could be a problem for you.

30. In Isaiah 44:20 it says *"...a deceived heart has turned him aside."* It's unlikely that you will be carving an idol out of wood and worshiping it, but it is very possible for your heart to be led astray. It's important that we take these warnings seriously so that we can stay alert and be wise. Write a brief summary of the advise you glean from the following scriptures.

Genesis 3:13

Obadiah 1:3a

2 Corinthians 11:3

Galatians 6:3

Colossians 2:8

James 1:14-16,26

1 John 3:7

2 John 1:7

Revelation 12:9, 19:20

31. How can you maintain a simple and pure devotion to Christ?

32. Picture one of Shakespeare's actors reading out Isaiah 44:12-20 in satire. God is really being witty and making fun of them. Write something comparable about an "idol" worshipper of today (cars, knowledge, money, superstars, medicine...). If it helps, go verse by verse through Isaiah 44:12-20 and write your own version.

> ## In everything, by prayer and petition... Philippians 4:6

... the simplicity and purity of <u>devotion</u> to Christ.
2 Corinthians 11:3

Ask the Lord to give you a heart that is wholly devoted to Him. Ask Him to put people on your heart who struggle with their devotion to Christ and pray for them. Ask Him to keep you and them from being deceived.

<u>Devote</u> yourselves to prayer, keeping alert in it with an attitude of thanksgiving...
Colossians 4:2

~ ~ ~ ~ **DAY 5** ~ ~ ~ ~
The Promise of Jerusalem Rebuilt

➤ <u>Draw near to God and He will draw near to you... James 4:8</u>

...He has granted to us His precious and magnificent promises...
2 Peter 1:4

No one can compare to our God. What wonderful promises He has made to us in His word! Think about all He has promised and planned for you. Let Him stir your heart today. Thank Him for His promise to make you like Him. Ask Him to grant you greater faith to trust Him.

Write your memory verse:

➤ <u>Study to show yourself approved ... 2 Timothy 2:15</u>

Isaiah chapter 44 ends with a glorious proclamation on God's part of what He will do for His people promising to rebuild Jerusalem, and the cities of Judah through a man who won't be born for 175 years! And this was prophesied when the city was still standing and flourishing. No idol worshiping false prophet could make a prediction like that!

33. Read Isaiah 44:21-28. Answer the following questions about the text.

What does the Lord exhort Jacob to do (v.21a)?

What does He want them to know (v.21b)?

What does God promise them in verse 22? See Isaiah 1:18.

Who will rejoice and how when the Lord redeems Israel (Isaiah 44:23)?

What did Jesus say in Luke 19:37-40 about this kind of worship?

How does the Lord identify Himself in Isaiah 44:24?

What does He do to the boasters, the diviners and the worldly wise men (v.25)?

The Lord says He will confirm the word of His servant. Make a note of each place or person mentioned and what He confirms about them:

verse 26

verse 27

verse 28

34. How were Isaiah 44:26,28 fulfilled? Fill in this chart.

Jerusalem	inhabitants	Temple
Nehemiah 2:4-6; 6:15	Ezra 1:1-3	Ezra 3:10-11

35. In Isaiah 44, the Lord makes a sharp contrast between Himself and idols. What are some of the differences you see in their power and the effect they have on those who serve them?

idols	God
verses 9-19, 25	verses 6-8, 24

➤ Prove yourselves doers of the word ... James 1:22

36. The Lord speaks of His redemption in three places in Isaiah 44, verses 22, 23 and 24. Can you hear the urgency of God's cry to His people in verse 22, *"Return to Me, for I have redeemed you."*? God has purchased us and wants full ownership of our lives. He belongs in the driver's seat. What do you need to yield to Him today?

37. In Isaiah 44:28, the Lord prophesied that the Temple and Jerusalem would be rebuilt and inhabited, before they had even been destroyed. Nowhere on earth is there a God like ours who can predict the future so accurately. Do you believe what He says? Do you take His word at face value? Ask the Lord to increase your faith.

➤ In everything, by prayer and petition ... Philippians 4:6

Pray for more faith to lay hold of the glorious promises of God. Ask Him to speak to you. Listen to what He says.

*For as many as are the promises of God, in Him they are yes;
therefore also through Him is our Amen to the glory of God through us.
2 Corinthians 1:20*

~ ~ ~ ~ ~ ~   Prayer Requests   ~ ~ ~ ~ ~ ~

Cyrus Comes, Babylon Falls
Isaiah chapters 45 – 47

Lesson 20

DAY 1 — Calling Cyrus

➢ *Draw near to God and He will draw near to you... James 4:8*

I know your deeds. Behold, I have put before you an open door which no one can shut, because you have a little power, and have kept My word, and have not denied My name.
Revelation 3:8

The Lord knew Cyrus' deeds before he did them. He knows about your deeds, too. Let this verse encourage you today. The Lord has planned good for you and He will equip you in every way to accomplish it. He will reward your faithfulness.

MEMORY VERSE Isaiah 46:4

Even to your old age and gray hairs I am He,
I am He who will sustain you. I have made you and I will carry you;
I will sustain you and I will rescue you. (NIV)

➢ *Study to show yourself approved... 2 Timothy 2:15*

Isaiah chapter 45 begins with a more detailed description of Cyrus, the future king of Persia – 175 years before he was born! – as the one who would come to conquer nations, free the Jewish exiles and decree that the Lord's Temple be rebuilt.

1. Read Isaiah 45:1-8.

How does God speak about Cyrus (v.1a)?

What did He say He would do for Cyrus (v.1b-2)?

What will God give him (v.3a)?

Read Ezra 1:7-11. What were some of the "*treasures of darkness*" that God was referring to?

2. What does God want Cyrus to know in Isaiah 45:3b?

Why has He done this (v.4a)?

What else did He give Cyrus (v.4b)?

> In Isaiah 45:1, God calls Cyrus His "anointed". In the Old Testament, God had the priests (Exodus 30:30, 40:15) and the kings anointed (1 Samuel 15:1). He also had a foreign king anointed by Elijah in 1 Kings 19:15. The word Messiah comes from the same root and means "Anointed One". Only God could anoint someone. It designated a consecrated form of leadership.

What does the Lord affirm strongly in both v.5a and v.6b?

What does He say He will do for Cyrus in verse 5b?

Why will He use Cyrus (v.6)?

In verse 7, what does the Lord say He creates and what does that prove?

How does the Lord describe the righteousness He creates in verse 8?

3. Read Daniel 5. Summarize the passage here briefly.

4. What job does God have for Cyrus to do? Read the following scriptures.
Ezra 1:1-4

Isaiah 44:28

Isaiah 45:13

5. Read Proverbs 21:1. How is this evident in Cyrus' life?

6. What kind of a man do you think Cyrus was? In Isaiah 44:28, God calls Cyrus His shepherd. He affirms that Cyrus will "*perform all My desire*". Look at our passage today, Isaiah 45:1-6, and try to describe him based on the clues you find.

For example, we can deduce he must be a courageous man, willing to face danger in battle because he conquers nations in verse 1.

7. Let's compare this king of Persia with the earlier king of Babylon, Nebuchadnezzar, who originally conquered Jerusalem and carried off the exiles and the treasures of the Temple.

What did it take for Nebuchadnezzar to acknowledge the Lord as God? Read Daniel 5:20-21.

What did it take for Cyrus to realize that the Lord is God? Read Isaiah 45:2-3.

8. Read Ezra 5:14-15. What did Nebuchadnezzar do with the Lord's treasures and what did Cyrus do with them?

Can you imagine becoming king and having a two hundred year scroll read to you with your own name in it? Can you imagine the astonishment he must have felt? His life story was known before he existed! We <u>know</u> he became a believer. Cyrus proved he was a man of faith by his deeds. He acted on the prophecies about himself.

➢ <u>Prove yourselves doers of the word . . . James 1:22</u>

9. In Isaiah 45:1 God calls Cyrus by name for a special purpose. God is calling you also. Are you listening, yielded to Him?

10. Has God given you *"a title of honor"* (Isaiah 45:4)? Do you use that place to glorify Him so that *"men may know…that there is no one besides Me"* (Isaiah 45:6)? Or do you use that title to bring glory to yourself?

11. Look at Isaiah 45:7. Why do you think God would create darkness and calamity as well as light and well-being? See Romans 8:28.

➢ <u>In everything, by prayer and petition . . . Philippians 4:6</u>

> *I am the LORD, and there is no other; besides Me there is no God.*
> *I will gird you, though you have not known Me; that men may know from the rising*
> *to the setting of the sun that there is no one besides Me. I am the LORD, and there is no other.*
> *Isaiah 45:5-6*

Praise the Lord now that there is no God besides Him. Pray that He would be glorified in your life and that you would give all honor back to Him. Ask Him to grant you deeds that prove your faith in Him. Ask the Lord to make you faithful to the calling He has placed on your life.

~ ~ ~ ~ **DAY 2** ~ ~ ~ ~
Don't Quarrel With Your Maker

➢ <u>Draw near to God and He will draw near to you . . . James 4:8</u>

A complaining heart is an unhappy one. Do you need a quiet and gentle spirit today? This is where we find our strength. We have no right to quarrel with our Maker and find fault with how He works. Ask Him to search your heart and forgive any attitudes that are against Him. Ask Him to fill you with trust in Him, in all His ways.

> … the hidden person of the heart, with the imperishable quality of a
> gentle and quiet spirit, which is precious in the sight of God.
> 1 Peter 3:4

Practice your memory verse:

> Even to your old _____ and _____ hairs __ ___ He,
> I am He who will _____ you. I have _____ you and I will _____ you;
> I will _____ you and I will _____ you.
> Isaiah 46:4

> ## Study to show yourself approved...2 Timothy 2:15

As we continue studying Isaiah 45 today, verses 9-10 begin with two woes. These are the final woes listed in Isaiah, (for a list of the others see page 165). The Lord is reminding His people of His plan for them and the power He has to fulfill it. Not only will He save them, but other nations will bow down to them because God is with them. But those who serve idols will be humiliated and those who complain about what He does with them will suffer woe.

12. Read Isaiah 45:9-19. Answer the following questions.

Who is described in verse 9 and how?

What foolish things does he say to his own Maker (v.9b)?

What does God pronounce "woe" on in verse 10?

In verse 9-10, how does Isaiah show the foolishness of arguing with God?

What names does the Lord use for Himself in verse 11a?

How does He advise them to pray instead of quarreling with Him in verse 11b?

What does the Lord remind them about Himself in verse 12?

Verse 13 is about Cyrus. How has the Lord aroused him and what will He do for him (v.13a)?

What will Cyrus do for the Lord (v.13b)?

13. Long before the time period we are studying, when God brought the children of Israel out of Egypt (Exodus 12:35-36), He had stirred the hearts of the Egyptians to give them whatever riches they asked for. They came out carrying the wealth of Egypt.
It's interesting that now God points out that His exiles will go free "*without any payment or reward*" (verse 13b). Why do you think they will take nothing extra with them this time, except for the riches of the Lord's Temple, when they return to their homeland?

14. According to Isaiah 45:14, what will the other nations do for Israel and why?

What does Isaiah 14:1-2 say?

15. What does Isaiah praise God for in Isaiah 45:15?

What will happen to the makers of idols (v.16)?

Describe Israel's salvation (v.17a).

How long is God going to care for Israel (v.17b)?

Why did God form the earth (v.18)?

Contrast how God has not spoken with what He has spoken (v.19).

16. Summarize all the things God creates in Isaiah 45.

verse 7

verse 8

verse 12

verse 18

God is appealing to the nations based on His identity as the Creator. This is the witness of Him they have had all along. Read Romans 1:19-20 and compare it to these verses in Isaiah 45. What message do you think He wants them to understand here?

➢ <u>Prove yourselves doers of the word... James 1:22</u>

17. We see the foolishness of quarreling with our maker, yet how many times do we doubt God and His plan for our life? (v.9)

18. Reread Isaiah 45:9-11. What thing(s) in your life are you arguing with your maker about? In what area are you saying to God "Why did you make me this way?" or "Why did you let this happen to me?"

19. Isaiah 45:11 has good, practical advice for someone who is struggling with who they are, or grieved over someone else's condition, like a handicapped child, or a poverty stricken family. When we reject ourselves or someone else, it is sin. We have no right to question God's wisdom in what He created. Asking God about it is OK, finding fault with our Creator is not. "Woe" the Bible says about this!

> *Why do you complain against Him that He does not give an account of all His doings?*
> *Job 33:13*

20. In Isaiah 45:11, God gives two principles. How can we apply them?

"Ask Me about the things to come concerning My sons..."

Jeremiah 33:3

James 1:5

"Commit to Me the work of My hands."

2 Timothy 1:12b

1 Peter 4:19b

➢ <u>In everything, by prayer and petition... Philippians 4:6</u>

Ask the Lord to speak to you "*about the things to come*" concerning your life and others'. Commit yourself to Him and intercede for others that they would be committed to Him.

Commit your way to the LORD, trust also in Him, and He will do it...
Psalm 37:5

~ ~ ~ ~   **DAY 3**   ~ ~ ~ ~
God's Plea To All People

➤ <u>Draw near to God and He will draw near to you... James 4:8</u>

The Lord longs for all people to be saved. Let Him share His heart with you. Offer yourself to Him to be a light to the lost. Ask Him to help you pray for them. You will bring comfort to His heart.

For I have no pleasure in the death of anyone who dies,"
declares the Lord GOD. "Therefore, repent and live."
Ezekiel 18:32

Practice your memory verse:

_____ to _____ old _____ and _____ hairs ___ am _____,
I ____ He _____ will _____ you. ___ have _____ you _____ I _____ carry _____;
I _____ sustain _____ and ___ will _____ you.
_____ 46: ___

➤ <u>Study to show yourself approved... 2 Timothy 2:15</u>

At the end of Isaiah chapter 45, the Lord again calls on the nations to present their case before Him. He warns them that they must bow before Him and makes an earnest plea to them to repent and accept His offer of salvation.

21. Read Isaiah 45:20-25.

Who is God calling together (v.20a)?

Who does He say has no knowledge (v.20b)?

What does God demand of the nations again (v.21a)?

What has God proved about Himself (v.21b)?

In verse 22 what is God's appeal, and to whom?

What has God sworn in verse 23?

How is this like Philippians 2:10-11?

22. Isaiah 45:22-23 are like the pinnacle of the mountain in this trial of the nations. All of the Lord's reasoning is intended for this one purpose, to call the nations to be saved! What does John 6:40 say?

23. Continuing with the passage, Isaiah 45:24-25:

What will those who come to Him say of the Lord (v.24a)?

What will happen to everyone who is angry at God (v.24b)?

How will Israel be justified (v.25)?

24. Remember that the Lord has all the nations in His courtroom. He is the Judge and now He is using His authority to make a legal pronouncement. Israel's offspring will be justified.
How does Romans 5:1-2 explain this justification?

Who are these offspring of Israel that will be justified?

Galatians 3:27-29

Galatians 4:28

25. In chapter 45, verses 5, 6, 14, 18, 21-22, declare *"There is no other God but Me"*. Why do you think this is important to understand?

26. In Isaiah 45 we see many examples of God's omniscience, which means 'all-knowing, (Ex: Isaiah 44:6-7, Jeremiah 1:5). He is able to predict the future. Read Jeremiah 29:11-12. How does this attribute of God comfort you?

> **Justification**... is the judicial act of God, by which He pardons all the sins of those who believe in Christ, and accounts, accepts, and treats them as righteous in the eye of the law... The law is not relaxed or set aside, but is declared to be fulfilled in the strictest sense; and so the person justified is declared to be entitled to all the advantages and rewards arising from perfect obedience to the law...
> Easton Bible Dictionary

> ➤ <u>Prove yourselves doers of the word ... James 1:22</u>

27. If you have not yet bowed the knee and sworn allegiance to God alone, <u>now</u> would be a really good time to do it. Someday every knee will bow and every tongue confess that Jesus is Lord. Listen to God's plea in Isaiah 45:22!!

Turn to Me and be saved, all the ends of the earth; for I am God, and there is no other.

28. Isaiah 45:24. What two things do you have that come from God alone?

29. Isaiah 45:25 says that all the offspring of Israel will glory in the Lord. Is this true of you?

When God is glorified, His true character is revealed and we rejoice. The Lord reveals His glory to us, not only so that we may rejoice, but also so that He may be glorified through us. Do you realize that you carry the Lord's glory? What do these scriptures say?

John 17:10,22

2 Corinthians 3:18

1 Peter 4:14

> ➤ <u>In everything, by prayer and petition ... Philippians 4:6</u>

Give glory to God and give praise to Jesus. He is worthy! Confess with your mouth that your righteousness comes from God alone. Ask Him to transform you into His image and pray that He would be glorified in your daily life.

"Father, glorify Your name." Then a voice came out of heaven:
"I have both glorified it, and will glorify it again."
John 12:28

DAY 4
Remember!

➢ **Draw near to God and He will draw near to you... James 4:8**

God challenges Israel to look back into the past and remember how He has proved Himself so that they can trust Him to take care of them in the future. He often had them set up altars as points of remembrance of when He did something special.

As you prepare your heart to study, ask God to remind you of all He has done for you, how He has been faithful to seek you out and take care of you. Ask Him to make your heart and mind open to what He wants to teach you today.

> Bless the LORD, O my soul, and forget none of His benefits;
> Who pardons all your iniquities, who heals all your diseases;
> Who redeems your life from the pit, who crowns you with lovingkindness and compassion;
> Who satisfies your years with good things, so that your youth is renewed like the eagle.
> Psalm 103:2-5

Practice your memory verse:

Even _____ your _____ age _____ gray _____ I _____ He, ___ am _____ who _____ sustain _____. I _____ made _____ and __ will _____ you; __ will _____ you _____ I _____ rescue _____ .

Isaiah _____ : 4

➢ **Study to show yourself approved... 2 Timothy 2:15**

Isaiah chapter 46 singles out the idols of Babylon as worthless. He proves He is God by declaring the end from the beginning. Why would they choose to carry a burden they have to pay for when God promises to carry them? "I will bear you!" He cries out to them. What will it take to get their attention? He wants them to be saved!!

30. Read Isaiah 46:1-13.

Bel and Nebo are two of the gods of Babylon. Who carries these idols and how are they described in verse 1?

What posture have they taken and how well have they rescued those who trusted in them (v.2)?

These gods have to be carried but God is never carried by His people! Notice the contrast. When did God begin to carry Israel (v.3)?

How long will He continue to carry them (v.4a)?

List the verbs He uses to describe His care for them in verse 4.

What question does the Lord ask in verse 5?

What investment do people make in their idols (v.6a)?

How do they take care of and honor their idols (v.6b-7a)?

What kind of help can an idol give in distress (v.7b)?

Who is God speaking to in verse 8 and what does He advise them?

What does God call them to remember in verse 9?

What has the Lord done to prove Himself (v.10a)?

What does the Lord affirm about His purposes in verse 10b?

31. Fill in the following chart comparing what God says about Himself and idols using Isaiah 46:1-7.

Bel and Nebo / Idols	God

32. In Isaiah 46:9, the Lord calls Israel to remember. What are some of the things that God has done for them in the past that reminds them of who God is and what He is capable of?
See Isaiah 37:36-37.

33. Continue answering questions about Isaiah 46:11-13.

Who does God again say He calls in verse 11a?

Who is this "*bird of prey from the east?*" See Isaiah 45:1 for help.

What does He again affirm in verse 11b?

What does God call those He is speaking to (v.12)?

How does God encourage people to turn to Him for salvation in verse 13?

➢ <u>Prove yourselves doers of the word... James 1:22</u>

34. Are you carrying too much on your shoulders? The Lord wants so much to bear you up and carry you. Are you letting Him? Read Matthew 11:28-30.

35. In Isaiah 46:4 the Lord promises to bear you "*even to your graying years*". Do you trust Him to care for you in your old age or does it frighten you? Commit to trusting Him.

36. We don't trust an idol for our future safety and deliverance. We don't give "*lavish gold*" to a goldsmith to make an idol we can pray to (Isaiah 46:6). But, do we put our trust in things other than God? A retirement account, a house, an expensive education? Is your heart right about these things God has given you? Have you stumbled by trusting in things that require labor and care from you, but can not save you in distress? What do you invest in? Ponder this.

➤ In everything, by prayer and petition... Philippians 4:6

Ask the Lord to help you remember all He has done and to not forget. Ask Him to strengthen your trust in Him. Pray for people you know who are "*stubborn-hearted*" or "*far from righteousness*" that God would reveal His great salvation to them.

> *I bring near My righteousness, it is not far off; and My salvation will not delay.*
> *And I will grant salvation in Zion, and My glory for Israel.*
> *Isaiah 46:13*

~ ~ ~ ~ **DAY 5** ~ ~ ~ ~
Babylon Will Be Judged

➤ Draw near to God and He will draw near to you... James 4:8

> *Therefore let him who thinks he stands take heed that he does not fall.*
> *1 Corinthians 10:12*

Have you let your heart grow distant from the Lord? Have you been comfortable and let your zeal for Him cool? Have you begun to take credit in your own heart for the blessings, skills or accomplishments your Lord has given you? Let this be the prayer of your heart:

Lord, You are able to keep me. Draw my heart back to You lest I stumble. You are the reviver of my heart.

Write down your memory verse:

➤ Study to show yourself approved... 2 Timothy 2:15

In Isaiah chapter 47, the Lord exposes Babylon's sin and arrogance. He clearly explains what they have put their trust in. God had used Babylon to judge His people, but they abused Israel far beyond what He had intended. Now they will experience God's wrath. We studied Babylon at length in Lesson 6. You may want to review that Lesson before you do today's study.

37. Read Isaiah 47:1-15.

What two names does God give the Babylonians in verse 1?

In verses 1-3, Babylon has lost her status. How is her new status described and how will she be exposed?

Who will bring this vengeance on her (v.4)?

What does the Holy One of Israel tell her to do in verse 5a?

What title has she lost (v.5b)?

Why did God let her have power over His people (v.6a)?

How did Babylon handle that freedom (v.6b)?

How does God repay them for their lack of mercy to His people? Read Isaiah 13:15-19.

38. Using Isaiah 47:7,8, and10, describe Babylon's boasting and attitude.

verse 7

verse 8

verse 10

39. What similarity do you see between Babylon's boasting in verses 7-10 and Isaiah 14:13-14?   Who was the force behind this way of thinking?

40. Using verses 9 and 11, contrast Babylon's methods of self preservation with God's prophecies.

	What Babylon counted on to protect her	What will come on her anyway
verse 9		
verse 11		

41. In verses 9 and 11 it says "*suddenly in one day*", how was this fulfilled in Daniel 5:23,30?

42. Continue answering questions about Isaiah 47:12-15.
What does verse 12a say Babylon will do? *Notice how it says "labored" implying it was hard work.* What is she hoping (v.12b)?

How has all this divination affected her (v.13a)?

Who does the Lord challenge to save Babylon (v.13b)?

What will happen to her astrologers in verse 14?

How long has Babylon trafficked with these people and what will the final result be (v.15)?

How is Isaiah 13:9-10 an appropriate judgment for Babylon?

43. Read Psalm 137:1-9. This is a psalm that was written by captive Jews in Babylon. What were some of the things they were feeling about their captivity and their captors?

44. How does Revelation 18:7-8 agree with and add to Isaiah's description of Babylon in Isaiah 47?

45. Babylon isn't just a city. Babylon also represents the world's religions and the world's system that has set itself up as "god" and against God. When God judges Babylon, what is the reaction of the multitudes in heaven? (Revelation 19:1-4)

➤ Prove yourselves doers of the word... James 1:22

46. In Isaiah 47 verse 8 and 10, Babylon said in her heart "*I am, and there is no one besides me.*", an imitation of the Lord's name. Notice how similar it is to Isaiah 46:9 "*I am God, and there is no other; I am God, and there is no one like Me.*" Babylon's heart was full of pride. Ask the Lord to keep you humble and teachable.

47. In some countries, people often wear amulets (charms) that are supposed to keep the evil spirits away. In our *knowledgeable, scientific* society we laugh at such things in scorn, but those things aren't that far away in our culture either. What goes through your mind if you hear of someone breaking a mirror, walking under a ladder or seeing a black cat? Why don't they make a floor 13 in hotels? As we see more and more people turning to these things, many of them not knowing they're connected to witchcraft and Satanism, what would God say to those who put their trust in them? See Isaiah 47:12-15.

48. What does 1 Corinthians 10:18-20 say about the connection between worshiping idols and the spiritual realm?

49. Did you ever use a Ouija board? Or tarot cards? Or consulted a psychic? Or had your fortune told? Or have you perhaps brought something home as a souvenir from another country that was used for a religious purpose (mask, amulet...)?

To use God's language from Isaiah 47:14b, "*...they have become like stubble, fire burns them; they cannot deliver themselves from the power of the flame...*" Watch out! You need to get rid of the item if it is in your home, and ask God to forgive you and cleanse you.

➤ In everything, by prayer and petition... Philippians 4:6

Do you know anyone who is involved in some demonic practices? Pray for them, that God will open their eyes before it's too late. That He will show them His mercy and draw them to Himself.

Pray for yourself that you won't be tempted to trust something other than God, that He will help you to be content with what He has chosen for you and that you will be a shining light to those around you.

*I heard another voice from heaven, saying, "Come out of her, my people,
so that you will not participate in her sins and receive of her plagues;
Revelation 18:4*

~ ~ ~ ~ ~ ~ Prayer Requests ~ ~ ~ ~ ~ ~

Inscribed on the Palms of My Hands
Isaiah chapter 48-50

Lesson 21

DAY 1 — For His Name's Sake

> ### Draw near to God and He will draw near to you... James 4:8

Jesus said "*Blessed are the poor in spirit, for theirs is the kingdom of heaven*". This is our true condition before God. We long to offer Him something of value, but we have so little. Sin, fear and doubts are much more abundant in our hearts. But, He will exchange our poverty for His riches in Christ Jesus. Isn't this wonderful? Give Him everything today. He will accept you.

I am writing to you, little children, because your sins have been forgiven you for His name's sake.
1 John 2:12

MEMORY VERSE Isaiah 49:15-16a

Can a mother forget the baby at her breast
and have no compassion on the child she has borne?
Though she may forget, I will not forget you!
See, I have engraved you on the palms of my hands. (NIV)

> ### Study to show yourself approved... 2 Timothy 2:15

The Lord has been presenting all the evidence against idols and proving that He alone is God. Now in Isaiah chapter 48, He explains more of the reasons for why He acts the way He does – because of Israel's obstinacy. He has chosen to hide what He will do until He is ready to create it so that they wouldn't claim their idols were responsible. And He restrained His wrath for His own sake, for the glory of His name.

1. Read Isaiah 48:1-11.

What unusual name does the Lord call His people in verse 1a?

How do they call on the Lord in verse 1b?

What do they call themselves after and what does it mean (v.2a)?

Who do they lean on (v.2b)?

> *Note – They assume God will look out for them just because they live in the "holy city" and use His name.*

What did the Lord declare and when (v.3a)?

How did He act on His promises (v.3b)?

Why did He do it that way and how does He describe them (v.4)?

2. Verse 4 describes the people of Judah as being obstinate, with iron necks and bronze foreheads. How does Psalm 78:8 describe them?

Read Ezekiel 22:17-21. What does "*iron and bronze*" signify in this passage?

Read Jeremiah 7:26-31. What did the people of Judah do to earn this description?

3. Continue answering questions about Isaiah 48:5-11.
When did God proclaim His deeds to them and why (v.5)?

As if presenting irrefutable evidence, what does the Lord ask in verse 6a?

What does God say He will proclaim to them in verse 6b?

Why is the Lord creating these things <u>now</u> instead of long ago (v.7)?

What was the condition of their ears and why did the Lord not let them know before now (v.8)?

4. According to verse 9, what does the Lord do for His own name's sake?

If the Lord hadn't restrained His wrath, what would've happened to them (v.9b)?

5. How has the Lord refined them (Isaiah 48:10)?

How was the time in Babylon a "*furnace of affliction*"? Considering how the Lord describes His people in verses 4 and 8, what "precious metal" do you think He desired?

6. What do these verses say about the result of the furnace of affliction?

unsuccessful	successful
Jeremiah 6:28-30	Zechariah 13:9
Ezekiel 24:11-13	Malachi 3:2-3

7. What reason does He give for His actions in Isaiah 48:11?

What do Exodus 34:14 and Isaiah 42:8 say about this?

8. Read Exodus 32:9-14. How does this story of Moses interceding for the people demonstrate what God means in Isaiah 48:9-11?

> The Lord didn't want other nations to take credit for what He was doing (Deuteronomy 32:26-27), and He was grieved by their captors who blasphemed His name (Isaiah 52:5).
> *"I acted for the sake of My name, that it should not be profaned in the sight of the nations among whom they lived, in whose sight I made Myself known to them by bringing them out of the land of Egypt. So I took them out of the land of Egypt..."* Ezekiel 20:9-10a

9. How should we represent the glorious name of our God? Read the following scriptures and make a note of the instruction they give.

Matthew 5:16

Colossians 1:10

> ➤ <u>Prove yourselves doers of the word... James 1:22</u>

10. God's people in Isaiah's day were "*obstinate*", with iron necks and bronze foreheads (Isaiah 48:4). How are we warned to avoid the same mistakes?

Proverbs 29:1

Romans 2:5-6

1 Timothy 4:1-2

Ask the Lord to keep you tender hearted towards God. What advice does James 1:21-22 give?

But to this one I will look, to him who is humble and contrite of spirit, and who trembles at My word. Isaiah 66:2b

11. The Lord refines us for our own good. What do these scriptures teach you about that?

Proverbs 17:3

Proverbs 27:21

1 Peter 1:7-8

12. Have you been in a "furnace" lately? Do you know someone who has? What encouragement did you find in today's lesson?

> ➤ <u>In everything, by prayer and petition... Philippians 4:6</u>

Ask the Lord to purify you and strengthen your faith which is more precious than gold. Ask the Lord to help you walk in such a way that His name is glorified among the nations. You can count on the Lord's help as you pray in His name.

"For My own sake, for My own sake, I will act; for how can My name be profaned? And My glory I will not give to another
Isaiah 48:11

DAY 2
Listen to the Lord!

> **Draw near to God and He will draw near to you... James 4:8**

*Yield now and be at peace with Him; thereby good will come to you.
Please receive instruction from His mouth and establish His words in your heart.
Job 22:21-22*

From the beginning the Lord has been faithful to direct you in the way you should go. He has never left you without His merciful care. Soften your heart towards Him today and accept His instruction. He wants to bless you.

Practice your memory verse:

Can a _____ forget the _____ at her breast
and have no compassion on the _____ she has borne?
Though she may _____, I will _____ _____ you!
See, I have _____ you on the palms of my _____.
Isaiah ___:15-16a

> **Study to show yourself approved... 2 Timothy 2:15**

In the second half of Isaiah 48, the Lord reveals Himself again declaring various names He has and things He has done. He shares His heart with His people, what His plans for them are and what would've happened if they had obeyed Him. Even as He laments their disobedience He promises once again to redeem them and care for them. This time, they must flee Babylon to reap the blessing.

13. Read Isaiah 48:12-22.

What does the Lord call Himself in verse 12?

The Lord calls Himself "*I am He*" 5 times in Isaiah alone. Read John 8:24,28. Who else uses this name and what is he saying?

"*The First and the Last*". This name is used in both Isaiah and Revelation. What does Jesus say in Revelation 22:13?

14. What does Isaiah 48:13 say and who is actually saying this, based on what you learned in the previous verse?

What does the Lord say about His servant in verse 14?

What does He say He has done for him in verse 15?

How does He call to His people in verses 14a and 16a?

After calling them to listen, what does He say to them in verse 16?

How does verse 16b reveal the trinity?

15. Read the following verses and make a note of how they reveal the three distinct persons of God.

Isaiah 61:1

Matthew 28:19

Luke 3:22

16. Continue answering questions about Isaiah 48:17-22.

Who speaks to Israel in verse 17a and what names does He use for Himself?

How does John 6:69 confirm who is talking?

What does He say He does for them in Isaiah 48:17b?

What lament does He make in verse 18a?

What would have been their condition if they had paid attention (v.18b)?

What heritage would they have had according to verse 19?

17. In Isaiah 48:18-19 we can see the cry of God's heart for His people. We see the same heart expressed in Jesus' words before He went to the cross. Read Matthew 23:37. What is God's heart's cry for His people?

18. Continue answering questions about Isaiah 48:20-22.

What does God want the Israelites to do when they leave Babylon (v.20)?

What does the Lord do for them in the deserts (v.21)?

Read Numbers 20:11. What was the Lord referring to?

What does 1 Corinthians 10:4 say this meant?

What sobering pronouncement does the Lord make in Isaiah 48:22?

Why do you think this warning is included here?

> ## Prove yourselves doers of the word ... James 1:22

19. We have seen Jesus in Isaiah 48 saying "*I am the first, I am also the last*". He refers to what He has done in the past to give them a picture of what He will do in the future. Look at God's work in the past. His track record is perfect. What confidence does this give you for the future?

20. Have you "*paid attention to My commandments*" as Isaiah 48:18 says? What benefits will you reap according to verse 17-19?

21. Isaiah 48:22 says "*There is no peace for the wicked*". How do the following verses show you the peace that is offered us?

John 14:27

Romans 5:1

Romans 8:6

Colossians 1:20

Based on these truths, why do you think there is no peace for the wicked?

Now may the Lord of peace Himself continually grant you peace in every circumstance.
2 Thessalonians 3:16

> ## In everything, by prayer and petition... Philippians 4:6

Ask the Lord to give you a heart devoted to following His commandments. Ask Him to fill you with peace. Praise Him for all the ways He cares for you.

Oh that they had such a heart in them, that they would fear Me and keep
all My commandments always, that it may be well with them and with their sons forever!
Deuteronomy 5:29

~ ~ ~ ~   **DAY 3**   ~ ~ ~ ~
Not in Vain

> ## Draw near to God and He will draw near to you... James 4:8

But I said, "I have toiled in vain, I have spent My strength for nothing and vanity..."
Isaiah 49:4a

Are you discouraged today? Even the Lord Jesus expressed discouragement at times. Yet He kept His focus on the Father's faithfulness, *"...Yet surely the justice due to Me is with the LORD, and My reward with My God."* Bring your discouragement to Jesus. He understands. He will help you find rest. Put your trust in the Father as He did.

And let this thought comfort you, that Jesus was comforted by thinking of you.

Practice your memory verse:

_____ ___ mother _____ the _____ at _____ breast
and _____ ____ compassion on the child _____ ____ borne?
_____ she _____ forget, I will ____ forget ____!
See, I have _____ you ___ the _____ of my hands.
_____ 49:___-16a

> ## Study to show yourself approved... 2 Timothy 2:15

In Isaiah chapter 49, Jesus speaks more openly than He did in chapter 48. He tells us how grieved He was over Israel's meager response to His ministry of salvation. The Lord promises Him a much greater harvest, extending His covenant to all the nations of the world. The glory and wonder of this promise brings great rejoicing to all of creation!

22. **Read Isaiah 49:1-13.** Answer the following questions about this Messianic prophecy.
Who is He calling to in verse 1a?

When did the calling on His life begin (v.1b)?

How does Matthew 1:20-21 show that this was fulfilled in Jesus' life?

How does He describe Himself in Isaiah 49:2?

23. How was verse 2 fulfilled in Jesus' life according to the following verses?
How was Jesus' *"mouth like a sharp sword..."* (Revelation 1:16, 2:16, 19:15)?

How did the Lord conceal Him *"in the shadow of His hand..."* (Isaiah 51:16)?

The reference verse 2 makes to *"a select arrow"* points to being a Son, (Psalm 127:4-5).

24. Considering that this prophecy is about Jesus, why do you think the Lord would conceal His *"sharp sword"* or hide His *"arrow... in His quiver"*? What does this mean?

In the Old Testament, the mystery of God's plan of salvation was kept secret. How does Romans 16:25-26 confirm that?

25. What did the Lord say to His Servant (Isaiah 49:3)?

   Note – In this passage the Messiah is called Israel because He has become their representative before God, their High Priest and He will fulfill God's purpose.

What is the Servant's response to the Lord (v.4)?

How does John 1:11 explain why Jesus could have said, *"...I have toiled in vain"* (Isaiah 49:4)?

Yet Jesus committed Himself to His Father's will and persisted. What insight does Hebrews 12:2 give you into how Jesus could go from discouragement to hope?

The Hebrew word for "salvation" is Yeshuah which is basically the same word as Jesus' Hebrew name (Yeshua). Every time you see a reference to salvation, you are seeing a connection to Jesus.

26. What was the Lord's purpose for the Messiah (Isaiah 49:5)?

How does the Lord express His approval of the Servant in verse 5b?

What more did the Lord want to achieve through Him (v.6)?

If the Lord hadn't decided to extend His salvation *"to the end of the earth"*, what would our condition have been? Read Ephesians 2:12

How do the following verses confirm the Servant's mission in Isaiah 49:6? Remember that 'gentiles' means 'nations'.

Luke 2:25-32

John 8:12

27. From Isaiah 49:7a, what names does the Lord give Himself and His Servant?

What will happen according to verse 7b and why?

Two very different pictures of the Messiah are presented in this verse. How do they contrast Jesus' reception by the world in His first and second coming?

28. What time and day has the Lord chosen to help His Servant (Isaiah 49:8a)?

What does verse 8b say God will do?

How does Paul apply verse 8 in 2 Corinthians 6:2?

29. Who is mentioned in Isaiah 49:9a and what will the Servant say to them?

How will He bless them and why, according to verses 9b-10?

What does Revelation 7:16-17 add to the description in Isaiah 49:9-10?

30. How will the Lord prepare the road in Isaiah 49:11?

Where will the people come from (v.12)?

In verse 12, the place called Sinim (or Aswan in NIV) might be the Sinai peninsula (in the south) or a place in southern Egypt or even China, as it is called today by Israelis, (representing the east).

Who will rejoice according to verse 13? Why?

31. In Isaiah 49:10 and 13, it says the Lord "*has compassion on them*". What do you learn about the Lord's compassion from these scriptures?

Psalm 103:13

Matthew 9:36

Isaiah 30:18

Mark 1:41

Micah 7:18-19

John 11:33-38

How can I give you up, O Ephraim? How can I surrender you, O Israel? ...
My heart is turned over within Me, all My compassions are kindled. I will not execute My fierce anger; I
will not destroy Ephraim again. For I am God and not man, the Holy One in your midst,
And I will not come in wrath.
Hosea 11:8-9

➢ <u>Prove yourselves doers of the word . . . James 1:22</u>

32. Have you ever felt like the Servant did in Isaiah 49:4, that your labor was in vain and you couldn't see any good results from it? Write about it.

33. The Lord had a calling on His Servant that was greater than Israel had imagined (Isaiah 49:6). God has vision for us and we can also limit it by our lack of our understanding. Is your vision too small? Do you need to let go of your ideas in order to be open to His? Are you willing to let Him change your focus or direction?

What are your thoughts about the Lord's vision for your life? Write down what you know about His calling.

➢ <u>In everything, by prayer and petition . . . Philippians 4:6</u>

Pray for the Lord to increase your vision. Ask Him to give you a willingness to serve even when it seems small or in vain. Lay your own expectations at His feet and pray for the fruit that He desires.

Even if I am being poured out as a drink offering upon the sacrifice
and service of your faith, I rejoice and share my joy with you all.
Philippians 2:17

~ ~ ~ ~   # DAY 4   ~ ~ ~ ~
Never Forgotten

➢ <u>Draw near to God and He will draw near to you . . . James 4:8</u>

For He Himself has said, "I will never leave you nor forsake you."
Hebrews 13:5b

The Lord will never forget you. He knows your every thought and has heard every prayer. He doesn't forget them. He loves you more than anyone who has ever lived. He is totally committed to you. Hope in Him and believe that He has dealt wonderfully with you.

Practice your memory verse:

_____ a _____ forget _____ baby _____ her _____
and _____ no _____ on _____ child _____ has _____ ?
Though _____ may _____ , I _____ not _____ you!
_____ , I _____ engraved _____ on _____ palms _____ my _____ .

Isaiah ___ : ___ - ___

> ## Study to show yourself approved...2 Timothy 2:15

In the second half of Isaiah chapter 49, the Lord promises to NEVER forget His people. He gives them mighty promises about the restoration He has planned for them and all their children.
In this passage, there is a dual application. God is talking about both the Jews and the Gentiles that have been adopted as His sons. He is talking about both the return from exile in Babylon and the return that will happen when Jesus comes back again.

34. Read Isaiah 49:14-26. Answer the following questions.

What did the people of Zion say in verse 14?

How did the Lord answer them in verse 15-16?

How did Jesus fulfill verse 16? Read John 20:24-27.

35. Who is coming to Jerusalem and who is leaving in Isaiah 49:17?

Note – Verse 17 says "Your builders hurry"(NAS). Most versions translate this word "sons". The Hebrew word can be translated either way. In this context (v.18,20) the word "sons" makes more sense.

What do they see when the Lord tells them to lift their eyes in verse 18a?

What does He promise in verse 18b? What will these "*jewels*" be (see v.20)?

How will their land be transformed (v.19)?

What will Zion's children say about her land (v.20)?

How is this a fulfillment of Genesis 22:17?

Summarize what Zion will say in her heart according to Isaiah 49:21.

In verses 22-23, who is going to take care of the children and how will they help them return to their land?

What does God want Israel to know through experiencing all of this? Isaiah 49:23b.

36. Continue answering questions about Isaiah 49:24-26. Before these sons can all come home, the Lord must intervene. Some of their captors will not release them willingly.
What is God going to do for their sons, according to verses 24-25?

37. How will the Lord deal with their oppressors (Isaiah 49:26a)?

What does God want all mankind to understand from verse 26b?

How is Revelation 16:4-7 a fulfillment of this verse?

➢ <u>Prove yourselves doers of the word . . . James 1:22</u>

38. In Isaiah 49:14, Zion said *"...the Lord has forgotten me"*. Are you tempted to believe this?

39. How do the following scriptures answer this concern about feeling forgotten?
Deuteronomy 31:8

Psalm 37:25, 28

Luke 12:6-7

40. The Lord promised *"...they will bring your sons in their bosom, and your daughters will be carried on their shoulders"* (v.22). God cares about our children. How does the promise of their children being brought back encourage you?

41. The Lord spoke of rescuing their sons from the mighty man and the tyrant in Isaiah 49:24-25. How are people being held captive today?
Colossians 2:8

2 Timothy 2:26

How does God deliver us from the mighty man and the tyrant?
Matthew 12:28-30

2 Corinthians 10:3-5

Ephesians 6:12-13

➢ <u>In everything, by prayer and petition . . . Philippians 4:6</u>

Pray for people you know who are feeling forsaken or forgotten. Ask the Lord to help you to be a comfort to them. The Lord hasn't forgotten the children who are far away from Him. Ask the Lord to bring them back to Him.

With all prayer and petition pray at all times in the Spirit...
Ephesians 6:18

~ ~ ~ ~ <u>DAY 5</u> ~ ~ ~ ~
The Servant Submits

➢ <u>Draw near to God and He will draw near to you. . . James 4:8</u>

...He awakens Me morning by morning, He awakens My ear to listen as a disciple...
Isaiah 50:4

Ask the Lord for a heart like this. You need to begin your day with His thoughts. He is willing and able to awaken you day by day. He wants to speak to you each morning. Submit your heart to His gentle instruction. Listen as Jesus did, with the intention of obeying.

Write out your memory verse.

➢ **Study to show yourself approved... 2 Timothy 2:15**

In Isaiah chapter 50, the Lord begins by explaining why He sent Israel away into exile. He found no one to intercede for them. He begins to describe His Servant, the Messiah, who alone is able to redeem the people. The Messiah, Himself, tells us His heart's attitude, how He is mistreated and how He finds the strength to go through it. He proclaims that He will be vindicated and those who condemn Him will be destroyed.

42. Read Isaiah 50:1-11.

What two questions does the Lord ask them in verse 1a?

How does Jeremiah 3:8a answer the first question?

How does the Lord explain what happened to them in Isaiah 50:1b?

The Lord asks four questions in verse 2. What does He ask in the first pair of questions (v.2a)?

What does He ask in the second pair of questions (v.2b), and what does He expose about their faith?

How does Ezekiel 22:30-31 show the truth of what the Lord is saying?

What evidence does He give of His power to contradict their lack of faith (Isaiah 50:2c-3)?

43. In Isaiah 50:4, we see the Messiah speaking again. What has the Lord given Him and what purpose does it serve in verse 4a?

(M)

How does the Lord minister to His Servant in verses 4b-5a?

How did the Messiah respond in verse 5b?

> *What a contrast the Lord is making between the open ear and obedient heart of the Servant vs. the deaf ears and rebellious spirits of Israel!*

How did the Servant demonstrate His willing and obedient spirit in verse 6?

How did Jesus fulfill this prophecy, Mark 14:65, 15:19?

What enabled Him to bear it (Isaiah 50:7), and how does He act on this help?

Page 254

44. In Isaiah 50:8, the Messiah returns to the theme of a court case. Notice the legal terms He uses and how they are applied. Who does He say is near (v.8a)?

What challenge does He offer in verse 8b?

Who helps Him in verse 9a?

What will happen to those who condemn Him (v.9b)?

Who condemned Jesus? What do the following scriptures say?
   Matthew 27:24-25

   Mark 14:55, 64

How was Jesus vindicated according to Acts 2:23-24?

45. How does the Messiah call out to those who are going through dark times in Isaiah 50:10?

What does He advise them?

How does verse 11a explain what some people do instead of *"trusting in the name of the Lord and relying on His God"*?

What warning does the Lord give them in verse 11b?

After all the remarkable revelations and promises of redemption that Isaiah had been prophesying, why do you think someone would *"kindle a fire"* or *"encircle themselves with firebrands"*?

➤ Prove yourselves doers of the word... James 1:22

46. Isaiah 50:4a says the Lord "...*has given Me the tongue of disciples, that I may know how to sustain the weary one with a word.*" What a beautiful ministry! Do you listen to the Lord as a disciple? He may give you a word to help sustain a weary soul.

47. In Isaiah 50:10, the Messiah offers wise counsel for those who *"fear the Lord...that walk in darkness and have no light..."* How can you put His advice into practice?

➤ In everything, by prayer and petition... Philippians 4:6

Pray for a listening ear and the tongue of a disciple. Ask the Lord to help you trust in His name and rely on Him. Ask Him to vindicate you and be near you.

*Then the LORD stretched out His hand and touched my mouth,
and the LORD said to me, "Behold, I have put My words in your mouth."
Jeremiah 1:9*

~ ~ ~ ~ ~ ~ ~   Prayer Requests   ~ ~ ~ ~ ~ ~ ~

Awake, O Zion!
Isaiah chapters 51 – 52

Lesson 22

DAY 1
Pursuing Righteousness

➤ <u>Draw near to God and He will draw near to you... James 4:8</u>

Righteousness is God's gift to us. It is meant to make it possible for us to know Him and be close to Him. Do you want to be close to Him? Ask Him to make you thirsty for Him. He wants you to pursue Him. He is pursuing you.

... but He loves one who pursues righteousness.
Proverbs 15:9

MEMORY VERSE   Isaiah 51:11

So the ransomed of the LORD will return and come with joyful shouting to Zion, and everlasting joy will be on their heads. They will obtain gladness and joy, and sorrow and sighing will flee away.

➤ <u>Study to show yourself approved... 2 Timothy 2:15</u>

In Isaiah 51, the Lord strongly exhorts an afflicted people to hope in Him and reminds them of His promises to them. He doesn't want them to be discouraged by those who revile them, because they won't last!

1. Read Isaiah 51:1-8. Use the following questions to draw out the meaning of the text.

Who is the Lord speaking to in verse 1a?

What does He advise them in verse 1b?

Who are they told to look to and what is the witness they should remember (v.2)?

What does Hebrews 11:8-12 say about Abraham and Sarah's example?

2. Having this example of God's faithfulness, who does the Lord promise to bless in Isaiah 51:3?

Write down the words that capture the blessings they will receive.

Whose attention does the Lord call for in verse 4a?

What does He promise in verse 4b and who is it intended for?

What does the Lord say in verse 5?

Where does the Lord tell them to look in verse 6a?

What does He prophesy about what they see in verse 6b?

What does He contrast this with in verse 6c?

When will this prophecy be fulfilled according to 2 Peter 3:10?

Who does the Lord appeal to in verse 7a and what does He say is in their heart?

What advice does the Lord give them in verse 7b?

What does He predict for those who reproach them (v.8a)?

What does He again contrast them with in verse 8b?

> **What is righteousness?**
> ISBE defines it as "...the intention to be and do right." Our relationship with God is dependent on righteousness because God is perfect. To have a relationship with Him we need to be "right" with Him. Unfortunately, people have been unable to live up to the standards of "rightness" that God established, so God created a righteousness that we could receive as a gift, where all that needed to be done right, was done for us. This is why the Bible speaks of the Lord putting on righteousness like a breastplate (Isaiah 59:17). He does this for our sake.

3. Verse 7 talks about "...*a people in whose heart is My law...*" referring to us, who have believed and have been sealed with His Spirit. This law in our hearts that "*will go forth from...*" the Lord (v.4) is different than Moses' Law. What do the following scriptures teach you about this law?

Galatians 3:24

Galatians 5:14

Galatians 6:2

> *I delight to do Your will, O my God; Your Law is within my heart."*
> Psalm 40:8

4. "*Do not fear the reproach of man...*" Isaiah 51:7 says. What do the following scriptures add to this?

Proverbs 29:25

Matthew 5:10-12

Luke 12:4-5

Acts 5:41

5. Isaiah 51:8a says "*the moth will eat them like a garment...*" referring to those who reproach and revile Israel. Isaiah contrasts the reproach and reviling of men with the righteousness of God that lasts forever. In view of this, how should we respond?

1 Corinthians 4:12

1 Peter 2:23, 4:14

6. In Isaiah 51:7 it says, "*You who know righteousness...*" Righteousness is mentioned 5 times in this passage. <u>Everyone</u> who believes in Jesus is made right with God. What do you learn about righteousness from the following scriptures?

Romans 3:22, 25

Romans 10:9-10

Philippians 3:9

7. "*Listen to Me, you who know righteousness...*" Isaiah 51:7 says. How can we guard our hearts against walking in self-righteousness?

Matthew 6:1

Matthew 23:28

Galatians 3:11

Ephesians 2:8-9

➤ Prove yourselves doers of the word... James 1:22

8. The Lord gave a beautiful promise in Isaiah 51:3 of how He would comfort Zion and "*all her waste places.*" This is what He does for our heart. How has the Lord comforted you and how is He restoring the waste places in your life to fruitfulness again?

In the same verse He also said He would make "*her wilderness... like Eden, and her desert like the garden of the LORD; Joy and gladness will be found in her, thanksgiving and sound of a melody.*" What evidence of transformation, joy, gladness, thanksgiving and melody, do you see in your heart?

➤ In everything, by prayer and petition... Philippians 4:6

Pray that you would walk in the Lord's righteousness. Ask Him to give you divine opportunities to make the free gift of His righteousness known to others. Pray for His Spirit to anoint this message with hope and joy.

Blessed are those who hunger and thirst for righteousness, for they shall be satisfied.
Matthew 5:6

~ ~ ~ ~ **DAY 2** ~ ~ ~ ~
I Am He Who Comforts You

➤ Draw near to God and He will draw near to you... James 4:8

And the ransomed of the LORD will return and come with joyful shouting to Zion,
With everlasting joy upon their heads. They will find gladness and joy,
And sorrow and sighing will flee away.
Isaiah 35:10

Dwell on the hope God offers you. Let His promises about your future comfort you. He has planned joy for you. He intends to wipe out every cause of sorrow and sighing. You need to remember these things because the sorrows and sighs you gather in your heart are too heavy for you. Release them and accept the comfort He offers you today.

Practice your memory verse:

So the _____ of the LORD will _____ and come with joyful _____ to Zion, and _____ joy will be on their _____. They will obtain _____ and joy, and sorrow and _____ will flee away.

Isaiah 51:11

> *Study to show yourself approved... 2 Timothy 2:15*

Today we continue studying in Isaiah 51. The Lord calls on the Arm of the Lord (another name for the Messiah) to awaken and intervene on behalf of His exiles. He continues to exhort them to hope in the Lord and take comfort from Him. He reasons with them telling them not to fear their oppressors.

9. Read Isaiah 51:9-16.

How does the Lord beckon in verse 9a and whom is He speaking to?

What does verse 9b say He did?

> *Note – See Lesson 11, Day 4 to review information about the dragon.*

What else did He do according to verse 10?

> *Note – This happened in Exodus 14:21-22.*

Who will return to Zion in verse 11a?

How does verse 11b describe them?

How does God reassure them in verse 12a?

What fear does He point out in verse 12b?

What has this fear led them to do (v.13)?

In what ways does the Lord contrast Himself with those they fear in verses 12-13?

What promise does the Lord give in verse 14?

> *Note – There are several applications we need to consider when we read this verse. First of all, in the time of Isaiah's prophesying, the northern kingdom of Israel was in exile and captivity. Second, many of these prophecies are about Judah's captivity in Babylon in the near future. And third, the release of captives from Satan's power and their return to the heavenly kingdom of God is the final fulfillment of the redemption described in this chapter.*

What does the Lord say to remind them of who He is and why they shouldn't fear (v.15)?

What does the Lord say in verse 16 and whom do you think He is speaking to?

10. Isaiah 51:9 speaks to the *"Arm of the Lord"*. This is a messianic reference. Jesus is the arm of the Lord. Let's look at some verses with this in mind. What has the arm of the Lord done?

Isaiah 59:15-16

Isaiah 63:5

11. *"...You cut Rahab in pieces..."* we read in Isaiah 51:9. How did God deal with Rahab in the following scriptures?

Job 26:12

Psalm 89:10

Ⓜ **Rahab** used here means "pride" in Hebrew. It is possible that it is a reference to *"...the fleeing serpent."* in Job 26:12-13. It is a <u>different</u> word than the name of the harlot who was saved by her faith in Joshua 6:25.

12. Isaiah 51:11 speaks of *"...the ransomed of the Lord will return and come with joyful shouting to Zion."* How do the following scriptures confirm this promise?

Revelation 7:9-10

Revelation 21:1-4

> ➤ <u>Prove yourselves doers of the word . . . James 1:22</u>

13. In Isaiah 51:12 the Lord says *"I, even I, am He who comforts you. Who are you that you are afraid of man who dies?"* Fear hinders their ability to be comforted by God. In Acts 9:31, it also draws a link between fearing the Lord and receiving His comfort. *"So the church... enjoyed peace, being built up... in the fear of the Lord and in the comfort of the Holy Spirit..."*

Have you forgotten the Lord your Maker? Have you let fear of man quench His comfort? What can you do about it?

How would Jesus' advice in Matthew 5:44 be helpful?

14. *"The exile will soon be set free..."* Isaiah 51:14 says. This verse has a spiritual application. Just as the Lord set the captives free from Babylon, Jesus sets people free from their bondage to sin and death. Is there someone you have been praying for who is in spiritual bondage? How does this verse encourage you? How can it strengthen your prayers?

> ➤ <u>In everything, by prayer and petition . . . Philippians 4:6</u>

Commit your fears to the Lord. Ask Him to comfort you. Ask Him to help you remember Him when you are going through difficult times.

But God, who comforts the depressed, comforted us...
2 Corinthians 7:6

~ ~ ~ ~ **DAY 3** ~ ~ ~ ~
The Cup of Anger

> ➤ <u>Draw near to God and He will draw near to you. . . James 4:8</u>

Therefore we do not lose heart, but though our outer man is decaying,
yet our inner man is being renewed day by day. For momentary, light affliction
is producing for us an eternal weight of glory far beyond all comparison...
2 Corinthians 4:16-17

Are you suffering? The Lord has not left you alone. Have you been burdened and grieved by trials? They are not the result of a punishment or God's wrath upon you. You have been spared from wrath. Your afflictions are a temporary condition that He wants to share with you. Trust Him.

Practice your memory verse:

So _____ ransomed _____ the _____ will _____ and _____ with _____ shouting _____ Zion, _____ everlasting _____ will ____ on _____ heads. _____ will _____ gladness _____ joy, _____ sorrow _____ sighing _____ flee _____.

Isaiah ____ :11

Page 261

> ## Study to show yourself approved... 2 Timothy 2:15

As we finish studying Isaiah chapter 51, the Lord calls to Jerusalem to rouse herself. She has suffered devastation and destruction but the Lord is going to take away His cup of anger and never make her drink it again. It will be put into the hands of those who tormented her.

15. Read Isaiah 51:17-23. Answer the following questions about the text.

Who is the Lord calling to rise in verse 17a?

Why is she in a fallen condition (v.17b)?

How does the Lord explain that she has none to help her in verse 18?

Verse 19 says that two things have befallen Jerusalem. These are 1- famine and 2- the sword. Before it names them, it uses two words to describe the effect they had: devastation and destruction. What two questions does the Lord ask in this verse?

What has happened to Jerusalem's sons and why (v.20)?

Who does the Lord speak to in verse 21 and what are they drunk with?

What does the Lord say about Himself in verse 22a?

What does He say He will take out of their hands in verse 22b?

What will He do to their tormentors (v.23a)?

How did their tormentors taunt them in verse 23b?

What does Proverbs 11:8 say about this?

16. In verses 17 and 22 of Isaiah 51, the Lord speaks of *"...the cup of His anger, the chalice of reeling..."* What do you learn about this from the following scriptures?

What is this cup and to whom was it given?
Psalm 75:7-8

Jeremiah 25:15-16

Revelation 14:9-10

Who was the cup given to here?

Jeremiah 25:17, 28-29

We would've had to drink this cup because of our sins, but the Lord intervened on our behalf. What do these verses show our Lord has done for us?

Mark 14:36

John 18:11

What cup has He offered us instead of the cup of wrath?
Luke 22:20

Page 262

17. Write down the words that show how the Lord beckons to His people in Isaiah 51. Why do you think God's tone is so urgent?

verse 1

verse 4

verse 7

verse 17

> <u>Prove yourselves doers of the word . . . James 1:22</u>

18. Thank God we have been spared the cup of His anger! What do these verses teach you about this?

John 3:36

Romans 5:9

Ephesians 2:3-6

Colossians 3:5-7

1 Thessalonians 5:9-10

> <u>In everything, by prayer and petition . . . Philippians 4:6</u>

Pray for those who are under God's wrath that He would reveal Himself to them and lead them to repentance. Ask Him for opportunities to share your testimony. Pray for those who are saved to live a life dedicated to God.

Have mercy on some, who are doubting; save others, snatching them out of the fire; and on some have mercy with fear, hating even the garment polluted by the flesh.
Jude 1:22-23

~ ~ ~ ~ **DAY 4** ~ ~ ~ ~
Loosing Chains of Captivity

> <u>Draw near to God and He will draw near to you . . . James 4:8</u>

Shake yourself from the dust, rise up, O captive Jerusalem;
Loose yourself from the chains around your neck, O captive daughter of Zion.
Isaiah 52:2

Are you still living as though you were enslaved? The Lord wants to reveal Himself to you as He really is, a God of comfort and compassion. He wants you shake off the dust of the past and rejoice in His news of peace and happiness. He is restoring you and He will surely finish what He has started.

Practice your memory verse:

____ the _____ of ___LORD____ return ____ come ____

joyful _____ to ____, and _____ joy ____ be ____ their _____.

They ____ obtain _____ and ____, and _____ and _____ will _____ away.

_____ 51: ____

Page 263

> ## Study to show yourself approved...2 Timothy 2:15

Isaiah chapter 52 begins with a stirring call to Zion. She has been enslaved but the Lord is calling her to rise up and loose her chains. The price of her redemption has been paid and the Lord will reveal His salvation in the eyes of the world!

19. Read Isaiah 52:1-10. Answer the following questions.

Who does the Lord call to awake in verse 1?

What does He tell her to do in this verse?

Who will no longer come into the city?

"Clothe yourself in your beautiful garments..." verse 1 says. How was this fulfilled according to the following scriptures?

   Galatians 3:27

   Revelation 7:9, 13-14

How does Revelation 21:27 show the fulfillment of *"For the uncircumcised and unclean will no longer come into you."* (Isaiah 52:1b)?

20. Continue answering the following questions about Isaiah 52:2-10.

Who does the Lord speak to in verse 2?

What does He tell her to do in this verse?

What does the Lord say about their slavery in verse 3?

What do these scriptures add to your understanding of this?

how they were redeemed from Egypt	1 Chronicles 17:21
<u>how</u> they were sold to Assyria and Babylon	Psalm 44:12
<u>why</u> they were sold to Assyria and Babylon	Isaiah 50:1
how they will be redeemed from Babylon	Isaiah 45:13
how they were redeemed eternally	Acts 8:20 1 Peter 1:18-19

21. Continue answering the following questions about Isaiah 52:4-10.

What two nations oppressed God's people in verse 4?

How does God say His people were taken away in verse 5a?

How were their conquerors acting in verse 5b?

What does the Lord plan to make known to His people (v.6a)?

What will He say to them "*in that day*" (v.6b)?

What does the Lord consider lovely in verse 7a?

What message is proclaimed in verse 7b?

Who rejoices in verse 8 and why?

Who are the watchmen? What do these verses say?
   Isaiah 62:6-7

   Ezekiel 3:17

22. Continue answering the following questions about Isaiah 52:9-10.
   Who also rejoices in verse 9 and why?

   What has the Lord done in verse 10 and to whom is He referring?

   Note – "Salvation of our God" is a reference to the name "Jesus" which means salvation.

23. In Isaiah 52:5-6, the Lord says "*My name is continually blasphemed all day long...*" and explains His intention, "*...My people shall know My name...*" Read Ezekiel 36:20-28 and answer the following questions to help you understand this better.
   How was the Lord's name profaned in Ezekiel 36:20?

   How did the Lord feel about it and why did He decide to do something about it (Ezekiel 36:21-23)?

   From Ezekiel 36, explain what God does to vindicate the holiness of His name:

   gathering them, v. 24

   cleansing them, v. 25

   transforming them, v. 26

   anointing them, v. 27

   His promise to them, v.28

➢ <u>Prove yourselves doers of the word...James 1:22</u>

24. In Isaiah 52:2, the Lord encourages His people to "*Loose yourself from the chains around you neck.*" They had been in Babylon for 70 years and most of them were born there and didn't know anything else. It was hard to rise up and leave. Do you find it hard to "*shake yourself from the dust*" and leave the past behind? What does Galatians 4:9 advise you?

25. When the "*nations*" look at you (Isaiah 52:5) – is God being honored in their eyes, or blasphemed? What kind of ambassador are you? What do you need to grow in?

26. Isaiah 52:8 says "*Your watchmen lift up their voices...*" Who are the watchmen mentioned in Hebrews 13:17 and what is required of them?

We read in Isaiah 62:6, that the watchmen "*remind the Lord*". This is a picture of prayer. How do these verses teach you about prayer and keeping watch?

Psalm 130:5-6

Habbakuk 2:1

Matthew 26:38-41

Luke 18:1-8

> ## In everything, by prayer and petition... Philippians 4:6

Pray for the Lord's holy name to be vindicated and for His people to be delivered of any remnants of captivity. Pray that chains will be broken and people set free. Give praise to the glorious and wonderful name of Jesus!!

Suddenly there came a great earthquake, so that the foundations of the prison house were shaken; and immediately all the doors were opened and everyone's chains were unfastened.
Acts 16:26

~ ~ ~ ~
# DAY 5
Purify Yourselves
~ ~ ~ ~

> ## Draw near to God and He will draw near to you... James 4:8

Our freedom is bought at a high price. When you consider how dearly the Lord paid to free us, it seems a small thing to honor His request to purify ourselves as vessels of the Lord. Ask the Lord to open your heart to what He is teaching you today.

...Christ Jesus, who gave Himself for us to redeem us from every lawless deed, and to purify for Himself a people for His own possession, zealous for good deeds.
Titus 2:14

Write your memory verse.

> ## Study to show yourself approved... 2 Timothy 2:15

In the second part of Isaiah 52, the Lord exhorts His people to leave Babylon without being tainted by its uncleanness. He reveals the cost of their freedom. He talks about how His Servant will astonish people by what happens to Him just as the nations were shocked at what happened to them. He begins to describe the incredible picture of the Messiah who becomes an offering for the sin of the nations.

27. Read Isaiah 52:11-15. Use the following questions to help you understand the passage.

What does the Lord command His people to do in verse 11a?

Who is He speaking to in verse 11b?

What will their exit be like (v.12a)?

Why is this possible (v.12b)?

These verses have a dual application. One was when Babylon was conquered in the 6th century B.C. and the other will take place when Babylon is destroyed in the end times.
Fill in the following chart to see how this was and will be fulfilled.

Leaving Babylon	in the 6th century B.C.	in the end times
Depart, depart, go out from there...	Ezra 2:1	2 Corinthians 6:17-18, Revelation 18:4
You who carry vessels of the Lord...	Ezra 8:28-30	2 Corinthians 4:7
For the Lord will go before you...	Ezra 8:21-23	Revelation 17:14, 19:11

28. What does the Lord say about His Servant in Isaiah 52:13?

How was this fulfilled?
John 3:14-15

Ephesians 1:20-23

Philippians 2:8-11

29. Continue answering questions about Isaiah 52:14-15.
How did many react to God's people (v.14a)?

Read the following scriptures to see why this was.
The warning - 1 Kings 9:8-9

The fulfillment - Lamentations 2:15-17

Describe what happens to the Messiah in Isaiah 52:14b.

How was Jesus' appearance "*...marred more than any man...*"?
Isaiah 50:6

Matthew 26:67, 27:29-30

John 19:1

30. What will the Servant accomplish according to Isaiah 52:15a?

In the Old Testament, the Lord gave very specific directions for the cleansing of sin according to Moses' Law. Animal sacrifices were to be offered daily, and once a year blood was brought into the holy of holies to atone for the sins of His people.
Read Leviticus 16:15-16. How does it describe this?

Note – the mercy seat is the place above the ark of the covenant, representing the Lord's throne where His presence abided.

How has Jesus fulfilled this according to Hebrews 9:12?

Isaiah says plainly that the Messiah will "*...sprinkle many nations...*" But the people of Jesus' day found it very difficult to accept that salvation was always intended for all the nations.

Jesus made it clear:

Matthew 24:14

Matthew 28:19

Jesus' disciples were surprised:

Acts 10:45

Acts 11:17-18

The Jews were livid at the idea! See Acts 22:21-22.

31. What impact will the message have (Isaiah 52:15b)?

Read Acts 26:26-28. What example of this does it give?

➤ <u>Prove yourselves doers of the word ... James 1:22</u>

32. Rather than carrying vessels, we have become the "*vessels of the Lord.*" How can we "*Depart, go out from there...purify yourselves...*" as Isaiah 52:11 says? What do these scriptures teach us?

Romans 12:1-2

2 Timothy 2:21

1 Peter 2:11

1 John 2:15

➤ <u>In everything, by prayer and petition ... Philippians 4:6</u>

Pray for a pure heart. Ask the Lord to cleanse your conscience and free you to serve Him.

Let us draw near with a sincere heart in full assurance of faith, having our hearts sprinkled clean from an evil conscience...
Hebrews 10:22

~ ~ ~ ~ ~ ~ Prayer Requests ~ ~ ~ ~ ~ ~

The Portrait of Our Redeemer
Isaiah chapters 53
Lesson 23

DAY 1 — A Tender Shoot

> Draw near to God and He will draw near to you... James 4:8

*Have this attitude in yourselves which was also in Christ Jesus,
who although He existed in the form of God,
did not regard equality with God a thing to be grasped, but emptied Himself,
taking the form of a bond-servant, and being made in the likeness of men.
Philippians 2:5-7*

Jesus chose to humble Himself and become poor. He took on the form of a bondservant. He wants you to know Him as He really is. He has written these things for you. Prepare your heart to learn today, to know Him better and value Him more. Ask Him to anoint His word today.

MEMORY VERSE   Isaiah 53:5

But he was pierced for our transgressions, he was crushed for our iniquities; the punishment that brought us peace was upon him, and by his wounds we are healed. (NIV)

> Study to show yourself approved... 2 Timothy 2:15

Isaiah chapter 53 covers the portrait of the suffering Messiah. Painted in vivid color, with great compassion and insight, Isaiah reveals to us the human and humble side of our glorious King of kings. What a privilege Isaiah was given!

This chapter is so detailed and accurate that many "scholars" in recent decades began to declare that it had been written by Christians after the fact. But God was prepared for them and in the mid 20th century, He brought to light a copy of this very chapter which has been proven to be older than the birth of Christ. It's found in the Dead Sea scrolls.

We have dedicated this whole week to studying this one chapter in detail so that we may behold our Savior.

1. Read Isaiah 53:1-2. Answer the following questions.

What question does Isaiah ask in verse 1a?

What question does he ask in verse 1b and what do you think it means?

How did the Servant of the Lord grow up according to verse 2a?

How is He described in verse 2b?

2. *"Who has believed our message?"* Isaiah asked in verse 1. How does John 12:34-38 show the fulfillment of this verse?

How does Paul present this verse in Romans 10:14-17? What encouragement does he give?

Why do they not believe the message? Read 1 Corinthians 1:23-24.

"And to whom has the arm of the Lord been revealed?" Isaiah continues in Isaiah 53:1. Answer this question using the following verses.

Matthew 11:25

Matthew 16:16-17

John 6:45

3. How did Jesus grow *"like a tender shoot"* according to Luke 2:40, 52?

In Isaiah 53:2, it says He was *"like a root out of parched ground"*? The word *'root'* is a reference to the Messiah meaning that He is the Son of David (see box on page 70). How do these verses show that Jesus is this person?

Isaiah 11:10

Romans 15:12

4. Jesus had *"no stately form or majesty nor appearance that we should be attracted to Him"* (Isaiah 53:2). Build a description of Him showing how He appeared to others as an ordinary human being.

shadow of impropriety	Matthew 1:18-25	
place of birth	Luke 2:7	
family status	Luke 2:22-24 with Leviticus 12:8	
reputation in home town	Matthew 13:54-58	
His trade	Mark 6:3	
rulers reaction to Him	Luke 2:46-47	
His town's reputation in Judah	John 1:45-46	
His brothers' reaction to Him	John 7:3-5	
His people's reaction to Him	Mark 3:20-22	
John the Baptist's first impression	John 1:33a	

In John 1:32-34, what sign was given so that John would recognize Jesus?

Note – This is significant because the word Messiah (Christ in the Greek) means 'anointed one' and anointing is symbolic of the Holy Spirit (Acts 10:38).

5. Read these verses and record some of the things that the Jews were looking for in a Messiah.

Matthew 2:6

Matthew 16:1

John 6:14-15

John 12:34

6. What else do you think the Jews were looking for in their Messiah? Think about the messianic prophecies we have studied (such as Isaiah 9:6-7, or Isaiah 11:1-5)

➢ <u>Prove yourselves doers of the word ... James 1:22</u>

7. *"Who has believed our message? And to whom has the arm of the Lord been revealed?"* Isaiah laments in 53:1. God wants to reveal Himself to you more and more as you draw close to Him. Ask the Lord to reveal Himself to you. What does Paul pray for in Ephesians 1:17-18?

If people don't believe the message, this prayer in Ephesians is a good way to prepare the soil of their hearts. What else can help them according to Romans 10:17?

8. In Isaiah 53:2 it says that Jesus grew up like a root in *"parched ground"*. He was surrounded by people with little or no faith. He had to rely on His relationship with His Father for spiritual fellowship. Are you living in *'parched ground'*, thirsty and longing for your spirit to be built up? How do these scriptures build you up?

Jeremiah 17:7-8

Revelation 7:17

> *I stretch out my hands to You; My soul longs for You, as a parched land.*
> *Psalm 143:6*

9. The Messiah had *"no stately form or majesty that we should look upon Him, nor appearance that we should be attracted to Him."* (Isaiah 53:2). What characteristic in Jesus drew you to Him?

➢ <u>In everything, by prayer and petition ... Philippians 4:6</u>

Ask the Lord to pour out a spirit of revelation on those who are unbelieving. Give praise to your Savior who became an "ordinary" man for your sake.

> *As to this salvation, the prophets who prophesied of the grace that would come to you*
> *made careful searches and inquiries, seeking to know what person or time the Spirit of Christ within*
> *them was indicating as He predicted the sufferings of Christ and the glories to follow.*
> *It was revealed to them that they were not serving themselves, but you,*
> *in these things which now have been announced to you through those*
> *who preached the gospel to you by the Holy Spirit sent from heaven*
> *-- things into which angels long to look.*
> *1 Peter 1:10-12*

~ ~ ~ ~ **DAY 2** ~ ~ ~ ~
A Man of Sorrows

➤ <u>Draw near to God and He will draw near to you… James 4:8</u>

*You search the Scriptures because you think that in them you have eternal life;
it is these that testify about Me;
John 5:39*

Jesus is the source of all joy and also your companion in all your sorrows. He wants you to know Him better so that you will trust Him more. Come into the Lord's presence with confidence. Let Him show you precious and beautiful promises in His word today.
Ask the Lord to reveal Himself to you through the scripture we read today.

Practice your memory verse:

But he was _____ for our transgressions, he was crushed for our _____;

the punishment that _____ us peace was upon _____,

and by his wounds we are _____.

Isaiah ____:5

➤ <u>Study to show yourself approved… 2 Timothy 2:15</u>   Ⓜ

Today as we consider the "*man of sorrows*" in Isaiah 53, ask the Lord to open your understanding and reveal Himself to you by the power of His Holy Spirit. There is no one like Him.

10. Read Isaiah 53:3-4. Answer the questions about the text.

How does verse 3 say that people treated our Savior?

How does the verse 3b describe His emotional condition?

How does Isaiah include himself in the last line of verse 3?

What did Jesus do for us in verse 4a?

How did we interpret what happened to Him in verse 4b?

11. Build a description of our Lord's <u>emotional</u> suffering using these scriptures.
He was despised…
   Psalm 22:6-8

   Matthew 27:39-43

   Luke 4:28-29

---

and forsaken of men…
   Matthew 26:21

   Mark 14:48-50, 70-72

   John 15:18

Page 272

a man of sorrows...
>Psalm 69:20

>Matthew 23:37

>Hebrews 5:7

and acquainted with grief... Matthew 26:37-38 Luke 19:41-42 John 11:33-35	How little was Jesus esteemed? In Matthew 26:14-16 we read that Judas betrayed Jesus to the chief priests for thirty shekels of silver. In Moses' Law, this was the value given to replace slaves who were accidentally killed. Free men, (when paying a vow) were valued at 50 shekels. Zechariah 11:12-13a shows how the Lord felt about their evaluation of Him.
like one from whom men hide their face... John 1:10-11 Acts 3:13	
and we did not esteem Him. Luke 8:52-53, 16:14 John 8:48-49	

12. How does 1 Corinthians 1:27-29 demonstrate God's wisdom in bringing the Messiah in such a humble fashion?

13. Read Isaiah 53:4. Why was the Lord was willing to go through so much? What do the following scriptures teach us about how these passages were fulfilled?

Surely our griefs He Himself bore, and our sorrows He carried...
>Jeremiah 8:21

>Matthew 8:16-17, 11:28-30

_____

Yet we ourselves esteemed Him stricken...
>Luke 23:35

>John 19:7

_____

smitten of God and afflicted.
>Deuteronomy 21:22-23

>Psalm 22:1-2

_____

14. How does Isaiah 62:4 show the outcome of the Lord being "*forsaken*" (Isaiah 53:3) on our behalf?

> <u>Prove yourselves doers of the word ... James 1:22</u>

15. Have you been "*despised and forsaken of men*" (Isaiah 53:3)? How does Hebrews 12:3 encourage you?

16. "*... like one from whom men hide their face He was despised, and we did not esteem Him*" (Isaiah 53:3). How can you esteem Jesus more?

Are there people you do not esteem as you should? What should you do about this?

17. "*...Surely our griefs He Himself bore, and our sorrows He carried....*"(Isaiah 53:4). Are you sorrowful today? Jesus knows what you are going through. Give Him your sorrow and receive His comfort. Read 2 Corinthians 1:3-5.

In all their affliction He was afflicted... Isaiah 63:9a

> <u>In everything, by prayer and petition ... Philippians 4:6</u>

Thank Him for bearing your sorrow. Pray for a willing spirit that would accept whatever suffering or humbling the Lord brings your way. Ask Him to give you compassion and effective prayer for those who are suffering. Pray that you wouldn't shrink back from sharing in His sorrows if He grants you this.

...fixing our eyes on Jesus, the author and perfecter of our faith, who for the joy set before Him endured the cross, despising the shame and has sat down at the right hand of the throne of God.
Hebrews 12:2

~ ~ ~ ~   **DAY 3**   ~ ~ ~ ~
The Price of Our Healing

> <u>Draw near to God and He will draw near to you... James 4:8</u>

...they will look on Me whom they have pierced;
and they will mourn for Him, as one mourns for an only son...
Zechariah 12:10

Have you contemplated the price that was paid for your healing and salvation? Precious blood of a pure and holy Lamb was poured out for you. If you have doubted His love for you, let this convince you. Make this the prayer of your heart:

Lord Jesus, grant me more love for You and more compassion for what You went through.

Practice your memory verse:

But ____ was _____ for _____ transgressions, ____ was _____ for _____ iniquities;
the _____ that _____ us _____ was _____ him,
_____ by _____ wounds _____ are _____.

Isaiah _____:5

Page 274

> ## Study to show yourself approved... 2 Timothy 2:15

The Messiah came so that He could become an offering for us. Our passage today, Isaiah 53:5-6, describes how He suffered in the hands of His own people and the gentiles.

18. Read Isaiah 53:5-6. Answer the following questions about the text.

What happened physically to the Messiah in verse 5?

What was the purpose according to this same verse (5)?

How does the Lord describe our spiritual condition in verse 6a?

What has the Lord done for us in verse 6b?

> Ⓜ Isaiah 53:5 uses two words referring to sin. *Transgression*, which means rebellion, and *iniquity* which means perversity, or depravity.
> BDB-Definitions

19. Look up the following scriptures and make a note of how each part of this prophecy in Isaiah 53:5-6 was fulfilled and how we benefited from it.

how it was fulfilled	benefit we received

He was pierced through for our transgressions...

Psalm 22:16	Ephesians 2:13
John 19:34,37	Hebrews 10:19

He was crushed (broken, bruised) for our iniquities...

Mark 14:22	Psalm 34:18
	Isaiah 53:10

The chastening for our well-being (peace) fell upon Him...

Matthew 27:46	2 Corinthians 5:19-20
Matthew 27:50-51	Colossians 1:20

By His scourging (wounds) we are healed.

Mark 15:15	Psalm 103:2-3, 147:3
John 19:1	1 Peter 2:24

20. How have we turned away from the Lord as Isaiah describes in 53:6? How has the Lord brought us back? Use the following scriptures to answer.

All of us like sheep have gone astray...

   1 Peter 2:25

Each of us has turned to his own way...

   Romans 3:10-12

But the Lord has caused the iniquity of us all to fall on Him.

   2 Corinthians 5:21

21. Jesus knew that He had come to suffer and die. He knew He would rise again. What do the following scriptures teach you about this?

Zechariah 12:10

Luke 9:22

Luke 24:25-27, 45

➢ Prove yourselves doers of the word... James 1:22

22. Do you have "*transgressions*" that need cleansing (v.5)? Do you have "*iniquities*" that need forgiving? Are you lacking peace? Jesus has provided a way for your healing. Come to Him and ask.

23. Have you "*gone astray*" or "*turned to your own way*" (v.6)? What hope do you find in today's scriptures? What should you do?

24. After Jesus rose from the dead, He appeared to two disciples who didn't recognize Him. He began to explain the scriptures to them, proving that He had to suffer and die before He could enter His glory. Our passage in Isaiah 53 must have been one of the main ones He discussed with them. In Luke 24:32 it says:

> They said to one another, "Were not our hearts burning within us while He was speaking to us on the road, while He was explaining the Scriptures to us?"

This is the effect Isaiah should be having on us! Jesus is also explaining the scriptures to us by His Spirit. Is your heart burning within you? Ask Him to speak to you and help you understand His word.

➢ In everything, by prayer and petition... Philippians 4:6

Praise God for replacing our filthy garments with robes of righteousness. He loves you so much. Spend time thanking God for all that He did to accomplish your salvation.

> *For all of us have become like one who is unclean,*
> *And all our righteous deeds are like a filthy garment;*
> *Isaiah 64:6a*

> *I will rejoice greatly in the LORD, my soul will exult in my God;*
> *For He has clothed me with garments of salvation, He has wrapped me with a robe of righteousness, As a bridegroom decks himself with a garland, and as a bride adorns herself with her jewels.*
> *Isaiah 61:10*

~ ~ ~ ~ **DAY 4** ~ ~ ~ ~
A Lamb Led to the Slaughter

➤ <u>Draw near to God and He will draw near to you... James 4:8</u>

Jesus was saying, "Father, forgive them; for they do not know what they are doing."
Luke 23:34

No wonder the thief said, *"Jesus, remember me when You come in Your kingdom!"* How lavish and abundant His grace is! Come to Him today. His blood washes you clean of every sin and He willingly, forgives and cleanses you.

Practice your memory verse:

____ he ____ pierced ____ our _____, he ____ crushed ____ our _____;

the _____ that _____ us _____ was _____ him,

_____ by _____ wounds _____ are _____.)

Isaiah ___ :5

Ⓜ

➤ <u>Study to show yourself approved... 2 Timothy 2:15</u>

There has never been a miscarriage of justice like the one that took place when Jesus was tried. In Isaiah 53:7-9, the Lord lays it out for us point by point. Let Him give you a spirit of wisdom and of revelation in the knowledge of Him as you study His word today.

25. Read Isaiah 53:7-9. Answer the following questions about Jesus' trial, judgment and sentencing.

How was the Servant treated in verse 7a?

How did Jesus respond to this treatment in Isaiah 53:7b?

How was He taken away (v.8a)?

What does it say about His generation (v.8b)?

Why did the stroke fall on Him (v.8c)?

Who was He assigned to the grave with (v.9a)?

Who was He buried with (v.9b)?

Why did God appoint this place for His burial (v.9c)?

26. Jesus *"was oppressed and He was afflicted..."* (Isaiah 53:7) in the final days of His earthly life. Look up the following scriptures about the standard set by Moses' Law to understand how greatly they abused the Law. Make a note of what you learn.

Leviticus 19:15-18

Deuteronomy 16:18-19

Deuteronomy 19:15-19

Deuteronomy 25:1-3

*Note – When Jesus says "If I have spoken wrongly, testify of the wrong; but if rightly, why do you strike Me?" in John 18:23. He was confronting their abuse of authority referring to standards in the Law that were well known to them.

What warning does 2 Chronicles 19:6-7 give to judges?

27. Look up the following scriptures to see how Jesus fulfilled Isaiah 53:7.

He did not open His mouth…
Matthew 27:12-14

1 Peter 2:23

Like a lamb that is led to slaughter…
John 1:29

Acts 8:32-35

28. Look up the following scriptures and make a note of how Isaiah 53:8 was fulfilled through Jesus.

By oppression…
Mark 15:14-15

Luke 23:8-11, 22

And judgment He was taken away…
Matthew 26:63-66

John 19:9-16

> To be oppressed is to be treated with great cruelty and injustice by the governing authorities.

He was cut off out of the land of the living…
Daniel 9:26

John 11:49-52

For the transgression of My people, to whom the stroke was due. (In other words, Jesus took the punishment that God's people deserved.)
1 Peter 3:18

29. How were these prophecies in Isaiah 53:9 fulfilled?

His grave was assigned with wicked men…   Matthew 27:38

Yet He was with a rich man in His death…   Matthew 27:57-60

Because He had done no violence, nor was there any deceit in His mouth.
Luke 23:4, 13-15

Hebrews 7:26

1 Peter 2:22

30. How terrible their judgment will be!! They knew Moses' Law and abused it anyway!! What does Hebrews 10:28 say about this?

➢ <u>Prove yourselves doers of the word . . . James 1:22</u>

31. Jesus set us an example in the way He handled the injustice He received. What do you need to remember from the following scriptures?

Matthew 5:38-45

Luke 23:33-34a

James 2:13

32. Our sins nailed Jesus to the cross. We also have received unmerited favor. We ought to be characterized by a great love because we have been forgiven so much. Read Luke 7:44-48 and write down your thoughts about it.

Our love for Christ should manifest itself in great mercy towards others. We have received freely and we should also give freely. Read these scriptures and write your thoughts about them.

Matthew 6:12

Matthew 18:23-33

➢ <u>In everything, by prayer and petition . . . Philippians 4:6</u>

Knowing that you were not redeemed with perishable things like silver or gold from your futile way of life inherited from your forefathers, but with precious blood, as of a lamb unblemished and spotless, the blood of Christ.
1 Peter 1:18-19

Jesus did this because of you. For the joy set before Him He endured the cross, because He loves you so much. Pray for those who still don't know Jesus.

~ ~ ~ ~ <u>DAY 5</u> ~ ~ ~ ~
He Justified the Many

➢ <u>Draw near to God and He will draw near to you. . . James 4:8</u>

After these things I looked, and behold, a great multitude which no one could count, from every nation and all tribes and peoples and tongues, standing before the throne and before the Lamb, clothed in white robes, and palm branches were in their hands; and they cry out with a loud voice, saying, "Salvation to our God who sits on the throne, and to the Lamb."
Revelation 7:9-10

A great multitude will be present in heaven because Jesus has justified the many. Thank the Lord that you are counted in that number! Ask Him to open your heart to hear what He has to say to you.

Write down your memory verse:

> <u>Study to show yourself approved… 2 Timothy 2:15</u>

Isaiah 53:10-12 tells us the outcome of the Messiah's terrible suffering and the injustice that sent Him to death. It also gives us insight into the Father's feelings about His Son's sacrifice, and the rewards He will give Him because of it.

33. Read Isaiah 53:10-12. Answer the following questions about the text.

Who was ultimately responsible for Jesus' death and how did He feel about it (v.10a)?

What did Jesus render Himself in verse 10b?

What will the Lord do as a result of it in verse 10c?

What will satisfy the Lord in verse 11a?

What will the Servant accomplish by His knowledge in verse 11b?

What will the Lord do for Him in verse 12a?

Why will He do this in verse 12b?

34. Read the following verses and explain how these passages were fulfilled.

But the Lord was pleased to crush Him, putting Him to grief…
   Romans 8:32

If He would render Himself as a guilt offering…
   Leviticus 17:11

   Ephesians 5:2

He will see His offspring…
   John 1:12

He will prolong His days…
   Psalm 16:10

   Acts 2:24-28

   Romans 6:9

   Revelation 1:18

> *Note – The guilt offering is one of the sacrifices that Jesus fulfilled. It consisted of either a ram or a lamb offered to cover personal guilt from breaking Moses' Law.

   *Note –The religious rulers <u>knew</u> these verses! This is why they put a guard on the tomb in Matthew 27:62-66!

The plan the Lord had from the beginning will be accomplished because of the Messiah's sacrifice. It will prosper in Jesus' hand. How will this "*good pleasure of the Lord prosper in His hand*" (Is 53:10)?
   Psalm 149:4

   Colossians 1:19-20

35. In Isaiah 53:11, we see that the Messiah will be satisfied with what is accomplished through the anguish of His soul. What do you learn about this from the following references?

As a result of the anguish of His soul...
   Luke 22:44

   John 12:27

He will see it and be satisfied...
   Hebrews 12:2

By His knowledge, the Righteous One, My Servant will justify the many...
   Matthew 20:28

   Romans 5:18-19

> Justify – a legal term in which the person is given credit for having fulfilled the Law completely.

As He will bear their iniquities.
   Hebrews 9:28a

36. How do these references explain what the Lord will do for His Servant in Isaiah 53:12?

Therefore, I will allot Him a portion with the great...
   Acts 5:31

   Ephesians 1:20-21

   Philippians 2:8-11

And He will divide the booty with the strong...
   Psalm 2:8

   Isaiah 49:24-25

Because He poured Himself out to death and was numbered with the transgressors...
   Mark 15:27-28

Yet He himself bore the sin of many, and interceded for the transgressors.
   Leviticus 16:21-22

   1 Timothy 2:5-6

   Hebrews 7:25

> *As far as the east is from the west, so far has He removed our transgressions from us.*
> *Psalm 103:12*

➤ **Prove yourselves doers of the word . . . James 1:22**

37. Jesus gave Himself up as an offering for us (Isaiah 53:10). In Ephesians 5:1-2, Paul advises us to "*...be imitators of God, as beloved children; and walk in love, just as Christ also loved you and gave Himself up for us, an offering and a sacrifice to God as a fragrant aroma.*" How can you put that into practice?

38. Not only was Jesus willing to be "*numbered with the transgressors*" (v.12), but He also interceded for them. How about you? Are you too holy to associate with sinners? Are you praying for them?

➤ **In everything, by prayer and petition . . . Philippians 4:6**

Ask the Lord to fill your heart with thanksgiving for what He has done for you. Pray that you would be given grace to follow His example and love others as He did. Pray that God's good pleasure would be accomplished in your life.

We see Jesus who was made for a little while lower than the angels...
because of the suffering of death crowned with glory and honor,
so that by the grace of God He might taste death for everyone.
Hebrews 2:9

~ ~ ~ ~ ~ ~ Prayer Requests ~ ~ ~ ~ ~ ~

Enlarge Your Tents
Isaiah chapters 54 – 55

Lesson 24

DAY 1   Your Husband is Your Maker

> ➢ **Draw near to God and He will draw near to you... James 4:8**

There was a prophetess, Anna... She was advanced in years and had lived with her husband seven years after her marriage, and then as a widow to the age of eighty-four. She never left the temple, serving night and day with fastings and prayers.
Luke 2:36-37

Anna knew the Lord as her husband. Her love for Him kept her living in His presence night and day. He kept her alive until she could see the infant who would grow into her King, her Bridegroom, and her Redeemer. Take her example to heart. Someday you will see your Bridegroom face to face, but take time now to seek His face in secret.

MEMORY VERSE   Isaiah 55:8-9

"For my thoughts are not your thoughts,

neither are your ways my ways," declares the LORD.

"As the heavens are higher than the earth, so are my ways

higher than your ways and my thoughts than your thoughts." (NIV)

> ➢ **Study to show yourself approved ... 2 Timothy 2:15**

Isaiah 54 speaks of the spiritual children that will be created as a fruit of the Messiah's sacrifice in chapter 53. The Lord promises to be a husband to His people and multiply their descendants.

1. Read Isaiah 54:1-6. Use the following questions to draw out their meaning.

Who does the Lord speak to in verse 1a and what does He tell her to do?

What reason does He give for this in verse 1b?

What preparations does He tell them to make in verse 2?

What promise does He make about their descendants in verse 3?

Why does the Lord tell them not to fear or feel humiliated (v.4)?

What names does the Lord give Himself in verse 5? What relationship does He emphasize?

How does the Lord describe their condition when He called (v.6)?

(H)

2. Why would the Lord call His people "*barren*"(v.1)?   Read Isaiah 26:17-18.

How does Paul apply Isaiah 54:1 in Galatians 4:26-28?

How else do we see this promise fulfilled in the following scriptures?
   Psalm 113:9

   Isaiah 49:20-21

3. The Lord says "*Enlarge the place of your tent; Stretch out the curtains of your dwellings, spare not; Lengthen your cords And strengthen your pegs.*" in Isaiah 54:2.
Read 1 Chronicles 4:9-10. (Jabez's name means 'grieving' or 'sorrowful'.)

> The tent referred to in Isaiah 54:2, has a spiritual significance. In the Old Testament it represents a tribe, clan or family.
> (see Psalm 78:67 or Isaiah 16:5)

What did he pray for?

How did God answer?

How did the sons of Joseph obtain what they needed in Joshua 17:14-18?

What does 1 Corinthians 2:9 say?

What principle is being taught in these passages?

4. Isaiah 54:4 says "*…you will forget the shame of your youth*". How does Jeremiah 31:16-19 explain the shame they felt?

"*…and the reproach of your widowhood you will remember no more*". What does Lamentations 1:1 say about this?

5. Isaiah 54:5-6 says "*…your husband is your Maker…the Lord has called you, like a wife forsaken…*" The best way to understand this picture is to read the story in Hosea. The following verses cover the main points. What do they say?

About Hosea's wife and children:
   Hosea 1:2-3,6,8-9

   Hosea 3:1-3

About Israel, the Lord's wife:
   Hosea 1:10

   Hosea 2:2-4, 14-17

   Hosea 2:19-20,23

   Hosea 3:5

6. How has Jesus fulfilled these prophecies according to Ephesians 5:25-27?

> ## Prove yourselves doers of the word... James 1:22

7. Isaiah 54:2 speaks of enlarging "*the place of your tent*". The Lord's tent includes all those who are saved, or the body of Christ. We can enlarge our tents when we participate in gathering people into His tent. Jesus said, "*The harvest is plentiful, but the workers are few. Therefore beseech the Lord of the harvest to send out workers into His harvest.*" (Matthew 9:37-38). What can we learn from the following examples?

How did Abraham enlarge his tent? There are two key factors here.

Genesis 15:5-6

Genesis 22:15-18

What was Jesus' heart for enlarging the kingdom? Read Luke 14:23.

What was Peter's example? Read Acts 2:38-41.

What was Paul's approach? Read 2 Corinthians 5:20.

Paul continually asked for prayer as he preached the gospel everywhere. This is a vital part of enlarging your tent. What did Paul ask for prayer for in 2 Thessalonians 3:1?

In summary, how can <u>you</u> "*Enlarge the place of your tent*"?

8. The context of our passage refers to Israel who was forsaken because of her sins, but it also reveals God's heart for godly wives who are "*...forsaken and grieved in spirit*". What do these scriptures say about it?

Psalm 34:4-8

Isaiah 62:4

9. Are you like a "*...wife forsaken and grieved in spirit*"? How does the Lord long to comfort you?

> ## In everything, by prayer and petition... Philippians 4:6

Ask the Lord to keep you pure and spotless, to make you faithful and to keep you from stumbling. Ask Him to enlarge your tents and grant you spiritual children for His sake.

Come here, I will show you the bride, the wife of the Lamb.
And he carried me away in the Spirit to a great and high mountain, and showed me
the holy city, Jerusalem, coming down out of heaven from God, having the glory of God...
Revelation 21:9b-11a

~ ~ ~ ~ **DAY 2** ~ ~ ~ ~
Precious Stones

➤ <u>Draw near to God and He will draw near to you... James 4:8</u>

Whoever possessed precious stones gave them to the treasury of the house of the LORD...
1 Chronicles 29:8

Jesus said that wherever our treasure was, there our heart would be also. Invest your heart in the Lord. Give to Him the things which are most precious to you. Ask Him to care for all those you love and to help you rest in trusting Him.

Practice your memory verse:

"For ____ thoughts are ____ your _____,
neither are ____ ways my ways," _____ the LORD.
"As the heavens are _____ than the earth, so are my _____
higher than your ways and my thoughts _____ your _____."
Isaiah 55:8-9

➤ <u>Study to show yourself approved... 2 Timothy 2:15</u>

Today, as we continue studying Isaiah 54, the Lord explains the grace He offers His people, describing how He will never be angry with them again and how He will adorn them and lavish them with compassion.

10. Read Isaiah 54:7-12. Answer the following questions.

How did the Lord deal with His people because of their sin in verse 7a?

How will He regather them (v.7b)?

How does the Lord, their Redeemer, explain this 'before and after' treatment again in verse 8?

What did the Lord promise Noah in verse 9a?

How does the reassure them now in verse 9b?

Use verse 10a to fill in the following chart.

may be removed or shaken	will not be removed or shaken

Why will He do this (v.10b)?

How does the Lord describe them in verse 11a?

How does He say He will adorn their stones, foundations, battlements, gates and wall (v.11b-12)?

11. *"For a brief moment I forsook you... In an outburst of anger I hid My face from you for a moment..."* Isaiah 54:7-8 says. Who bore the brunt of this and how, according to Mark 15:33-34?

12. How does Deuteronomy 30:1-6 show that the Lord knew from the beginning that they would be exiled and regathered as described in Isaiah 54:7?

13. What did the Lord mean when He said "For this is like the days of Noah to Me..." in Isaiah 54:9 and why do you think He chose that example? See Genesis 8:21, 9:11-16.

14. Isaiah 54:10 promises that even if the earth shakes, "*My lovingkindness will not be removed from you and My covenant of peace will not be shaken*". Contrast this promise with the fear of those who reject the Lord in Revelation 6:12-17.

15. It's clear that the Lord's heart is moved by His people's sufferings. He mentions His compassion 3 times (in verses 7, 8, 10), and calls her "...*O afflicted one, storm-tossed and not comforted*" in Isaiah 54:11. How do the following scriptures help you understand why He allowed their affliction?

Psalm 119:67, 71

Lamentations 3:31-33

Hosea 6:1

16. "*I will set your stones in antimony, and your foundations I will lay in sapphires. Moreover, I will make your battlements of rubies, and your gates of crystal, and your entire wall of precious stones.*" Isaiah 54:11b-12 says. How is this described in the following references?

Exodus 24:10

Revelation 21:10-11, 18-21

> Prove yourselves doers of the word... James 1:22

17. Are you "*afflicted... storm-tossed and not comforted*"? (Isaiah 54:11) What does the Lord want you to know?

What hope does 2 Corinthians 4:17-18 give you?

18. What does the "*entire wall of precious stones*" (Isaiah 54:12) represent?

Ephesians 2:20-22

1 Peter 2:5

What does this mean to you personally?

> In everything, by prayer and petition... Philippians 4:6

Pray for those who are afflicted and storm-tossed. Ask the Lord to establish them on the foundation of Christ. Pray that they would only turn to Him and cling to Him.

And the LORD their God will save them in that day as the flock of His people;
For they are as the stones of a crown, sparkling in His land.
Zechariah 9:16

DAY 3
The Vindication of the Lord

> ➤ <u>Draw near to God and He will draw near to you... James 4:8</u>

For the LORD will vindicate His people, and will have compassion on His servants...
Deuteronomy 32:36

Are you troubled by accusations? Is your conscience burdened by sins? In His compassion the Lord vindicates you. He clears all charges against you and declares you right with Him. He won't tolerate any attack or accusation against you. Let Him cleanse you and protect you. Turn to Him now.

Practice your memory verse:

"For _____ thoughts _____ not _____ thoughts, _____ are _____ ways _____ ways," _____ the _____. "As _____ heavens _____ higher _____ the _____, so _____ my _____ higher _____ your _____ and _____ thoughts _____ your _____."

Isaiah _____:8-__

> ➤ <u>Study to show yourself approved... 2 Timothy 2:15</u>

In the beginning of Isaiah 54, we saw the Lord describing the harvest that would come from the Messiah's sacrifice and the way He would adorn and care for them as a living city. These precious stones are the sons of the kingdom. Today the chapter wraps up with a description of the protection from the enemy they will receive.

19. Read Isaiah 54:13-17. Answer the following questions.

> *'Shalom',*
> *the Hebrew*
> *word for peace*
> *(well-being, NAS)*
> *means 'wholeness,*
> *or completeness'.*

Who will teach their sons (children) and what will be the outcome (v.13)?

How will they be established and why will they not fear (v.14)?

How does the Lord reassure them about possible assailants (v.15)?

What does the Lord affirm He has created in verse 16?

What is His point? See Exodus 9:16.

What will God not allow in verse 17a?

What heritage does He promise them in verse 17b?

20. *"All your sons will be taught of the Lord"* (Isaiah 54:13a). How has the Lord done this?
Jeremiah 31:33-34

Luke 24:45

John 6:44-45

1 Thessalonians 4:9

1 John 2:27

21. *"And the well-being (peace) of your sons will be great"* (Isaiah 54:13b). What do these scriptures teach you about that?

Psalm 119:165

John 14:27

22. *"You will be far from oppression"* (Isaiah 54:14). How do these verses explain this?

Job 1:6-10

Zechariah 2:4-5

23. The Lord doesn't promise them that they will never be attacked. But He does promise complete vindication. What do you learn about this from the following verses?

Isaiah 54:15-17   scriptures

If anyone fiercely assails you it will not be from Me.	Romans 8:31 1 Corinthians 4:3-4
Whoever assails you will fall because of you.	Revelation 12:10
… I have created the destroyer to ruin.	Proverbs 16:4
No weapon that is formed against you will prosper;	Matthew 16:18
And every tongue that accuses you in judgment you will condemn.	Deuteronomy 19:16-19 Zechariah 3:1-2
This is the heritage of the servants of the LORD,	Psalm 16:5-6
"And their vindication is from Me," declares the LORD.	Isaiah 50:8-9

> Prove yourselves doers of the word … James 1:22

24. Read Isaiah 54:13 again. How can you claim this verse for your children?

25. *"No weapon that is formed against you will prosper…"* (Isaiah 54:17). Isn't it encouraging the way the Lord defends us? How do the following scriptures show you the powerful protection and deliverance He gives us from Satan, our great enemy?

Ephesians 6:11-12

James 4:7

1 Peter 5:8-9

Revelation 12:10b-11

26. Isaiah 54:17 also speaks of accusing tongues. Are you under condemnation? The Lord wants to lift you up and fill you with joy. He doesn't condemn you, therefore no one else can!! How can you apply these scriptures?

Exodus 14:14

Colossians 2:16-19

➢ In everything, by prayer and petition... Philippians 4:6

Thank the Lord for His protection from the enemy. Thank Him that no weapon formed against you will prosper. Thank Him that this is our heritage that He has provided. Lift up to Him any circumstance in which you are being treated unjustly. Ask Him to vindicate you.

> *Vindicate me, O Lord, for I have walked in my integrity,*
> *And I have trusted in the Lord without wavering.*
> *Psalm 26:1*

~ ~ ~ ~ **DAY 4** ~ ~ ~ ~
Come and Live!

➢ Draw near to God and He will draw near to you... James 4:8

> *I came that they may have life, and have it abundantly.*
> *John 10:10b*

How generous is our God! All that makes life wonderful comes from Him and He has given it so freely. We don't have to fear condemnation or death. We are not left as orphans in the world, but the Holy Spirit is a comforting companion to us in everything. We have hope and love poured out in our hearts, and unity with other believers. We have a home in heaven to look forward to. How great is our God!

Consider all that He has done to make your life rich and let it fill your heart with thanksgiving.

Practice your memory verse:

"____ my _____ are ____ your _____,
neither ____ your ____ my ____," declares ____ LORD.
"____ the _____ are ____ than ____ earth, ____ are ____ ways
_____ than ____ ways ____ my _____ than _____ thoughts."
_____ 55: __ -9

➢ Study to show yourself approved... 2 Timothy 2:15

Isaiah 55 is the message of the gospel preached before it was revealed through Jesus! It begins with an invitation to take freely of the abundant gift of life God offers without paying anything. All that's required is that you forsake your wicked thoughts and turn to the Holy One of Israel. He will abundantly pardon.

27. Read Isaiah 55:1-7. Answer the following questions.

What is the message the Lord preaches in verse 1?

How does God reason with His people in verse 2?

How does the Lord appeal to them in verse 3a?

What does He promise to do for them (v.3b)?

What has the Lord done for David in verse 4?

Note – Here the name of David is a Messianic title because the son of David would inherit the throne and reign forever. See 2 Samuel 7:12-13 and Ezekiel 37:24.

What will His people do for the Lord once they accept the everlasting covenant (v.5a)?

Why will this happen (v.5b)?

Note – When Jesus is glorified through His servants' preaching, nations will run to Him. See Psalm 18:43 and Zechariah 2:11, 8:20-23.

What message will His people preach in verse 6?

What should the wicked do (v.7a)?

How will the Lord receive him according to verse 7b?

28. In the following scriptures, who is speaking and what does He say?
Revelation 21:6

Revelation 22:17

God's people were hungry. How does John 6:48-51,58 define the bread that they needed?

When Isaiah 55:2 says "*Why do you spend money for what is not bread, and your wages for what does not satisfy?*", it wasn't speaking literally of bread. How do the following scriptures help you understand what were they "spending their wages" on, in a spiritual sense?

Matthew 15:9

Matthew 16:11-12

Romans 9:31-32

Romans 10:2-3

Now what do you think the Lord meant when He said "*Why do you spend money for what is not bread?*"

29. What are "*the faithful mercies shown to David*" (Isaiah 55:3) according to these scriptures?
2 Samuel 7:12-13

Ezekiel 37:24-26

30. How did the Lord fulfill His promises to David in Isaiah 55:4?

leader - Matthew 2:6	witness - Revelation 1:5a	commander - Revelation 19:11-14

Page 291

31. "*Let the wicked forsake his way and the unrighteous man his thoughts*" it says in Isaiah 55:7. What is the condition of the thoughts of our hearts without God's grace?

Genesis 6:5

Psalm 10:4

Matthew 15:18-19

How does this affect our relationship with God? Read Psalm 66:18.

32. Isaiah 55:7 shows that there are two steps the wicked need to follow. Forsaking our sin is the first step, "*Let the wicked forsake his way*" and the second is "*return to the Lord*". Read the following scriptures

Deuteronomy 30:2

Joel 2:12-13

> Prove yourselves doers of the word ... James 1:22

33. The message is so clear. Have you answered the Lord's call to you? Have you sought Him "*while He is near*"? Have you turned from wicked thoughts? Look up these scriptures and glean the truth you need from them today.

2 Chronicles 16:9a

Psalm 27:8

Jeremiah 29:12-13

34. Three times in Isaiah 55:2-3, the Lord appeals to His people saying "*Listen carefully to Me... Incline your ear to Me... Listen that you may live..*" Are you coming to the Lord listening to Him? He has so much abundance to give.

> In everything, by prayer and petition ... Philippians 4:6

Ask the Lord to feed you from His abundance and satisfy all the desires of your heart. Pray that He would make you as generous towards others with His truth and His lovingkindness as He has been to you.

*He who did not spare His own Son, but delivered Him over for us all,
how will He not also with Him freely give us all things?
Romans 8:32*

~ ~ ~ ~ **DAY 5** ~ ~ ~ ~
Knowing His Thoughts

> Draw near to God and He will draw near to you... James 4:8

*Oh, the depth of the riches both of the wisdom and knowledge of God!
How unsearchable are His judgments and unfathomable His ways!
Romans 11:33*

Have you assumed you know what the Lord is thinking? Or have you neglected to pursue Him when you needed to know His thoughts on some matter? We can err in judgment on either side, thinking too small of Him, presuming we know, or thinking He is too great and distant for us to connect with Him.

The Bible is full of His thoughts and His Holy Spirit is ready and willing to reveal them to us. Lay down your own assumptions and ask the Lord to reveal new understanding to you today. He is so much more wonderful than we realize!

Write down your memory verse:

➤ <u>Study to show yourself approved... 2 Timothy 2:15</u>

Yesterday we read the Lord's appeal to the wicked man to turn from his thoughts. Today the second half of Isaiah 55 continues this discussion. The Lord compares His thoughts to the people's. They estimate His thoughts to be similar to their own. *"You thought that I was just like you..."* (Psalm 50:21). We also try to understand and grasp the Lord with our own finite mind. This is foolish.

35. Read Isaiah 55:8-13. Answer the following questions.

Compare our thoughts and ways to the Lord's in verses 8-9.

What analogy does the Lord present in Isaiah 55:10?

What does He compare the rain and snow to in verse 11a?

What does it accomplish (v.11b)?

How does Isaiah 55:12 describe the joy that lies ahead for the redeemed?

What does Isaiah 55:13 promise and what do you think it means?

36. The Lord says *"My thoughts are not your thoughts"* in Isaiah 55:8. What do the following scriptures say about the thoughts of the Lord?

Psalm 40:5

Psalm 92:5

Psalm 139:17

1 Corinthians 2:11

Isaiah 55:9 makes it clear that God's thoughts are higher than ours. What does the Lord do for us so that we can know His thoughts? See 1 Corinthians 2:12-16.

37. The Lord promises *"My word which goes forth from My mouth will not return to Me empty, without accomplishing what I desire"* in Isaiah 55:11. How does Isaiah 46:10 affirm this promise?

John 1 tells us that Jesus is the Word of God. With this in mind, read John 4:34. How does Jesus show that He fulfills this prophecy in Isaiah about the word from God's mouth?

38. "*For you will go out with joy*" Isaiah 55:12 says. How do these verses describe this?

    1 Chronicles 16:32-33

    Isaiah 35:10

> ## Prove yourselves doers of the word … James 1:22

39. Isaiah 55:8 says that the Lord's thoughts are higher than our thoughts, but He has granted us His Holy Spirit so that we can be changed. Do you allow the Holy Spirit to transform your mind? What evidence do you see that you have the mind of Christ?

40. John 16:22 says "*Therefore you too have grief now; but I will see you again, and your heart will rejoice, and no one will take your joy away from you.*" Do you have grief now? Are you longing for the fulfillment of the joy the Lord promises in Isaiah 55:12 ("*You shall go out with joy*")? How does this verse comfort you?

> ## In everything, by prayer and petition … Philippians 4:6

Ask the Lord to show you any presumptuous thoughts you have about Him. Ask Him to give you a hunger for His word and to open your understanding. Pray that He would season your conversation richly with His word so that you would be sowing and watering with your speech.

…but let him who boasts boast of this, that he understands and knows Me.
Jeremiah 9:24a

How precious also are Your thoughts to me, O God! How vast is the sum of them!
Psalm 139:17

~ ~ ~ ~ ~ ~   Prayer Requests   ~ ~ ~ ~ ~ ~

Prepare the Way For My People

Isaiah chapters 56 – 57

Lesson 25

DAY 1 House of Prayer

> ➤ Draw near to God and He will draw near to you... James 4:8

The Lord has a place for you in His house of prayer. The world may regard you as an outcast or you may feel as if you'll never fit in, but the Lord welcomes you. He wants you. Remember what He has done to purchase you back from the enemy. Ask Him to make you spotless and beautiful – the way He sees you in Jesus. Ask Him to open your heart and mind to what He wants to say to you today.

Even those I will bring to My holy mountain and make them joyful in My house of prayer.
Isaiah 56:7a

MEMORY VERSE Isaiah 57:15b

I live in a high and holy place, but also

with him who is contrite and lowly in spirit,

to revive the spirit of the lowly and to revive the heart of the contrite.

> ➤ Study to show yourself approved... 2 Timothy 2:15

Isaiah chapter 56 begins with an encouragement from the Lord to all foreigners and eunuchs who love the Lord and honor His covenant. Traditionally, these people were excluded from the covenant of the Lord in Moses' Law unless they converted to Judaism and even then, they were limited in how close they could come to the Lord. The Lord is making very plain here that He has a covenant for them that makes their offerings acceptable on His altar. He wants them to hope in His salvation: Jesus.

1. Read Isaiah 56:1-7. Answer the following questions.

What does the Lord recommend and why in verse 1?

Who does He say is blessed in verse 2 and what does he do?

What two kinds of people does He mention in verse 3 and what does He tell them not to say?

What behavior does He look for in eunuchs that seek Him (v.4)?

What will He give them in verse 5?

What is the desire of the foreigners (v.6a)?

What does He require of them (v.6b)?

> The Jews developed an attitude against the Gentiles and eunuchs because they saw them as outcasts and inferior, and saw themselves as privileged by God.

Page 295

What does He promise them in verse 7?

2. Verse 1 advises us to "*Preserve justice and do righteousness, for My salvation is about to come.*" What insight do the following verses give you into this message?

    Matthew 4:17

    Romans 13:11-14

3. The Lord chose two specific things that are important to him in Isaiah 56:2. What do the following scriptures teach you about them?

    "*…who keeps from profaning the sabbath…*"

        Exodus 31:13-16

    "*…and keeps his hand from doing any evil.*"

        Romans 12:9

        1 Thessalonians 5:22

4. The Lord is making clear that eunuchs who choose what pleases Him (Isaiah 56:4-5) have a place in His kingdom. What does Moses' Law say about eunuchs according to Deuteronomy 23:1-3?

5. Jesus taught about eunuchs in Matthew 19:10-12 when the disciples were questioning whether it was better not to marry at all. What did He say?

6. The Bible has two examples of righteous, God-fearing eunuchs, both of them Ethiopians. Make a brief note of what they did that pleased God.

    Jeremiah 38:7-13

    Acts 8:27-39

7. The Lord also says that foreigners who join themselves to Him are acceptable to Him (Isaiah 56:6-7). What did Moses' Law say about them in Numbers 18:4,7?

What do you learn about the standing of "*foreigners*" in the new covenant from these verses?

    Galatians 3:27-29

    1 Peter 2:10

8. Cornelius is a good example of a God-fearing Gentile. Read Acts 10:1-4 and describe him.

9. The Lord saw foreigners and eunuchs who were seeking Him and honoring Him more than His own people. What does Romans 9:30-32 say about this?

10. Isaiah 56:7 says "*My house will be called a house of prayer for all the peoples*". Jesus quotes this verse in Mark 11:15-17. The outer court of the temple was the only place that the "nations" or Gentiles could enter. They weren't allowed to enter into the inner courts. This is the place where the money changers and merchants set up their tables – as a '*service*' to those who had to change money to pay temple taxes and to buy an animal for sacrifice.
Why do you think Jesus was upset about this?

11. Isaiah 56:2,4,6 speaks of keeping the sabbath. This was an important part of Moses' law. What did Jesus say about keeping the law in Matthew 5:17-20?

What do you think God is trying to say? Are we as foreigners supposed to keep the Law or not?

12. Let's see what the word teaches about the Law. What does God really want from us?
Matthew 7:12

Matthew 22:37-40

Matthew 23:23

Galatians 5:14

Galatians 6:2

13. The Bible teaches us plainly that the sabbath was merely a shadow of the reality that we receive in Jesus. Keeping the sabbath and holding fast the covenant (Isaiah 56:4,6) are references to faith in Christ. How do the following scriptures confirm that?
Mark 2:23-28

Colossians 2:16-17

Hebrews 4:3, 9-11

Therefore the Law has become our tutor to lead us to Christ, so that we may be justified by faith.
But now that faith has come, we are no longer under a tutor.
Galatians 3:24-25

➢ Prove yourselves doers of the word... James 1:22

14. Is it your heart's desire to "*choose what pleases Me and hold fast My covenant*" (v.4b)? Do you pursue the Lord from a heart of love or do you prefer rules that you can measure your performance with? Have you stumbled over trying to please God by works rather than faith?

15. Isaiah 56:7 says "*I will bring them to My holy mountain and make them joyful in My house of prayer.*" Do you spend time in the Lord's holy presence? Do you have joy in prayer?

16. How is God making us into a "house of prayer"? Read 1 Peter 2:5.

➢ In everything, by prayer and petition... Philippians 4:6

Ask the Lord to help you live in His house of prayer. Pray for a heart that lives by faith and not by superficial rules. Ask the Lord to reach out to those who feel unworthy of Him and bring them into His house of prayer.

For My house will be called a house of prayer for all the peoples.
Isaiah 56:7c

DAY 2
Shepherds Who Have No Understanding

➢ <u>Draw near to God and He will draw near to you... James 4:8</u>

The Spirit of the LORD will rest on Him, the spirit of wisdom and understanding...
Isaiah 11:2a

God's ways are not our ways... We NEED His Spirit to be able to understand even the smallest spiritual truth! Ask Him to fill you with the Holy Spirit and to breathe LIFE into the words that you study today.

Practice your memory verse:

I _____ in a high and _____ place, but also with him who is _____ and lowly in spirit, to _____ the spirit of the _____ and to revive the _____ of the contrite.
Isaiah 57:___

➢ <u>Study to show yourself approved... 2 Timothy 2:15</u>

As we finish studying Isaiah 56 today, the Lord continues with the theme of gathering outcasts to Himself. The truth is that the people of Israel must consider themselves on the same footing as foreigners and eunuchs (discussed yesterday in verses 1-7). They have been brought low and their "*watchmen*", their religious leaders, have let them down.

17. Read Isaiah 56:8-12. Answer the following questions.

Who does the Lord speak of gathering in verse 8?

Who does He call to eat (v.9)?

How does the Lord describe the watchmen in verses 10-11?

What do they say in verse 12?

*Note – See Isaiah 28:1-8 to review the drunkards of Ephraim.

18. Isaiah 56:8 says "*...yet others I will gather to them...*". How does Jesus explain this in John 10:16? Who was He referring to?

19. Isaiah 56:9 says "*All you beasts of the field, all you fields in the forest, come to eat.*" In the context of the passage, verses 7-8, this probably refers to the nations. But it could also be interpreted in other ways. Fill in the following chart about what it could mean.

scripture	what the beasts signify
Jeremiah 34:20	
Acts 10:9-15,35	
Acts 20:29	

20. We have studied Israel's watchmen or religious leaders before (Isaiah 28). Let's review what we've learned using the description given in Isaiah 56:10-11. Make a note of how they fulfilled this description from the scriptures listed.

watchmen are blind	Matthew 15:14	
all of them know nothing	Jeremiah 14:13-14	
mute dogs unable to bark	Ezekiel 33:6	
dreamers lying down who love to slumber	Isaiah 29:10	
greedy dogs	Jeremiah 6:13	
not satisfied	Ecclesiastes 5:10	
shepherds who have no understanding	John 8:43-44	
turned to their own way	Jeremiah 23:13	
unjust gain	Micah 3:11	

21. Read Ezekiel 33:1-3 and write down what the job of these watchmen was supposed to be. Compare it to the chart above. How did these leaders in Isaiah 56:10-11 fall short of this?

22. Twice in our passage, the Lord calls these watchmen "*dogs*". He doesn't use this term lightly. What do you learn about this label from the following verses?

Psalm 22:16

Proverbs 26:11

Matthew 7:6

Philippians 3:2

Revelation 22:15

23. What does Ezekiel 34:2-6 say about these "*shepherds who have no understanding*" (Isaiah 56:11)?

24. Read Matthew 7:15-20 and Acts 20:28-31. What dangers does the flock face when the shepherds fail?

➢ <u>Prove yourselves doers of the word . . . James 1:22</u>

25. Who are you a shepherd or watchman for?

26. How can you be a better watchman? How can you avoid the mistakes Israel's leaders made? How can you shelter the flock from wolves? Read Matthew 7:15 and Acts 20:29.

27. Today we covered some of the sins of Israel's watchmen. We need to be aware of our weaknesses so that we won't fall into any of the same sins. Is the Holy Spirit convicting you of any specific weakness here? Do you have any of those same characteristics? Which quality would God like to weed out of your life?

➢ <u>In everything, by prayer and petition . . . Philippians 4:6</u>

Ask the Lord to make you a faithful watchman, a godly shepherd. Ask Him to fill you with understanding. Pray for your spiritual leaders.

> *On your walls, O Jerusalem, I have appointed watchmen;*
> *All day and all night they will never keep silent.*
> *You who remind the LORD, take no rest for yourselves.*
> *Isaiah 62:6*

~ ~ ~ ~   **DAY 3**   ~ ~ ~ ~

The Idolaters of Judah

➢ <u>Draw near to God and He will draw near to you . . . James 4:8</u>

Consider how great the Lord's compassion and kindness are that He continues to reach out to us even though He has seen us at our worst! Open your heart today to what He has to say to you remembering how He treasures you and longs to be your first love. He desires an intimate relationship with you. Make up your mind to respond to His loving hand as He draws you.

> *The LORD appeared to him from afar, saying,*
> *"I have loved you with an everlasting love;*
> *Therefore I have drawn you with lovingkindness.*
> *Jeremiah 31:3*

Practice your memory verse:

I _____ in _____ high _____ holy _____, but _____
with _____ who _____ contrite _____ lowly _____ spirit, _____ revive _____
spirit _____ the _____ and _____ revive _____ heart _____ the _____.
Isaiah ___:___

➢ <u>Study to show yourself approved . . . 2 Timothy 2:15</u>

Isaiah chapter 57 begins with a reminder about what death means for the righteous. It is not to be feared. Perhaps Isaiah was referring to the death of King Hezekiah. It then goes into a description of terrible, blatant idolatry. It is thought that this takes place during the reign of King Manasseh who led the people into great evil, unlike any king before him.

The people of Israel were to be married unto God. God likened their relationship with Him to a love between a husband and wife. It should have been an exclusive, devoted relationship, but they were worshiping other gods.

28. Read Isaiah 57:1-7. Answer the following questions.

What happens to the righteous in verse 1a and what impact does it have on those left?

Where is he taken from and what is he given (v.1b-2)?

What does God call the people in verse 3 and what do you think He means?

How have they been acting according to verse 4a?

What are they children of and how does this explain their behavior (v.4b)?

Use the following diagram to lay out what they have done and where it was done, verses 5-7.

their deeds	where they were done

What does the Lord ask them in the last line of verse 6 and what do you think He means?

29. Read II Kings 21:1-9 and make a note of some of the sins of Manasseh.

30. Isaiah 57:1 says "*The righteous man perishes and no man takes it to heart.*" People hardly seem to notice. Who does notice when a godly person dies? Read Psalm 116:15.

31. Isaiah 57:4 asks "*Against whom do you open wide your mouth and stick out your tongue?*"
How is this prophecy echoed in Psalm 22:7-8,13?

When was this fulfilled according to Matthew 27:39-43?

32. In Isaiah 57:5 it says "*...who slaughter the children in the ravines.*" We would say this is barbarian and inhumane. What kind of deception and evil could lead a person to sink to such a deed? Yet there have been an estimated 45 million abortions in the United States since 1973. How does God see this sin? Use the following scriptures to answer.

Exodus 20:13

Leviticus 18:21

Leviticus 20:2-5

Ezekiel 16:20

33. If you have been a part of a decision leading to abortion, you can be sure that the child is safe with the Lord in heaven. But the Lord also wants to heal you. What comfort do the following scriptures give?

1 John 1:9

Revelation 21:4

➢ Prove yourselves doers of the word ... James 1:22

34. Isaiah 57:1b-2a says "...*The righteous man is taken away from evil, he enters into peace...*" Sometimes the wickedness of the world is so grieving, but the Lord wants to give us peace in the midst of it. For a short time we have trials but the day will come when the Lord will take us away from evil. How can you have peace now? How can you rest in knowing the Lord will soon come for you?

➢ In everything, by prayer and petition ... Philippians 4:6

The Lord has given us righteousness and we know that we have a home with Him when we die. But in this life, we want to honor Him in all our ways. Ask the Lord to make you loyal to Him as your first love. Pray for deeds that are loving, from the heart.

But I have this against you, that you have left your first love.
Therefore remember from where you have fallen, and repent and do the deeds you did at first...
Revelation 2:4-5a

~ ~ ~ ~ ## DAY 4 ~ ~ ~ ~
Worrying and Lying

➢ Draw near to God and He will draw near to you ... James 4:8

But the Lord answered and said to her, "Martha, Martha,
you are worried and bothered about so many things; but only one thing is necessary,
for Mary has chosen the good part, which shall not be taken away from her."
Luke 10:41-42

Are you worried? Are you finding it hard to come and sit at Jesus' feet? Only you can distance yourself from the joy of His presence, His wisdom and comfort. Come to Him. The time you spend with Him is precious. It will ease your heart and satisfy your soul. Rest and listen.

Practice your memory verse:

" ____ live __ a _____ and _____ place, ____ also
_____ him ____ is _____ and _____ in _____ , to _____ the
_____ of ____ lowly ____ to _____ the _____ of ____ contrite.
_____ 57: 15b

➢ Study to show yourself approved ... 2 Timothy 2:15

Isaiah chapter 57 continues describing the wickedness of God's people. It wasn't enough for them to pursue the idols of the nations around them, they actually sent envoys to distant lands to make unholy alliances with them and their gods. The Lord makes it clear He considers this adultery.

35. Read Isaiah 57:8-13. Answer the following questions.

What have God's people set up and where in verse 8a?

What else have they done in verse 8b?

Who do you think they have "*made an agreement*" with (in verse8)?

What lengths did they go to, to pursue their sins (v.9)?

How does verse 10 show their perseverance?
What emotions did they feel in verse 11a and what did they do because of it?

Why did they not fear the Lord (v.11b)?

What kind of a witness will the Lord be for them and what good will it do them (v.12)?

Who must they turn to and what good will it do them (v.13a)?

What will be given to those who take refuge in the Lord (v.13b)?

36. "*…far removed from Me, you have uncovered yourself…*" Isaiah 57:8 says. Read the following scriptures about the adulteress woman to see what they looked like to the Lord. Make a note of what you learn.
Proverbs 2:16-19

Proverbs 7:18-23

In Isaiah 57:8 it also says "*…you have made an agreement for yourself with them, you have loved their bed…*" What examples of this does the Lord give in Ezekiel 16:25-29?

37. "*Of whom were you worried and fearful?*" Isaiah 57:11 asks. How do these verses show the danger of fearing others besides the Lord?
  Proverbs 29:25

  Matthew 10:28

  Matthew 26:69-70

  Galatians 2:11-13

"*when you lied…*" Isaiah 57:11 says. What does the word teach about lying?
  Proverbs 12:22

  Proverbs 26:28

  John 8:44

"*… and did not remember Me nor give Me a thought…*" Isaiah 57:11 continues. What do you learn about this from Jeremiah 2:32?

38. Isaiah 57:11 says *"Was I not silent even for a long time so you do not fear Me?"* People often mistake God's longsuffering for indifference. Read the following scriptures and make a note of what you learn.

   Isaiah 30:18

   Habakkuk 2:3

   Romans 9:22-23

   Hebrews 10:37

   2 Peter 3:9

➤ Prove yourselves doers of the word ... James 1:22

39. Consider Isaiah 57:11. When do you become worried or fearful? In what circumstances do you tend to forget the Lord?

How does Ephesians 4:15 encourage us to speak the truth and not lie?

➤ In everything, by prayer and petition ... Philippians 4:6

Ask the Lord to increase your love for the truth and your trust in Him. Ask Him to keep lies far from you. Pray that you would always remember Him and turn to Him first.

*Be anxious for nothing, but in everything by prayer and supplication
with thanksgiving let your requests be made known to God.
Philippians 4:6*

~ ~ ~ ~   **DAY 5**   ~ ~ ~ ~
A High and Holy Place

➤ Draw near to God and He will draw near to you... James 4:8

*And I, if I am lifted up from the earth, will draw all men to Myself.
John 12:32*

    Let this wonder soften your heart today. Jesus referred to how He would be killed not to ask for sympathy, or to express bitterness – but to reveal the intent of His heart, to draw all men to Himself. This is still the intent of His heart.
    The phrase "lifted up" here means 'to elevate.' Jesus wants to be elevated above all other things and voices pressing into our lives. As we exalt Him in our hearts, it humbles us and drawing close to Him becomes possible.

Praise the Lord He is high and lifted up and yet, He chooses to dwell with the lowly and contrite!

Write down your memory verse:

> ## Study to show yourself approved...2 Timothy 2:15

In Isaiah 57 today the Lord shares His heart for the lost. He will do everything possible to make a way for them. He will humble Himself and dwell with them and He will restrain His anger. He will heal their sinful ways and restore peace to those who mourn over them.

40. Read Isaiah 57:14-21. Answer the following questions.

What does verse 14 say should be done for those who take refuge in the Lord (mentioned in v.13)?

How does the Lord describe Himself in verse 15a?

Where does He dwell and why (v.15b)?

What hope does the Lord offer those He is punishing in verse 16a?

What reason does He give for His restraint (v.16b)?

Why did He strike His people according to verse 17?

What action did the Lord choose to take after seeing their ways (v.18)?

What results will this have (v.19)?

As a contrast to those who benefit from His discipline, how does He describe the wicked (v.20)?

What conclusion does the Lord draw about them in verse 21?

As long as there is life, there is hope. No matter how they have sinned, Jesus' blood is sufficient to cover it and the offer will stand as long as a person lives. However, for those who continually reject the grace of forgiven sin and an invitation to live eternally, there will be no peace. Nothing more can be offered them.

How much severer punishment do you think he will deserve
who has trampled under foot the Son of God, and has regarded as unclean the blood
of the covenant by which he was sanctified, and has insulted the Spirit of grace?
Hebrews 10:29

---

41. *"...prepare the way, remove every obstacle out of the way of My people"* Isaiah 57:14 says. How did the Lord accomplish this according to these verses?

Isaiah 40:3

Mark 1:2-5

42. The *"high and holy place"* (Isaiah 57:15) is natural for *"the high and exalted One"*, but why does God also dwell with *"the contrite and lowly of spirit"*? Read the following definitions.

Contrite: literally "crushed," is only the superlative of "broken"; "a contrite heart" is "a heart broken to pieces." In Holy Scripture, the heart is the seat of all feeling, whether joy or sorrow. A contrite heart is one in which the natural pride and self-sufficiency have been completely humbled by the consciousness of guilt. (from ISBE)

Lowly: humble, poor, afflicted, inferior.

What does this tell you about God's character?

43. What do these scriptures teach us about this character quality?

    Matthew 11:29-30

    Matthew 23:12

    Romans 12:3,16

    Philippians 2:3-4

    I Peter 5:5-6

> ## Prove yourselves doers of the word . . . James 1:22

44. How can you be more like the Lord in the area of humility?

45. Describe what true humility and contrition look like today.

46. God wants to make our lives a highway, an express lane to Him, whereby others can find Jesus. What are the obstacles that need to be removed from your life so you won't hinder others but draw them to God?

> *Enter by the narrow gate; for wide is the gate and broad is the way*
> *that leads to destruction, and there are many who go in by it.*
> *Matthew 7:13*

47. Are you grieved over someone who "*went on turning away, in the way of his heart*" (Isaiah 57:17)? The Lord offers you great hope and comfort in our passage today. What promises from Isaiah 57:18-19 do you need to hold onto?

    How do these verses add to this encouragement?

        Jeremiah 3:22

        Hosea 14:4

> ## In everything, by prayer and petition . . . Philippians 4:6

Ask the Lord to make you genuinely, sincerely humble and to keep you from false humility. Pray for a heart willing to associate with the lowly and the lost. Pray for those have turned away in their hearts and ask Him to heal them. Pray that you would be a drawing influence and not an obstacle. Pray for your life to be a highway to lead others to Christ.

> *Though He was God, He did not demand and cling to His rights as God.*
> *He made himself nothing; He took the humble position of a slave and appeared in human form.*
> *Philippians 2:6-7 (NLT)*

~ ~ ~ ~ ~ ~   Prayer Requests   ~ ~ ~ ~ ~ ~

The Fasting God Desires
Isaiah chapters 58 – 59

Lesson 26

DAY 1   Why The Lord Doesn't Answer

➤ <u>Draw near to God and He will draw near to you... James 4:8</u>

*Blessed are those who hunger and thirst for righteousness,
for they shall be satisfied.
Matthew 5:6*

There is a true hunger which God recognizes, validates and answers. There is also another kind of hunger that James talks about (*James 4:3*) where he says "*You ask and do not receive, because you ask with wrong motives, so that you may spend it on your pleasures.*"

Ask the Lord to answer the hunger within you that comes from a desire to be right with Him. Ask Him to overlook and overcome the desires that are worldly and a stumbling block to you. It is so easy for Him and He is so willing! He waits to help you, not condemn you.

Offer your heart to Him today.

MEMORY VERSE   Isaiah 58:11

And the Lord will continually guide you, and satisfy your desire in scorched places, and give strength to your bones, and you will be like a watered garden, and like a spring of water whose waters do not fail.

➤ <u>Study to show yourself approved... 2 Timothy 2:15</u>

Isaiah 58 begins with God exposing the true motives of His people when they fast. Moses' Law was the standard the Lord set for every aspect of their lives. He never prescribed any fasts although there were solemn days set aside during the year for seeking the Lord and abstaining from all labor. Fasting was a voluntary humbling of oneself that was pleasing to God when the heart was right.

During this time the attendance at the temple had not dwindled. People were still going through the outward forms of religion and rituals. On the surface it looked like people were doing the right thing. But the Lord knew their hearts were far from Him. They still worshipped their own idols and lived after the flesh, holding onto "*a form of godliness, but denying its power*" (2 Timothy 3:5).

1. Read Isaiah 58:1-7. Answer the following questions about the text.

What does the Lord tell Isaiah to do in verse 1?

Note – Isaiah is being faithful as a watchman to warn the people. See Ezekiel 3:17-21.

What have they done, as if they were a righteous nation (v.2)?

What do they ask of God in verse 3a?

What is God's answer in verse 3b?

What is the motive for their fast and what is lacking (v.4)?

How does the Lord describe their fasting (v.5)?

What kind of fasting was He looking for in verses 6-7?

2. It's not very often we see sarcasm in the Lord's words, but verse 2 is certainly sarcastic. "*...as a nation that has done righteousness... they delight in the nearness of God*" It is obvious that they aren't truly near the Lord, so their concept of nearness to God is way off. Look up the following scriptures to review what their worship was like in God's eyes.

Isaiah 1:11-15

Isaiah 29:13

Jeremiah 42:20-21

3. "*Why have we fasted and You do not see?*" (Isaiah 58:3) they ask of God. He isn't cooperating with their church game. How does James 4:3 answer their question to God?

Isaiah 58:3 says "*On the day of your fast you find your desire and <u>drive hard all your workers</u>.*" Why do you think this was offensive to God?

> Any day set aside to seek the Lord was called a sabbath and the Law required that no work be done on that day. Fasting was optional.

4. The first example of fasting in the Bible speaks of the tribes of Israel grieving over the sin of the tribe of Benjamin in Judges 20:26. It was an outward show of the attitude of their hearts.
How does Daniel 9:3 describe fasting?

Daniel's fasting was pleasing to the Lord and his prayers were powerful. How does Joel 2:12-13 explain the kind of fasting the Lord desires?

What advice does Jesus gives us in Matthew 6:16-18 about fasting?

5. "*Behold, you fast for contention and strife and to strike with a wicked fist.*" Isaiah 58:4 says. How do the following verses demonstrate this?

1 Kings 21:9-13

Proverbs 21:27

John 18:28

6. How does Jesus condemn the leaders who were guilty of this kind of false religion? Read Matthew 23:25-28 make a note of what He says about them.

7. Look up the following verses and fill in the chart. Add some if you wish.

Fasting for the purpose of intense, concentrated prayer.

Occasions to Fast	Scriptures	Your Thoughts
Testing or trial	Esther 4:3	
Distress	Nehemiah 1:3-4 Daniel 6:17-18	
for repentance	1 Samuel 7:6	
To humble yourself	Jonah 3:5-6	
Preparation for ministry	Luke 4:1-2	
For direction	Acts 13:2-3	
Commissioning ministers	Acts 14:23	

8. Consider Isaiah 58:6-7. How is this a picture of the ministry of the Messiah? See Isaiah 61:1-3.

What did Jesus teach about this in Matthew 25:35-40?

➤ <u>Prove yourselves doers of the word . . . James 1:22</u>

9. Fasting should be from a pure motive to seek after God and wanting more of God in my life. Not an outward display to try and coerce God into doing your will (Isaiah 58:3a). Have you ever fasted hoping to gain an advantage with God – i.e. 'forcing' God to give me the answer I want because I'm fasting? Explain.

10. Is God asking you to fast right now? If so commit to a time when you will fast, and what you will fast about with the Lord.

How is fasting a part of your walk with God?

➤ <u>In everything, by prayer and petition . . . Philippians 4:6</u>

Pray for a heart that is humbled before God so that when you fast, He will <u>listen</u> and accept your prayer. Ask Him to give you a spiritual hunger for Him so that you would seek Him earnestly every day.

Then you will call upon Me and come and pray to Me, and I will listen to you.
You will seek Me and find Me when you search for Me with all your heart.
Jeremiah 29:12-13

DAY 2
Take Delight in the Lord

➤ <u>Draw near to God and He will draw near to you... James 4:8</u>

"The LORD your God in your midst, The Mighty One, will save;
*He will **rejoice over you** with gladness, He will quiet you with His love,*
*He will **rejoice over you** with singing."* NKJ
Zephaniah 3:17

Can you imagine Him singing over you? Why is it that the Lord rejoices so much over us? Does it seem hard to believe that He takes delight in you? Ask Him to help you trust in Him more and to believe what He says. He is the source of all joy.

Practice your memory verse:

And the Lord will _____ guide you, and _____ your desire in _____ places, and give strength to your _____, and you will be like a _____ garden, and like a _____ of water whose _____ do not fail.

Isaiah 58:11

➤ <u>Study to show yourself approved... 2 Timothy 2:15</u>

The second half of Isaiah 58 focuses on the blessings the Lord will pour out on those who seek Him with true honor, turning away from wickedness. Their repentance would lead to spiritual healing, restoring and rebuilding of their land, and finding delight in the Lord.

11. Read Isaiah 58:8-14. Answer the following questions.

What result would the fasting God describes bring in verses 8-9a?

What does He want them to get rid of (v.9b)?

What more does He desire of them in verse 10a?

What will happen to their darkness if they take His advice (v.10b)?

How will He care for them in verse 11?

Note – See John 4:11-14 to review the symbolism of the water.

What long-term benefits will this have (v.12a)?

What will they be called (v.12b)?

Fill in this chart showing how God calls on them to honor the sabbath using verse 13.

turn away from	choose to

What result will it bring (v.14)?

12. "*Your light will break out like the dawn and your recovery will speedily spring forth*" it says in Isaiah 58:8. This is the Lord's heart for them, what He longs to do for them. What promises do you find in these scriptures?

Proverbs 4:18-19

Jeremiah 33:6

13. "*If you remove the yoke from your midst, the pointing of the finger and speaking wickedness*" it says in Isaiah 58:9. What does Proverbs 6:12-19 teach about this yoke of wickedness?

14. "*If you give yourself to the hungry and satisfy the desire of the afflicted...*" it says in Isaiah 58:8. Using Proverbs 11:24-30, fill in the following chart describing the generous righteous and the wicked.

generous	wicked

15. Isaiah 58:12 says "*Those from among you will rebuild the ancient ruins... and you will be called the repairer of the breach...*" How was this fulfilled in the following verses?

Nehemiah 2:5, 17, 6:1

Daniel 9:2-3, 18-22, 25 *Note – Daniel's role was different but just as important.

16. "*...turn your foot from doing your own pleasure on My holy day and call the sabbath a delight*" Isaiah 58:13. In this verse 'your own' is used four times. Who is at the center here?

The sabbath was meant as a day to rest from their labors and habitual pursuits and to turn their hearts to the Lord. This is what He desired. Physical fasting didn't achieve this. What does Colossians 2:21-23 say about the effectiveness of self-made religion?

God wanted them to stop seeking their own pleasure. Read Galatians 5:13. What did He set us free <u>for</u>?

17. "*Then you will take delight in the Lord...*" Isaiah 58:14 says. Do you notice how the passage teaches that turning from our own ways and honoring the Lord leads to <u>our</u> delight? How can we delight in the Lord?

Psalm 37:4

1 Peter 1:8

How does Psalm 16:3 show you how the Lord feels about those who are set apart for Him?

➢ <u>Prove yourselves doers of the word ... James 1:22</u>

18. In Isaiah 58:11, the Lord promises to continue to guide us and satisfy our desire, and make us a like a watered garden. Where are you feeling dry and arid, needing God to soften you with the water of His Holy Spirit? In your marriage? Your devotional life?

19. How could Isaiah 58:12 about rebuilding "*the ancient ruins*" and "*raising up the age-old foundations*" be applied to our times?

Nehemiah 3:28 says "*…the priests carried out repairs, each in front of his house.*". The repairing of the wall starts at home first. What needs to be repaired in your home? What do you think you should do?

20. Do you delight in the Lord? When it comes to doing your Bible study each week do you approach it as a merely academic process to finish and cross off your list? God wants to be your delight. He longs to be your first passion. If you feel weak in this area and you can't conjure up this emotion, remember God is simply asking for a willing and available heart.

➤ In everything, by prayer and petition... Philippians 4:6

Ask the Lord to help you "*give yourself to the hungry and satisfy the desire of the afflicted*". Pray that He would make you a well-watered garden and a "*repairer of the breach*" for His glory. Ask Him to help you make Him your delight.

For then you will delight in the Almighty and lift up your face to God.
You will pray to Him, and He will hear you…
Job 22:26-27

~ ~ ~ ~ **DAY 3** ~ ~ ~ ~
Separation From God

➤ Draw near to God and He will draw near to you... James 4:8

I regard wickedness in my heart, The Lord will not hear;
But certainly God has heard; He has given heed to the voice of my prayer.
Psalm 66:18-19

We have free access to the presence of God. The only thing that hinders us is our sin. But Jesus has torn down the wall that separated us and His blood cleanses us from all sin. Ask the Lord to cleanse you today of any unrighteousness He sees in your heart. Rest in the assurance He gives you. Nothing can separate you from the love of God.

Practice your memory verse:

And ____ Lord ____ continually _____ you, _____ satisfy _____ desire ___ scorched _____, and _____ strength ___ your _____, and ____ will ___ like ___ watered _____, and _____ a _____ of _____ whose _____ do ____ fail.

_____ 58: ___

➤ Study to show yourself approved... 2 Timothy 2:15

Isaiah 59 is God's explanation to His people of why He isn't listening to their prayers. They wanted to be able to indulge in all kinds of evil and have God's protection and blessings as well. They may have even been tempted to think that their God couldn't help, that He was weak. The Lord sets them straight and exposes what He sees in them.

21. Read Isaiah 59:1-8. Use the following questions to draw out the meaning of the text.
How does verse 1 show that God is able to save His people?

What has hindered His response to them (v.2)?

What do their hands look like (v.3a)?

What are their mouths like (v.3b)?

How does verse 4 describe their lack of integrity?

What parable does the Lord tell of their behavior and what do you think it means (v.5)?

What good will it do them and why (v.6a)?

What are their evil deeds (v.6b-7)?

What are they lacking in verse 8?

22. "*...the Lord's hand is not so short that it cannot save, nor is His ear so dull that it cannot hear*" Isaiah 59:1 says. What do you learn about this from the following verses?
Proverbs 15:29

Jeremiah 32:17

Hebrews 7:25

23. "*...your iniquities have made a separation between you and your God*" Isaiah 59:2 says. Then Isaiah goes on to list their sins. How do the following scriptures add to this description?
2 Kings 21:6, 16

Proverbs 4:14-16

24. "*They hatch adder's eggs...*" (Isaiah 59:5). An adder is a viper, a very poisonous snake. It also refers to a malicious or treacherous person. The eggs they hatch are the evil plans and lies they lay to ensnare others. What do you learn about these kinds of people from the following references?
Psalm 140:1-3

Matthew 3:7-10

25. In Isaiah 59:6 it says "*Their webs will not become clothing, nor will they cover themselves with their works...*" What does Isaiah 64:6 say about how God sees our works that we clothe ourselves with?

Read these verses and write what their condition is and what clothing has been provided for the believer.

Isaiah 61:10

Revelation 3:17

Revelation 19:8

26. "*Their works are works of iniquity...*" (Isaiah 59:6b). What does James 1:13-15 teach you about how these works come into being?

➢ Prove yourselves doers of the word... James 1:22

27. We have seen a distressing description of wicked people in this passage. Do you see these things around you today? Is your heart grieved over those who walk in these ways? What comfort do you find in Psalm 37:7-11?

28. Have you allowed yourself to lay "*adder's eggs*" or "*weave spider's webs*"? Evil deeds begin in the heart. Are you indulging evil thoughts that hinder your prayers and will eventually give birth to wickedness? What should you do?

➢ In everything, by prayer and petition... Philippians 4:6

Give praise to God that He is able to save you! Ask Him to search your heart and cleanse you of evil intentions and sins that have not yet given birth to deeds. Pray that He would cover you with His righteousness and accept your prayers.

Search me, O God, and know my heart; Try me and know my anxious thoughts;
And see if there be any hurtful way in me, and lead me in the everlasting way.
Psalm 139:23-24

~ ~ ~ ~   **DAY 4**   ~ ~ ~ ~
Hoping For Light

➢ Draw near to God and He will draw near to you... James 4:8

This is the message we have heard from Him and announce to you,
that God is Light, and in Him there is no darkness at all.
1 John 1:5

Are you longing for light today? The Lord Himself will answer you. Ask Him to fill you with His light. Offer Him free access to every area of your heart that needs light. His presence banishes the darkness.

Practice your memory verse:

_____ the _____ will _____ guide ____, and _____ your _____ in _____ places, ___give _____ to _____ bones, ____you _____ be _____ a _____ garden, ____like __ spring ___water _____ waters ___ not _____.

Isaiah ____ :11

Page 314

> ## Study to show yourself approved... 2 Timothy 2:15

As Isaiah continues with the description of the state of his people in chapter 59, he talks about the darkness they are living in and the emptiness it has brought them. They moan under their spiritual condition and they live without justice and truth. They cannot save themselves but their hearts will begin to long for the Lord and repentance.

29. Read Isaiah 59:9-15a. Answer the following questions about the text.

In verse 8 we saw God's people were lacking peace. What else are they lacking (v.9a)?

What do they hope for and what do they get (v.9b)?
What effect does this have on them (v.10)?

How do they express their need in verse 11 and what is their need?

Why is it far from them (v.12)?

What are these transgressions according to verse 13?

What result did it bring (v.14)?

What is lacking and who becomes a prey (v.15a)?

30. In Isaiah 59:9 it says "*We hope for light but behold, darkness...*" They want the benefits of light, but they don't want to give up the deeds of darkness. What does 1 Thessalonians 5:2-3 say about this kind of hope?

31. "*We grope along the wall like blind men... we stumble at midday...*" Isaiah 59:10 says. This is one of the consequences of breaking Moses' Law. As it says in Deuteronomy 28:28-29:

The LORD will smite you with madness and with blindness and with bewilderment of heart; and you will grope at noon, as the blind man gropes in darkness, and you will not prosper in your ways; but you shall only be oppressed and robbed continually, with none to save you.

What do you learn about this condition from the following scriptures?

Proverbs 4:19

John 11:9-10

32. Isaiah 59:11 says "*All of us growl like bears and moan sadly like doves...salvation is far from us.*" What does this mean? How do these verses add insight into what this means?

Psalm 32:3

Psalm 119:155

33. "*...our sins testify against us...we know our iniquities*" Isaiah 59:12 says. Their consciences are convicting them. They are aware of their own sin. How do these verses portray this?

Ezra 9:6

Jeremiah 14:7

Page 315

What would it be like living with a nagging conscience?   *Note – This is why they have no peace.*
(Isaiah 59:8)

Read Psalm 32:1-5. In contrast, describe the remedy God has provided for a guilty conscience.

34. Isaiah 59:13 says "*...speaking oppression and revolt, conceiving in and uttering from the heart lying words.*" Matthew 12:34 is a fitting explanation for this behavior. "*You brood of vipers, how can you, being evil, speak what is good? For the mouth speaks out of that which fills the heart.*" What do you learn about this from James 3:8,14-16?

35. In Isaiah 59:15 it says, "*...he who turns aside from evil makes himself a prey.*" This has been true from the beginning. The wicked hate the ones who turn to righteousness. What do you learn about this from these scriptures?
Acts 9:1

Hebrews 11:36-38

1 John 3:11-12

> ## Prove yourselves doers of the word... James 1:22

36. "*...we know our iniquities*" Isaiah 59:12 says. The scripture has a wealth of teaching about the conscience. Summarize the wise counsel given in these scriptures.
Acts 23:1

Romans 2:15, 13:5, 14:22

1 Corinthians 8:12

2 Corinthians 4:2

1 Timothy 1:5

Titus 1:15

Hebrews 9:14, 10:22, 13:18

37. When we don't want to hide or justify our sin, we must come to the light. In the light, the blood of Christ covers our deeds and we are given credit for practicing the truth. If you are struggling with lying or another sinful weakness, keep bringing it to the light. Expose it before the Lord in prayer. What do the following scriptures tell you?
John 3:21

1 John 1:7

38. In Isaiah 59:14 it says "*For truth has stumbled in the streets.*" Do you ever find yourself telling a little white lie? ("*It wouldn't hurt anyone!*") Or what about an exaggeration?

39. Make a commitment to memorize one or both of the following scriptures:

"*Speak the truth in love.*" Ephesians 4:15

"*Even a fool, when he keeps silent, is considered wise.*" Proverbs 17:28

➤ In everything, by prayer and petition... Philippians 4:6

Pray for repentance and revival in your area. Ask the Lord to bring light so that darkness won't overtake them. Pray that you would keep a clean conscience before God. Ask Him to put a guard over your tongue to keep you from speaking lies.

*But you, brethren, are not in darkness, that the day would overtake you like a thief;
for you are all sons of light and sons of day. We are not of night nor of darkness;
So then let us not sleep as others do, but let us be alert and sober.*
1 Thessalonians 5:4-6

~ ~ ~ ~ **DAY 5** ~ ~ ~ ~

The Intercessor

➤ Draw near to God and He will draw near to you... James 4:8

Today you need an intercessor, someone to be an advocate for you, to speak for you before the Almighty God. You have sin that needs to be cleansed and help you need to obtain. God will accept only One person as your representative – Jesus. What a joy to know that we have such a wonderful intercessor!

Take time right now to ask for His willing help and trust in all He has done for you. Ask the Lord to reveal any areas where you aren't trusting in Him and are relying on yourself or some other approach to God, besides Jesus.

*For there is one God, and one mediator also
between God and men, the man Christ Jesus,*
1 Timothy 2:5

Write down your memory verse:

➤ Study to show yourself approved... 2 Timothy 2:15

Isaiah chapter 59 ends with a description of the beautiful response the Lord makes to the pitiful spiritual condition of His people. They can't save themselves, so He accomplishes salvation for them.

40. Read Isaiah 59:15b-21. Answer the following questions.

What displeased the Lord in verse 15b?

What did He see in verse 16a and how did it affect Him?

What did He do about it in verse 16b?

How did He prepare His "*own arm*" in verse 17?

What will He do to restore justice in verse 18?

Page 317

What benefit will it bring in verse 19?

What promise does He give in verse 20?

What covenant does the Lord make with those He redeems in verse 21?

41. In Isaiah 59:16 it says, "*And He saw that there was no man.*" Read Romans 3:10-12 and write down how it sheds light on this passage.

42. It continues in Isaiah 59:16: "*And was astonished that there was no one to intercede.*" To intercede is to plead on another's behalf, or to act as a mediator. Why do you think it says the Lord was astonished?

And He wondered at their unbelief... Mark 6:6

43. An intercessor is like a lawyer who pleads on behalf of another before a righteous judge. The following scriptures paint a beautiful picture of intercession. What do they say?

Exodus 28:29-30

Ezekiel 22:30

What does 1 Samuel 2:25 ask and how does 1 Timothy 2:5 answer it?

*I have prayed for you, that your faith may not fail;
and you, when once you have turned again, strengthen your brothers.
Luke 22:32*

44. In Isaiah 59:16 it continues and says, "*Then His own arm brought salvation to Him.*" Read the following scriptures and write down how Jesus fulfilled this prophecy in Isaiah.

Matthew 18:11

John 12:47

45. In Isaiah 59:17 is a discussion of what the Messiah will put on to bring salvation. In Ephesians 6:11-18, we are also admonished to put on similar armor to bring about God's victory. Read this passage and write what you think each piece represents in the believer's life.

Loins girded with Truth-

Breastplate of Righteousness-

Shod feet with Gospel of Peace-

Shield of Faith-

Helmet of Salvation-

Sword of the Spirit -

46. In Isaiah 59:17 it continues: "*He put on garments of vengeance for clothing and wrapped Himself with the zeal as a mantle.*" How did Jesus demonstrate this zeal in John 2:13-17?

47. *"...This is My covenant with them..."* the Lord says in Isaiah 59:21. What more does the Bible teach about this covenant before it was revealed in Christ? Read these scriptures and write what you learn.

Jeremiah 31:33-34

Jeremiah 32:38-41

Ezekiel 36:25-27

➢ <u>Prove yourselves doers of the word . . . James 1:22</u>

48. When the Lord saw that "...*that there was no one to intercede...*" He stepped in and "*His own arm brought salvation to Him.*" (Isaiah 59:16) This should be a great comfort if you are discouraged with your prayers for others. Jesus – the Arm of the Lord – has done the work for you. The armor He put on in Isaiah 59:17 is our spiritual clothing as well (see 1 Thessalonians 5:8).
Clothed in His righteousness, we can intercede for others effectively.
How does James 5:16-18 explain show us how to pray?

49. The Lord has made a wonderful promise to you in Isaiah 59:21, *"...My words which I have put in your mouth shall not depart from your mouth, nor from the mouth of your offspring, nor from the mouth of your offspring's offspring,"* says the LORD, *"from now and forever."*. What encouragement does this give you regarding the future of your offspring?

➢ <u>In everything, by prayer and petition . . . Philippians 4:6</u>

Ask God to make you a better intercessor like Aaron keeping the people on his heart before the Lord.

*Therefore He said that He would destroy them, Had not Moses His chosen one
stood in the breach before Him, To turn away His wrath from destroying them.
Psalm 106:23*

*I searched for a man among them who would build up the wall
and stand in the gap before Me for the land, so that I would not destroy it...
Ezekiel 22:30*

~ ~ ~ ~ ~ ~   Prayer Requests   ~ ~ ~ ~ ~ ~

Page 320

The Favorable Year of the Lord
Isaiah chapters 60 – 61

Lesson 27

DAY 1 — The Everlasting Light

> ➤ *Draw near to God and He will draw near to you... James 4:8*

Is the Lord your light? Do His thoughts shape how you see the world? Do you share in His joy and pride as He considers His redeemed ones, (including you)? Sometimes we view people and situations based on ordinary human light and understanding. Ask Him to give you eyes to see and ears to hear so that His glory will be revealed to you today in His Word, and lay down whatever pride or light you have that doesn't come from Him.

I will make you an everlasting pride, a joy from generation to generation.
Then you will know that I, the LORD, am your Savior
And your Redeemer, the Mighty One of Jacob
Isaiah 60:15-16

This is the message we have heard from Him and announce to you,
that God is Light, and in Him there is no darkness at all.
1 John 1:5

MEMORY VERSE   Isaiah 60:20

Your sun will no longer set, nor will your moon wane;

for you will have the LORD for an everlasting light,

and the days of your mourning will be over.

> ➤ *Study to show yourself approved... 2 Timothy 2:15*

Isaiah 60 begins with a call to God's people to rise up and shine with the glory of the Lord that is coming to them. It will overcome the darkness and draw all nations to them. They will come bringing wealth and their descendants from around the world.

1. Read Isaiah 60:1-9. Answer the following questions about the passage.

What proclamation is made in verse 1?

What will happen to the earth in verse 2a?

What will the Lord do to overcome it in verse 2b?

Who will come to the light in verse 3?

As their sight is restored, what do they see (v.4)?

How will this sight affect them (v.5a)?

Why will they feel this way (v.5b)?

Who will come in verse 6 and what will they bring?

Who else will come (v.7a)?

How will the Lord receive them in verse 7b and for what reason?

In verse 8 the Lord is looking into the future and using poetic language to describe how He sees the people He will gather. How does He describe them?

Who else is mentioned and what will they bring the Lord (v.9a)?

Why will they do this (v.9b)?

2. "*Arise, shine; for your light has come...*" Isaiah 60:1 says. What does John 12:46 say about this light?

3. "*...darkness will cover the earth and deep darkness the peoples...*" Isaiah 60:2 says. One of the reasons the Lord says they were in deep darkness is because of their evil deeds. Ephesians 5:11 calls them "*unfruitful deeds of darkness.*" What do you learn about darkness from these verses?

Psalm 107:10-11

John 3:19-20

Acts 26:18a

Romans 1:21

Ephesians 4:17-18

4. "*...they come to you. Your sons will come from afar, and your daughters will be carried in the arms.*" Isaiah 60:4 says. What do these scriptures say about where these children come from?

Isaiah 43:6-7

Matthew 28:19

5. "*Then you will see and be radiant and your heart will thrill and rejoice...*" it says in Isaiah 60:5. How do these verses show how this is being fulfilled?

Philippians 4:1

1 Thessalonians 2:19-20

6. "*All the flocks of Kedar will be gathered to you, the rams of Nebaioth will minister to you. They will go up with acceptance on My altar...*" it says in Isaiah 60:7. Who are these people that the Lord accepts according to Genesis 25:12-13?

Read Genesis 21:9-13 and see how the Lord remembered Abraham's heart for his son, Ishmael.

Write down the words God uses in Isaiah 60:7 to show how He receives these sons.

> ## Prove yourselves doers of the word... James 1:22

7. "*Arise, shine ...*" Isaiah 60:1 says. How are we to shine? What does this mean in a practical sense? Read these scriptures and summarize what's important.

Matthew 5:14-16

Romans 13:11-14

Ephesians 5:8-14

8. Isaiah 60:2 tells us that the glory of the Lord rises up and overcomes the darkness. Read the following verses and summarize how we deal with darkness in our lives.

John 8:12

Ephesians 6:11-12

1 John 1:7

9. Isaiah 60:5 speaks of the thrill you will have in your heart when you see your spiritual children in heaven. Do you rejoice over people coming to Christ, or do you underestimate its significance in the spiritual realm? Ask God to give you a heart for lost souls.

> ## In everything, by prayer and petition... Philippians 4:6

In Isaiah 60:1-3, it says the light and the glory of the Lord has risen upon you. Don't underestimate how the Lord will use you to draw others out of darkness to His light. Ask the Lord to shine through you for His glory. Pray that His Light would shine brightly in your heart, mind and life.

The people who were sitting in darkness saw a great light,
and those who were sitting in the land and shadow of death, upon them a light dawned.
Matthew 4:16

~ ~ ~ ~   # DAY 2   ~ ~ ~ ~
The City of the Lord

> ## Draw near to God and He will draw near to you... James 4:8

You have come to Mount Zion and to the city of the living God, the heavenly Jerusalem,
and to myriads of angels, to the general assembly and church of the firstborn who are enrolled in
heaven, and to God, the Judge of all, and to the spirits of the righteous made perfect,
and to Jesus, the mediator of a new covenant...
Hebrews 12:22-24

What a glorious kingdom we have come to! Consider the great community of servants of the living God who share your devotion to Him. If you are feeling discouraged, remember that you belong to a family of believers, a home that your heart yearns for. We all long for our true home. Ask the Lord to make it more real to you today.

Practice your memory verse:

Your sun will no _____ set, nor will your moon _____;
for you will have the _____ for an everlasting _____,
and the days of your _____ will be over.
Isaiah 60:___

> ## Study to show yourself approved... 2 Timothy 2:15

Today as we continue studying Isaiah 60, we see a description of the transformation of Jerusalem, the holy city. It's a beautiful picture of the heavenly city, the Bride of Christ, spoken of by John the apostle in Revelation 21:2, "*And I saw the holy city, new Jerusalem, coming down out of heaven from God, made ready as a bride adorned for her husband.*"

10. Read Isaiah 60:10-18. Answer the following questions about the passage.

Who will reach out to them and what will they do (v.10a)?

What does the Lord say He did in verse 10b?

How will the city be kept and why in verse 11?

What will the Lord require of the nations and what are the consequences of disobedience (v.12)?

In verse 13, the Lord again uses the imagery of trees to describe people (Psalm 92:12). Who will come and what effect will they have (v.13)?

Who else will come in verse 14a and why is this significant?

What will their city be called (v.14b)?

How has Jerusalem been treated formerly in verse 15a?

How will it be regarded now (v.15b)?

How will it be nurtured and cared for in verse 16a?

What will this confirm to it in verse 16b?

What will the Lord take and what will He replace it with in verse 17a-b?

instead of _____	I will bring	_____
instead of _____	I will bring	_____
instead of _____	I will bring	_____
instead of _____	I will bring	_____

What will oversee them in verse 17c?

How does the Lord contrast what they were like before with what He will give them in verse 18?

11. Using our passage today, fill in the following chart contrasting the way Jerusalem used to be with the way it will be once God has transformed it. Some are implied, not stated.

verse	before	after
10		
11		
12		
13		
14		
15		
16		
17		
18		

12. These scriptures also describe the holy city of Jerusalem, Zion. What do they add to the description of what it will be like?

Isaiah 4:5

Isaiah 49:16-23

Isaiah 51:11

Zechariah 8:3-5, 21-23

Revelation 21:3-4

Revelation 22:3-4

13. Isaiah 60:11 says "*Your gates will be open continually; they will not be closed day or night.*" Read Revelation 22:14. Who has the right to enter the city gates?

14. In Isaiah 60:17 the Lord talks about exchanging their bronze and iron for gold and silver, and replacing their wood and stone with bronze and iron. This is a picture for us. The Lord takes our natural strengths as well as our weaknesses and replaces them with His much greater spiritual strengths and grace. He takes whatever we have and replaces it with things of much greater value. Make a note of what these verses teach.

2 Corinthians 12:9-10

Philippians 3:7-8

➢ <u>Prove yourselves doers of the word . . . James 1:22</u>

15. This passage in Isaiah could be the story of your life. Once the Lord has finished all the wonderful work He is doing in you, you will be like the holy city, beautiful, "*an everlasting pride, a joy from generation to generation*" (v.15). What transforming work is the Lord doing in you right now? What are you looking forward to?

> In everything, by prayer and petition... Philippians 4:6

Ask the Lord to help you keep your focus on eternal things, on your real home. Pray that He would help you make good use of the time you have to prepare for it.

Sing for joy and be glad, O daughter of Zion; for behold I am coming and I will dwell in your midst," declares the LORD.
Zechariah 2:10

~ ~ ~ ~ **DAY 3** ~ ~ ~ ~
Reflecting the Glory of the Lord

> Draw near to God and He will draw near to you... James 4:8

For the earth will be filled with the knowledge of the glory of the LORD, as the waters cover the sea.
Habakkuk 2:14

One of the ways the knowledge of the Lord will fill the earth is through us, His people. This starts with us reflecting His light, basking in the knowledge of Him, beholding His glory. Take a moment to quiet your heart and ask Him to fill you, reveal Himself to you and show you His glory today. This is His will for you and you can ask with confidence knowing you will receive it!

Don't be distressed if His light and glory expose some things in your heart. Trust in His faithfulness, confess your sins and start fresh today with a clean conscience. His pure light will be a joy!

Practice your memory verse:

_____ sun _____ no _____ set, _____ will _____ moon _____;

for ____ will _____ the _____ for ___ everlasting _____,

and _____ days ___ your _____ will ___ over.

_____ 60: ___

> Study to show yourself approved... 2 Timothy 2:15

Chapter 60 ends with a glorious description of the light we will live by when the Lord has gathered His people and transformed His city in Zion.

16. Read Isaiah 60:19-22. Answer the following questions about the passage.

What sources of light are no longer needed (v.19a)?

What will be their source of light (v.19b)?

How does the Lord explain the permanence of this light in verse 20a?

What days will be finished in verse 20b?

What will this people be like in verse 21?

How does verse 22a describe their fruitfulness?

When will it happen (v.22b)?

In Jesus' day, the Jews had been waiting and yearning for their Messiah for a long time. Because of passages like Isaiah 60 they were looking for a someone who would bring about the glorious Kingdom. Other scriptures like Isaiah 53 about the suffering Messiah, they spiritualized. So when Jesus came on the scene and died on the cross many didn't believe in Him. They expected a Messiah who would make Israel great and glorious and do it immediately. They had no idea there would be two comings of the Messiah, the first as a Lamb and the second as a Righteous King.

Even after His death and resurrection when Jesus had told His disciples to wait in Jerusalem for the Holy Spirit to come upon them, they still didn't understand:

So when they had come together, they were asking Him, saying,
"Lord, is it at this time You are restoring the kingdom to Israel?"
Acts 1:4-6

They did not understand that God had a plan to gather in the Gentile nations of the world into a body of believers He would call His Church.

For I do not want you, brethren, to be uninformed of this mystery
– so that you will not be wise in your own estimation –
that a partial hardening has happened to Israel
until the fullness of the Gentiles has come in.
Romans 11:25

God allowed the partial hardening so you and I might be saved. But in His second Coming Jesus will reign here on earth and Israel will be restored to glory and prominence among the nations.

17. List everything Isaiah chapter 60 says about light in the following verses.

verse 1

verse 2

verse 3

verse 5

verse 19

verse 20

18. Read Revelation 21:22-27 and 22:5. Describe light and dark in the New Jerusalem.

19. "*And the days of your mourning will be over*" Isaiah 60:20 says. What kind of mourning do you think this is referring to? What did Jesus say about this in Matthew 5:4?

20. "*...you will have the Lord for an everlasting light and your God for your glory*" Isaiah 60:19 says. Make a note of the references to the Lord's glory in Isaiah 60 (glorious, glorify, etc.)

verse 1	verse 13
verse 2	verse 19
verse 7	verse 21
verse 9	

Glory, (kabod in Hebrew) refers to abundance, wealth, treasure and honor. When speaking of the Lord, it refers to His splendor, brightness and majesty, His glorious moral attributes and His infinite perfections.

from the Easton Bible dictionary

Look up Exodus 40:34-38. Where did God's glory once dwell?

Why did His glory depart from there? Read I Samuel 4:4,10-11,19-22.

Read I Kings 8:6, 11. Where did God's glory dwell next? _____

When the Bible speaks of the Lord's glory dwelling over the cherubim, it is referring to the lid of the ark sitting in the temple which had two cherubim molded out of gold. These represented the throne of God in heaven where the four cherubim (or four living creatures described by John in Revelation 4:6-8), are around the Lord. Read these verses to explain how the glory of the Lord departed when the nation refused to turn away from idols.

Ezekiel 10:4,18

Ezekiel 11:22-23

Read John 1:14. Where does it say God's glory was beheld? _____

Where does 1 Peter 4:14b say God's glory dwells now?

What are we to do with God's glory?

Matthew 5:16

1 Corinthians 6:20.

➤ <u>Prove yourselves doers of the word . . . James 1:22</u>

21. How are you a light in darkness? Is your lamp dim, waning? Are you hiding it from anyone?

22. How are you exemplifying the glory of the Lord at home or work?

23. Consider how great the Ark of the Covenant and the Temple were! Isn't it humbling to be the vessel God chose for His glory to dwell? Do you realize how great an honor this really is? What is the Lord saying to you about this?

➤ <u>In everything, by prayer and petition . . . Philippians 4:6</u>

Ask the Lord to help you simply reflect His glory.

> *But we all, with unveiled face, beholding as in a mirror the glory of the Lord,*
> *are being transformed into the same image from glory to glory,*
> *just as from the Lord, the Spirit.*
> *2 Corinthians 3:18*

~ ~ ~ ~ **DAY 4** ~ ~ ~ ~
The Favorable Year of the Lord

> ### Draw near to God and He will draw near to you... James 4:8

Thus says the LORD, "In a favorable time I have answered You,
And in a day of salvation I have helped You..."
Isaiah 49:8

You have been granted the Lord's favor. He is waiting to minister to you today, to give you good news, to bind up your brokenness, to free you from the things that have held you captive and to comfort you in whatever you mourn over. Listen to Him and trust Him.

Practice your memory verse:

Your _____ will _____ longer _____, nor _____ your _____ wane;
_____ you _____ have _____ LORD _____ an _____ light,
_____ the _____ of _____ mourning _____ be _____.
Isaiah ____:20

> ### Study to show yourself approved... 2 Timothy 2:15

Isaiah 61 begins with a very famous passage quoted by Jesus in the gospels. It contains a succinct description of the ministry of the Messiah when He comes to earth. In verse 2 Isaiah prophesied of both the first and second comings of Jesus.

24. Read Isaiah 61:1-4. Answer the following questions about the passage. (M)

Who has anointed Him with the Spirit of the Lord (v.1a)? *Note – anointed is the root word for Messiah.*

What healing and deliverance will He bring (v.1b)?

What will He proclaim in verse 2a? (M)

How will He comfort those who mourn in verses 2b-3a?

	Jesus gives
instead of ashes	
instead of mourning	
instead of a spirit of fainting	

What will they be called and what will it bring the Lord (v.3b)?

What will they do for the old cities in verse 4?

25. Read Luke 4:16-22. Imagine yourself being there that day in the synagogue. This was the custom of the time for rabbis to read from the scriptures. Jesus stood up and read this passage about Himself. Notice where Jesus stops reading.

Read Matthew 11:2-5 and explain how Jesus perfectly fulfilled Isaiah 61:1-2a.

26. "*...the Lord has anointed Me to bring good news to the afflicted*" Isaiah 61:1 says. What is good news to an afflicted person (Isaiah 61:1)?

According to Webster afflicted means; "affected with often repeated or continued pain, suffering, grief or distress." (Webster Dictionary 1828) How did Jesus share good news with the afflicted?

Psalm 34:18-19

Psalm 149:4.

Luke 8:29-33

John 5:4-9

27. What does it mean to "*bind up the broken hearted*" (Isaiah 61:1)?

How did Jesus do this?
Psalm 147:3

Luke 18:10-14

John 19:26-27

28. To whom did Jesus "*proclaim liberty to captives and freedom to prisoners*" (Isaiah 61:1)?
Luke 23:39-43.

John 8:3-11

29. How did Jesus "*comfort all who mourn*" (Isaiah 61:1)?
Luke 8:49-56

John 11:32-44

30. In Isaiah 61:2b it says "*the day of vengeance of our God*." This is the part of the prophecy that Jesus did not read in Luke 4:19-20 because it referred to an event yet to be fulfilled. Will we experience this event? Read these verses and make a note of what you find out.
Romans 5:9

I Thessalonians 5:9

31. Instead of ashes, mourning, and fainting (Isaiah 61:3), God gives us beauty, joy and praise (NKJ). How has God made beauty from ashes in your life?

I came that they may have life, and have it abundantly.
John 10:10

32. In Isaiah 61: 4 they will rebuild, restore and repair. Read these definitions:

rebuild – is to build again something which has been broken down or dismantled.
restore – is to raise up something that has fallen, return it to its original condition.
repair – make something like new again after it has been damaged

What do these verses teach you about how the Lord rebuilds, restores and repairs through believers?

Romans 14:19

1 Corinthians 3:10-11

Ephesians 2:20-22

> ## Prove yourselves doers of the word ... James 1:22

33. Write down a time when the Lord gave good news to your afflicted heart. Maybe it was a promise or a word from a fellow believer He sent your way.

34. How has Jesus bound up your broken heart? Share with the group.

35. What has Jesus freed you from? What do you need Him to free you from currently, such as an addiction, a critical spirit, complaining, anger, fear, etc.?

36. There are people who are afflicted, brokenhearted and prisoners in your life.
Who is He sending you to?

37. How can you help rebuild, restore, and repair others? Are you being faithful?

38. What area does God want to rebuild in your own life so you can effectively minister to others?

> ## In everything, by prayer and petition ... Philippians 4:6

The Lord wants so much to give you beauty, joy and praises in exchange for your mourning. Ask Him to take your mourning and make you beautiful to Him. Give thanks for the way He is transforming your life.

*You have turned for me my mourning into dancing;
You have loosed my sackcloth and girded me with gladness,
Psalm 30:11*

DAY 5
Priests of the Lord

> ➤ <u>Draw near to God and He will draw near to you... James 4:8</u>

Let Your priests be clothed with righteousness,
And let Your godly ones sing for joy.
Psalm 132:9

God has given us the most amazing robes of righteousness! He has provided all we need so that we can be His priests and have open access to His holy presence. He has made Himself so accessible!!!
This is unlike the way the world guards its treasures, locking them up in secret. But through Jesus we can have bold access to our Heavenly Father and all the riches of His grace. Now take time to enjoy access to your Father!

Through Him we have our access in one Spirit to the Father. Ephesians 2:18

In whom we have boldness and confident access through faith in Him. Ephesians 3:12

Write down your memory verse:

➤ <u>Study to show yourself approved... 2 Timothy 2:15</u>

Isaiah chapter 61 continues with a description of the people the Lord chooses as His priests and ministers. They will be robed in wonderful garments, filled with everlasting joy and greatly blessed by God.

39. Read Isaiah 61:5-11. Answer the following questions about the passage.

Who will minister to them and how (v.5)?

What will they be called (v.6a)?

How will they be provided for in verse 6b?

What will they no longer have and what will they receive instead in verse 7?

What does the Lord say He loves and hates in verse 8a?

What will He do for them in verse 8b?

How will they be known among the nations in verse 9?

Why does this person rejoice in verse 10a?

What analogy does he use to describe his joy in verse 10b?

The earth is also used as an analogy. What does verse 11 explain?

> In Isaiah 61:10, it says "I will rejoice..." It isn't clear who is speaking. It could be Isaiah or any believer rejoicing in what God has done.

40. "*But you will be called the priests of the Lord*" Isaiah 61:6 says. What do you think this means?

In order to understand our priestly role, let's review the roles of priests in the Bible.
How does Hebrews 5:1-3 explain the duties of the Levitical priests in the Old Testament?

How did Jesus fulfill a much higher priesthood according to these verses?
   Hebrews 4:14-16

   Hebrews 10:10-12

What Jesus accomplished rendered the former sacrifices unnecessary and yet the Lord still desires that His people would be a priesthood set apart for Himself. He calls us to come before Him on behalf of others in prayer as the Levites did, only we rely on the perfect sacrifice of Jesus' blood.

What do these scriptures teach you about our role as a priest of the Lord?
   Romans 12:1

   1 Peter 2:5

   Revelation 5:10

   Revelation 20:6

41. In Isaiah 61:6 it also says, "*…you will be spoken of as ministers of our God.*" The word minister in the Hebrew means servant. Jesus is our example of a servant. What does His example look like in these scriptures?
Mark 10: 44-45

John 13:5-17

42. Isaiah 61:7 says, "*Therefore they will possess a double portion in their land, everlasting joy will be theirs.*" Look up the following scriptures and write down what they teach us about joy.
Nehemiah 12:43

Psalm 16:11

John 15:11

1 Peter 1:8

43. "*He has clothed me with garments of salvation, He has wrapped me with a robe of righteousness…*" Isaiah 61:10 says. Isaiah 61:3 speaks of the "*mantle of praise*".
How do these scriptures describe the clothing God has provided for you?
Psalm 132:9,16

Galatians 3:27

> ### Prove yourselves doers of the word... James 1:22

44. How are you practicing being a "*priest of the Lord*", going to the Lord on behalf of others?

45. Read Matthew 25:34-40. How are you doing in this area of being a minister to God, a servant? How about giving something to eat or drink in the name of Jesus? Do you readily share? When called on, do you respond "Yes" to providing a meal for those in need?

How are you at inviting strangers in? Or do you only invite the beautiful and lovely?

When did you last visit those in prison? Or shut-ins who can't physically get out?

Jesus says its as easy as simply giving a child a glass of water. Small steps of obedience. What small step do you need to make this week?

46. Is your life characterized by joyfulness? Are you experiencing everlasting joy? Some joy robbers are: expectations, ungratefulness, tyranny of the urgent. What would you add to this list that robs you of your joy?

> ### In everything, by prayer and petition... Philippians 4:6

Which joy-robber are you struggling with right now? Give it to the Lord and ask Him to restore to you the joy of your salvation.

Restore to me the joy of Your salvation.
Psalm 51:12

Pray that you will recognize your high priestly service of ministering to others in your daily life. Ask the Lord to make you a servant especially at home where we long to act as we should. Ask Him to increase your love for Him.

~ ~ ~ ~ ~ ~   Prayer Requests   ~ ~ ~ ~ ~ ~

My Delight is in Her
Isaiah chapters 62 – 63

Lesson 28

DAY 1   New Names

➢ <u>Draw near to God and He will draw near to you... James 4:8</u>

I have called you by name; you are Mine!
Isaiah 43:1

Your name is more than just a name. It is associated with your identity – who you are, how you feel about yourself. When Jesus calls us by our name, He isn't just acknowledging the name and identity we wear everyday. He also calls the secret person of our heart.

This name reflects the things that only He knows about us, the identity He created for us in the beginning and that we are longing to be, and the deeply personal relationship He desires to have with us.

Ask the Lord to free you from the constricting walls of your ordinary name and to speak to your heart – calling you by His name for you.

MEMORY VERSE   Isaiah 62:3

You will also be a crown of beauty in the hand of the LORD,

and a royal diadem in the hand of your God.

➢ <u>Study to show yourself approved ... 2 Timothy 2:15</u>

In the beginning of Isaiah chapter 62, the Lord proclaims that He will change the names of His people and their land. These names reflect the new creation He will make them into.

1. Read Isaiah 62:1-5. Answer the following questions.

The Lord is probably the one speaking in verse 1. The context supports this assumption (see v.6). For whose sake will He not keep quiet (v.1a)?

What is He waiting for (v.1b)?

Who will see? What will they see (v.2a)?

What will the Lord give her and why do you think that is (v.2b)?

What will the city be in the Lord's hand (v.3)?

What names will be taken away and what new ones will be given in their place (v.4a)?

Why (v.4b)?

"and to Him your land will be married" Isaiah 62:4 says. Revelation 21:2 makes it clear that the Lord refers to Jerusalem, the holy city, as the Bride of Christ. In other words, the Church or the body of believers will be married to Christ.

Page 335

What relationship does the Lord use to describe the bond and joy between them in verse 5?

2. *"For Zion's sake I will not keep silent and for Jerusalem's sake I will not keep quiet..."* Isaiah 62:1 says. God doesn't forget His promises. We are the ones who need constant reminding so that we won't give up on them. How do these verses show that He is glad to do this for us?

Philippians 3:1

2 Peter 1:12

3. *" And you will be called by a new name which the mouth of the LORD will designate."* Isaiah 62:2 says. Read Hosea 1:9-10 and make a note of another name that the Lord had given His people and how He will change it.

4. Isaiah 62:3 says *"You will also be a crown of beauty in the hand of the Lord, and a royal diadem in the hand of your God."* This is a precious object of great worth. What do the following scriptures add to this amazing truth?

Isaiah 28:5

1 Thessalonians 2:19

5. The following is a list of all our "new names" given in Isaiah chapter 62, (including verse 12). It's important to understand that the names given to the land or the city are referring to the Lord's redeemed people and they apply to us. Read the definitions and their corresponding scriptures. Make a note of what you consider important.

name - definition	references	your notes
Delight v.4 – a high degree of pleasure, joy, rapture	Psalm 16:3	
Married v.4 – united in covenant, wedlock	Isaiah 54:5 2 Corinthians 11:2	
Rejoice over you v.5 – to experience joy or gladness in a high degree	Zephaniah 3:17	
Holy people v. 12 – devoted to the service of God	I Peter 2:9	
Redeemed v.12 – ransomed by paying a specific sum, to recover	Isaiah 43:1	
Sought out v.12 – to look for, to try to find, to try to acquire	Matthew 13:45-46	

6. In Isaiah 62:4 it says we will not be called Forsaken or Desolate. Read the definitions and their opposites.

Definition	Opposite
Forsaken – abandoned	inhabited, occupied, populated, settled
Desolate – devastation, utter waste	preserved, saved, cheerful

How does this encourage you?

> ### Prove yourselves doers of the word... James 1:22

7. The Lord looks at us with eyes of faith and calls us by a new name because He sees what we are in Christ. His words build us up and we should treat one another the same way. How do you treat God's precious possession? What do you call people in your family? Is it edifying?

8. When you read the definitions of the "new names" which one blessed you the most and why?

> ### In everything, by prayer and petition... Philippians 4:6

Take some time to give thanks to the Lord and praise Him because you are "Sought Out". He didn't just wait for you, He pursued you, and He bought you!!

The kingdom of heaven is like a treasure hidden in the field, which a man found and hid again; and from joy over it he goes and sells all that he has and buys that field. Again, the kingdom of heaven is like a merchant seeking fine pearls, and upon finding one pearl of great value, he went and sold all that he had and bought it.
Matthew 13:44-46

~ ~ ~ ~   ## DAY 2   ~ ~ ~ ~
Keeping Watch

> ### Draw near to God and He will draw near to you... James 4:8

I wait for the LORD, my soul does wait, and in His word do I hope.
My soul waits for the Lord more than the watchmen for the morning;
Indeed, more than the watchmen for the morning.
Psalm 130:5-6

How earnestly do you long to see the Lord, to hear from Him, to receive His answer no matter how long it takes? There are burdens on your heart that God has given you for prayer. Are you waiting on Him or do you take matters into your hands and resolve those burdens of the heart in a human way?

Surrender now. Just give up your ways. Join with the chorus of God's people around the world, whose voices He hears night and day, calling out "You, Lord! I wait for You alone! Hear me and don't delay!" His heart yearns towards the cry of your heart.

Practice your memory verse:

You will also be a _____ of beauty in the _____ of the LORD, and a royal _____ in the hand of your _____.

Isaiah 62:___

> ## Study to show yourself approved... 2 Timothy 2:15

Isaiah chapter 62 continues with an exhortation to the watchmen God has appointed to intercede for Jerusalem. He reminds them of what His will for the city is and how they should pray.

9. Read Isaiah 62:6-12. Answer the following questions.

Who has God appointed in verse 6a?

What is their task (v.6b-7)?

What do you think this means?

What has the Lord sworn never to do again (v.8)?

Who will enjoy the fruits of their labor (v.9)?

How is the way to be prepared for God's people (v.10)?

What has the Lord proclaimed in verse 11 and how far has His message extended?

What will these people be called and what will their city be called (v.12)?

10. Isaiah 62:6 says "*On your walls, O Jerusalem, I have appointed watchmen; all day and all night they will never keep silent.*" Read Luke 18:1-7 and make a note of what you learn about this kind of persistence.

11. "*You who remind the Lord, take no rest for yourselves and give Him no rest until He establishes and makes Jerusalem a praise in the earth.*" Isaiah 62:6-7 continues. What does Psalm 122:6-7 say about what they were to pray for?

12. What encouragement does Isaiah 52:8 give these watchmen?

How does Psalm 134:1-2 describe the ongoing ministry of the watchmen to the Lord?

13. *'The LORD has sworn by His right hand and by His strong arm, "I will never again give your grain as food for your enemies; Nor will foreigners drink your new wine for which you have labored."'* Isaiah 62:8 says. Enemies had done this to them many times in their history. Judges 6:3-4 gives an example of this. What does it say?

14. In Isaiah 62:10 it says *"Clear the way for the people, build up, build up the highway."* Read Isaiah 35:8 and make a note of what it says about this highway.

15. Isaiah 62:11 says *"Behold, the LORD has proclaimed to the end of the earth, Say to the daughter of Zion, "Lo, your salvation comes..."* How is this being fulfilled according to Matthew 24:14?

➢ Prove yourselves doers of the word... James 1:22

16. *"On your walls I have appointed watchmen...you who remind the Lord, take no rest for yourselves..."* verse 6 says. God doesn't forget but He chooses to let prayer affect His work. How do these scriptures show Moses' example of being a watchman who reminds the Lord of His promises?

    Exodus 32:7-14

    Numbers 14:11-20

    Psalm 106:23

What promises are you reminding the Lord, laying hold of and claiming for His glory?

How do these scriptures affirm the wisdom of trusting in the promises of God?

    Joshua 21:45

    2 Corinthians 1:20

    2 Peter 1:4

17. Look again at Isaiah 62:8-9. If the Lord were to make a promise like this to you, consider what it would be like. Fill in the blank:

"The Lord has sworn by His right hand and by His strong arm, I will never again . . .

_____

_____

18. *"Build up the highway..."* verse 10 says. How can you <u>build up</u> the high way to God? Consider the following scripture in your answer.

But you, beloved, <u>building yourselves up</u> on your most holy faith, praying in the Holy Spirit, keep yourselves in the love of God, looking for the mercy of our Lord Jesus Christ unto eternal life.
Jude 20-21

> ## In everything, by prayer and petition... Philippians 4:6

Ask the Lord to make you a faithful watchman on the wall interceding on behalf of others. Recognize that this is a work of the Holy Spirit and is only possible as you abide in Christ. Ask the Lord to strengthen you and keep you from growing weary or giving up.

*Therefore, my beloved brethren, be steadfast, immovable,
always abounding in the work of the Lord, knowing
that your toil is not in vain in the Lord.
1 Corinthians 15:58*

*Let us not lose heart in doing good, for in due time
we will reap if we do not grow weary.
Galatians 6:9*

~ ~ ~ ~
# DAY 3
The Day of Vengeance
~ ~ ~ ~

> ## Draw near to God and He will draw near to you... James 4:8

God is not in a hurry. He delays judgment as long as possible so that He might show mercy on us. Perhaps you have underestimated the grace He has shown you and the judgment you've been spared. Slow down now, and wait on Him. Learn of Him. He is beautiful in all His ways.

*But You, O Lord, are a God merciful and gracious,
Slow to anger and abundant in lovingkindness and truth.
Psalm 86:15*

Practice your memory verse:

You _____ also _____ a _____ of _____ in _____ hand _____ the _____,
and _____ royal _____ in _____ hand _____ your _____.
Isaiah _____:3

> ## Study to show yourself approved... 2 Timothy 2:15

Isaiah chapter 63 begins with a description of the day of vengeance of the Lord. It is a picture of the Messiah that we prefer not to think about. As we study this passage today, let's remember how the Lord restrains His wrath and holds back as long as possible but He is holy and can't leave the evils and the bloodshed of the earth unpunished. God is the only one who is able to be truly just. Not only that, but Jesus Himself has drunk the cup of God's wrath so that no one else will have to and the only ones who will suffer this wrath are those who reject His great mercy and compassion.

19. Read Isaiah 63:1-6. Answer the following questions.

Someone is coming in verse 1a. Where is He coming from?

How is He described (v.1b)?

How does He answer when they ask "*Who is this who comes...*" (v.1c)?

What do His garments look like (v.2)?

Who helped Him to tread the wine trough (v.3a)?

What motivated Him in this task (v.3b)?

How did He stain His garments (v.3c)?

Why did He do it (v.4a)?

What is linked to this day and why do you think that is the case (v.4b)?

What did He look for in verse 5a?

What was His reaction to what He found and why do you think He felt this way (v.5b)?

How did He respond to this and what upheld Him in verse 5c?

What did He do in verse 6?

20. *"Who is this who comes from Edom, with garments of glowing colors from Bozrah…?"* verse 1 says. How does Isaiah 34:5-6 explain what He did in Bozrah?

21. *"Why is your apparel red, and your garments like the one who treads in the wine press?"* Isaiah 63:2 asks. The next verse explains that His robes are stained with blood. What do you learn about this wine press and who it is for in the following scriptures?

Revelation 14:9-11

> Edom is named here as a representative of the nations that have oppressed the Jews. Bozrah was one of its main cities and its name means *"grape gathering"*. This is significant since the image here is that of a wine press. The name Edom means red and is another name for Esau. (Genesis 25:30)

Revelation 14:17-20

22. How does Jesus fulfill this prophecy in Isaiah 63:3 according to Revelation 19:11-13?

23. Isaiah 63:4 says *"For the day of vengeance was in My heart"*. What do you learn about this from these scriptures?

Isaiah 61:2

Luke 21:20-22

Who will experience this day of vengeance?

Deuteronomy 32:41

Psalm 75:8

Micah 5:15

24. In Isaiah 63:4 it continues, "... *and My year of redemption has come*". For some the day of vengeance becomes the year of redemption. Look up the following scriptures and write what you learn about God's mercy and grace even in the midst of judgment.

Joel 2:30-32

Joel 3:13-14

Jude 1:23

25. "*I looked and there was no one to help, and I was astonished and there was no one to uphold...*" Isaiah 63:5 says. What does Isaiah 59:16-17 say about this?

> Put in the sickle, for the harvest is ripe. Come, tread, for the wine press is full;
> The vats overflow, for their wickedness is great.   Joel 3:13

26. Isaiah 63:6 says "*I trod down the peoples in My anger... and I poured out their lifeblood on the earth.*" It is hard for us to understand how this picture is consistent with a loving and compassionate God. How do these verses show that this is an appropriate response for our Savior?

What commandment did God give to all people in Genesis 9:6?

How does Jesus confirm this truth in Matthew 26:52?

How does Hebrews 9:22 show that sins are forgiven through the shedding of blood?

Jesus shed His own blood to pay for all the bloodshed and sin of the world. But if someone rejects His gift of grace, what is the only thing left for him according to Hebrews 10:29-30?

27. This description of God's wrath could be frightening if we weren't forgiven of our sins. Read the following scriptures and fill in the chart.

what we are saved from	what we are saved for
John 3:16-18	John 4:23
Romans 5:9	Ephesians 2:8-10
	Revelation 7:15-17

> ➤ Prove yourselves doers of the word... James 1:22

Praise God that He has not destined us for wrath but for salvation! God has bestowed on us His mercy and grace!

28. Jesus is the only One who can show anger appropriately. We may get angry, but Ephesians 4:26 says "*Be angry and yet do not sin...*" Our anger causes problems. How awful is your wrath? Is anyone afraid of you?

What does James 1:19-20 say about this?

How about when you're managing people or parenting? Are you threatening or nagging? Do you say what you mean and mean what you say? What does Ephesians 6:4, 9 say about this?

29. Do you demonstrate God's long suffering when given an opportunity?   Or are you characterized by being inflexible and unreasonable?

30. Read Romans 12:14-21. What instruction do we receive from the Lord regarding vengeance from this passage?

31. Reading today about the day of vengeance, does this give you greater urgency in wanting to share your faith? To whom do you need to apply this urgency to?

32. These passages about the day of vengeance can be sobering. How can this sober perspective be helpful to you?

> <u>In everything, by prayer and petition . . . Philippians 4:6</u>

Take time right now to pray for those who still don't know the Lord and God's wrath is still in their future. Pray through each of your answers on the previous questions. Ask the Lord to search your heart and show you your heart.   Give this to the Lord, He alone is able to change you and make you truly longsuffering.

*What if God, although willing to demonstrate His wrath and to make His power known,
endured with much patience vessels of wrath prepared for destruction? And He did so to make known
the riches of His glory upon vessels of mercy, which He prepared beforehand for glory.*
Romans 9:22-23

~ ~ ~ ~   # DAY 4   ~ ~ ~ ~
Isaiah's Prayer

> <u>Draw near to God and He will draw near to you. . . James 4:8</u>

Welcome the Lord to examine your motives today. Invite the Lord in to judge your heart. Give Him permission to do a thorough check-up, as you meditate on these scriptures.

*All the ways of a man are clean in his own sight,
But the LORD weighs the motives.*
Proverbs 16:2

*Therefore do not go on passing judgment before the time, but wait until the Lord comes
who will both bring to light the things hidden in the darkness and disclose the motives
of men's hearts; and then each man's praise will come to him from God.*
1 Corinthians 4:5

*… in whatever our heart condemns us; for God is greater
than our heart and knows all things.*
1 John 3:20

Practice your memory verse:

_____ will _____ be ___ crown ___ beauty ___ the _____ of _____ LORD,
_____ a _____ diadem ___ the _____ of _____ God.
Isaiah _____ : ___

> ### Study to show yourself approved . . . 2 Timothy 2:15

Isaiah was moved to pray for his people after seeing the vivid image of God's vengeance described in the beginning of chapter 63,. He remembers the Lord's great lovingkindness and compassion and begins to intercede. This is a window into Isaiah's heart, one of the few in the whole book of Isaiah.

33. Read Isaiah 63:7-14. Answer the following questions.

What does Isaiah say here in verse 7a?

What does he say the Lord has granted His people (v.7b)?

What did the Lord say about His people in verse 8a?

What did He become in verse 8b?

List the things the Messiah did for them in verse 9.

What was their response to His care in verse 10a?

What did He have to do because of it (v.10b)?

What effect did this have on them (v.11a)?

Isaiah begins to cry out to God after remembering what He has done for His people in the past. What did Isaiah ask in verses 11b-13a?

What were they compared to in verses 13b-14a?

What had the Lord done for them and why in verse 14b?

34. Verse 7 says "*I shall make mention of the lovingkindnesses of the Lord, the praises of the Lord, according to all that the Lord has granted us...*" Considering this beautiful response is after the vision of the vengeance of the Lord, how do these scriptures shed light on why Isaiah would respond this way?

Deuteronomy 9:13-14, 18-20

Deuteronomy 10:10

Psalm 106:23

35. Isaiah 63:9 says "*In all their affliction He was afflicted...*" Jesus fulfilled this perfectly. How do these scriptures show this?

Isaiah 53:3-7

Luke 22:63-64

36. "*But they rebelled and grieved His Holy Spirit,*" it says in Isaiah 63:10. What do you learn about this from these verses?

Psalm 78:8, 40, 56

Ezekiel 6:9

Acts 7:51

In the New testament, we are warned "*Do not grieve the Holy Spirit of God by whom you were sealed for the day of redemption.*" (Ephesians 4:30) Read through Ephesians 4:17-32, and summarize in a few words what kind of behavior grieves the Spirit of God.

37. Isaiah 63:11 says "*...He who put His Holy Spirit in the midst of them...*" What does this teach us about the Holy Spirit in the Old Testament? How is this different than the New Testament? See Acts 2:2-4.

➢ Prove yourselves doers of the word... James 1:22

38. Isaiah said "*I shall make mention of the lovingkindnesses of the Lord*" in 63:7. What can you learn from Isaiah's example of remembering the Lord's wonderful deeds even when faced with a vision of God's wrath?

What deeds of the Lord can you look back on to strengthen you for prayer?

What encouragement does James 5:16b give you?

39. In Isaiah 63:10 it says "*But they rebelled and grieved His Holy Spirit.*" Ask the Lord if there is some area in which you are grieving the Holy Spirit. What should you do about it? Do you know someone who is grieving the Spirit? What can you do for them?

40. Isaiah 63:14 says "*The Spirit of the Lord gave them rest.*" The Lord wants to give you rest also. How has the Lord given you rest? How do you need rest today?

> In everything, by prayer and petition... Philippians 4:6

It has been said that "judgment that is invited never destroys". Ask the Lord to expose, reveal and uncover any area of sin in your own heart. Ask Him to guard your heart against grieving the Holy Spirit. Take time to thank Him for how He has been good to you today. Consider how has He borne your affliction, how has He carried you, led you, given you rest, and put His Spirit in you. (Isaiah 63:9-14)

*In all their affliction He was afflicted, and the angel of His presence saved them;
In His love and in His mercy He redeemed them, and He lifted them
and carried them all the days of old.
Isaiah 63:9*

~ ~ ~ ~   ## DAY 5   ~ ~ ~ ~
You Are Our Father

> Draw near to God and He will draw near to you... James 4:8

*Because you are sons, God has sent forth the Spirit of His Son
into our hearts, crying, "Abba! Father!"
Galatians 4:6*

Your Father in heaven is waiting to hear the cries of your heart. He sent His Spirit to help you call on Him. Turn to Him in confidence and ask Him to anoint your time in the word today.

Write down your memory verse:

> Study to show yourself approved... 2 Timothy 2:15

In the end of Isaiah chapter 63, Isaiah continues to pour out his heart and plead with the Lord for help. He appeals to him as a son to his father and questions why the Lord has hardened the hearts of His people. The most moving thing about this is that Isaiah was pleading for restoration before any of this had come to pass.

41. Read Isaiah 63:15-19. Answer the following questions.

How does Isaiah appeal to God in verse 15a?

What does he ask the Lord in verse 15b?

What has the Lord restrained towards him in verse 15c?

What does he call God in verse 16a,c?

What two people does he say may not recognize them in verse 16b?

How does he question the Lord in verse 17a?

What does he ask for in verse 17b?

What does verse 18 say has happened to the Lord's sanctuary (i.e. Temple)?

What have God's people become like in verse 19?

42. *"Where are your zeal and Your mighty deeds? The stirrings of Your heart and Your compassion are restrained toward me"* verse 15 says. Isaiah is taking this very personally. His heart will only be comforted by the Lord's intervention. What do these verses tell you about the stirrings and compassion of God's heart?

Jeremiah 31:20

Hosea 11:8

2 Corinthians 1:3-4

43. *"For You are our Father..."* Isaiah says in 63:16. How could Isaiah make such a claim? How does Deuteronomy 32:6b show that God offered this privilege from the beginning?

God's people forgot this beautiful promise and never laid claim to it. By praying in this way, Isaiah was prophetically looking ahead to the promise of becoming children of God through faith in Jesus. He didn't know how it would happen but he believed that God was his Father.
What do these scriptures say about the fatherhood of God?

John 1:12

1 John 3:1

*Note – When Isaiah says *"though Abraham does not know us and Israel does not recognize us"* in Isaiah 63:16, this is also a prophetic look ahead to the harvest among the Gentiles. They are not from the bloodline of Abraham and Israel, so the people of Israel wouldn't recognize their claim to being their offspring.

44. In Isaiah 63:17 he says *"Why do You cause us to stray from Your ways and harden our heart from fearing You?"* God doesn't arbitrarily harden people's hearts. Their hearts become harder when they resist the Lord and His word of truth. How did the Lord answer the cry of Isaiah's heart and bring good out of the spiritual condition of his people? Read Romans 11:25 and write your thoughts.

45. In Isaiah 63:19 *"We have become like those over whom You have never ruled, like those who were not called by Your name."*. How was this scripture fulfilled in Jesus' lifetime?

John 19:14-15

John 19:19-21

> ➢ Prove yourselves doers of the word... James 1:22

46. Isaiah says *"For You are our Father,"* in 63:16. How do you address the Lord? Is He your Father? Read Isaiah 64:8.

47. Isaiah 63:18-19 express the discouragement Isaiah felt. Have you ever felt like this? How could you turn these kinds of emotions into something positive?

> <u>In everything, by prayer and petition . . . Philippians 4:6</u>

Ask the Lord to help you lean on Him more as your Father. Your Father knows what you need before you ask Him.

Pray, then, in this way:
Our Father who is in heaven, hallowed be Your name.
Your kingdom come. Your will be done, on earth as it is in heaven.
Give us this day our daily bread. And forgive us our debts, as we also have forgiven our debtors.
And do not lead us into temptation, but deliver us from evil.
For Yours is the kingdom and the power and the glory forever. Amen.
Matthew 6:9-13

~ ~ ~ ~ ~ ~   Prayer Requests   ~ ~ ~ ~ ~ ~

Found by Those Who Did not Seek Me
Isaiah chapters 64 – 65

Lesson 29

DAY 1 — Righteousness and Good Deeds

➢ <u>Draw near to God and He will draw near to you . . . James 4:8</u>

Today as we read about the miserable condition of our own good deeds and righteousness, let's rejoice in the precious gift of God – clean linen, righteousness by faith in Jesus, good deeds that are acceptable to our Lord! We don't have to mourn over our lack, He has shared His abundance with us!

*"Let us rejoice and be glad and give the glory to Him,
for the marriage of the Lamb has come and His bride has made herself ready."
It was given to her to clothe herself in fine linen, bright and clean;
for the fine linen is the <u>righteous acts</u> of the saints.
Revelation 19:7-8*

MEMORY VERSE   Isaiah 64:4

For from days of old they have not heard nor perceived by ear,

nor has the eye seen a God besides You,

who acts in behalf of the one who waits for Him.

➢ <u>Study to show yourself approved . . . 2 Timothy 2:15</u>

In chapter 64 Isaiah continues the prayer he began in the previous chapter adding intensity as he thinks about the power of God. He begs the Lord to act as He has before so that their enemies would fear His name, even though he admits that they have all sinned and become unclean. All their righteous deeds are worthless.

1. Read Isaiah 64:1-6. Answer the following questions.

What does Isaiah long for in verse 1a?

What analogy does he use to describe the effect this would have (v.1b-2a)?

What would it accomplish (v.2b)?

What does verse 3 say God did in the past?

How is God unlike anyone else in history in verse 4?

Who does the Lord "*meet*" or help (v.5a)?

In contrast, how have God's people acted and what question does Isaiah ask (v.5b)?

What have God's people and their deeds become like (v.6a)?

What will happen to them (v.6b)?

2. Isaiah cries out to God "Oh, that You would rend the heavens and come down, that the mountains might quake at Your presence… to make Your name known to Your adversaries, that the nations may tremble at Your presence!" in Isaiah 64:1-2. His plea is based on what he knew God has done in the past (v.3).

What event in Israel's history is Isaiah remembering? Read Exodus 19:18-20a.

How does this demonstration of God's power impact the nations? Read Nahum 1:5-6.

How can this be a benefit to Israel according to Deuteronomy 2:25?

3. Isaiah 64:3 says "*When You did awesome things which we did not expect…*" What is one of the ways God did something that they did not expect in Deuteronomy 4:36?

4. What are some of the ways "*from days of old*" that the nations have seen God act "*on behalf of the one who waits for Him.*" as Isaiah mentions in 64:4? Use these verses to answer.

Psalm 78:12-15

Psalm 78:23-27

Psalm 78:42-53

5. Isaiah was thinking of the past, but when Paul quotes Isaiah 64:4 loosely in I Corinthians 2:9, (not word for word), he was thinking of the future. How does he use it in context?

6. Isaiah says to the Lord "*You meet him who rejoices in doing righteousness*" in 64:5. What does Acts 10:35 say about this?

Isaiah knew the Lord would accept them if they remembered His ways, but he acknowledges that they are very far from this. "*For we sinned, we continued in them for a long time.*" verse 5 says. In his prayer, Isaiah honors the Lord by stating the truth plainly and agreeing with what God has shown him about his people. What did the Lord reveal to Isaiah about this in Isaiah 59:1-2?

7. Isaiah 64:6 says "*For all of us have become like one who is unclean, and all our righteous deeds are like a filthy garment.*" literally, menstrual rags. This is what their best deeds look like to God. Nothing we do can make us righteous. Righteousness is a gift that God gives us because of our faith in Jesus. Read the following scriptures and summarize what they say about this.

Romans 4:3-8

Romans 10:9-10

Galatians 2:16

8. If anyone had a reason to boast it was Paul, yet look at how he describes his righteous deeds. Read Philippians 3:4-9. What does he say about them in verse 8?

> ## Prove yourselves doers of the word... James 1:22

9. "*You did awesome things which we did not expect*" Isaiah says in verse 3. God wants to do things beyond your highest expectation. Read Ephesians 3:20-21. Ask God to do exceedingly, abundantly beyond all you could even think to ask for.

10. As Isaiah began to pray he found himself strengthened by remembering the mighty deeds of the Lord who "*acts on behalf of those who wait for Him*" Isaiah 64:4. What do you need to remember to encourage your faith? Write it here.

11. "*All our righteous deeds are like a filthy garment.*" Isaiah says in 64:5. Do you find yourself putting hope in your good deeds thinking they will impress Him and get the answer you want? Or how about thinking that He hasn't answered your prayers because you weren't good enough to earn an answer?

God acts because of His own goodness and faithfulness, not because of your good deeds. Ask Him to help you commit your cares to Him and trust Him for the answers.

12. In Isaiah 64:5 it says "*You meet him who rejoices in doing righteousness...*" Are you rejoicing in doing righteousness? Are you growing weary? What does 1 Corinthians 15:58 say?

> ## In everything, by prayer and petition... Philippians 4:6

Bring your cares, burdens, needs and longings to the Lord and ask Him to do far more abundantly than you could think, ask, or even imagine.
Pray for those you know who are satisfied with their own righteousness and don't realize how they need the gift of the Lord. May the Lord open their eyes and their understanding! Ask Him to use you to reach them.

I advise you to buy from Me gold refined by fire so that you may become rich,
and white garments so that you may clothe yourself, and that the shame of your nakedness
will not be revealed; and eye salve to anoint your eyes so that you may see.
Those whom I love, I reprove and discipline; therefore be zealous and repent.
Revelation 3:18-19

~ ~ ~ ~   # DAY 2   ~ ~ ~ ~
The Work of His Hands

> ## Draw near to God and He will draw near to you... James 4:8

We need to be softened. The Lord loves to work with us gently, shaping us into His image and healing the broken places within us. Do you have any hardness of heart? Bring it to Him and let Him have His way. Don't resist Him.

The vessel that he was making of clay was spoiled in the hand of the potter;
so he remade it into another vessel, as it pleased the potter to make.
Jeremiah 18:4

Practice your memory verse:

> For from days of old _____ have not heard nor _____ by ear,
> _____ has the eye seen a God _____ You,
> who acts in _____ of the one who _____ for Him.
> Isaiah 64: __

> ## Study to show yourself approved... 2 Timothy 2:15

In chapter 64 Isaiah continues with his intercession. The Lord has shown him the future of his people and it is so real to him that he is grieving over the destruction of his city and the Lord's Temple. He pleads with the Lord as his Father and as his Potter.

13. **Read Isaiah 64:7-12.** Answer the following questions.

What does Isaiah say about his people in verse 7a?

What has God's response been in verse 7b?

What bold claim does Isaiah make on the Lord in verse 8a?

What other aspect of their relationship with Him does he mention in verse 8b?

How does he plead with God in verse 9?

What has happened to their cities (v.10)?

What has happened to the Temple in verse 11?

What does he ask the Lord in verse 12?

14. Isaiah is grieving over the condition of his people. "*There is no one who calls on Your name*" he says in verse 7. Elijah felt the same way. What does he say about it in 1 Kings 19:14?

15. Isaiah 64:7 says "*For You have hidden Your face from us...*" How do the following verses show people responding to God hiding His face?

Psalm 13:1-4

Psalm 69:17-18

16. What does "*delivered us into the power of our iniquities*" mean (Isaiah 64:7)?
Read Romans 7:15-25 to find out.

17. In Isaiah 64:8, it says "*We are the clay and You our potter.*" Look up the following scriptures and describe the power and authority of the potter versus the attitude of the clay.

reference	Potter	Clay
Isaiah 29:16		
Jeremiah 18:1-10		
Romans 9:20-23		

18. Isaiah 64:8 says "*All of us are the work of Your hand.*" Isaiah is acknowledging God's authority as the Creator. In light of this, what should our attitude be?

Psalm 119:73

Ephesians 2:10

19. Isaiah mourned over "*our holy and beautiful house*" which "*has been burned by fire*" (Isaiah 64:11). He prophesied that the Temple would be destroyed. Look at timeline #2.

When was this fulfilled?

2 Chronicles 36:11-21 explains how the last king of Judah brought this tragedy on Jerusalem. What does verse 19 in this passage say?

Why would those who love God's Temple grieve over its destruction?

Psalm 26:8

Psalm 65:4

Psalm 84:2

Why did the Lord allow His Temple to be destroyed?

Ezekiel 22:26

Ezekiel 23:37-39

20. How do you think the Lord might be stirred by Isaiah's plea? "*Will You restrain Yourself at these things, O Lord? Will You keep silent and afflict us beyond measure?*" (Isaiah 64:12)

➢ Prove yourselves doers of the word... James 1:22

21. In Isaiah 64:7 it says "*There is no one who calls on Your name, who arouses himself to take hold of You.*" Are you faithfully rising up to take hold of the Lord? He longs to be loved by you.

22. "*You have hidden Your face from us*" Isaiah says in 64:7. Have you ever felt like that? What encouragement does Psalm 27:8-9,14 give you?

23. God is the potter and "*All of us are the work of His hands.*" (Isaiah 64:8). Clay that is soft is easy to work with but hard lumps must be broken down until they can be shaped. Are you soft and pliable in His hands? Have you yielded your will to His?

24. When God is fashioning and molding you, do you resist or sit still? What area are you resisting Him in right now?

➤ <u>In everything, by prayer and petition . . . Philippians 4:6</u>

*Now in a large house there are not only gold and silver vessels,
but also vessels of wood and of earthenware, and some to honor and some to dishonor.
Therefore, if anyone cleanses himself from these things, he will be a vessel for honor,
sanctified, useful to the Master, prepared for every good work.
2 Timothy 2:20-21*

Ask the Lord to make you a vessel for honor, sanctified and useful, prepared for every good work. Isaiah pours out his heart in prayer and reminds God of His promises. Take this time to pour out your heart to the Lord and claim the promises that He has given you.

~ ~ ~ ~   **DAY 3**   ~ ~ ~ ~
A Plan For the Gentiles

➤ <u>Draw near to God and He will draw near to you. . . James 4:8</u>

*Behold, you will call a nation you do not know, and a nation which knows you not will run to you,
because of the LORD your God, even the Holy One of Israel; for He has glorified you.
Isaiah 55:5*

How it must comfort the Lord that there are people who will run to Him when the message is preached! His longing for us is so much greater than we know. Turn to Him with all your heart today. Ask Him to draw you closer to Him as you study His word.

Practice your memory verse:

*For _____ days of ____ they _____ not _____ nor _____ by ____,
nor _____ the _____ seen ___ God _____ You,
_____ acts ___ behalf ___ the _____ who _____ for _____.
Isaiah ____:4*

➤ <u>Study to show yourself approved . . . 2 Timothy 2:15</u>

In Isaiah chapter 65, in answer to Isaiah's prayer in the previous chapters, the Lord explains how He will bring good out of His people's sin. He shows us His heart with the moving description of how He has reached out to them and He explains how He will turn to those who haven't known Him or sought Him. He will open up His arms to those who have been far away, the Gentiles.

25. Read Isaiah 65:1-7. Answer the following questions.

What did the Lord permit in verse 1a?

What did He say and to whom in verse 1b?

How does He explain why He has done this in verse 2?

Note – Pause for just a moment and consider this verse. Can you feel God's father heart towards His children? Have you noticed how patiently He reaches out to people?

List how the people provoked Him to His face in verses 3-4.

What do they boast about in verse 5a?

What are they like to God (v.5b)?

What is written in verse 6-7a?

Why will He do this (v.7b)?

26. Fill in the following chart about the sin of God's people.

their sin	scriptures about this
A people who continually provoke Me to My face	Deuteronomy 32:16-17 Psalm 78:58
offering sacrifices in gardens	Isaiah 57:5 Isaiah 66:17
burning incense on bricks	Exodus 20:24-25 Exodus 30:1,8-9
who sit among graves and spend the night in secret places	Numbers 19:11
who eat swine's flesh, and the broth of unclean meat is in their pots	Deuteronomy 14:8
who say 'Keep to yourself, do not come near me, for I am holier than you!'	Luke 5:30, 7:39 Luke 18:9-14

27. God says "*I permitted Myself to be found by those who did not seek Me*" in Isaiah 65:1. This is a prophecy concerning the Gentiles, you and I. Verse 2 explains why the Lord did this. "*I have spread out My hands all day long to a rebellious people.*" Read Romans 10:19-21 and make a note of what His purpose was.

Jesus explained it with a parable. What does Luke 14:16-24 teach?

How does Acts 18:5-6 demonstrate the Jews attitude and God's response?

What does Paul ask in Romans 11:1?

How does he answer the question in Romans 11:11,25?

28. Because of these things the Lord says "*I will not keep silent, but I will repay; I will even repay into their bosom, both their iniquities and the iniquities of their fathers together*" in Isaiah 65:6-7. This speaks of generational sin. What does Exodus 34:7 teach you about this?

29. Does generational sin exist under the New Covenant in Jesus' blood? Read the following scriptures and summarize your answer.
Jeremiah 31:29-30

Romans 5:12-21 (especially v.18)

➤ <u>Prove yourselves doers of the word . . . James 1:22</u>

30. Has the Lord been saying "*Here am I, here am I*" to you? Has He been "*spreading out My hands all day long*" to you and you are resisting Him? Are you walking in "*the way which is not good, following your own thoughts*"? (Isaiah 65:1-2) Ask Him to soften your heart.

31. As Gentiles, what should our attitude be about Israel? Read Romans 11:11-28 before you answer.

32. Jesus has set us free from generational sin but we still suffer the consequences of sin in our lives. Is there a consequence of sin you're still dealing with even though you're forgiven (Galatians 6:7)?

> *I, even I, am the one who wipes out your transgressions*
> *for My own sake, and I will not remember your sins.*
> *Isaiah 43:25*

➤ <u>In everything, by prayer and petition . . . Philippians 4:6</u>

Pray a prayer of gratefulness and thankfulness for Israel. Pray for the peace of Jerusalem.

> *I say then, they did not stumble so as to fall, did they? May it never be!*
> *But by their transgression salvation has come to the Gentiles, to make them jealous.*
> *Now if their transgression is riches for the world and their failure is riches for the Gentiles,*
> *how much more will their fulfillment be!*
> *Romans 11:11-12*

Thank God for your salvation. Everyday is different because of Him; we experience peace, joy, purpose, forgiveness....

~ ~ ~ ~ <u>DAY 4</u> ~ ~ ~ ~
Those Who Are Blessed vs. Those Who Are Cursed

➢ <u>Draw near to God and He will draw near to you... James 4:8</u>

*Moreover the LORD your God will circumcise your heart and the
heart of your descendants, to love the LORD your God with all your heart
and with all your soul, so that you may live.
Deuteronomy 30:6*

*Create in me a clean heart, O God,
And renew a steadfast spirit within me.
Psalm 51:10*

*And I will give them one heart and one way, that they may fear Me always,
for their own good and for the good of their children after them.
I will make an everlasting covenant with them that I will not turn away from them,
to do them good; and I will put the fear of Me in their hearts
so that they will not turn away from Me.
Jeremiah 32:39-40*

The Lord has made a way for His people, not based on their own deeds of righteousness but on His mighty gift. He is able to grant us a heart that will not turn away from Him. Ask and you will receive so that your joy may be complete!!!

Practice your memory verse:

_____ from ___ of old _____ have _____ heard _____ perceived ____ ear,

_____ has ____ eye _____ a _____ besides _____,

who _____ in _____ of ____ one _____ waits _____ Him.

Isaiah ____ : ___

➢ <u>Study to show yourself approved ... 2 Timothy 2:15</u>

Isaiah chapter 65 continues with a vivid description of the difference between how the servants of the Lord will be treated and how those who turn away from the Lord will be treated. This isn't meant to show God's vindictiveness, but rather the astonishing hardness of those who choose their own way after being shown such grace by God.

33. Read Isaiah 65:8-16. Answer the following questions.

What hope does the Lord give in the midst of this prophecy of judgment (v.8)?

Who will inherit the land and dwell there (v.9)?

What will He provide for those who seek Him (v.10)?

Who does He speak to in verse 11 and what does He say they've done?

What destiny will the Lord give them in verse 12a?

Why will He do this (v.12b,c)?

What does the Lord expect when He calls and speaks (v.12b)?

Contrast what the Lord will do for His servants vs. those who did evil in His sight using verses 13-15.

God's servants	those who did evil in His sight

What does verse 16a say about those who are blessed?

What does verse 16b say about those who swear?

Why is this the case (v.16c)?

34. Isaiah 65:9-10, talks about what God promises to do for those who seek Him. What does 2 Chronicles 7:14 say about this?

35. Read the story about the valley of Achor from Joshua 7 and summarize it here.

> The word "Achor" in Hebrew means "trouble".

36. Isaiah 65:10 says "*the valley of Achor (will be) a resting place for herds, for My people who seek Me*". Israel understood what this meant. How would making this a resting place be a huge comfort?

37. Isaiah 65:11 refers to sacrifices they offered to false gods. In question 26, we saw that they were sacrificing to demons (Deuteronomy 32:17). What admonition does Paul add to this in 1 Corinthians 10:20-21?

38. In Isaiah 65:15, it says "*My servants will be called by another name.*" What do these verses say about this?

Isaiah 44:5

Isaiah 62:2-4

Acts 11:26b

39. In Isaiah 65:16 it says "*the former troubles are forgotten and they are hidden from My sight!*" Write down what Jeremiah 31:34b says about this.

➢ <u>Prove yourselves doers of the word . . . James 1:22</u>

40. What does God replace our former troubles with? Read Isaiah 61:3.

41. How has God taken your valley of Achor (Valley of Troubles, v.10) and made them forgotten?

42. In Isaiah 65:13-15 it says that the servants of the Lord will eat, drink, rejoice, shout joyfully and be called by a new name. Read John 10:10 and see how God wants your life to be. Does this describe your life? Write your thoughts about this.

➢ <u>In everything, by prayer and petition . . . Philippians 4:6</u>

Thank God for taking away your former troubles and replacing them with His joy.

> *When the LORD brought back the captive ones of Zion, we were like those who dream.*
> *Then our mouth was filled with laughter and our tongue with joyful shouting; then they said among the nations, "The LORD has done great things for them."*
> *The LORD has done great things for us; we are glad.*
> *Psalm 126:1-3*

~ ~ ~ ~
# DAY 5
The Messiah's Reign

➢ <u>Draw near to God and He will draw near to you . . . James 4:8</u>

> *But we all, with unveiled face, beholding as in a mirror the glory of the Lord,*
> *are being transformed into the same image from glory to glory,*
> *just as from the Lord, the Spirit.*
> *2 Corinthians 3:18*

> *Therefore I urge you, brethren, by the mercies of God,*
> *to present your bodies a living and holy sacrifice, acceptable to God,*
> *which is your spiritual service of worship. And do not be conformed to this world,*
> *but be transformed by the renewing of your mind, so that you may prove*
> *what the will of God is, that which is good and acceptable and perfect.*
> *Romans 12:1-2*

> *For those whom He foreknew, He also predestined to become conformed*
> *to the image of His Son, so that He would be the firstborn among many brethren;*
> *Romans 8:29*

> *.... and have put on the new self who is being renewed to a true knowledge*
> *according to the image of the One who created him –*
> *Colossians 3:10*

> *Just as we have borne the image of the earthy,*
> *we will also bear the image of the heavenly.*
> *1 Corinthians 15:49*

God is transforming our lives into His image. Praise Him for this truth.

Write down your memory verse:

➢ <u>Study to show yourself approved... 2 Timothy 2:15</u>

Isaiah chapter 65 concludes with a prophecy about the 1000 year reign of Christ and the creation of a new heavens and a new earth. It includes all the blessings God has promised about His people that have yet to be fulfilled.

43. **Read Isaiah 65:17-25.** Answer the following questions.

What will God do (v.17a)?

What will happen to the former things (v.17b)?

What should our attitude be because of this (v.18a)?

What will the Lord create Jerusalem and her people for (v.18b)?

How will the Lord feel about it (v.19a)?

What will no longer be found in this city (v.19b)?

How does verse 20 describe the longevity of those who live there?

How will the people labor and what benefit will they receive (v.21-22)?

What does verse 23a say about them?

Why will this happen in verse 23b?

What wonderful promise does the Lord give them in verse 24?

What else will characterize the Lord's holy mountain (v.25)?

44. Isaiah 65:17 says "*I create new heavens and a new earth.*" Look up the following scriptures and make a note of how this will be fulfilled.

2 Peter 3:10-13

Revelation 21:1.

45. Isaiah 65:18-25 goes on to describe the millennial kingdom when Jesus will reign here on earth, <u>before</u> it is destroyed by fire. Look up these verses and describe the millennial kingdom.

Isaiah 2:4

Isaiah 9:6-7

Isaiah 11:6-9

Micah 4:3

Revelation 20:1-5

46. In Isaiah 65:24 it says *"It will also come to pass that before they call, I will answer; and while they are still speaking, I will hear."* Look up the following scriptures and make a note of how God answers prayer.

Psalm 91:15

Isaiah 58:9

Daniel 9:20-23

47. Are there prayers you're asking for? He says He will answer. Believe Him.

> Prove yourselves doers of the word ... James 1:22

48. Look at Isaiah 65:17. In 2 Peter 3:11, Peter asks a very insightful question. *"Since all these things are to be destroyed in this way, what sort of people ought you to be?"* (2 Peter 3:11) What is the answer according to the following scriptures?

Matthew 6:19-21

Philippians 1:27a

1 Timothy 4:12

1 Peter 2:12

2 Peter 3:11-14

49. In Isaiah 65:17b it says *"the former things will not be remembered or come to mind."* Praise God that He puts our past and our sorrows behind us, and the former things do not come to mind! How does John 16:22 explain why this will happen?

> In everything, by prayer and petition ... Philippians 4:6

Thank God for the answers to your prayers. Give Him your concerns and things that are weighing you down. He is trustworthy.

Do not be afraid, Daniel, for from the first day that you set your heart on understanding this and on humbling yourself before your God, your words were heard.
Daniel 10:12

~ ~ ~ ~ ~ ~   Prayer Requests   ~ ~ ~ ~ ~ ~

New Heavens and a New Earth
Isaiah chapter 66
Lesson 30

DAY 1 — Where the Lord Dwells

> Draw near to God and He will draw near to you... James 4:8

How lovely are Your dwelling places, O LORD of hosts!
My soul longed and even yearned for the courts of the LORD;
My heart and my flesh sing for joy to the living God.
Psalm 84:1-2

Nothing is more joyful than being in the presence of God. He has chosen you for His dwelling place! Take a moment to ponder this. Ask Him to transform you more and more each day into the home He desires.

MEMORY VERSE — Isaiah 66:2

For My hand made all these things, thus all these things came into being," declares the LORD. "But to this one I will look, to him who is humble and contrite of spirit, and who trembles at My word.

> Study to show yourself approved... 2 Timothy 2:15

In Isaiah chapter 66, the Lord answers Isaiah's prayer for the Temple (Isaiah 64:10-11). He makes it clear that when the people are filled with evil, there is no place for His presence to rest. The destruction of the Temple building is merely symbolic of the much more terrible destruction that has happened in the souls of His people.

1. Read Isaiah 66:1-6. Answer the following questions.

How does the Lord view heaven and the earth (v.1a)?

What does the Lord ask in verse 1b?

What does the Lord say about everything in heaven and earth (v.2a)?

To whom will the Lord look (v.2b)?

How does the Lord view His people's sacrifices, offerings and incense (v.3a)?

What reason does He give in verse 3b?

What will He do in verse 4a?

Why will He do it (v.4b)?

Who does the Lord speak to in verse 5a?

What have their brothers said to them in verse 5b that was particularly offensive to the Lord?

What attitude do you think this comment reveals in the scoffers?

What will happen to the scoffers (v.5c)?

Where does the voice of the Lord come from in verse 6 and what does it bring?

2. Isaiah 66:1 says "*Where then is the house you could build for Me?*" How do these references show where God's presence does <u>not</u> dwell?
Acts 7:48-50

Acts 17:24-25

3. Isaiah 66:1 makes it clear that the Lord doesn't dwell in a physical temple made with human hands. What does Ephesians 2:20-22 say?

What does I Corinthians 6:19-20 add to this?

What do you think it means to "*tremble at His word*" (Isaiah 66:2,5)? Read Acts 16:29-32.

In Isaiah's day people weren't trembling at His word. What does Isaiah 29:13 say they were doing?

4. According to Isaiah 66:5, their brothers mocked them saying "*Let the Lord be glorified that we may see your joy.*" This is the same attitude that the scoffers in Jerusalem showed towards Jesus. Read Matthew 27:39-44. Then make a note of what 1 Peter 2:23 says.

How could anyone be so foolish as to mock God's people in this way? What do these verses say?
Psalm 10:3-4,11

Psalm 14:1

Psalm 36:1

Psalm 52:7

Romans 1:21-22

Read what will happen to scoffers in Proverbs 1:22-32. Write one sentence to summarize it.

5. We may also have to bear the Lord's reproach. Read these scriptures. How do they encourage you?

Matthew 5:10-12

1 Peter 4:14

> ➤ Prove yourselves doers of the word... James 1:22

6. *"But to this one I will look, to him who is humble and contrite of spirit and who trembles at My word"* Isaiah 66:2. This is what the Lord longs and looks for. Read these scriptures.

2 Chronicles 34:27

Psalm 51:17

Isaiah 57:15

How does God look upon those who demonstrate this kind of humility?

7. Do you allow yourself to scoff at the things of God? Have you ever scorned someone else's style of worship and relationship with the Lord? What should you do?

> ➤ In everything, by prayer and petition... Philippians 4:6

Ask God to give you a greater respect for His word, to learn to regard it with awe and respect. Pray that the Lord would cleanse and transform you into a dwelling place that is pure and holy, a joy for Him. Ask Him to change any attitudes of scorn or cynicism. Ask Him to fill you with praise.

The bird also has found a house, and the swallow a nest for herself,
where she may lay her young, even Your altars, O LORD of hosts, My King and my God.
How blessed are those who dwell in Your house! They are ever praising You.
Psalm 84:3-4

~ ~ ~ ~ # DAY 2 ~ ~ ~ ~
Born in One Day

> ➤ Draw near to God and He will draw near to you... James 4:8

That which is born of the flesh is flesh, and that which is born of the Spirit is spirit.
Do not be amazed that I said to you, 'You must be born again.' The wind blows where it wishes
and you hear the sound of it, but do not know where it comes from and where it is going;
so is everyone who is born of the Spirit.
John 3:6-8

The Lord has created us as spiritual beings to live in a spiritual kingdom. Our true home is not in this world. We will always have an element of sorrow in our hearts because we are longing for our eternal home. But the Lord is always here encouraging us and helping us to be patient until the day He takes us home. Take a moment to give thanks for the Lord's comforting presence.

Practice your memory verse:

> For My _____ made all these things,
> thus all these _____ came into being," _____ the LORD.
> "But to this one I will _____, to him who is _____ and contrite of spirit,
> and who _____ at My word.
> Isaiah ____:2

➢ <u>Study to show yourself approved . . . 2 Timothy 2:15</u>

Isaiah chapter 66 continues with a description of the nation God will create in one day. He encourages His people who are hoping in His promises to not doubt. He assures them that they will see Jerusalem when it is restored and will be cared for and comforted by it.

8. Read Isaiah 66:7-14. Answer the following questions.

What word picture does the Lord use to describe the deliverance He will accomplish for His people in verse 7?

(M)

What amazing thing will the Lord do in verse 8?

How does He encourage Isaiah not to lose hope in verse 9?

How does the Lord encourage those who mourn over Jerusalem (v.10)?

How will the Lord nurture them in verse 11 and what does He mean by this word picture?

How will He bless them? List the things you find in verses 12-14.

9. In verses 7-9, Isaiah uses the metaphor of a woman giving birth to describe the nation of Israel being born in one day. How does Isaiah 26:17-18 describe what they were going through?

Israel couldn't bring deliverance to the earth. They were never meant to. But they did bring the Deliverer to earth. Read Revelation 12:1-2, 5. This refers to Israel. Verse 5 makes this clear. How is Israel described in verses 1-2?

How is her Child described in does Revelation 12:5?

Note – The political Israel was born on May 14, 1948 but the new Israel will be born in a day when they believe in the Lord Jesus Christ. Jerusalem will experience joy, peace, and satisfaction.

10. In Isaiah 66:7 it says *"she gave birth to a boy"* and we saw that this referred to Jesus. Then in verse 8 it says *"As soon as Zion travailed, she also brought forth her sons."* This refers to those who would believe in Jesus. The verses that follow after it describe how these sons will be lovingly cared for.

"Can a nation be brought forth all at once?" Isaiah 66:8 asks. Yes!! Jesus saved us in one day! How did He accomplish such a great thing *"in one day"*?

Jesus had one purpose from the beginning. What was it?	John 1:29
Who took His life from Him?	John 10:17-18
What did He accomplish on the day He died?	Hebrews 9:12
What did He become for us?	John 11:25-26
What response is needed from us?	John 1:12, 3:3

11. Isaiah 66:9 says *"Shall I bring to the point of birth and not give delivery?"* We are meant to rejoice in what God is doing even before it is done. The nation will go through some very hard times but the birth of the nation will happen! What exhortations does God give in these verses?

Genesis 18:14a

Zechariah 8:6

Matthew 14:30-32

Matthew 19:26

12. The Lord calls us to *"Be joyful with Jerusalem and rejoice for her, all you who love her; be exceedingly glad with her, all you who mourn over her"* in Isaiah 66:10. How do these scriptures show you that this is speaking to us?

John 16:20-22

Romans 8:22-23

13. In Isaiah 66:11 –13, Isaiah continues with the idea of a mother taking care of her young. This is how the Lord will deal with Israel. She will be restored. What blesses you the most about this description?

14. Isaiah 66:14 says *"Your bones will flourish like the new grass."* Ezekiel 37:1-14 gives an incredible description of this. Summarize what it says.

➢ <u>Prove yourselves doers of the word … James 1:22</u>

15. *"Shall I bring to the point of birth and not give delivery?"* (Isaiah 66:9) God is saying here, 'You can count on Me. I always do what I say. I always complete what I begin.' Read Philippians 1:6. How does this encourage you?

16. Isaiah 66:10 encourages us to rejoice because of what the Lord will do. After all you've studied today, what do you look forward to the most?

17. The Lord wants to care for you as a mother would her young baby (Isaiah 66:12). He promises to comfort you (v.13). What area do you need comfort in? Tell the Lord.

➤ <u>In everything, by prayer and petition . . . Philippians 4:6</u>

Thank God, our Father cares for us as gently as a mother. Praise Him that He will deliver what He has promised.

> *Blessed be the God and Father of our Lord Jesus Christ,*
> *who according to His great mercy has caused us to be born again to a living hope*
> *through the resurrection of Jesus Christ from the dead, to obtain an inheritance which*
> *is imperishable and undefiled and will not fade away, reserved in heaven for you.*
> *1 Peter 1:3-4*

~ ~ ~ ~   **DAY 3**   ~ ~ ~ ~
A Grain Offering

➤ <u>Draw near to God and He will draw near to you. . . James 4:8</u>

> *For thus says the LORD, 'David shall never lack a man to sit on the throne of the house of Israel;*
> *and the Levitical priests shall never lack a man before Me to offer burnt offerings,*
> *to burn grain offerings and to prepare sacrifices continually.'*
> *Jeremiah 33:17-18*

Jesus, the Son of David, is always present with the Father on our behalf. Whatever we offer to God, whether our prayers, burdens or fears, Jesus always makes our offerings acceptable to the Father. What do you want to bring to Him today? He welcomes you with open arms.

Practice your memory verse:

_____ My _____ made _____ these _____ ,
thus _____ these _____ came _____ being," _____ the _____ .
"But _____ this _____ I _____ look, _____ him _____ is _____ and _____ of _____ ,
and _____ trembles _____ My _____ .
Isaiah 66: ___

➤ <u>Study to show yourself approved . . . 2 Timothy 2:15</u>

Isaiah chapter 66 describes two gatherings, one for judgment and one for grace. The Lord will gather the nations to see His glory and He will judge them. But there will be survivors and He will use them to declare His glory among the nations that have never heard of Him. They will return to Jerusalem bringing back the sons of Israel as a grain offering. This could well be a picture of the gospel being preached in all the world and the harvest of the word of God.

18. Read Isaiah 66:15-22. Answer the following questions.

The last line of verse 14 said "*He will be indignant toward His enemies.*" How does verse 15 say the Lord will come and for what purpose?

How will the Lord deal judgment (v.16)?

Who will He target according to verse 17?

What does the Lord know (v.18a)?

What has the time come for (v.18b)?

What will the Lord do according to verse 19a?

Where will He send them (v.19b)?

What will their purpose be (v.19c)?

What will they do in verse 20a?

What does the Lord compare this offering to (v.20b)? Why do you think He says this?

What will the Lord do with this offering (v.21)?

How long will their offspring and their name endure and what does He compare them to (v.22)?

19. "*I will set a sign among them and will send survivors from them to the nations*" the Lord says in Isaiah 66:19. How does Ephesians 3:8 give an example of the fulfillment of this prophecy?

Note – the nations mentioned are some of the most distant known at that time spreading out in all different directions from Jerusalem.

Read Psalm 126. How does this song show that survivors like these would be a perfect witness to the nations?

20. Isaiah 66:20 says "*Then they shall bring all your brethren from all the nations as a grain offering to the Lord.*" How do the following verses explain the grain offering?

Leviticus 2:1-5

Leviticus 2:11, 13-14

The grain offering is full of rich symbolism for the believer in Christ. Each element of it represents an aspect of our spiritual life. Fill in the following chart to learn what the symbols mean.

symbol	scripture	what it means
bread or flour	Luke 22:19	
oil	1 Samuel 16:13 Acts 10:38	
incense	Revelation 5:8b	
salt	Matthew 5:13a Colossians 4:6	
unleavened	Matthew 16:11-12	

How do these verses make it clear that the Lord considers those who are saved a grain offering?
Matthew 9:37-38

Matthew 13:24-30, 36-43

"For from the rising of the sun even to its setting, My name will be great among the nations, and in every place incense is going to be offered to My name, and a grain offering that is pure; for My name will be great among the nations," says the LORD of hosts.
Malachi 1:11

> ## Prove yourselves doers of the word ... James 1:22

21. Are you praying for a "*grain offering*" to bring to the Lord? Who or what people group is on your heart?

22. Isaiah 66:16 says "*the Lord will execute judgment by fire*" because of "*their works and their thoughts*" (v.18). Then he says that there will be survivors declaring the glory of God among the nations. How has the Lord used your suffering to soften your heart and give you compassion for the lost people in the world?

23. Isaiah 66:18 says "*For I know their works and their thoughts.*" Read Joshua 7:1, 19-20. God sees our hidden sin. Confess your sins to God. He's ready to forgive.

24. In Isaiah 66:20-21 we see that God is going to take people from all around the world and make them priests unto the Lord. How is 1 Peter 2:9 a fulfillment of this?

> ## In everything, by prayer and petition ... Philippians 4:6

Ask the Lord to grant you an abundant "*grain offering*". Offer yourself to Him and ask Him to use your former trials and suffering for His glory. Pray for the Lord to send more workers into the harvest.

Those who sow in tears shall reap with joyful shouting. He who goes to and fro weeping, carrying his bag of seed, shall indeed come again with a shout of joy, bringing his sheaves with him.
Psalm 126:5-6

~ ~ ~ ~   **DAY 4**   ~ ~ ~ ~
Eternal Destiny

> ➢ <u>Draw near to God and He will draw near to you... James 4:8</u>

Therefore if anyone is in Christ, he is a new creature;
the old things passed away; behold, new things have come.
2 Corinthians 5:17

And He who sits on the throne said, "Behold, I am making all things new."
And He said, "Write, for these words are faithful and true."
Revelation 21:5

Lay the past behind you and believe God is making all things new. Accept forgiveness for yourself. God forgives you. He loves you.

. . . to the praise of the glory of His grace, by which He has <u>made us accepted in the Beloved</u>.
Ephesians 1:6

Practice your memory verse:

For ____ hand ____ all ____ things,
____ all ____ things ____ into ____ ," declares ____ LORD.
" ____ to ____ one ____ will ____ , to ____ who ____ humble ____ contrite ____ spirit,
____ who ____ at ____ word.
Isaiah ____ : ____

> ➢ <u>Study to show yourself approved... 2 Timothy 2:15</u>

Isaiah chapter 66 finishes with a dramatic contrast between the righteous who worship the Lord and the wicked whose corpses become an abhorrence to all mankind. Today we will look at the eternal destiny of those who have not chosen God.

25. Read Isaiah 66:23-24. Answer the following questions.

What measure of time does the Lord use in verse 23a?

What will happen (v.23b)?

What will the people do when they come to worship the Lord (v. 24a)?

How are these corpses described (v.24b)?

26. In Isaiah 66:24 we see a picture of Hell. Read another description of hell in Mark 9:43-48. How is it described?

27. Read Luke 16:19-31. Before Christ died, all those who died went to a place of waiting, either to Abraham's bosom for the righteous dead or Hades for the unrighteous dead. Briefly describe each place.

28. After Jesus died He went to their place of waiting. Read the following scriptures and summarize what you learn about this.

Ephesians 4:8

1 Peter 3:18-19

1 Peter 4:6

29. Because of Jesus' death and resurrection, we have immediate entrance into the presence of the Lord when we die. Read these scriptures and write down what you learn.

Luke 23:43

2 Corinthians 5:8

30. God never intended to send man to hell, but when we reject Christ and align ourselves with the interest of Satan's, He has no choice but to justly judge us. Who was hell prepared for? Read Matthew 25:41.

> In John 3:19-20 it says that men love the darkness rather than the light because their deeds are evil. They have preferred the filthy rags of their own righteousness over the clean robes of righteousness Jesus offers. They are unfit for heaven and the presence of God which is such a joy for the believer is a torment to them.

31. What will be the final destiny of Satan? Read the scriptures below and summarize them.

Revelation 20:10

Revelation 20:13-14. *(Notice Hades is thrown into the Lake of Fire.)*

32. There is comfort for us who have chosen Jesus. Read Revelation 21:4.

33. But there is an urgency and responsibility to share this good news that Jesus has saved us from the wrath to came. Read the flowing scriptures and write down their promises.

John 3:18

2 Peter 3:9

Revelation 22:12

> ➤ Prove yourselves doers of the word... James 1:22

34. Read what Jesus has commanded us in Matthew 10:28. What advice does He give us?

35. Write out Hebrews 10:31 here.

36. Have you truly chosen the righteousness given to us freely in Jesus? If you have then you need not ever fear God's wrath. If not, then do it NOW. Don't put it off any longer. Pray, confess your sins and ask Jesus to forgive you. Proclaim with your mouth your belief that He rose from the dead. Tell someone about it.

*For God has not destined us for wrath, but for obtaining
salvation through our Lord Jesus Christ.
1 Thessalonians 5:9*

*For this is the will of My Father, that everyone who beholds the Son and believes in Him,
may have eternal life; and I Myself will raise him up on the last day.
John 6:40*

➢ <u>In everything, by prayer and petition . . . Philippians 4:6</u>

There are still many who don't know Him. Let this give you a greater resolve to share your hope of heaven with those destined for hell.

Pray and ask God to give you His heart for the lost. Pray right now for each one by name.

Comfort, O comfort My people," says your God. Isaiah 40:1

~ ~ ~ ~ **DAY 5** ~ ~ ~ ~
Conclusion

➢ <u>Draw near to God and He will draw near to you. . . James 4:8</u>

Read the following scriptures with a thankful heart and take joy in all the Lord has done for you.

*Shout for joy, O heavens, for the LORD has done it! Shout joyfully, you lower parts of the earth;
Break forth into a shout of joy, you mountains, O forest, and every tree in it;
For the LORD has redeemed Jacob and in Israel He shows forth His glory
Isaiah 44:23*

*Shout for joy, O heavens! And rejoice, O earth! Break forth into joyful shouting, O mountains!
For the LORD has comforted His people and will have compassion on His afflicted.
Isaiah 49:13*

*"Shout for joy, O barren one, you who have borne no child;
Break forth into joyful shouting and cry aloud, you who have not travailed;
For the sons of the desolate one will be more numerous than the sons of the married woman,"
says the LORD.
Isaiah 54:1*

*Instead of your shame you will have a double portion,
and instead of humiliation they will shout for joy over their portion.
Therefore they will possess a double portion in their land, everlasting joy will be theirs.
Isaiah 61:7*

Write down your memory verse:

➤ <u>Study to show yourself approved ... 2 Timothy 2:15</u>

Congratulations! You have finished the book of Isaiah. As a wrap up, we will read the conclusion and look back at what God has taught you through Isaiah.

37. Read the *Conclusion to Isaiah* located at the end of this study. Summarize your thoughts about the book of Isaiah.

38. One of the themes in Isaiah was God's great love for all nations and His plan to redeem them. Look up the following verses and summarize what they teach about this.

Isaiah 2:2

Isaiah 11:10

Isaiah 42:6

Isaiah 49:6

Isaiah 52:14-15

Isaiah 53:11

Isaiah 61:11

39. How do these scriptures summarize the Lord's patience and long-suffering?

Isaiah 30:18

Isaiah 42:14

Isaiah 48:9

Isaiah 57:11

Isaiah 65:2

Why is the Lord so patient and long-suffering? Read 2 Peter 3:9.

40. Another theme in Isaiah is God's restoration, His promise of abundant waters in the wilderness. How do these verses show that?

Isaiah 32:2

Isaiah 41:17-18

Isaiah 43:19-21

Isaiah 48:21

Isaiah 49:10

> ### Prove yourselves doers of the word... James 1:22

41. Praise God for His promise of fruitfulness in a parched land! How has He refreshed you with His living waters? How have His promises revived your hope and comforted you in trials?

42. *"You thought I was just like you."* the Lord says in Psalm 50:21. We don't even realize how limited our view of God can be. How has studying Isaiah increased your understanding of who our Lord is and what He is like? Is He more real to you?

43. Has your view of the teachings in God's word changed in any way? How?

44. What impact do you think this study has made on your life?

How would you like to apply what you've learned?

Do you have any questions you would like the Lord to answer? What are they?

> ### In everything, by prayer and petition... Philippians 4:6

Praise God for His patience and long-suffering towards all nations! Ask Him to reveal Himself to them and soften their hearts. Ask Him to help you redeem the time you have, boldly sharing your faith about "your Redeemer, the Holy One of Israel, who is called the God of all the earth." (Isaiah 54:5b)

*For you will go out with joy and be led forth with peace;
the mountains and the hills will break forth into shouts of joy before you,
and all the trees of the field will clap their hands.
Isaiah 55:12*

~ ~ ~ ~ ~ ~   Prayer Requests   ~ ~ ~ ~ ~ ~ ~

In Conclusion

"Holy! Holy! Holy!" the seraphim called out to each other as they hovered around the presence of the Living God in His appearance to the greatest prophet Judah had ever known. This gripping revelation of the Lord forever changed Isaiah's life, coloring and shaping everything he said or did to the end of his days. He referred to the Lord repeatedly as the Holy One of Israel, a name used first by King David in the Psalms and rarely used anywhere else.

This is the one theme that ties together the whole message of Isaiah. In His holiness the Lord called Isaiah and purified his lips so that he could speak the word of the Lord. Because of His holiness, judgment was predicted (and came) to the nations who had seen His glory. In holiness, the Lord made a plan to save all Israel and the nations from their sin and judgment, one that wouldn't compromise His purity, His truth, His very identity. He, Himself, the Holy One of Israel, would reach down and redeem His people. *Your Redeemer is the Holy One of Israel, who is called the God of all the earth.* (Isaiah 54:5b) And He even made clear that He would welcome other nations in these promises.

> *I permitted myself to be sought by those who did not ask for me;*
> *I permitted myself to be found by those who did not seek me.*
> *I said, 'Here am I, here am I,' to a nation which did not call on My name.*
> Isaiah 65:1

God's incredible plan of salvation was revealed more vividly and thoroughly in this book than anywhere else in the Old Testament. David described Jesus' suffering in Psalm 22 but who understood how it would be fulfilled? Isaiah revealed its significance when he clearly explained the sacrifice of the Messiah and proclaimed "... *the LORD has caused the iniquity of us all to fall on Him.*" (Isaiah 53:6)

But that's not all!! God's holiness demanded a holy sacrifice, but the intent of His loving heart was eternal redemption. A rescue more wonderful, more beautiful, more spectacular than anything people could imagine! Isaiah doesn't just tell us of the sin that was so contrary to the Lord's holiness, or the judgment coming because of it. He didn't just proclaim a Redeemer who would spare all those who repent – He proclaimed even louder the glorious inheritance and restoration of Israel and all those who would turn to the Holy One of Israel! He testified to the flowing of healing waters and rebirth of life in the desert, a picture of the life that would come from the outpouring of the Holy Spirit of God – this Living Spirit Who could now come upon all flesh because of the perfect sacrifice, without compromising His holiness!! How beautiful and majestic are the ways of God!! How glorious His redemption!! No wonder the Lord cries out "... *I am God, and there is no one like me.*" (Isaiah 46:9)

Can you see how great Isaiah's plea is? Having witnessed such an incredible demonstration of who God is and what He planned for us, how earnest the call to repent becomes! Every aspect of waywardness is touched on; those who worship idols, those who fear men, those who pretend to worship the Lord but whose hearts are far away, those who rebel and those who are complacent or self-indulgent. What anguish we hear in Isaiah's voice when he realizes that many aren't listening! *Who has believed our message?* (Isaiah 53:1) Yet for the sake of those who will listen, yesterday, today and until He comes back, the message will most certainly be proclaimed. *"You are My witnesses," declares the LORD.* (Isaiah 43:10a) and *How lovely on the mountains are the feet of him who brings good news, who announces peace and brings good news of happiness, who announces salvation, and says to Zion, "Your God reigns!"* (Isaiah 52:7)

Our prayer for you is that having studied this book, <u>you will never be the same</u> and that you will flourish in the fruitfulness of the Lord as He promised:

> *'For I will pour out water on the thirsty land and streams on the dry ground;*
> *I will pour out My Spirit on your offspring, and My blessing on your descendants;*
> *And they will spring up among the grass like poplars by streams of water.'*
> *"This one will say, 'I am the LORD'S'; and that one will call on the name of Jacob;*
> *and another will write on his hand, 'Belonging to the LORD,'*
> *and will name Israel's name with honor.*
> Isaiah 44:3-5

Isaiah Study Appendix

Historical Summaries   page

- Overview of the History of the Ancient World   380
- History of Aram   384
- History of Assyria   385
- History of Babylon   386
- History of Edom   387
- History of Egypt   388
- History of Israel   389
- History of Moab   390
- History of Tyre & Sidon   391

Optional study tools

- Messianic Prophecies in Isaiah   393
- The Day of the Lord Prophecies   395
- The Holy One References   397

Overview Of The History Of The Ancient World

     In Genesis, the Bible describes for us how man was created, how he multiplied and filled the earth, and how he grew increasingly evil until every living person, from their youth on was filled with evil thoughts. The Lord was grieved in His heart and decided to start over. There was only one man left who was righteous, a man of God, a man of faith – not perfect, but definitely dedicated to the Lord with all his heart. This man, Noah, became the beginning of a new era on earth. Everyone else was destroyed in the flood. He spent a hundred years building a large ship and had three sons during that time. He, his wife, his sons and their wives, were the only people to survive.

     When Noah descended from the ark and offered a sacrifice to the Lord, God decided to never again curse the land because of man. He commanded them to multiply and fill the earth, just as He had commanded Adam, and then He added something new:

> *Whoever sheds man's blood, by man his blood shall be shed,*
> *for in the image of God He made man.*
> *Genesis 9:6*

     The precedent God had set before the flood provided protection for murderers (Genesis 4:15, 23), but now, men were to be held accountable for this sin. It's as if God was proving that this kind of mercy was not merciful since it allowed evil to flourish and take over the earth in an extremely short period of time. After the flood, murderers were held accountable and to some extent, evil was restrained. The other way in which the Lord restricted the spread of evil was to greatly shorten men's lives.

     In the earliest years after the flood, the worship of the Lord was the only religion on earth. But it wasn't long before people rebelled. Instead of spreading out and filling the earth as God had commanded, they decided to gather in one place and make a name for themselves. They began building a city with a tower, and with it a new religion. The Lord effectively ended their unity and propelled them into following His command by confusing their languages so they couldn't understand each other. Even now language is a living, changing thing and today there are thousands of languages on earth. Unable to work together or share knowledge and skills, they abandoned their city and their tower and began to spread out gradually filling the continent as the generations passed and their numbers increased.

     Think of it as ripples in the water. When a stone falls into the water, the surface is disturbed and a small wave bursts out from the spot where the stone fell. This wave ripples outwards in circular form, growing increasingly larger in diameter until it bounces against some surface. It is followed by a series of other waves in the same form. The spread of ancient civilization followed a similar pattern. The first wave being the pioneers, and those who followed in increasing numbers filled the land. When the migrating tribes came against a mountain range or an ocean coast, it hindered and delayed their advance. Eventually, the waves washed over or around these obstacles. If you study the history of the ancient world in chronological order, (not by cultures the way it is often presented today), you will see this effect. The earliest wave, a brave adventurous, often nature loving people. Later waves, more civilized, more organized, either filling in the land, or driving the first ones back, or conquering. The way Europeans spread across the Americas is a good example of this.

     This is important to understand because otherwise we won't see how the Lord revealed Himself to ALL the nations of the ancient world and how He was right to hold them accountable to what they knew of Him.

The earliest civilization we know of was birthed in the valley of Shinar, an ancient kingdom known to us as Sumer. Archeology has uncovered tens of thousands of clay tablets, most of which haven't been translated yet, and numerous evidences of the sophistication of their learning and culture. They had advanced mathematics and astronomy, as well. This is the land of the Chaldeans, in which the city of Ur is found -- from which Abram came.

Several other civilizations were birthed almost simultaneously, Egypt, Ashur, Canaanites, Amorites and others. It is interesting to note that these people, in their own historical records have a definite beginning and a first king. They had a highly complex civilization. Not only did they develop central government, division of labor, religious beliefs and practices, they also had their own method of writing. Again let me stress that they believed these had a beginning, not an evolution over time from a simpler lifestyle. Archeological evidence has an abrupt beginning, as well. There is no obvious transition from the simple to the complex.

These early cultures had not forgotten their heritage in the teachings of Noah and his sons. In fact, according to the genealogical records of Genesis, Noah's son Shem was still alive when Abram was born.

Some noteworthy examples: in Egypt, one of the early Pharaohs had the custom of taking beautiful women to be his wives. When Abram and his wife Sarai traveled there, they pretended she was his sister because she was so beautiful that he was afraid he would be killed for his wife. Pharaoh took her into his harem and God punished him. Then he was angry with Abram because of the deceit, implying that he would not have touched a married woman. (Genesis 12:10-20) Notice what he did NOT say. He didn't ask who the Lord was or question His existence or authority. Neither did he dispute the Lord's complaint against him. He understood the moral standard that God was holding him accountable to and submitted to it. In contrast, hundreds of years later, Moses' contemporary had no knowledge of God.

We see the same moral standard and understanding of God in King Abimelech in Genesis 20:1-12 when he made the same mistake Pharaoh had made; in fact, it is described in even more detail. The king spoke with God defending himself and the Lord responded, "*I know that you acted in the integrity of your heart...*" (v.6)

They knew what God expected of them and they knew who He was.

Abram was recognized by all as a great prince among the ancient peoples and as a man of God. You can be sure that when God spoke to him and promised that <u>all</u> the nations of the world would be blessed through him, the nations of that time heard about it and were watching him to see if it were true. He had a son at the age of a hundred and his wife was 90, everyone who heard of it laughed.

These things did not take place in a vacuum or a small corner of the planet. They occurred in the center of the world, at a time when all people groups had the opportunity of hearing about them.

All the nations were going their own way, creating their own religions as it suited them. Many of them had roots derived from the religion of Babel. The Lord longed to reveal Himself to them in a new way. They knew of Him only as the Creator and the author of the flood. He chose Abraham (as Abram came to be called) to be the father of many nations, one in particular, through whom He would reveal Himself. He chose Abraham's son Isaac, and then Jacob, Isaac's son. Jacob became the father of the nation of Israel, God's chosen people.

They had a difficult beginning. As they multiplied from merely a large family, to twelve tribes, to a vast multitude, they were mistreated by the nation that had originally welcomed them. Egypt enslaved them out of fear of their numbers and began to kill their newborn sons. The Lord chose Moses out of these babies doomed to die and set him apart to be their Redeemer. He led the people of Israel out of Egypt with mighty plagues and miracles in the name of the Lord.

The Lord made a name for Himself. He went out of His way to demonstrate that He ruled over all the gods of Egypt. His plagues specifically attacked the authority of those gods. All the nations on earth heard of it, because they had not yet spread over the world. This was the beginning of how God brought blessing to all nations through Abraham's seed.

The Lord gave the children of Israel His law, a mighty and powerful document, full of wisdom, designed to take slaves and make them a free people. He was very firm with them in the beginning when they rebelled against Him because it was the only way His law could be established.

He led them through the desert for forty years, feeding them with bread from heaven and brought them to the land of Canaan. In this land the people had turned to more evil than any other land on earth. They sacrificed their children to idols and Nephilim were among them, giants such as the ones who had been on the earth before the flood.

They had broken covenant with the Lord. He had decreed that "*Whoever sheds man's blood, by man his blood shall be shed . . .*" So He brought Israel, the people He had chosen, to fulfill this promised judgment, wiping out or driving out the Canaanites and taking their place in Canaan. This privilege did not come without a cost. The same measure they used for others would be used for them.

All the world was watching. They were terrified of the people of the Lord. One of the nations (Moab) hired a prophet of the Lord to come and curse them but he was unable to do so. But he was a very crafty man and he taught them how to get Israel in trouble (Numbers 31:16, Deuteronomy 23:4-5). This story is important because it reveals how the knowledge of the Lord was being spread. All of their usual methods of cursing enemies were worthless before the living God, but if they could get Israel to sin against the commandments they had been given, then God Himself would judge them.

This is what they did. They used their newfound knowledge of God to ensnare the children of Israel and watched in glee as the Lord punished them. It was a short-lived delight. The Lord dealt with the sin and continued to bless Israel – and He did not forget Moab's treachery.

Once Israel had conquered most of their land, they settled down to enjoy it. From then on their history is a succession of seasons of revival and true worship of God and seasons of apostasy, falling into the worship of idols and following evil practices. All the time they lived in the land, the covenant and the law of the Lord ruled over them – and the nations watched and learned something of the ways of the Lord.

For four hundred years, judges that the Lord raised up by His Spirit ruled the people of Israel. After that, kings ruled them. When the third king of Israel, Solomon, turned away from the Lord in his old age, the Lord divided the land into two nations. Ten of the twelve tribes broke away from the rest and established their own monarchy. They became the northern kingdom of Israel and their capitol city was Samaria. Judah and Benjamin remained in the hands of the dynasty of King David and their capitol was Jerusalem. They were known as Judah.

These nations were revealed by their deeds. God had chosen Jerusalem from among all the cities of the land, as the place where His name would dwell. The Lord promised to bless the northern kingdom if they would follow Him and continue to worship at His temple in Jerusalem. No sooner had they broken off, than they set up two golden calves to worship (1 Kings 12:26-29); one in their northernmost city and one near their southern border, to keep their people from traveling to Jerusalem to worship the Lord. They continued in this evil for the rest of their years as a nation. Not one of their rulers followed the Lord though He sent many prophets to bring them back.

Judah flip-flopped back and forth between following the Lord and serving idols. Their well being as a nation was directly affected by it. The Lord sent them some of the mightiest prophets of all. Among them Isaiah was considered the greatest.

At the time our study covers, the northern kingdom of Israel was carried away into captivity by Assyria, the ruling world power of that generation. This was the beginning of the dispersion of the Jews, (a term which came to refer to all twelve tribes even though it comes from the word "Judah").

The kingdom of Judah also ended up being taken captive by Babylon. Isaiah prophesied about this though it happened long after his death.

The nation which the Lord had set apart to bless the world became a source of shame to Him. "*The name of God is blasphemed among the Gentiles because of you,*" (Romans 2:24).

Jesus is a good example of how distressing this really was to the Lord. He chased the merchants and money changers out of the Lord's Temple with a whip, crying out, "*Is it not written: 'My house shall be called a house of prayer for all nations'? But you have made it a 'den of thieves.'*"

The ancient world had been growing, spreading, and the stories of the God of Israel and Judah were no longer reaching the farthest ones. The Lord, in His infinite wisdom, used the shame of His people for good. He scattered them abroad. When Judah was in Babylon, they established the worship of the Lord, the practice of the law and the study of the Bible without the Temple and without sacrifices. Synagogues popped up wherever there were Jews. As it says in Acts 15:21 "*For Moses from ancient generations has in every city those who preach him, since he is read in the synagogues every Sabbath.*" In this way the knowledge of the Lord was spread.

Looking ahead, after the time of Isaiah and his prophecies, consider how the Lord prepared the world for the gospel.

Assyria began the dispersion (or Diaspora). Babylon continued it and caused the Jews to adapt their religion to one that works in exile. Then the Medes and the Persians came, conquered Babylon, and sent the people of Judah back to Jerusalem to rebuild their home and the Temple of the Lord. This time they took the law more seriously and the Lord prepared the way for the coming of His Messiah, the Anointed One.

When Alexander the Great conquered the known world, he hellenized the nations, teaching them the Greek language, culture, ideologies and way of thinking. The whole world learned their way of debating truth.

Rome's roads, iron rule and vast commerce made it possible to travel all over the empire. When Jesus sent the disciples out to preach the gospel to ALL THE NATIONS, He had already made it possible. They needed only one language. They traveled greatly in one empire. They came to cities where their own people had lived for a long time and established a witness. And each nation still had a sense of God that they could appeal to.

God never left the world without a witness.

History of Aram

Aram is the ancient name for Syria, and Damascus, their capital city, has existed and been lived in since the earliest days of civilization (after the Tower of Babel). We tend to think of it as Muslim and hostile to the things of God, or perhaps unacquainted with them, but throughout history the Lord has revealed Himself in many ways to this nation. Abraham's brother, Nahor, settled in that area, bringing with him the knowledge of God. Abraham won a great victory there when he fought the armies of the four kings of the East and recovered his nephew Lot and all of Sodom and Gomorrah. Isaac's wife was from the area. The children of Israel were told their father was a wandering Aramean, probably because of Jacob who lived and married there.

Over 400 years later, when the children of Israel came up out of Egypt, the knowledge of God was still in the land of Aram. We know this because there was a prophet of the Lord there named Balaam – a man who sold out for personal profit. He used his knowledge of God to teach the Moabites how to bring a curse on Israel, even after having just prophesied some incredible promises over Israel, words directly from the mouth of God!

The main reason that the Lord wanted Israel to conquer the peoples of Canaan was to destroy their false religions and any nations they didn't conquer became a stumbling block to them. During the times of the Judges, Israel turned away from the Lord and followed, among others, the gods of Damascus. The Lord had promised the territory of Aram to them but they didn't conquer it until David was king. Solomon ruled over them most of his life until in his old age he turned away from the Lord, and the Lord raised up an adversary (Rezin) against him who took control of Damascus and established a new line of kings. After Solomon's death, Israel was split into two kingdoms (Israel and Judah) and then Aram grew as a threat to both of them.

During the period of the kings of Israel (the northern kingdom), a little over 200 years, Aram was a major antagonist who spent most of that time at war with Israel. This started when King Asa of Judah was being threatened by Israel, and took gold from the Lord's treasury in the Temple and sent it to Aram to ask for help. From then on there was war between Aram and Israel until they finally made an alliance against Judah, during the reign of King Ahaz, in Isaiah's day. (Beware when you end up making alliances with former enemies because you have ended up being like them! The destruction of Israel followed quickly on the heels of this "diplomatic victory".)

The Lord went to great lengths to reveal Himself in mighty ways, not only to Israel, who had turned aside to worship two golden calves and lots of other gods, but also to Aram. Whether it was stopping rain for three years, revealing the king of Aram's secret battle plans, taking whole armies captive without any fighting, healing lepers, miraculously ending lengthy sieges and famine in a single day or predicting the next king of Aram; the Lord showed Himself to be the God who lives and has power over the affairs of men. The war between Israel and Aram was a witness to God's authority, judgment and grace, to them as well as to the surrounding nations. In the end, Israel and Aram both shared the judgment from the Lord's hand, brought by the Assyrian army.

In Isaiah 7, Aram and Israel had made an alliance and attacked Judah and the Lord prophesied that He would bring Assyria to judge them, but King Ahaz decided to take matters into his own hands, a witness to his unbelief and his rejection of the Lord's promise. He sent money from the Lord's temple to Assyria and begged for help. The Assyrians came, as the Lord promised they would, but after conquering both Aram and Israel, they went after Judah.

Damascus was humbled, most of their people taken into exile, but not utterly wiped out. In Jeremiah 49:23-27, the Lord spoke judgment over them again since they still hadn't turned to Him.

But, this is not the end of the story. May God be praised!! Jesus came to this region and preached the gospel and healed many. Paul was converted there and the church flourished there for many centuries, becoming a major leader of the church of the East from the times of the apostles until being conquered by Muslims in the early Middle Ages. There remains to this day a community of Christians in this land who haven't turned aside from the faith.

History of Assyria

Assyria was one of the earliest civilizations founded, nestled along the banks of the ancient rivers of Mesopotamia, the Tigris and the Euphrates. Its name comes from Asshur, the son of Shem and grandson of Noah, but its most famous cities were founded by Nimrod, the son of Cush and grandson of Ham.

Nimrod is the first world leader mentioned after the flood and may well have been the instigator of the building of the tower of Babel. He is described as a "*mighty hunter before the Lord*" and his name means "we will rebel". He founded Babel and several cities around it before moving north and founding Nineveh and other cities in the area of Assyria. Assyria and Babylon ended up being similar in religion and culture.

In its early history, Assyria was under Babylon's power, but by the time we see it mentioned again in the Bible, (2 Kings 15), it had become a major force in the ancient world and Babylon was living in its shadow. They were known for their great cruelty in war. The Assyrians invented flaying (skinning a person alive) and often led their captives away with a hook through the nose (such as King Manasseh - 2 Chronicles 33:11-13). Notice the Lord's sense of justice when He tells the Assyrian commander "*Because of your raging against me, and because your arrogance has come up to My ears, therefore I will put My hook in your nose, and My bridle in your lips, and I will turn you back by the way which you came.*" II Kings 19:28.

In Assyria, the king was all-powerful, the head of the religion of the city as well as the head of government and of the army. Each city had one particular god they worshiped and eventually the city itself became worshiped because of its association with that god (ISBE).

Around 780 BC, a prophet from Israel, named Jonah, was sent to Nineveh to predict its destruction. His appearance (having survived three days in the belly of a fish) when he came to preach and walk through the city was so shocking and his message so frightening that the king and all the people of the city fasted and repented of their evil before the Lord God of Israel, their Creator. Isn't it interesting that after many centuries of worshiping their own gods, they all recognized the debt they owed the Lord (the God of another nation) and responded to this message! Jesus commended them when He rebuked the Pharisees for their hardness of heart. "*The men of Nineveh shall stand up with this generation at the judgment, and shall condemn it because they repented at the preaching of Jonah; and behold, something greater than Jonah is here.*" Matthew 12:41. What a witness to the Lord's heart! "*...who desires all men to be saved and to come to the knowledge of the truth.*" 1 Timothy 2:4.

Assyria grew in power and around the time of King Ahaz of Judah, Tiglath-Pileser III (also known as Pul) was ready to come and conquer Aram, needing perhaps only the excuse that Ahaz's invitation gave him. Damascus fell, as Isaiah predicted, in 733 BC. He also carried away several Israelite tribes into captivity, the Reubenites, the Gadites and the half-tribe of Manasseh.

In 725 B.C., the son of Tiglath-Pileser, King Shalmaneser V, campaigned against the rest of the northern kingdom of Israel and laid siege to Samaria. The city fell after three years, in 722 BC, and its inhabitants were carried away. In their place, Assyria brought people from the region of Babylon to live in Israel's cities and cultivate their fields, though their numbers were small and most of their fields lay fallow and wild animals roamed the land.

The next king of Assyria, Sennacherib, targeted Judah. Ahaz had become a vassal and paid tribute, but his son Hezekiah rebelled against the pagan ruler when he began the great reform and restoration of the worship of the Lord in Judah. He succeeded in overcoming a number of Judean cities but failed to conquer Jerusalem because of the intervention of God.

During Sennacherib's reign, he razed the ancient city of Babylon, utterly destroying it, because of a rebellion there. But though its walls were torn down, its spirit was not and Babylon continued to cause Assyria trouble.

When Scythians invaded from the north, and encamped around the walls of Nineveh, the attitude of the people was much different than it had been in Jonah's day. They were confident until flooding from the Tigris left a huge hole in the city walls and the enemy's army marched in and destroyed them in 606 BC.

As the Lord had spoken about Nineveh in Nahum 2:6:
"*The gates of the rivers are opened, and the palace is dissolved.*"

Then Babylon was ready to rise up in its place as a world power.

History of Babylon

Babylon was the greatest city of the Chaldeans, a people who lived in the land of the two rivers, the Euphrates and the Tigris – modern day Iraq. It represents the earliest civilization known today. According to Genesis, it was founded by Nimrod, and is the site of the Tower of Babel in the valley of Shinar, which we know of as Sumer. Archaeological digs have uncovered tens of thousands of their written documents. Their cuneiform alphabet and Semitic language are known to us. The Bible tells us it was from this location that all the peoples of the earth spread out.

After the Lord divided the peoples of the world at the Tower of Babel, (the Hebrew word for confusion), they dispersed and founded cities along the fertile crescent all the way to the Nile River in Egypt. Abraham, the patriarch of the people of Israel, came from Ur of Chaldea. He left when the Lord called him out and traveled to the land of Canaan. While he was living there, his nephew Lot was taken captive in a war between Sodom and Gomorrah and the king of Shinar (Babylon). Abraham rose up and pursued them with only the 300 men of his household and defeated the combined armies of four kings, rescuing his nephew Lot as well as all the people and possessions of the conquered cities. Early Babylon saw the glory of the Lord through this victory.

In later years, when Assyria rose to power and conquered Babylon, it proved to be a difficult vassal because of their long history of battling for dominance with each other. Assyria ended up destroying their city and tearing it down completely in an attempt to subdue it. They took some of the inhabitants of the area of Babylon to live in the land of Israel, which was empty because their people had been defeated and taken into exile. An Assyrian prince was given the task of ruling and rebuilding Babylon.

Babylon retained the desire to rebel against Assyria and throw off its yoke and Assyria was ill equipped to control its empire after the devastation of its army (Isaiah 37) and as their power waned, Babylon grew in strength. When King Hezekiah of Judah was miraculously healed of his mortal illness, the king of Babylon sent emissaries to him to find out more about it – so they said. This was after the destruction of Assyria's army and Jerusalem represented the single greatest threat to their thirst for world domination. By receiving them as honored guests and showing them all the treasures and defenses of his realm, Hezekiah showed great foolishness and pride. The information they took home gave Babylon all they needed to prepare for conquest when the time was right.

The people of Jerusalem assumed, after their miraculous victory over Assyria, that no enemy could ever enter their gates (Lam.4:12). This arrogance reached its height during the reign of Manasseh, Hezekiah's son. He led the people into more evil than any other king of Judah had before but God greatly humbled him. Assyria took him prisoner and then returned him to Jerusalem as a vassal under their power.

When Nineveh, Assyria's capital, fell to invaders from the north, Babylon was ready to take its place as ruler of the world. Nebuchadnezzar, the Babylonian king, came and lay siege to Jerusalem. He captured it three times, carrying away captives each time in an attempt to subdue it. The third time, he destroyed the Temple, and tore down and burned the city walls. Judah was carried into exile for seventy years and only a remnant would return to their land.

Babylon became known as one of the seven wonders of the ancient world. It straddled the Euphrates River, with walls thick enough for five chariots to ride abreast on top, and gates adorned with brilliant blue, ceramic tiles that made the city glisten like a jewel in the desert. Nebuchadnezzar stumbled over its majesty, claiming all the glory for himself. God humbled him giving him the mind of an animal for seven years. When he was restored to his throne, the Lord proved that He alone establishes kings.

His son, Belshazzar, didn't learn from this. He was so arrogant and confident that when the Lord brought the Persian army against him, he hosted a feast for his nobles, wives and concubines, and toasted their false gods with consecrated vessels from the Lord's Temple. The Lord sent a hand to write a message of judgment on the wall and even as Daniel interpreted it for him, the Persian army successfully diverted the Euphrates River. They marched in under the walls of the city and took Babylon that same night – as Isaiah had prophesied. Babylon fell.

But in the last days, prophecy says that Babylon will again be a world influence. She will "become a dwelling place of demons and a prison of every unclean spirit…" and all the nations will drink of the wine of her immorality and be deceived by her sorcery. Then Babylon will be judged and destroyed because of her sin. *"And in her was found the blood of prophets and of saints and of all who have been slain on the earth."* Revelation 18:24

History of Edom

In the days of the Patriarchs, when Abraham wandered like a nomad through the land he would inherit, a son was born to him by the name of Isaac. This son had twin boys, named Esau and Jacob, who wrestled with each other in the womb. Esau was born a few minutes before Jacob, but Jacob came out grasping his heel. Two nations were born that day. Jacob, the younger, coveted his brother's position as the firstborn son and as heir to Abraham's promise and used deceit and manipulation to gain both his father's blessing and the rights of the firstborn.

Jacob became the nation of Israel, inheritor of the promise of the blessing to all nations, which refers to Jesus, the Messiah. Esau became the nation of Edom, named after the word for 'red' in Hebrew because he was covered with red hair. Jacob had many faults but he believed in and wanted the Lord's promises whereas Esau despised them, selling his birthright for a bowl of stew when he was hungry. Isaac prophesied over Esau that his brother would rule over him but the day would come when he would shake off his yoke.

While the descendents of Jacob were living in the land of Egypt, multiplying and becoming a huge slave community, Edom was flourishing in the area of Mt. Seir, southwest of the Dead Sea. This land was given to them by God and when Moses led the Israelites out of Egypt to the land promised originally to Abraham, (over 500 years after the promise had been given), the Lord warned them not to disturb Edom as they passed by his land. They sent a message asking to pass through their borders peacefully, but Edom came out with a great army to resist them, so they detoured far out of their way, by the Red Sea, to avoid battle with them. This hostility on the part of Edom wasn't pleasing to the Lord.

When Israel camped in between Moab and the Jordan River, just across from the Promised Land, Moab hired a prophet of God from Aram, named Balaam, to come and curse them because they were afraid of them. This prophet was unable to curse them and instead prophesied great blessings over them, including an interesting one about Edom. He said that in the distant future, a ruler from the tribe of Judah would possess Edom. King David was the one who fulfilled this prophecy. His commander, Joab, conquered Edom and put all their males to death (1 Kings 11:15-16); only an Edomite prince and a few of his servants survived and escaped to the land of Egypt. He returned after David's death to be an adversary to Solomon, but didn't succeed in establishing independence.

During the reign of King Joash, Edom finally threw off the yoke of servitude to the house of David. Whenever there was war between them, if the King of Judah was a man who followed the Lord, then Edom was defeated and suffered great losses.

In the words of the prophets we find the truth about Edom's hostility towards Jacob. As time went on and Edom became more and more hardened in envy and a desire to see Israel crushed, the Lord talks more and more about how His soul was grieved by Esau. In the end, He says, "I have loved Jacob but I have hated Esau..." (Malachi 1:2-3), because Edom's hatred against Judah was so violent, and they gloated over Judah in the day of their disaster and destruction. They rejoiced over Judah's destruction, the word says, with vengeance and an everlasting enmity (Ezekiel 35:5). They also spoke arrogantly against the Lord, but He warned them that they would drink the same cup that was given to Judah.

Edom diminished to one of the smallest of nations with very few people, and in the Roman era, they were displaced into Judah's territory and called Idumea. One of them was actually made King of Judeah by the Romans, a man by the name of Herod. This was the same Herod who had all the boys age two and younger in the vicinity of Bethlehem put to death in an attempt to kill Jesus, the promised King of the Jews who was the fulfillment of God's greatest promise to Abraham, the birthright Jacob had coveted and Esau had despised.

How great is the wisdom of God who foreknew the descendents of these brothers, Jacob and Esau, and gave the promise to the one who would value it!

History of Egypt

Egypt is perhaps the most well known of all the earliest civilizations because of the wealth of its artifacts and ruins. Pyramids built thousands of years ago are still standing and museums are filled with statues and sarcophagi of their ancient pharaohs. Their culture – art, hieroglyphs, architecture, religion, etc. – stands out vividly from all the others in mystique and originality.

Mizraim, the Hebrew name for Egypt, was a son of Ham, the son of Noah. He founded a kingdom along the banks of the Nile River. This was a lush farmland nourished by yearly flooding which enriched the fields with silt from the upper regions of the river. It made them a wealthy and powerful nation.

Our first contact with Egypt in the Bible was when Abram went there with his wife Sarai looking for food in a time of famine. She was so beautiful that he feared Pharaoh would put him to death to take his wife. The Lord defended her striking Pharaoh's house with plagues. He sent Abram away with many gifts including an Egyptian slave girl named Hagar.

Egypt comes into the limelight again when Abraham's great-grandson, Joseph, was sold into slavery by his brothers. This young man was put into prison, but the Lord raised him up to be the ruler of Egypt, second only to Pharaoh himself (Genesis 39-41). A terrible seven-year famine came on the whole world and Joseph was used by God to prepare for it. During seven years of plenty, he stored up the extra grain and when the famine began, there was enough food for everyone.

It was during this period that the Lord solidified Pharaoh's absolute power in Egypt – through His servant Joseph. As the aristocratic landowners used up their private stores of food, they began to buy grain from Pharaoh. When their money ran out, they sold him their property and in the end, offered themselves to him as slaves. Pharaoh ended up owning all of Egypt and most of the wealth of the world. This was the Lord's doing!

Joseph brought his family to Egypt and settled them in Goshen where they grew into a mighty nation over the next four hundred years. During that time, they fell out of favor with Pharaoh's house. They had become so numerous and powerful, that the Egyptians feared they would join with an enemy and conquer them. Pharaoh enslaved them and put them to forced labor building cities. He also put their infant sons to death.

In their misery, the descendants of Jacob, or Israel as the Lord had named him, cried out to the Lord and He sent them a deliverer by the name of Moses. Moses was a Hebrew who had been raised by Pharaoh's daughter as a son. He confronted Pharaoh and demanded his people be set free in the name of the Lord. Pharaoh was unwilling until the Lord had humbled him and destroyed his land, his strength, his army and his people with terrible plagues. The Lord's people left carrying the wealth of Egypt with them. But Egypt became a symbol to them of everything the Lord wanted His people to avoid. Their idolatry, their sin, their pride and their armies, were things God's people were to never seek.

It was a long time before Egypt could raise its head again after the children of Israel had left.

About five hundred years later, King Solomon, the foremost world power of his day, made an alliance with Egypt and married Pharaoh's daughter, bringing Egyptian commerce, culture and influence into Israel. This was the beginning of his apostasy which led to the splitting of his kingdom. God raised up Jeroboam to rule the ten tribes of Israel in the north. He had spent years in Egypt, in exile. When he came to power, he disobeyed God and set up two golden calves in Israel and told the people "This is your god who brought you up out of Egypt."

In Isaiah's day, Hezekiah made an alliance with Pharaoh to protect himself from the king of Assyria. This was displeasing to the Lord. He points out that all of Pharaoh's advisors were fools. The proof came when Egypt failed and was conquered by Assyria.

In later years when Babylon became the dominant world power, survivors from Judah fled to Egypt to hide from Babylon, against the Lord's advice. Babylon came and conquered Egypt. They were in exile for forty years. Then the Lord gathered them back to their land. But they were never a world power again (Ezekiel 29:14-16), and Israel was never tempted to put their trust in them again.

When Alexander the Great conquered the ancient world, he founded the city of Alexandria and instituted many aspects of Greek learning. It was in Alexandria that 70 Jewish scholars were gathered to translate the Hebrew Bible into Greek so that the nations could study it. Ptolemy, one of Alexander's generals, set up a new dynasty in Egypt. The notorious Cleopatra was the last queen of the Ptolemies. Egypt was then conquered by Rome.

Jesus was born in Judea during the height of Roman power. When King Herod tried to have Him killed, his parents fled with him into Egypt. They lived in Egypt until Herod was dead and it was safe to return to their homeland. This is why prophecy says, *"Out of Egypt I called My Son"* (Hos 11:1).

When the Holy Spirit was poured out at Pentecost, there were Jews from Egypt present who believed and took the gospel back to their land. Egypt became home to a thriving body of believers for hundreds of years, very influential in the early history of the church, until they were conquered by Muslims in the 7th century. They are still home to a small Christian community today.

History of Israel

Israel was named for their fore-father Jacob, who received the name directly from God after wrestling with Him one night (Genesis 32:28). He was Abraham's grandson and the inheritor of the great promises of God. He had twelve sons and each one became a tribe within Israel.

Israel and his descendents moved to Egypt because Joseph, his eleventh son, achieved great power and influence there. They lived there for 430 years (Exodus 12:40-41), increasing in numbers until they became a great multitude and a threat to Egypt. Pharaoh enslaved them and began killing their infant sons. One of the babes was taken in by Pharaoh's daughter, named Moses, and raised as a prince of Egypt.

At the age of 40, Moses left Egypt and went to Midian where he married and worked as a shepherd. When he turned 80 years old, God sent him back to Egypt to bring out the children of Israel. God performed many miracles through Moses and led the people to Mt. Sinai where He gave them the Law. This laid down the commandments and instructions to govern every aspect of their lives. God was to be their king.

The children of Israel rebelled and broke the main commandments even while God was still explaining them to Moses. Because of their unbelief, the Lord could not give them the land he had promised to their fore-fathers. Moses led them in circles in the desert for forty years until that generation died off. Then Joshua, his successor, led them into the land of Canaan.

The children of Israel conquered most of Canaan and followed the Lord all the days of Joshua, but after that generation died, they did not continue to drive out the inhabitants of the land and they became a stumbling block to them. They intermarried with them and played the harlot by worshiping idols and indulging in sinful practices. So God gave them into the hands of their enemies.

For the next 400 years, the Lord raised up judges to govern the people, bring them back to the Lord and deliver them from their enemies. When the judge died, the people went back to idolatry and God gave them into the hands of their enemies again.

The worship of the Lord at the Tabernacle in Shiloh deteriorated until one day, the ark of the Testimony was actually captured by the Philistines because the priests took it into battle with them like the heathen nations. God plagued the Philistines and they returned the ark but it never went back to Shiloh.

The Lord raised up Samuel as a judge to bring the people back to Him but they clambered for a king. God had Samuel anoint Saul as king. He told Samuel, "*For they have not rejected you, but they have rejected Me from being king over them.*" (1 Samuel 8:7)

Saul was a tall, handsome man but he did not follow the Lord and he lost the throne because of disobedience. Samuel anointed David in his place. David was a mighty man of God and at first Saul loved him, but he soon became jealous of him and tried to kill him. In the end, Saul and his sons died and David became the king of Israel.

David brought peace to the nation of Israel, conquering their enemies, making alliances and ruling justly (2 Samuel 8:14-15). He captured Jerusalem and made it his capital city. Then he brought the ark there and made plans to build a Temple for the Lord. He designed and gathered all the materials necessary. He loved the Lord, but the Lord didn't let him build the Temple because he was a man of war. His son Solomon would build it.

At the height of his reign, David committed adultery and murder and brought disaster into his family. He didn't lose the throne because he repented, but he lost four sons and the sword would never depart from his house (2 Samuel 12:10).

Solomon, David's son, was the greatest king Israel ever had with respect to wealth, power, influence and the extent of their borders. He was also the wisest man who ever lived according to worldly wisdom. But he married many foreign women and they turned him away from the Lord in his old age. He built temples to their idols so they could offer incense in them.

The Lord took ten of the tribes away from the house of David because of Solomon's sin (1 Kings 11:1-13) and made Jeroboam their king. God promised to bless them if they would follow him. They retained the name of Israel. The son of Solomon ruled over the tribe of Judah and the small tribe of Benjamin. There was war between Israel and Judah for years.

Israel (the northern kingdom) chose to set up two golden calves just like their fore-fathers had done at the foot of Mt. Sinai. None of their kings ever followed the Lord, though He was very patient with them and sent them prophets like Elijah and did many miracles to draw them back to Himself. In the days of Ahaz, king of Judah, the Assyrian army lay siege to Samariah and after three years Israel fell and was taken away into exile because of their continued hardness of heart (2 Kings 17:6-18). Israelites spread throughout the Assyrian empire and continued to spread during later empires, the Babylonian, the Persian, the Greek and the Roman empires. This is called the Diaspora (or scattering).

Assyria brought people from the area of Babylon and settled them in the cities of Israel and they worshiped their own gods. They also learned some of the ways of the Lord and blended the teachings (2 Kings 17:24-33). Their descendents became known as the Samaritans in Jesus' day.

When Judah returned from exile in Babylon in the fifth century B.C., a remnant of Israel came with them and in the time of Christ, all twelve tribes were represented in the Promised Land. Moses had prophesied their entire history and given them this promise:

...in all nations where the LORD your God has banished you, and if you return to the LORD your God and obey Him with all your heart and soul according to all that I command you today, you and your sons, then the LORD your God will restore you from captivity, and have compassion on you, and will gather you again from all the peoples where the LORD your God has scattered you.
Deuteronomy 30:1-3

History of Moab

The nation of Moab had a rather unpleasant beginning, 2000+ BC. When the Lord decided to judge the ancient cities of Sodom and Gomorrah, Abraham's nephew, Lot, was living there with his family. He had become an influential man, a judge, probably because he was trustworthy. The Lord rescued him and his two daughters from the fire and brimstone that He rained down on the area and they escaped into the surrounding hills. But though they had escaped the judgment, they weren't free of Sodom's influence. Frustrated with the isolated life they were now living, Lot's two daughters each got him drunk and seduced him so that they could get pregnant. Moab was the resulting son of Lot and his oldest daughter. (The second daughter's son became the Ammonites.)

The Lord gave Moab his own territory in the area that today we know of as Jordan. When the children of Israel came up out of Egypt and were heading towards the land of Canaan, after they had spent forty years in the desert, the Lord told them to pass through the land of Moab without attacking them (1405 BC).

Moab, however, was very afraid of the horde of people that encamped on the edge of their territory and the king of Moab summoned Balaam, a prophet from Aram, to come and curse them so that they could defeat them in war. Balaam came but was unable to curse them and blessed them instead. One of his prophecies from the Lord stated that Israel would crush the forehead of Moab. The Lord went even farther and specified through Moses that no Moabite (or Ammonite) would be allowed to enter His assembly even down to the tenth generation, because they tried to curse the children of Israel instead of receiving and blessing them, (Gen 12:3).

Moab did more than just try to curse Israel. They learned from Balaam that if they could get Israel to sin, the Lord Himself would punish them, so they hosted huge feasts and sent their women into the Israelite camp to invite them. They came and sacrificed to idols and played the harlot with their women. This brought a terrible plague on Israel that was stopped by Phinehas, the high priest's son.

Moab continued to be a stumbling block to Israel. In the time of the judges, when they turned away from the Lord and served other gods (including the god of Moab), the Lord brought Moab against the land to conquer it and rule over it. They served Moab for 18 years until the Lord raised up a judge to deliver them.

During the latter part of the time of the judges (1400 to 1020 BC), a man from Bethlehem in Judah settled in Moab to escape a famine in his homeland. While there, his two sons married Moabite women. Soon after that, he and his sons died and his widow decided to return to Judah. One of her daughters in law, Ruth, wanted to follow the Lord and chose to come back with her. She ended up marrying a close relative of the family and having a son. This boy became King David's grandfather and a direct ancestor of Jesus, the Messiah.

In his early years, David was pursued by Saul, the first king of Israel, because the Lord had chosen him to be king in Saul's place. He was concerned for his parents' welfare and took them to Moab and asked the king there to take care of them. No mention was made of them again and the next we see of David's dealings with Moab, he was defeating Moab in battle and putting two thirds of the men to death (2 Samuel 8:2). The rest became his servants and paid tribute to Israel (~1000 BC).

In his old age, King Solomon built a high place for Chemosh, the idol of Moab (~925 BC), that wasn't destroyed until the time of King Josiah, one of the last kings of Judah, who defiled it so that it couldn't be rebuilt (~600 BC).

When the kingdom was divided after Solomon's death, Moab continued to pay tribute to the northern kingdom of Israel – 100,000 lambs and the wool of 100,000 rams – for about 80 years. At that time, the king of Moab rebelled (~850 BC). The king of Israel made an alliance with the king of Edom and with the king of Judah (which wasn't pleasing to the Lord) and came against Moab, utterly defeating it. But, the king of Moab sacrificed his own son, the heir to the throne and this inspired the people's wrath against Israel, so the armies of Israel left without reestablishing the tribute.

After this, Moab allied with Ammon and Edom and came against Judah. They were defeated in a mighty miracle of the Lord (2 Chronicles 20:1-29).

Assyria came (~ 720 BC) and conquered Moab and left only a remnant, as Isaiah prophesied, but Moab still resisted the Lord and didn't repent of his pride. When Babylon came up against it (~610 BC) and Jeremiah sent word that the Lord had told them to surrender to Babylon and live, they didn't and were destroyed. Moab as a nation vanished from the land, though perhaps a few survivors were taken into captivity and absorbed by the conquering nation.

"Therefore, as I live," declares the LORD of hosts, the God of Israel,
"Surely Moab will be like Sodom..."   Zephaniah 2:9

History of Tyre and Sidon

Tyre and Sidon were the two most powerful cities in the ancient land of Lebanon. This land was known as Phoenicia by the Greeks because of the purple dye they traded in, and was famous for their cedars, their ships and their wealth in commerce.

Sidon, their oldest city, was founded by one of the sons of Canaan in the earliest days of civilization. It was a sea-faring, merchant community whose influence, power and wealth spread throughout the Mediterranean world. They founded many colonies along their shipping routes in places like Crete, Cyprus, Carthage, Spain, and Sicily. They traveled over incredible distances, circumnavigating Africa, trading with Britain and even making small settlements in North America. (Nelson's)

The area of these Canaanite cities had been promised to the children of Israel, but was never conquered and the people were never driven out. As a result, the Israelites stumbled over their influence and worshiped their gods.

Sidon founded the city of Tyre and by the time of King David, it had become even greater than Sidon. Hiram, the king of Tyre in those days was the first ruler to recognize King David and ended up becoming a great friend and ally. It appears that David's witness made an impact on him because when Solomon became king and sent a message asking for help building the Temple of the Lord, the Tyrian king honored the Lord saying "Blessed be the LORD today, who has given to David a wise son over this great people." and he rejoiced greatly. He supplied vast amounts of high quality cedar, all kinds of raw materials, and laborers. Sadly, Solomon succumbed to a reverse influence. He ended up worshiping Ashtoreth, the goddess of the Sidonians.

Several generations later, King Ahab, who ruled the northern kingdom of Israel, married Jezebel, a princess of the ancient city of Sidon, and she brought in the worship of Baal with a vengeance. Israel had followed after these gods before but she searched the land and actively put to death the prophets of the Lord, instituting Baal worship as the main religion of the land. She would've put Elijah to death, too, if she could have found him. The Lord hid him for a couple of years at a widow's house in her home city of Sidon.

Her daughter, Athalia, married a king of Judah and when the Lord brought Jezebel to a violent death, her daughter had all the royal offspring slaughtered (including her own) so that she could rule Judah unchallenged. She missed one, a six-month-old baby, and when this boy, Josiah, was seven years old, the high priest made him king and Jezebel's daughter was put to death.

In Ezekiel we find the ruler of Tyre boasting in his heart that he is a god and the Lord calling the king of Tyre the fallen cherub of Eden, a reference to Satan. The Lord was holding them accountable and He warned them to submit to Nebuchadnezzar when he came conquering, but they resisted and were destroyed as Isaiah had predicted.

Nebuchadnezzar and his army worked very hard laying siege to and conquering Tyre and the Lord noticed that. He promised to pay them with booty from Egypt. They tore down and burned the walls of Tyre and took them into captivity. But the Tyreans returned after 70 years and went back to their trade, their religion and their greed, rebuilding their city on an island half a mile out into the sea so that they would never be taken again.

When Alexander the Great came and laid siege to this water locked fortress, he actually tore down all the debris of the ancient ruins of Tyre, scraping it down to the bare rock, and built a causeway from the shore to the walls of the city. He utterly destroyed it and it was never rebuilt again. Ezekiel had prophesied this "...*And they will destroy the walls of Tyre and break down her towers; and I will scrape her debris from her and make her a bare rock...*" Ezekiel 26:4

What did Jesus think of them? He loved them, of course! He traveled there and ended up delivering a woman's daughter from a demon and praising her for her faith. Multitudes were coming from there to see Him and He healed and delivered them all. He even said that if the miracles He had performed in Chorazin had taken place in Tyre and Sidon, they would've repented long ago. Some of the earliest Christian converts were in these cities and there are believers there to this day.

Messianic Prophecies in Isaiah

Reference	Description
4:2	Called the Branch of the Lord. Will be beautiful, glorious, the pride and adornment of the survivors of Israel.
6:13	
7:14	
9:6-7	
11:1-5, 10	
16:5	
19:20	
22:21-23	
28:16	
30:20	
32:1	
33:17	
35:4-6	
40:5, 9-11	

Messianic Prophecies in Isaiah

Reference	Description
42:1-4, 6-7	
48:12,16	
49:1-8	
50:4-7	
51:9	
52:10,13-15	
53:1-12	
55:4	
59:16-17,20	
61:1-2	
62:11	
63:1-6,8	
66:7	

"Day of the Lord" Prophecies in Isaiah

Reference	Description
2:2,10-11, 17-20	House of the Lord will be the chief of mountains. All nations will stream to it. Proud man will be humbled before the terror of the Lord. God alone exalted. Idols will vanish. Men will hide in caves. The Lord makes the earth tremble.
3:17-26	
4:1-6	
7:18-25	
10:20	
11:10-12	
12:1-4	
13:6-13	
17:4,7-9	
19:16-25	
22:12,20-25	

Page 395

"Day of the Lord" Prophecies in Isaiah

Reference	Description
24:21-23	
25:6-9	
26:1-2, 20-21	
27:1-6, 12-13	
28:5-6	
29:18-20	
30:26 (possibly 19-33)	
31:7	
34:8	
51:6,	
52:6-12	
63:1-6	

"The Holy One" References in Isaiah

Reference	Description
1:4	The people of Israel despised Him and turned away from Him.
5:19,24	
10:17, 20	
12:6	
17:7	
29:19, 23	
30:11, 15	
31:1	
37:23	
40:25	
41:14-16,20	

"The Holy One" References in Isaiah

Reference	Description
43:3, 14-15	
45:11	
47:4	
48:17	
49:7	
54:5	
55:5	
60:9, 14	

REFERENCES

Biblesoft's New Exhaustive Strong's Numbers and Concordance with Expanded Greek-Hebrew Dictionary. Copyright © 1994, Biblesoft and International Bible Translators, Inc.

Constance, T.M. (1988). *Explorer's Bible Study.* Dickson, TN. Explorer's Bible Study.

Nelson's Illustrated Bible Dictionary, Copyright (c)1986, Thomas Nelson Publishers.

Wiersbe, Warren. (1992). *Be Comforted*. Colorado Springs, Colorado. Chariot Victor Publishing.

EAST - Easton Bible Dictionary, Third Edition, 1897 by M. G. Easton, M.A., D.D., ASCII edition, 1988 Ellis Enterprises, Inc. Public Domain.

ISBE, The International Standard Bible Encyclopedia, 1915, 1st Edition, from Dr. Stanley Morris, IBT, 1997. Original unabridged edition. James Orr, M.A., D.D. General Editor. John L. Nuelsen, D.D., LL.D. Edgar Y. Mullins, D.D., LL.D. Assistant Editors. Morris O. Evans, D.D., PhD. Managing Editor. (Melvin Grove Kyle, D.D., JJ.D. Revising Editor. Revision published in 1939 by Wm. B. Eerdmans Publishing Co.)

BDB-Definitions, THE ONLINE BIBLE THAYER'S GREEK LEXICON AND BROWN DRIVER & BRIGGS' HEBREW LEXICON.
Copyright © 1993,
Woodside Bible Fellowship, Ontario, Canada.
Licensed from the Institute for Creation Research.
Used by permission.
First published in Canada by Online Bible.

Dictionary definitions for 'delight', 'married', 'rejoice', redeemed', and 'sought' were adapted from Webster's New Twentieth Century Dictionary, second Edition.
Copyright © 1975 by William Collins+World Publishing Co., Inc.

American Psychological Association (APA):
   dross. (n.d.). WordNet® 3.0. Retrieved September 20, 2007, from Dictionary.com website:
   http://dictionary.reference.com/browse/dross
Chicago Manual Style (CMS):
   dross. Dictionary.com. WordNet® 3.0. Princeton University.
   http://dictionary.reference.com/browse/dross (accessed: September 20, 2007).
Modern Language Association (MLA):
   "dross." WordNet® 3.0. Princeton University. 20 Sep. 2007. <Dictionary.com
   http://dictionary.reference.com/browse/dross>.

www.ingramcontent.com/pod-product-compliance
Lightning Source LLC
Chambersburg PA
CBHW051349070526

44584CB00025B/3700